Rapid Deployment of SAP® Solutions

SAP PRESS is a joint initiative of SAP and Galileo Press. The know-how offered by SAP specialists combined with the expertise of the Galileo Press publishing house offers the reader expert books in the field. SAP PRESS features first-hand information and expert advice, and provides useful skills for professional decision-making.

SAP PRESS offers a variety of books on technical and business-related topics for the SAP user. For further information, please visit our website: *www.sap-press.com*.

Lars Teuber, Corina Weidmann, and Liane Will
Monitoring and Operations with SAP Solution Manager
2014, 694 pp., hardcover
978-1-59229-884-6

Nathan Williams
IT Service Management in SAP Solution Manager
2013, 903 pp., hardcover
978-1-59229-440-4

Ann Rosenberg et al.
Applying Real-World BPM in an SAP Environment
2011, 698 pp., hardcover
978-1-59229-343-8

Marc Schäfer and Matthias Melich
SAP Solution Manager (3rd Edition)
2012, 724 pp., hardcover
978-1-59229-388-9

Bernd Welz, Stefan Hänisch, Stefan Kätker, Thomas Reiss, Elvira Wallis, et al.

Rapid Deployment of SAP® Solutions

Galileo Press

Bonn • Boston

Galileo Press is named after the Italian physicist, mathematician, and philosopher Galileo Galilei (1564—1642). He is known as one of the founders of modern science and an advocate of our contemporary, heliocentric worldview. His words *Eppur si muove* (And yet it moves) have become legendary. The Galileo Press logo depicts Jupiter orbited by the four Galilean moons, which were discovered by Galileo in 1610.

Editor Laura Korslund
Acquisitions Editor Florian Zimniak
Copyeditor Laura Schreier
Cover Design Graham Geary
Photo Credit iStockphoto.com/12225091/© RobKints
Layout Design Vera Brauner
Production Kelly O'Callaghan
Typesetting SatzPro, Krefeld (Germany)
Printed and bound in the United States of America, on paper from sustainable sources

ISBN   978-1-59229-910-2
© 2014 by Galileo Press Inc., Boston (MA)
1st edition 2014

Library of Congress Cataloging-in-Publication Data
Welz, Bernd.
Rapid deployment of SAP solutions / Bernd Welz. -- 1st edition.
pages cm
ISBN-13: 978-1-59229-910-2 (print)
ISBN-10: 1-59229-910-5 (print)
ISBN-13: 978-1-59229-911-9 (e-book)
ISBN-13: 978-1-59229-912-6 (print and e-book) 1. Management information systems.
2. SAP ERP. 3. Business--Data processing. I. Title.
HF5679.W46 2014
658.4'038028553--dc23
2013033828

Contents at a Glance

1   Why Rapid Deployment of SAP Solutions? 19

2   Smarter, Faster, Simpler: The New Implementation
    Paradigm 33

3   Value Case Studies around the Rapid Deployment
    of SAP Solutions 85

4   Content Architecture: Foundation of SAP Rapid
    Deployment Solutions 185

5   Tools for an End-to-End Experience: From Discovery to
    a Running System 225

6   Support Services for the Rapid Deployment
    of SAP Solutions 271

7   The Rapid Deployment Partner Program 311

Dear Reader,

Who doesn't dream about a custom house? It's all your idea, come to life, and the first of its kind. However, you might be so focused on the novelty of this new, custom house that you forget the myriad of cons: high expense, the need to find answers to one-of-a-kind questions, and a long build time.

Now imagine this with your IT system solutions: sure, a custom implementiation is 100 % yours, but it takes a long time, has higher cost, and has the potential to encounter many roadblocks. Understanding the predicament of balancing innovation and efficiency, your helpful thought leaders and IT experts at SAP came up with the answer to getting what you need at a fraction of the cost and effort: SAP Rapid Deployment solutions. Guaranteed to assuage the doubts that any prefabricated solution can be the best solution, this book will answer questions like: How can my business realize cost and time savings, while driving business innovation?

As always, we appreciate your business and welcome your feedback. What did you think about *Rapid Deployment of SAP Solutions*? Your comments and suggestions are the most useful tools to help us improve our books for you, the reader. We encourage you to visit our website at *www.sap-press.com* and share your feedback.

Laura Korslund
Editor, SAP PRESS

Galileo Press
Boston, MA

laura.korslund@galileo-press.com
www.sap-press.com

Contents

Introduction 15

1 Why Rapid Deployment of SAP Solutions? 19

1.1 Evolution of the New Paradigm 21
    1.1.1 From Individual Projects to ASAP 22
    1.1.2 From ASAP to Best Practices for the
    Mid-Market 22
    1.1.3 Introducing SAP Rapid Deployment Solutions 23
    1.1.4 Assemble-to-Order of Solution Landscapes
    with SAP Rapid Deployment Solutions 25
    1.1.5 From A2O to the Simplified Rapid-Deployment
    Solution Experience 27
1.2 Key Benefits of the Rapid-Deployment Approach 28
1.3 Is IT (Still) Strategic? 30
1.4 Summary 31

2 Smarter, Faster, Simpler: The New Implementation Paradigm 33

2.1 Key Essentials to the New Implementation Paradigm 34
2.2 SAP Best Practices, SAP Business All-in-One, and
    SAP Rapid Deployment Solutions 37
    2.2.1 SAP Best Practices 38
    2.2.2 SAP Business All-in-One 45
    2.2.3 Rapid-Deployment Solutions 47
2.3 The Assemble-To-Order Approach 50
2.4 Pre-Assembled Rapid-Deployment Solutions and
    the Cloud 51
    2.4.1 Definition of a Pre-Assembled Rapid-
    Deployment Solution 51
    2.4.2 Usage Scenarios of Pre-Assembled Rapid-
    Deployment Solutions 54
    2.4.3 Impact of Pre-Assembled Rapid-Deployment
    Solutions on Project Setup and Timeline 55

2.5   Use-Cases and Delivery Options for Rapid-Deployment
      Solutions   56
      2.5.1   New Business Processes   58
      2.5.2   Infrastructure Enhancements   62
      2.5.3   Database Migration   63
      2.5.4   Evaluation of Use-Cases and Delivery Options
              for Rapid-Deployment Solutions   65
2.6   The Simplified Rapid-Deployment Solution Experience ...   66
      2.6.1   Explore   68
      2.6.2   Scope   70
      2.6.3   Deploy   73
      2.6.4   Run   77
2.7   Services Complementing Rapid Deployment   78
2.8   The Role of SAP Partners in the New Implementation
      Paradigm   79
2.9   Benefits   80
2.10 Summary   83

3   Value Case Studies around the Rapid Deployment of SAP Solutions **85**

3.1   Database Migration to SAP NetWeaver BW Powered by
      SAP HANA   85
      3.1.1   Background   87
      3.1.2   Results   91
3.2   Data Migration to the SAP Business Suite Powered by
      SAP HANA   93
      3.2.1   Background   94
      3.2.2   Deployment   96
      3.2.3   Results 101
3.3   Rapid Deployment of SAP ERP with SAP ERP Rapid
      Deployment Solutions and the Assemble-to-Order
      Approach 101
      3.3.1   Background 102
      3.3.2   Solution-Deployment Planning 103
      3.3.3   Deployment 104
      3.3.4   Results 107

3.4   Deploying SAP CRM with SAP HANA   108
        3.4.1   Background   108
        3.4.2   Deployment   109
        3.4.3   Results   112
3.5   Combining SAP Rapid Deployment Solutions with an
        Incremental Rollout Strategy to Integrate Disconnected
        CRM Systems   113
        3.5.1   Background   114
        3.5.2   Deployment   117
        3.5.3   Results   120
3.6   Assemble-to-Order Deployment of SAP ERP   120
        3.6.1   Background   121
        3.6.2   Deployment   122
        3.6.3   Results   123
3.7   Telco Accelerates Billing Project Using a
        Rapid-Deployment Solution   124
        3.7.1   Background   125
        3.7.2   Deployment   127
        3.7.3   Summary   129
3.8   Consumer Products Company Deploys SAP Demand
        Planning in Weeks   130
        3.8.1   Background   130
        3.8.2   Deployment   131
        3.8.3   Results   133
3.9   Deploying Integrated Supply Chain Solutions Rapidly   133
        3.9.1   Background   134
        3.9.2   Deployment   135
        3.9.3   Results   136
3.10   Integrating Multiresource Scheduling into SAP ERP
        and Plant Maintenance   137
        3.10.1   Background   137
        3.10.2   Deployment   139
        3.10.3   Results   140
3.11   Assemble-to-Order Finance on SAP HANA   142
        3.11.1   Background   142
        3.11.2   Solution-Deployment Planning   145
        3.11.3   Deployment   147
        3.11.4   Results   148

3.12 SAP Business Intelligence Adoption Rapid-Deployment
Solution 151
3.12.1 Background 152
3.12.2 Deployment 153
3.13 Enterprise Performance Management 157
3.13.1 Background 158
3.13.2 Deployment 159
3.13.3 Results 162
3.14 Mobile Apps and Infrastructure 164
3.14.1 Background 165
3.14.2 Solution-Deployment Planning 165
3.14.3 Deployment 167
3.14.4 Results 168
3.15 SAP HANA Enterprise Cloud 170
3.15.1 Background 170
3.15.2 Deployment 170
3.15.3 Results 175
3.16 Case Study for a Rapid-Deployment Solution
Implementation of SAP Fiori 175
3.16.1 Background 176
3.16.2 Solution-Deployment Planning 177
3.16.3 Deployment 178
3.16.4 Results 178
3.17 Winning the Ratings War with SAP Personnel
Administration and Organization Management
Rapid-Deployment Solution 180
3.17.1 Background 182
3.17.2 Deployment 183
3.17.3 Results 183

4 Content Architecture: Foundation of SAP Rapid
Deployment Solutions 185

4.1 Content Architecture Defined 187
4.1.1 Business Value of Content Architecture 187
4.1.2 Objectives of Content Architecture 188
4.1.3 Key Concepts of Content Architecture 189
4.1.4 Content Architecture Example 192
4.1.5 The Asset Type Inventory (ATI) 194

4.2   Content Architecture of Rapid-Deployment Solutions   196
       4.2.1   Meta Model   197
       4.2.2   Key Entity Type Definitions   198
       4.2.3   Rapid-Deployment Solution Bill of Materials   200
       4.2.4   Layered Architecture of Implementation
                Building Blocks   208
4.3   Rapid-Deployment Solution Domain in the Context
       of SAP Taxonomy   210
       4.3.1   Meta Model   210
       4.3.2   Definition of Key Entities   211
4.4   Assemble-to-Order Content Architecture Principles   217
       4.4.1   Structure Content Around Scope Items   218
       4.4.2   Structuring Content around Scope Items   219
       4.4.3   Creating a Network of Scope items   221
4.5   Summary   223

**5   Tools for an End-to-End Experience: From Discovery
       to a Running System** **225**

5.1   Exploring SAP's Solutions with SAP Solution Explorer   226
       5.1.1   Value Maps   228
       5.1.2   Catalog of Fnd-to-End Solutions and Solution
                Capabilities   229
5.2   Scoping Your Solution with the SAP Solution
       Configurator   232
       5.2.1   The SAP Solution Configurator for Customers   233
       5.2.2   The SAP Solution Configurator for Bidding
                Teams   238
5.3   ASAP Methodology for Implementing SAP Rapid
       Deployment Solutions   244
       5.3.1   Overview and Benefits of ASAP 8   245
       5.3.2   The Taxonomy of the ASAP 8 Methodology   246
       5.3.3   Agile Delivery with the ASAP Methodology   248
5.4   Project Execution with the Rapid Deployment Cockpit,
       SAP Solution Manager, and Solution Builder Tool   251
       5.4.1   Collaborative Project Execution with the Rapid
                Deployment Cockpit   253

5.4.2   Supporting Your Implementation with SAP Solution Manager ... 259

5.4.3   Activating SAP Rapid Deployment Solutions Pre-Configuration Content with the Solution Builder ... 261

5.5   Operating Your Solution with SAP Solution Manager ... 265

5.6   Summary ... 269

6   Support Services for the Rapid Deployment of SAP Solutions ... 271

6.1   Engineered Services ... 272

6.1.1   Why Engineered Service? ... 272

6.1.2   Structure of Engineered Services ... 274

6.1.3   Delivery Approach ... 275

6.2   Services for Solution Implementation ... 276

6.2.1   Services for Solution Implementation and Operations ... 276

6.2.2   Reduce Implementation and Operational Costs with SAP Maintenance ... 282

6.3   Services for Enablement ... 291

6.3.1   SAP Ramp-Up Knowledge Transfer: Supporting SAP Solution Launches ... 292

6.3.2   SAP Education: Accelerating Time-to-Market and Time-to-Value ... 293

6.3.3   SAP Certifications: Key for Achieving Technology Value ... 295

6.3.4   SAP Education Software: Improve Learning Management, Knowledge Transfer, and Performance ... 296

6.3.5   SAP Enterprise Support Academy: Expert-to-Expert Training ... 298

6.3.6   SAP Rapid Deployment Solutions Enablement Program ... 301

6.3.7   SAP University Alliance and SAP Student Academy: Next-Generation SAP Experts ... 303

6.3.8 Educating the Crowd: openSAP "Enablement of
Innovation Adoption at Scale" 304

6.3.9 Information and Collaboration 306

6.4 Summary 310

7   The Rapid Deployment Partner Program 311

7.1 SAP Rapid Deployment Solutions for Partners 313

7.1.1 Adopting the Methodology to Conduct
State-of-the-Art Implementations 313

7.1.2 Adopting the Delivery of SAP Rapid
Deployment Solutions 314

7.1.3 Bringing It All Together: Partner-Led
Rapid-Deployment Solutions 315

7.2 Getting There Fast: Enablement and Qualification 320

7.2.1 Core Methodology Program 321

7.2.2 Enablement 321

7.2.3 Qualification 322

7.3 Sample Partner Case: F.I.T. Consulting 323

7.3.1 How the Engagement Started 323

7.3.2 How the Qualification Went 324

7.3.3 Qualifications for F.I.T. 324

7.3.4 Experiences and Expectations 325

7.4 Sample Partner Case: Fujitsu 325

7.4.1 How the Engagement Started and Developed 326

7.4.2 Experiences and Expectations 327

7.5 Sample Enablement Session 327

7.5.1 SAP Rapid Deployment Solutions Methodology
Premium Enablement Sessions 328

7.5.2 SAP Rapid Deployment Solutions Premium
Enablement Workshops 329

7.6 Summary 331

Appendices 333

A   SAP Rapid-Deployment Solutions: Packages 333

A.1 SAP ERP Rapid-Deployment Solutions 335

A.2 SAP Business Suite Powered by SAP HANA 336

Contents

A.3   Line-of-Business Rapid Deployment Solutions 340
A.4   Industry-Specific Packages 361
A.5   Mobile Packages 365
A.6   Technology Packages 366
A.7   SAP Business All-in-One 377
B   The Authors 387
B.1   Chapter Authors 389

Index 395

Introduction

SAP Rapid Deployment solutions enable a new paradigm for the way we approach the implementation of SAP solutions today: faster, at lower cost and risk, and above all, using the experience of the largest customer base and ecosystem in the software industry to guide the project from day one. The aim of this book is to give you, the reader, an insight into this new paradigm. Throughout the book, we'll describe in detail the many facets of SAP Rapid Deployment solutions that can significantly reduce the timescale of a project, from evaluating a solution to productive use (time-to-value), while at the same time dramatically reducing implementation efforts and increasing predictability, in terms of how the solution fits the customer's business and the business value it generates.

Before we start, we'll briefly sketch who this book will benefit, and discuss what each of the chapters covers.

Book Overview

Everyone dealing with the implementation and extension of SAP solutions will benefit from reading this book. If you're an SAP professional dealing with SAP implementations at your company, or an SAP consultant, this book will help you understand the new implementation paradigm based on the concepts related to SAP Rapid Deployment solutions, their evolution, and the benefits they offer to all SAP customers and prospects.

This book also provides case studies to illustrate in detail how deployment of SAP Rapid Deployment solutions has added value and reduced risk for its customers.

Reading Guidelines

Within the chapters of this book, you'll find explanations, insight, and examples assembled to increase your understanding of what SAP offers with the rapid deployment of business solutions. You will learn about the extensive offerings and infrastructure created by SAP to enable businesses to run faster, smarter, and better.

Chapter 1 will give you an overview of the new implementation paradigm, the key principles it is built on, and how it evolved over recent years.

After this introduction, we start **Chapter 2** by looking in detail at how the new implementation paradigm works. First, we examine some of the key essentials of the new implementation paradigm, including cloud, mobility, and Suite on SAP HANA solutions, before considering SAP Best Practices and its place in rapid-deployment solutions. Then we take a look at the rapid-deployment implementation approach, focusing in particular on the Simplified Rapid-Deployment Solution Experience, and how this extends and further simplifies the deployment approach in the cloud. It begins with a walk through of the implementation process, from the point where customers explore SAP solutions, through scoping, deploying, and running the solution. There is also a section on the latest version of the ASAP methodology and how this supports the delivery of rapid-deployment solutions, as well as examples.

Chapter 3 demonstrates how SAP made it possible for the deployment teams, using the methodology and tools described in this book, to produce fast, efficient, and effective deployments. The 17 case studies contained in this chapter span a variety of solutions, customers, and geographies to substantiate that the deployment teams were able to quickly and predictably unlock the power of the solution and accelerate that time-to-value.

SAP Rapid Deployment solutions in the context of the assemble-to-order approach is the focus of **Chapter 4**. It explains the content of a rapid-deployment solution package and how the content is gathered. This in turn leads to a focus on the tools that support the new methodology, which are the topic of **Chapter 5**. This section describes the discover-deploy-run process and the tools that support it, such as the SAP Solution Explorer, SAP Solution Configurator, SAP Solution Manager, and the Solution Builder. It features a checklist and step-by-step guide that helps you to assess how to best go about using or implementing rapid-deployment solutions, including an overview of the services that are detailed in the next chapter.

Chapter 6 surveys the latest SAP services that support customers and their teams, including SAP Partners that may be included in the deployments. Through engineered services, solution implementation, operation services, and enablement services, SAP has the infrastructure to support rapid deployments. These services are discussed in detail.

Chapter 7 reviews the role of the SAP Partner in the rapid deployment of SAP solutions, as well as the support, resources, and qualification programs that SAP makes available to SAP Partners. This infrastructure helps partners deploy and use the SAP Rapid Deployment solutions methodology to build and deliver new and useful solution packages in the market.

Finally, **Appendix A** contains a comprehensive overview of the current SAP Rapid Deployment solutions portfolio. It is structured by related topics, including ERP (Enterprise Resource Planning), SAP Business Suite powered by SAP HANA, line-of-business, industry, mobility, and technology packages, with analytics, migration, integration, and SAP HANA solutions too numerous to mention here.

In this chapter we'll explain the new implementation paradigm for SAP solutions, based on SAP Rapid Deployment solutions. We'll also provide an overview to frame the whole book and to guide you through reading it.

1 Why Rapid Deployment of SAP Solutions?

In this chapter, we'll provide the information you need to understand the essence of the new paradigm, SAP Rapid Deployment solutions: what they are, how they work, and their potential benefits to you. In essence, the new paradigm is based on the realization that it is faster and less risky for businesses to leverage available best business practices with SAP Rapid Deployment solutions for the majority of their business processes. This involves performing a fit/gap analysis, and restricting additional customizing, add-ons, and interfaces to only those areas of a company's operations where significantly more business value and differentiation can be achieved.

By leveraging SAP Rapid Deployment solutions and cloud services, it's now possible to have a system up and running within hours, pre-configured with all the relevant best practices as the starting point for the implementation project. Blueprinting is not done from scratch on a blank sheet of paper. Instead, the pre-configured best practice functionality is explored in the actual system to decide which parts of the best-practice proposals should be retained and which parts should be changed, extended, or discarded. This approach is not only much faster, but also leaves less room for misunderstanding between business users and IT. The question is no longer "What do you need?" but rather "Where should we depart from, or extend, the best practice?" The logical consequence of this approach is a higher degree of standardization, making the system easier to maintain and reducing the total cost of

Faster, fewer errors

ownership. Deviations from the SAP standard are only made where they add significant business value, based on the premise that there is little to be gained from inventing new solutions to problems that have been solved many times before.

Easy maintenance and expansion

Because the resulting solution is based on tried and tested SAP Best Practices that are used by many companies, it's more robust and easier to maintain. This also makes it much easier to incorporate new technological innovations, as well as adapt to changing business requirements. Business-process monitoring is simple to set up, because all the required content, such as process key performance indicators and intelligence measurements, comes pre-configured with the best-practice processes.

Best practice-based implementation

Best-practice business content has been available for a number of years. But now is the right time to move to the new implementation paradigm. With the rapid pace of change in business models and innovations, it has become an absolute imperative for any company to be able to react in real-time to market changes. As a consequence, the ability to build a solution landscape quickly, and change it almost instantly when required, has become a key success factor in running a real-time business. With a best practice-based implementation, time-to-value is shorter and the turnaround time to adapt to changes in processes and business models is much faster. Effort is not wasted on unnecessary, customer-specific modifications and add-ons. In addition, many business users are now well-versed in the use of IT, and are very capable of distinguishing between processes that are good enough to fit their requirements, and processes that offer genuine differentiation—that give the company a competitive edge—and therefore justify additional investment. Many companies are rethinking their IT strategies due to the influx of new technologies that support innovations like big data, mobility, and the cloud, so now is the right time to think about a best-practice-based approach.

SAP is ready to help companies make this change. It has a broad portfolio of proven best practices, and content is growing by the day. This includes core pieces across SAP's entire product portfolio as well as SAP's latest innovations. With SAP HANA Enterprise Cloud, customers do not have to wait until they have the requisite hardware in place and the SAP software installed before they can start the implementation. A fully configured, best-practice solution is available in a matter of hours, and the implementation process can start immediately. The project team is supported by a sophisticated tool landscape that covers the evaluation and scoping of the solution, fit/gap analysis, realization, testing, and go-live.

1.1 Evolution of the New Paradigm

Traditionally, software implementation focused on the perceived uniqueness of every project. Customers believed that when designing and implementing software solutions, every aspect of their business needed equal attention, and consequently had to be defined from scratch. Even though standard software is built on the premise that common best practices exist, designing a customer-specific business blueprint of all processes at the start of a project was the main approach.

Custom systems

However, this approach had inherent pitfalls. Implementation times were very long, with many projects taking 15 months or longer to complete. Often, the blueprinting phase alone exceeded nine months before the software was even touched. The technological requirements of the differentiated solution took priority over business needs. This in turn meant escalating costs, scope creep, and the danger of projects running well over budget. A considerable amount of time elapsed before a solution was attained to address these business needs. Worse still, by the time the solution was finally rolled out, the actual business priorities might have changed.

In the following sections, we'll go over some of the earlier approaches SAP has used to help customers with their implementations, leading up to the new best-practice-based approach. We'll also introduce SAP Rapid Deployment solutions and the evolution they went through, from delivering point solutions to being the foundation for any implementation project.

1.1.1 From Individual Projects to ASAP

AcceleratedSAP The earlier approach to software implementation projects was to treat each project as unique. There was no standard implementation methodology to fall back on, with customers and partners using a diverse range of generic implementation methodologies instead. To address some of the shortcomings of this earlier approach, SAP introduced an implementation methodology for SAP software in 1996, known as AcceleratedSAP (ASAP). The main aim behind ASAP was to gather the experience gained from past projects and mold this into a structured, deliverable-oriented implementation procedure. Based on a pre-designed project roadmap, ASAP provided clear, structured guidance through every phase of an implementation project. The roadmap also provided a detailed description of the work packages, activities, and tasks that accompany each phase, with recommendations on how best to implement the solution. In addition, it specified the tools and accelerators (content) that can assist project team members in every phase of the project, and included services to support knowledge transfer and the smooth execution of the project.

Blueprint Overall, the focus of the ASAP approach was on determining a blueprint based on the customer's own business processes, and mapping this to the capabilities of the SAP solution in a second step. In many cases, customer add-ons and modifications were included to fill the perceived gaps in the solution.

1.1.2 From ASAP to Best Practices for the Mid-Market

With ASAP, SAP developed the first structured, SAP-specific approach to software implementation. Having identified the necessary tasks, and how best to perform them, it was now possible to add more "content" so that the system could be configured in the best possible way for a specific business process. ASAP provided a framework for this configuration content, known as SAP Best Practices packages. This evolution towards best practices meant that SAP was not only able to fine-tune the tasks involved in every phase of a project, it was also able to define the optimum ways of configuring the system to run a wide range of business processes within a company.

Initially, best practices were aimed at mid-market customers. These customers have business requirements that are no less sophisticated than large companies. However, they do not have the resources to embark on large-scale enterprise implementations, and were therefore in effect excluded from deploying such solutions. By introducing best-practice coverage for all core SAP ERP processes, SAP was able to provide its ERP application in a form that enabled it to be deployed in a straightforward, fast, and cost-efficient way. With SAP Business All-in-One solutions, customers choose from best practices for more than 90 business processes spanning from financials and accounting to manufacturing, materials management, and logistics in one preconfigured bundle.

On top of the SAP Business All-in-One solutions delivered by SAP, partners can add additional content to make the solution fit to specific verticals that are not fully covered by best practices alone. Thus, partners can either develop their own qualified SAP Business All-in-One solutions, adapted to country or industry-specific needs, or use these offerings out of the box. Partners typically sell these solutions at a fixed price, including re-selling SAP's software, services and, if applicable, best-practice enhancements, or even hosting services as a value-added reseller (VAR).

Today, there are 166 SAP Business All-in-One packages on the market, with 1,050 SAP Business All-in-One partners and over 700 qualified partner solutions for more than 44 industries and industry segments available—an indication of how well the approach has been accepted by mid-market companies.

1.1.3 Introducing SAP Rapid Deployment Solutions

SAP Best Practices solutions and SAP Business All-in-One were initially targeted at the mid-market. However, it soon became apparent that the content was already being used and requested beyond the mid-market. The rationale behind SAP Best Practices was simple and attractive for large customers, too.

SAP software can typically be configured in many different ways. However, exploring and selecting the best options for a company is time-consuming and costly. This raises the question: Is the effort really justified for all processes? Why spend a lot of time and effort on blueprinting business processes that ultimately do not give you a competitive advantage? Why not use the knowledge acquired by SAP in delivering software solutions for industries that reflect the most efficient ways of performing certain business tasks by implementing standardized processes? By adopting preconfigured business scenarios, you not only reduce the time and effort required to implement the solution, you also profit from adapting your own processes to tried and tested formulas that offer genuine gains. Not only are the business processes themselves refined and improved; the implementation method can also be streamlined and standardized.

Consequently, there was increasing demand for SAP to make best practices available for large enterprise customers, too.

Expand existing scenarios

Extending the target customer space meant that additional aspects needed to be considered for the approach. While the large majority of SAP Business All-in-One projects address companies new to SAP that want to start with SAP ERP, most large enterprises already run an SAP application. Typically, such large enterprises want to extend their footprint beyond core SAP ERP components and into areas of SAP Business Suite that are more line-of-business focused, such as SAP Customer Relationship Management (CRM), SAP Human Capital Management (HCM), or SAP Product Lifecycle Management (PLM), to name but a few. They also want to deepen the footprint of existing scenarios; for example, by expanding SAP Financial Accounting into SAP Treasury and Risk Management, SAP Dispute Management, and SAP Collections Management, or more sophisticated planning and reporting solutions. And they want to adopt new technologies, such as SAP Mobile Platform or SAP HANA, quickly and safely as well. Furthermore, this market segment is sold to and serviced largely outside the VAR channel, so elements of the fixed-price approach that are prominent in SAP's indirect business had to be made available through SAP's own services organization and large ecosystem of system integrators (SIs) too.

In 2010, SAP Rapid Deployment solutions were introduced to address these broadened requirements. Like SAP Business All-in-One, SAP Rapid Deployment solutions bundle SAP software with SAP Best Practices content, including configuration guides and business process procedures or documents, and use the same concepts and tools for guided and automated activation of preconfigured content. SAP Rapid Deployment solutions go beyond the SAP Business All-in-One approach, however, bringing software and best-practice content together with engineered services that can be provided by SAP consultants or qualified partners.

A rapid-deployment solution contains the following content:

- A simplified implementation methodology based on ASAP, tailored exactly to fit delivery of the respective solution scope.

- Service content, such as the project schedule, project accelerators, statement of work (SOW) detailing the exact service scope, and so on.

SAP Rapid Deployment solutions content

The engineered service component of a rapid-deployment solution is normally available at a fixed price. Of course, this may be adjusted in a specific bid, for example if the project extends the scope of the rapid-deployment solution to include additional functionality.

An SAP Rapid Deployment solution partner program was also launched in parallel. This program enables SAP Partners to leverage rapid-deployment solution content in their implementation projects. It also enables partners to build their own rapid-deployment solutions on top of SAP content to fill niche market needs, such as micro-verticals, and areas that require a local or regional focus. The partner program has been hugely successful, with approximately 250 partners and more than 170 SAP-qualified partner-implementation services to date. Several thousand rapid-deployment solutions are currently in operation.

Solution partner program

1.1.4 Assemble-to-Order of Solution Landscapes with SAP Rapid Deployment Solutions

Each rapid-deployment solution comes with a clearly defined scope, targeted at a specific business requirement, usually with a fixed price for the engineered service that is included. However, in many cases customers are not just looking to deploy a small "point solution" for a "point problem"; instead, they want a larger end-to-end solution, while still looking for the benefits of the SAP Rapid Deployment solutions approach.

Assemble-to-order

To address this, rapid-deployment solutions have been designed in a modular, combinable way. When faced with large and complex requirements, customers can then assemble their end-to-end solution by deploying a combination of several rapid-deployment solutions, bundled with additional services on top. This is known as the assemble-to-order (A2O) approach, which was introduced in 2012.

A2O can address both broad and detailed customer requirements:

▶ Customers new to SAP often want to start with a broad scope, combining the SAP ERP backbone with procurement, human capital management, and risk and compliance management capabilities. The A2O model gives them the chance to start with a combination of several rapid-deployment solutions as a foundation, while providing the flexibility to make additional adjustments on top.

▶ For line-of-business requirements such as procurement, customer relationship management, or supply chain management, a single rapid-deployment solution provides value as a solid entry point. If a customer is looking for a deeper, more comprehensive solution, a combination of several rapid-deployment solutions related to the particular area again provides a strong, pre-packaged foundation.

In general, the A2O approach helps meet a customer's end-to-end business needs more simply and efficiently by "assembling to order" multiple rapid-deployment solution components plus extra functional scope, integration, governance, and testing. By combining multiple rapid-deployment solutions with engineered services, rapid data-migration services, and custom development services, even the most unique requirements can benefit from a package approach to their foundational elements and deliver competitive differentiation. Ideally, 80 percent of the solution scope can be covered with rapid-deployment solutions best practices, with the remaining 20 percent requiring additional effort for customer-specific blueprinting and realization. The reduction in time and the predictability of the business outcome is substantial. Some SAP customers that reduced the customer-specific part of the implementation to a bare minimum reportedly managed to reduce the time and effort required to implement a full SAP ERP application by a factor of 10 compared with the traditional implementation approach.

A2O is not simply intended for new installations, however. It can also be adopted to extend existing SAP solution landscapes.

1.1.5 From A2O to the Simplified Rapid-Deployment Solution Experience

The availability of cloud services makes it even faster and easier to deliver rapid-deployment solutions to customers. Cloud services provide customers with a working system in the cloud to help evaluate the solution, and then jump-start the implementation by providing a pre-assembled rapid-deployment-solutions-based system in the cloud within hours. This has enabled SAP to take the next step on the rapid-deployment solution journey by launching the simplified rapid-deployment solution experience in 2013.

Now, the customer experience begins with the exploration and selection of the SAP solutions required to move forward from a customer perspective. Leveraging new tools, namely the SAP Solution Explorer and SAP Solution Configurator, customers can themselves explore which solutions are available to address their business requirements, down to the level of solution scope items. The SAP Solution Explorer allows navigation of the entire SAP solution portfolio, and enables customers and prospects to view the capabilities that each solution provides.

In conjunction with the SAP Solution Explorer, there is a built-in solution configurator that allows you to drill deeper into this portfolio and select the capabilities and solutions you need. You can then get clear advice on the required licenses and the coverage of the rapid-deployment solution best-practice content. It also allows you to document gaps in the solution capabilities or the available rapid-deployment solution coverage, if required. Based on the configuration results, you can then order a test and evaluation system with the selected scope and best-practice content in the cloud. To simplify the assemble-to-order process, the typical combinations of rapid-deployment solutions are available in the cloud as pre-assembled SAP Rapid Deployment solutions.

The bundle of requisite rapid-deployment solutions can then be deployed in a preassembled fashion extremely quickly, either on-premise or in the cloud, to provide a running solution as a starting point for the implementation project. Instead of the customer installing the product, loading content, and activating and integrating the multiple rapid-deployment solutions together, the pre-assembled rapid-deployment solution is installed within hours.

SAP Solution Manager

All the content in the preassembled rapid-deployment solution and all the selections made in SAP Solution Explorer and SAP Solution Configurator appear in SAP Solution Manager, which is the main implementation tool. There is no need to reinvent or re-document anything, because no data is lost between the evaluation and the deployment phase. There is therefore a cohesive, consistent flow of data from exploration and selection down to deployment. Also, the best-practice content is reused in the run phase to perform business-process monitoring, thus closing the loop.

> **Note**
>
> Chapter 2 describes the new approach in detail.

1.2 Key Benefits of the Rapid-Deployment Approach

When customers deploy SAP solutions the rapid-deployment way, they gain a wide range of benefits. These include hard time and cost savings and reduced project risk on the one hand, and increased solution value and flexibility for the business on the other. With the rapid-deployment approach, you can focus your time and effort on those parts of the business that give you differentiation and significant additional business value by drawing up a blueprint from scratch. For the majority of other processes, you can benefit from the proven business best practices. Overall, this gives you shorter time-to-value with a predicable business outcome in the initial implementation, and lays a solid foundation for further extensions and changes as business requirements develop.

Time and money savings

The blueprinting phase, in particular, shrinks dramatically. Pre-configuration and implementation accelerator content provides significant savings during the realization and testing phases. The deployment of best practices, solution accelerators, step-by-step project guides, and end-user enablement also helps to align business and IT requirements, resulting in a solution that meets the customer's business needs without any unpleasant surprises. At least 40% less time and effort is required compared to traditional projects with a similar scope. The assemble-to-order approach extends these savings to entire solution landscapes. Thousands of customers have already bought into the rapid-deployment approach; many of those implementation projects took less than 12 weeks.

The rapid-deployment approach supports smarter innovation by enabling incremental adoption with clearly defined solution scopes and costs. SAP Rapid Deployment solutions provide a starting point from which to move forward with breakthrough SAP solutions and technologies, such as SAP HANA and SAP mobility and cloud solutions. The rapid-deployment approach has been particularly well-received by customers who went live with SAP HANA.

Smarter innovation

The role of rapid-deployment solutions in the deployment of technological innovations is not necessarily to provide proven best practices (which, when these innovations are released, cannot exist), but rather to show a way to achieve business value using the respective innovation. For example, the SAP HANA Operational Reporting rapid-deployment solution shortens the technical deployment of the new technology. It also offers a collection of relevant example dashboards and reports that can be used out of the box and later extended and adapted. Kennametal, an American tooling and industrial materials supplier, deployed this rapid-deployment solution in just five weeks, and extended it to cover their unique use-cases over another two months. Of course, customers often combine a rapid-deployment solution with additional elements in their project, which extends the implementation time for the combined deployment, but still typically provides faster time-to-value.

Achieve business value

The rapid-deployment approach is designed to stay as close to the standard solution as possible, which improves the maintainability and flexibility of the solution dramatically. This in turn reduces the related operating costs and therefore the overall total cost of ownership.

Communication between IT and business users is often challenging. The rapid-deployment approach, with a pre-configured, running system in the cloud, makes communication between the teams very efficient and

IT/business communication

reduces the risk of misunderstandings dramatically. We often use the analogy of a prefabricated house to describe how rapid-deployment solutions actually work. With a prefabricated house, the components are manufactured to standard models and sizes. Once they have been delivered to your site, all that remains is for them to be assembled according to a predetermined plan, and the house is ready to walk into. At this point, you can identify the changes you want, such as larger windows or a double garage, to meet your most important needs. Even after you move in, you still have the possibility to extend the house further if your situation changes and you need to adapt your living arrangements.

From a software perspective, SAP Rapid Deployment solutions enable both the IT and the business specialists to identify what needs to be changed on the basis of a real, working example, rather than discussing abstract concepts and misunderstanding each other's requirements. Even if the best practices only cover, say 60 percent to 80 percent of the final solution, having a running system available makes the discussion and specification of the missing parts much more efficient.

1.3 Is IT (Still) Strategic?

Nicolas Carr declared in his acclaimed book "*Does IT Matter? Information Technology and the Corrosion of Competitive Advantage*" (Harvard Business Review Press, 2004) that IT in business is no longer of strategic importance. Because IT has all the characteristics of an infrastructure technology, he argues, it too has become commoditized, and the advantages of distinction have disappeared. While his book spurred a hot debate, it seems with the new implementation approach based on best practices in SAP Rapid Deployment solutions, that IT is indeed now becoming a commodity when all companies are using the same best practices. The question is therefore again: Is IT strategic or not? Can companies achieve a competitive edge with IT?

Our answer to that is a clear-cut "yes"!

There is a constant stream of IT innovations, such as in-memory computing, that have the potential to continue to change the way business is done. Companies that are fast to adopt innovations and see the business potential that these innovations can drive have a competitive advantage. However, not all areas supported by IT in a company require differentiating. It does not make sense to reinvent best practices where no additional business value is to be expected.

Customers are now adept when it comes to distinguishing between differentiating and non-differentiating activities. The rapid-deployment approach gives customers the freedom to go with best practices, but adapt and extend the solution in areas where they expect fine-tuning or additional functionality to realize a business benefit. They also have the choice of implementing the best practices at the outset, and then investing more in additional customization and customer-specific add-ons at a later stage, when they have a better idea of how additional benefits can be achieved. With the rapid-deployment approach, the customer has the best of both worlds—simplicity and speed where best practices are sufficient, and the possibility to go beyond them when and where there is a real business benefit.

1.4   Summary

In this introductory chapter, we've seen how the SAP Rapid Deployment solutions approach evolved from previous implementation methodologies, and is further evolving to meet the new opportunities it uncovers. We've also seen how this approach significantly reduces time-to-value, offers predictable business value to customers, promotes efficient communication between business users and IT project teams, and supports smarter innovation by laying a solid foundation for further extensions and changes as business requirements develop. The following chapters of this book will explain the various facets of this methodology in greater detail. Case studies based on the experiences of SAP customers offer real-life examples that demonstrate how the theory is transformed into a practice that has radically transformed our approach to software implementations today.

*Here's your introduction to the new implementation para-
digm—find out how this approach supports the rapid deployment of SAP solutions. The key is standardized and engineered
implementation of pre-defined Best Practices as the foundation
of every SAP solution implementation.*

2   Smarter, Faster, Simpler: The New Implementation Paradigm

In the first chapter, you received a general overview of what SAP Rapid Deployment solutions are, how they work, and what their benefits are. This chapter will take the next step and explain in greater detail how the new implementation paradigm works and what the measurable benefits for customers are.

First, we'll introduce the key essentials of the new implementation paradigm. Next, in Section 2.2, we will introduce the foundation, and the concepts of SAP Best Practices, SAP Business All-in-One, and SAP Rapid Deployment solutions. In Section 2.3 and Section 2.4 we will introduce the assemble-to-order approach, i.e., how multiple rapid-deployment solutions are tied together to address the scope of a customer implementation project and the concept of pre-assembled rapid-deployment solutions, respectively. Section 2.5 provides a brief description of the different implementation use-cases addressed by the rapid-deployment approach, such as a new implementation of an SAP solution (e.g., a new SAP customer implements the SAP ERP core), adding a new SAP Business Suite component to an existing landscape (e.g., a customer already using SAP ERP is additionally implementing SAP CRM), or more technology-oriented use-cases such as migrating from a traditional relational database to SAP HANA.

After that, we explain how all these concepts and approaches tie together and provide the Simplified Rapid-Deployment Solution Experience—the core of the new implementation paradigm, in Section 2.6.

Section 2.7 introduces the service portfolio around rapid-deployment solutions implementations and Section 2.8 addresses the role of SAP Partners in that context. This chapter closes with an overview of the benefits that the new implementation paradigm can provide to customers.

2.1   Key Essentials to the New Implementation Paradigm

Today, more than ever, a company's software strategy is heavily influenced by business rather than by IT alone. Line-of-business leaders are in the driver's seat, and they care most of all about the business outcomes of the solution—and about how quickly and simply these can be achieved. Long projects with unpredictable post-implementation results and costs are no longer accepted. Instead, both business and IT leaders want to know up-front what they get, and get it fast and at predictable cost: A new implementation paradigm is required.

Benefit from past knowledge/experience

A key factor that influences this paradigm and creates one of its main pillars is that companies don't want to start designing their solutions from scratch in long blueprinting cycles, but instead benefit from the knowledge and experience of the ones who have done it before. They ask for best practices, the thought being that if the business problem is not totally unique for that customer or business, there is no reason that they can't simply take over the best-practice experience from the hundreds—or thousands—of others who have done it before, rather than re-inventing the wheel. Of course, this needs to be paired with the flexibility to add individualized "own practices"—but only where they really provide value. Companies have gotten smarter about where to stick close to the standard and where to individualize.

Reduce TCO

Next to significant risk reductions concerning cost over-run and scope creep, they aim to reduce complexity and the total cost of ownership (TCO) of maintaining a heavily individualized solution. Not the least, best-practice solutions will often beat individual designs in terms of effectiveness and business value by bringing in others' experience of what "good" looks like—if they also give customers the flexibility to add individual aspects where they are really beneficial.

To address this and make it smarter, faster, and simpler to deploy SAP solutions, SAP has introduced SAP Rapid Deployment solutions. To simplify the explanation, SAP has picked out the core building blocks of their offering and used their extensive experience with the largest customer base in the industry to identify best practices for how the solution could be best run. Based on this, SAP brings together the respective SAP product with pre-configuration, enablement content, and services—by SAP consulting or qualified partners—some available at a fixed price.

Many solutions already provide value if deployed by themselves alone. Typical examples for the large variety include:

- **Getting productive, fast, in a new solution area like sales-force automation or self-service procurement.**
  Rapid-deployment solution offerings are available to get customers up and running in mere weeks—and that even integrate into the existing SAP footprint, for instance, if they have an existing SAP ERP system. Even for companies entirely new to SAP, rapid-deployment solutions are available to get them from zero to a fully loaded SAP ERP system in context of their respective industry.

- **Lay a foundation for a bigger solution.**
  Even for the most complex of industry-specific end-to-end solutions—like billing and revenue innovation management in telecommunications, loans management in banking, or complex logistics processes—rapid-deployment solutions can dramatically reduce project risk and costs by providing a stable and integrated foundation for the solution. In cases with highly individualized needs, the rapid-deployment solution can naturally never be the final solution, but will rather serve as the starting point for the project.

- **Expand an existing solution.**
  Rapid-deployment solutions are not only available for "greenfield" projects, where the deployment starts into an "empty" system. Many solutions specifically deploy scenarios into existing components to

expand the footprint of already implemented solutions, e.g., adding treasury and risk management capabilities to an existing finance solution.

▶ **Enhance the infrastructure.**
This includes the deployment of a new technology, usually in addition to the current infrastructure—like a mobile infrastructure to extend the solution with mobile business scenarios that add a business intelligence platform for analytical capabilities.

▶ **Database migration.**
These solutions support the migration from one database to another, like the migration from a traditional relational database to an in-memory database like SAP HANA.

▶ **Adopt SAP's new innovations like SAP HANA.**
For example, for SAP Business Suite powered by SAP HANA, rapid-deployment solutions are available to address all important use-cases from new customers implementing SAP ERP on SAP HANA or SAP CRM on SAP HANA from scratch, as well as for customers who want to migrate their existing landscapes.

Modular solutions
-> assemble-to-
order

Not the least, SAP Rapid Deployment solutions provide much more than "point solutions for point problems." In fact, these solutions are designed in a modular way—so that for many use-cases, multiple rapid-deployment solutions can be combined like Lego blocks, working together to enable a bigger end-to-end solution. We refer to this as "assemble-to-order." Typical examples are companies that start with a broad footprint combining several rapid-deployment solutions for SAP ERP, SAP HCM, SAP SRM, mobile, etc., from the beginning.

Whether you want to address individual requirements or lay the foundation for large-scale, end-to-end solutions, SAP Rapid Deployment solutions make it simpler and faster, and provide significant reduction in cost, time, and risk. In addition to this, never underestimate the added business value of designing the solution based on best-practice experiences. As an SAP customer put it after implementing a large-scale extended warehouse management solution: "At the end of the day, we only left 70 percent of the scope according to the rapid-deployment solution, and the rest we changed and expanded; however, had we not seen the complete best-practice scope that came with the solution, we wouldn't have been able to make the right decisions for our business on which 30 percent really to individualize."

2.2 SAP Best Practices, SAP Business All-in-One, and SAP Rapid Deployment Solutions

In this section, we will introduce SAP Best Practices, SAP Business All-in-One, and SAP Rapid Deployment solutions in more detail. We will introduce what actually will be delivered with SAP Best Practices and how this concept relates to the SAP Business All-in-One offering for the mid-market and the rapid-deployment solutions offering. Before we dive into details, here is the explanation of the key offerings in a nutshell: With SAP Best Practices, we refer to the core content platform that describes the business best practices for specific areas like procurement, manufacturing, and different industries. SAP Best Practices are business-oriented, tried-and-tested, modular packages with pre-configuration, documentation, and built-in methodology that allow for out-of-the box deployment of integrated business capabilities.

Key offerings in a nutshell

Now let's review how SAP Business All-in-One and SAP Rapid Deployment solutions both build on the powerful content platform that SAP Best Practices provide.

SAP Business All-in-One is the offering for the mid-market. These packages are offered to customers and implemented via partners, i.e., the implementation service based on the pre-configuration content and documentation is performed by an SAP Partner.

Content platform

SAP Rapid Deployment solutions is the offering for enterprise customers also building on the content platform provided by SAP Best Practices. Rapid-deployment solutions add another component to the SAP Best Practices. They explicitly include an implementation service for the scope of the solution. This service is performed either via SAP Partners or directly by SAP consulting,

Figure 2.1 illustrates this relationship. We'll discuss these offerings individually in the following sections.

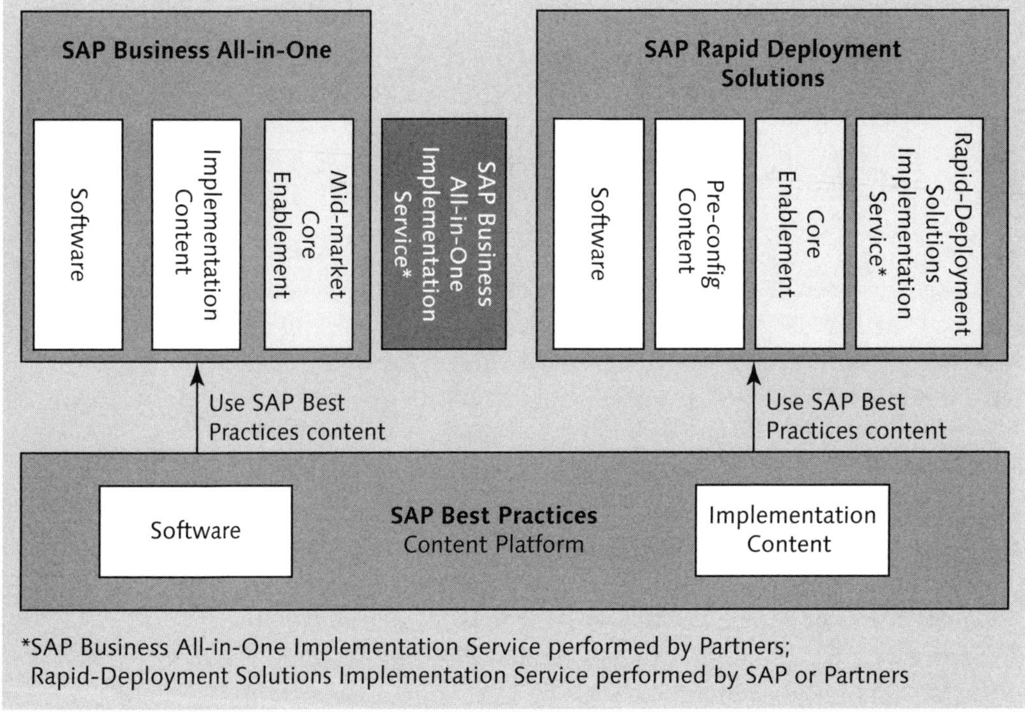

Figure 2.1 Relationship of SAP Best Practices, SAP Business All-in-One, and SAP Rapid Deployment Solutions

2.2.1 SAP Best Practices

The SAP Best Practices content platform captures the experience of more than 35 years of SAP implementation projects performed by SAP and partners around the globe for companies of all sizes and over a large variety of industries. SAP Best Practices document these experiences in a structured, well-designed, and extensible fashion that is available for customer projects. SAP Best Practices are continuously updated to cope with newest industry business trends and to include the latest technology innovations in the underlying products.

Best practice elements In essence, the SAP Best Practices content platform is comprised of two major elements:

1. The description of the best business practice, such as the best-practice business process for a certain area and industry, e.g., what are order-management best practices for the consumer-products industry.

2. A detailed documentation that describes how the SAP software should be configured and set up in order to execute the best business practices in the system. This includes detailed documentation like configuration and installation guides as well as pre-defined master data and configuration settings that can be uploaded in the system.

SAP Best Practices are structured into packages. Each package has a well-defined and self-contained functional scope that delivers a tangible business value and is suitable as scope for a separate implementation project. This means that the scope provides a complete base from which to launch an implementation project.

Packages

Content of an SAP Best Practice Package

An SAP Best Practice package consists in principle of a couple of documents and some scripts and files required to upload configuration settings and sample data (e.g., sample master data and organizational structures) into the system. These assets are defined via a standardized bill of material (BOM). Each asset type follows a common template.

The following list shows the key assets of a package and their purpose:

Package key assets

▸ **Software**
A list of the SAP software products and license materials that are required to run the scope of the package. This defines the software installation and software license requirements of the rapid-deployment solution.

▸ **Implementation Content**
The Implementation Content cluster contains assets that describe in detail how the best practice business process should be configured in the system.

▸ **Business Process Description**
A document describing the best-practice business process in graphical and textual form. See Figure 2.2 for an example of a best-practice business process diagram.

▶ **Configuration Guide**
A document describing in detail how to configure the system manually.

▶ **Quick Guide for Package Implementation**
A procedure to implement the complete package scope.

▶ **Pre-configuration settings**
The configuration settings for the package in a format that allows automatic upload of the settings into the system. The pre-configuration settings contain exactly the same settings as described in the configuration guide. If the automated upload of the configuration data can be used, the detailed steps in the configuration guide do not have to be executed manually.

▶ **Master data**
The relevant sample master data for the best-practice process. This incudes a so-called "model company" that serves as an example company with a sample organizational structure, chart of account, company and subsidiary setup, etc. This model company is shared across packages to simplify the combination of packages in one installation.

▶ **Test cases**
Test cases ready-to-use for the project to perform end-to-end tests for the best-practice business processes.

▶ **Learning material**
Material that can be leveraged by the project teams to conduct end-user training for the best-practice business process.

For a complete list of the assets contained in an example rapid-deployment solutions bill of material, see Section 4.2.3. In the following subsection, we will introduce some examples of key assets.

Key Assets

Business Process Description   The Business Process Description (BPD) comes in two flavors. A business-process diagram provides a graphical representation of the business processes of the rapid-deployment solution (see Figure 2.2).

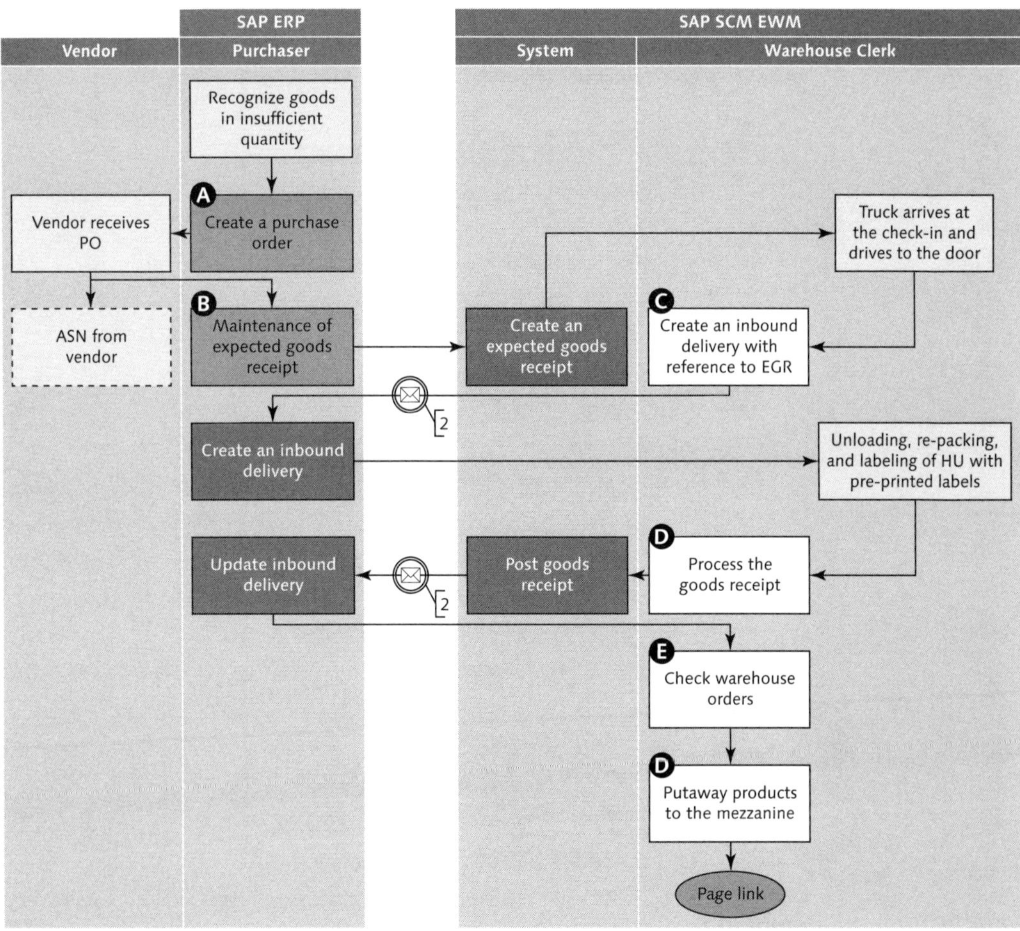

Figure 2.2 Process Diagram Example from Extended Warehouse Management Package

In addition, a textual document describes the process in detail and also describes how the process will be executed from the end-user perspective. This document is also well-suited for training and testing purposes. Figure 2.3 shows an excerpt of the Business Process Description document for the SAP Extended Warehouse Management rapid-deployment solution.

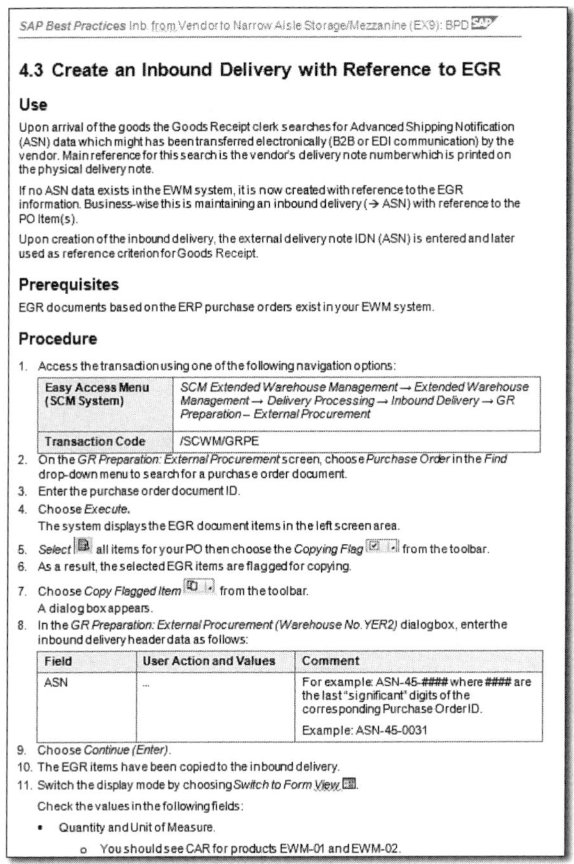

SAP Best Practices Inb. from Vendor to Narrow Aisle Storage/Mezzanine (EX9): BPD

4.3 Create an Inbound Delivery with Reference to EGR

Use

Upon arrival of the goods the Goods Receipt clerk searches for Advanced Shipping Notification (ASN) data which might has been transferred electronically (B2B or EDI communication) by the vendor. Main reference for this search is the vendor's delivery note number which is printed on the physical delivery note.

If no ASN data exists in the EWM system, it is now created with reference to the EGR information. Business-wise this is maintaining an inbound delivery (→ ASN) with reference to the PO Item(s).

Upon creation of the inbound delivery, the external delivery note IDN (ASN) is entered and later used as reference criterion for Goods Receipt.

Prerequisites

EGR documents based on the ERP purchase orders exist in your EWM system.

Procedure

1. Access the transaction using one of the following navigation options:

Easy Access Menu (SCM System)	*SCM Extended Warehouse Management → Extended Warehouse Management → Delivery Processing → Inbound Delivery → GR Preparation – External Procurement*
Transaction Code	/SCWM/GRPE

2. On the *GR Preparation: External Procurement* screen, choose *Purchase Order* in the *Find* drop-down menu to search for a purchase order document.
3. Enter the purchase order document ID.
4. Choose *Execute*.
    The system displays the EGR document items in the left screen area.
5. *Select* all items for your PO then choose the *Copying Flag* from the toolbar.
6. As a result, the selected EGR items are flagged for copying.
7. Choose *Copy Flagged Item* from the toolbar.
    A dialog box appears.
8. In the *GR Preparation: External Procurement (Warehouse No. YER2)* dialog box, enter the inbound delivery header data as follows:

Field	User Action and Values	Comment
ASN	...	For example: ASN-45-#### where #### are the last "significant" digits of the corresponding Purchase Order ID. Example: ASN-45-0031

9. Choose *Continue (Enter)*.
10. The EGR items have been copied to the inbound delivery.
11. Switch the display mode by choosing *Switch to Form View*.

    Check the values in the following fields:

    *   Quantity and Unit of Measure.

        o   You should see CAR for products EWM-01 and EWM-02.

Figure 2.3 Business Process Description Excerpt from Extended Warehouse Management Package

Configuration Guide

The Configuration Guide describes the detailed steps that are required to configure the business processes that are in the scope of the package. Each configuration setting, and how to access it, is described in detail. In the example of the SAP Extended Warehouse Management rapid-deployment solution package, a pre-defined sample warehouse layout is given and it is explained how project teams can configure exactly this layout in the Configuration Guide. Project teams use this sample layout in projects to adapt it to the actual layout. It is often easier to change a provided sample than to configure from scratch. Figure 2.4 shows an excerpt of the configuration guide and Figure 2.5 shows the provided sample of the layout in combination with the business process.

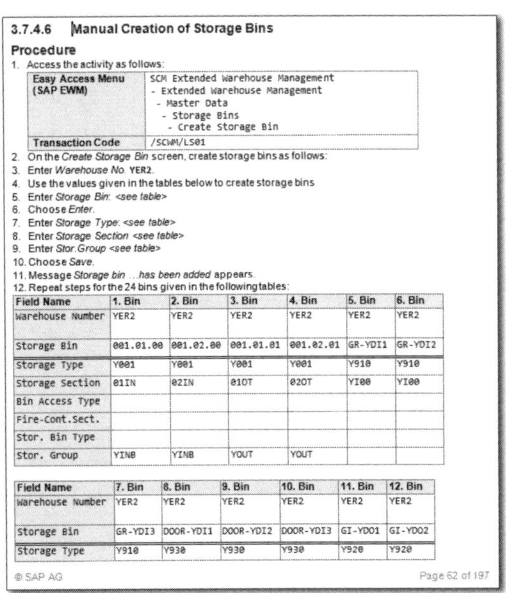

3.7.4.6 Manual Creation of Storage Bins

Procedure

1. Access the activity as follows:

Easy Access Menu (SAP EWM)	SCM Extended Warehouse Management
	- Extended Warehouse Management
	  - Master Data
	    - Storage Bins
	      - Create Storage Bin

Transaction Code	/SCWM/LS01

2. On the *Create Storage Bin* screen, create storage bins as follows:
3. Enter *Warehouse No.* YER2.
4. Use the values given in the tables below to create storage bins
5. Enter *Storage Bin*: <see table>
6. Choose *Enter*.
7. Enter *Storage Type*: <see table>
8. Enter *Storage Section* <see table>
9. Enter *Stor.Group* <see table>
10. Choose *Save*.
11. Message *Storage bin ...has been added* appears.
12. Repeat steps for the 24 bins given in the following tables:

Field Name	1. Bin	2. Bin	3. Bin	4. Bin	5. Bin	6. Bin
Warehouse Number	YER2	YER2	YER2	YER2	YER2	YER2
Storage Bin	001.01.00	001.02.00	001.01.01	001.02.01	GR-YDI1	GR-YDI2
Storage Type	Y001	Y001	Y001	Y001	Y910	Y910
Storage Section	01IN	02IN	01OT	02OT	YI00	YI00
Bin Access Type						
Fire-Cont.Sect.						
Stor. Bin Type						
Stor. Group	YINB	YINB	YOUT	YOUT		

Field Name	7. Bin	8. Bin	9. Bin	10. Bin	11. Bin	12. Bin
Warehouse Number	YER2	YER2	YER2	YER2	YER2	YER2
Storage Bin	GR-YDI3	DOOR-YDI1	DOOR-YDI2	DOOR-YDI3	GI-YDO1	GI-YDO2
Storage Type	Y910	Y930	Y930	Y930	Y920	Y920

© SAP AG   Page 62 of 197

Figure 2.4 Configuration Guide Excerpt for Extended Warehouse Management Package

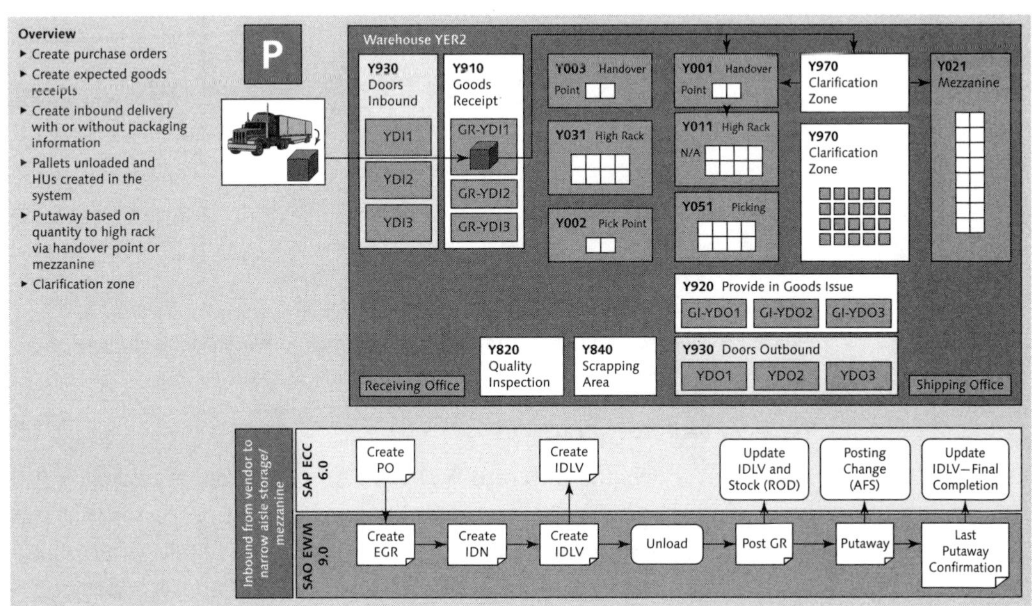

Figure 2.5 Sample Goods Receipt Process with the Usage of the Pre-Delivered Sample Warehouse Layout

Quick Guide for Package Implementation

The Quick Guide for Package Implementation summarizes the procedure of the package implementation and its prerequisites. It serves as the key document describing the implementation methodology, especially for the package in scope. Figure 2.6 shows an excerpt from SAP's example package.

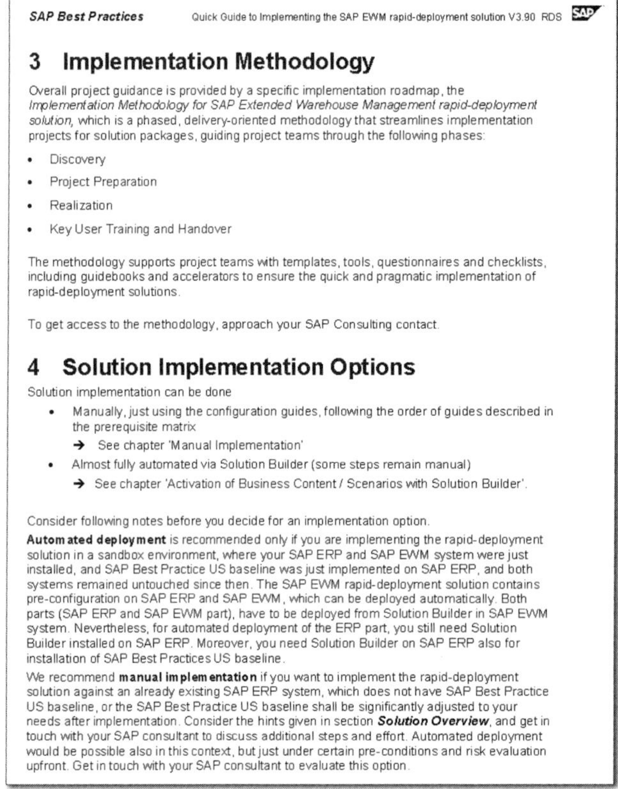

Figure 2.6 Quick Guide Excerpt from Extended Warehouse Management Package

Types of SAP Best Practices

Baseline packages

Figure 2.7 shows the different types of SAP Best Practice packages. The baseline packages provide the generic, core business processes that support the most important business needs. They are available in more than 50 different country localizations. These localizations are developed according to the legal requirements and country-specific needs. The baseline packages carry the core localization features. A separate baseline package, e.g., for SAP ERP, exists for each country. These baseline packages can be combined with any industry or cross-industry package.

See Appendix A, Section A.7, Table A.24, for a list of the baseline packages.

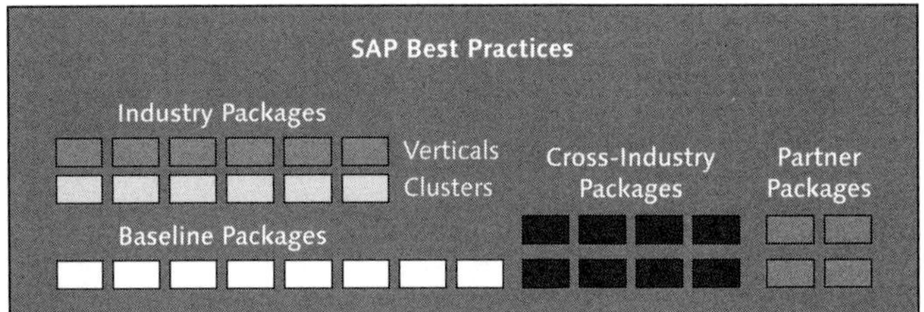

Figure 2.7 SAP Best Practices Package Types

Industry packages are configured to the needs of a specific industry. They are based on best practices developed with industry leaders. Industry packages are deployed on top of the respective baseline package for a specific country or cross-industry package. The automotive industry package, for example, could be deployed on top of the USA baseline package to build an automotive solution for a customer based in the USA.

Cross-industry packages contain predefined business processes relating to areas generally in use across multiple industries, such as C-parts procurement. They can be used in conjunction with baseline or industry packages.

The portfolio is extended by partners that offer their own partner packages; for example to address the configuration needs of specific partner extensions to the SAP solutions (see Chapter 7).

2.2.2 SAP Business All-in-One

SAP Business All-in-One is a solution that combines the SAP Best Practices content platform with a lifecycle workbench that assists project teams with a set of tools to ease the implementation tasks in the project, and has mid-market-specific, go-to-market assets that help position the business value of the SAP Business All-in-One packages. See Figure 2.8 for an overview of the structure.

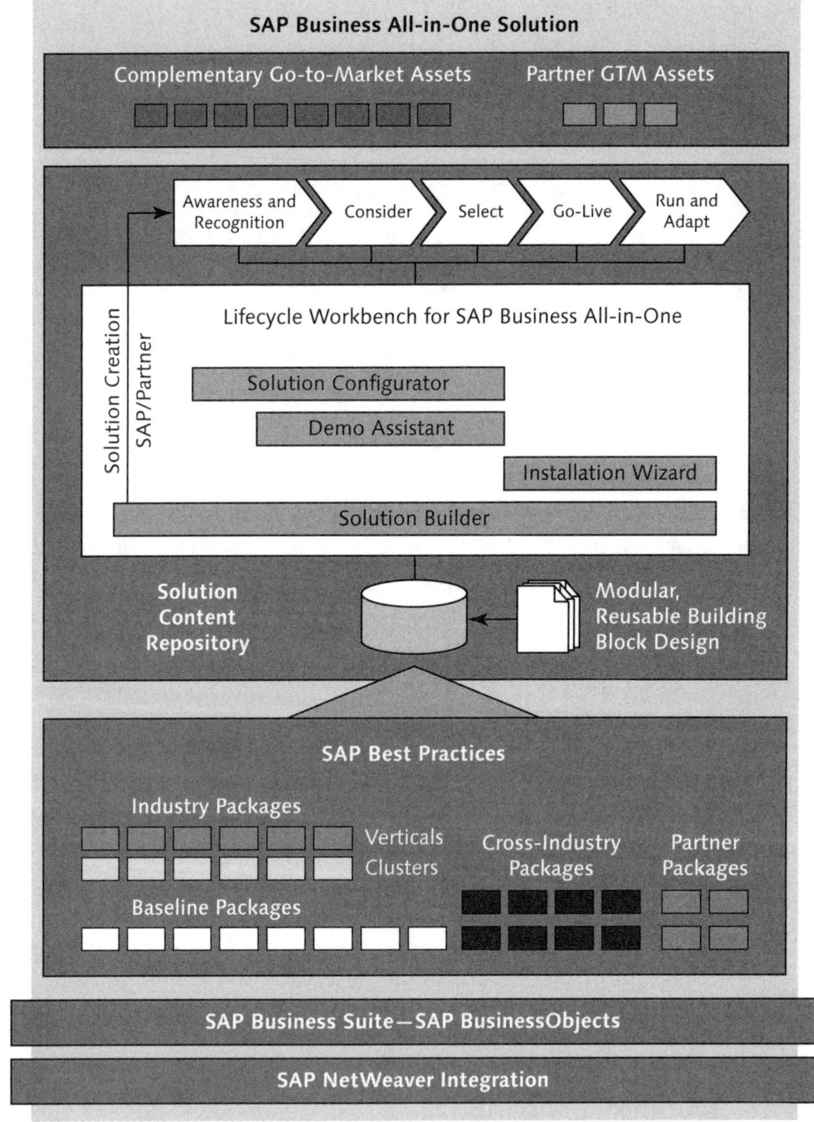

Figure 2.8 Structure of the SAP Business All-in-One Solution

As stated in the introduction of this section, the SAP Business-All-in-One solution represents the brand and the offering of the SAP Best Practices content for the mid-market. The implementation services for this content are performed via SAP Partners.

2.2.3 Rapid-Deployment Solutions

Rapid-deployment solutions are also based on the SAP Best Practices content platform. They also provide solutions based on this content for enterprise customers. In addition, rapid-deployment solutions adds two more elements to the SAP Best Practices content: the general go-to-market content and pre-defined implementation services.

Go-to-market content, pre-defined implementation services

Each rapid-deployment solution comes with a set of so-called services assets that define—often at a fixed price—implementation service for the scope of the solution. This service can be performed by SAP Partners or by SAP consulting.

Services assets

The key services assets consist of:

- **Work breakdown structure, schedule, and effort**
  A decomposition of work defined as a list of tasks to be done by the project team to complete project objectives.

- **Statement of Work**
  A document that describes the work that SAP delivers in an implementation project for the solution, and also any aspects that the customer must honor.

- **Scope document**
  A definition of the package used to understand the agreed-upon scope as a basis for handling changes to it.

- **Step-by-step guide**
  A standardized sequence of activities for the rapid deployment of the solution, with assets to support these activities.

Figure 2.9 shows an excerpt of a work breakdown structure (WBS) for the SAP Extended Warehouse Management rapid-deployment solution.

The WBS describes the different tasks that have to be executed in the project, grouped into project phases including testing, change management, user training, etc. Documents that describe further details on what and how to accomplish this task, or templates of deliverables of these tasks, are associated to the tasks in the WBS. These documents are called accelerators.

Work breakdown structure

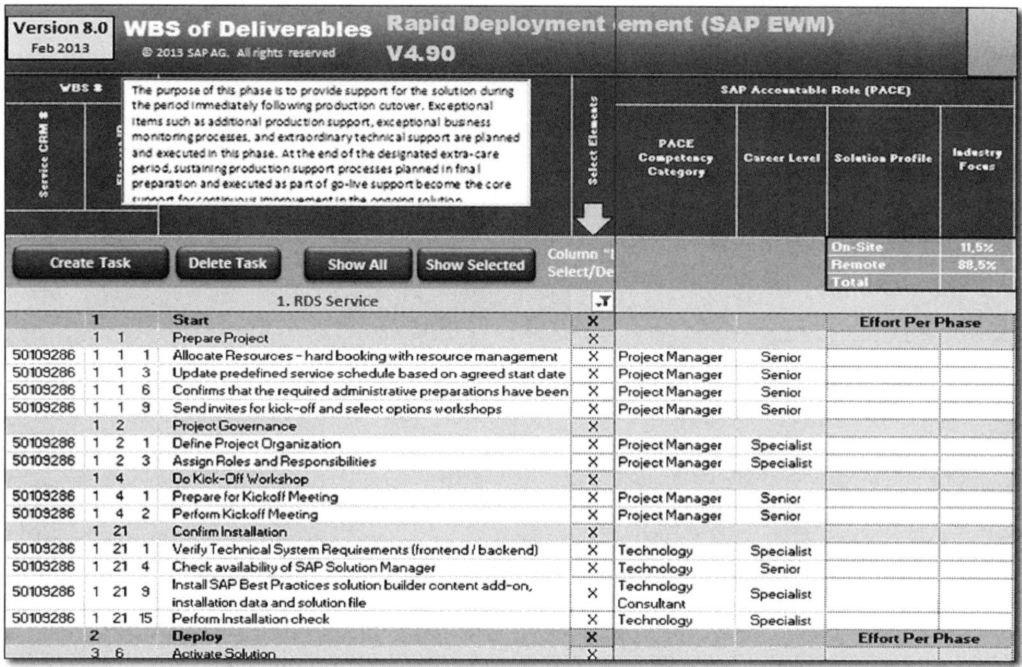

Version 8.0 Feb 2013	WBS of Deliverables © 2013 SAP AG. All rights reserved	Rapid Deployment…ement (SAP EWM) V4.90			

The purpose of this phase is to provide support for the solution during the period immediately following production cutover. Exceptional items such as additional production support, exceptional business monitoring processes, and extraordinary technical support are planned and executed in this phase. At the end of the designated extra-care period, sustaining production support processes planned in final preparation and executed as part of go-live support become the core support for continuous improvement in the ongoing solution.

Create Task	Delete Task	Show All	Show Selected		On-Site	11.5%
					Remote	88.5%
					Total	

Service CRM #		WBS #			Task	Select	PACE Competency Category	Career Level	Effort Per Phase
	1				Start	X			
	1	1			Prepare Project	X			
50109286	1	1	1		Allocate Resources – hard booking with resource management	X	Project Manager	Senior	
50109286	1	1	3		Update predefined service schedule based on agreed start date	X	Project Manager	Senior	
50109286	1	1	6		Confirms that the required administrative preparations have been	X	Project Manager	Senior	
50109286	1	1	9		Send invites for kick-off and select options workshops	X	Project Manager	Senior	
	1	2			Project Governance	X			
50109286	1	2	1		Define Project Organization	X	Project Manager	Specialist	
50109286	1	2	3		Assign Roles and Responsibilities	X	Project Manager	Specialist	
	1	4			Do Kick-Off Workshop	X			
50109286	1	4	1		Prepare for Kickoff Meeting	X	Project Manager	Senior	
50109286	1	4	2		Perform Kickoff Meeting	X	Project Manager	Senior	
	1	21			Confirm Installation	X			
50109286	1	21	1		Verify Technical System Requirements (frontend / backend)	X	Technology	Specialist	
50109286	1	21	4		Check availability of SAP Solution Manager	X	Technology	Senior	
50109286	1	21	9		Install SAP Best Practices solution builder content add-on, installation data and solution file	X	Technology Consultant	Specialist	
50109286	1	21	15		Perform Installation check	X	Technology	Specialist	
	2				**Deploy**	X			Effort Per Phase
	3	6			Activate Solution	X			

Figure 2.9 WBS Excerpt from Extended Warehouse Management Package

The WBS also captures which role in the project should execute the task and where it should be performed (on-site or in a near- or off-shore delivery center) together with the usual effort for the task based on experience from past projects. The WBS strictly follows the general structure and implementation methodology defined by the Accelerated SAP (ASAP) methodology. The ASAP 8 version contains a specific variant for the implementation of SAP Rapid Deployment solutions that is the master WBS for all the solutions. The specific WBS contains the specific refinement and the specific accelerators for the scope of the individual rapid-deployment solution. See Section 5.3 for a more detailed discussion on the ASAP implementation methodology.

Step-by-step guide

Figure 2.10 shows an example of a step-by-step guide. It provides a more simplified view on the WBS and lists the different project accelerators, i.e., the documents that help the consulting teams perform the various tasks in the project, structured around the project lifecycle.

The example shows the solution-activation step in the Deploy phase where either automated configuration content or the Configuration Guide for manual activation is used. The related accelerator assets like Business Process Description or manual configuration and activation (the Configuration Guide) and others are listed and are directly accessible from the step-by-step guide.

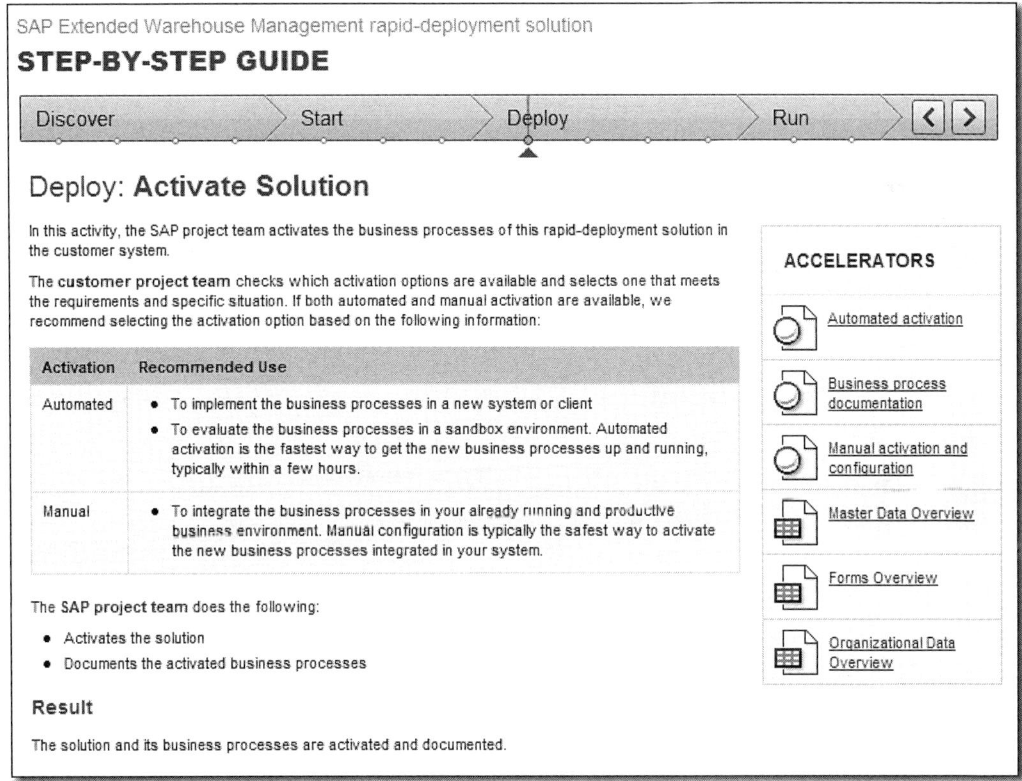

Figure 2.10 Step-By-Step Guide for SAP Extended Warehouse Management Rapid-Deployment Solution

While the SAP Business All-in-One solution is pretty much focused on SAP ERP and business objects, rapid-deployment solutions are available across SAP's product portfolio, including line of business, industry, technology, and analytics solutions. Please see Appendix A, Section A.1 for the SAP Rapid Deployment solutions portfolio.

2.3   The Assemble-To-Order Approach

Usually, the scope of a customer project is not covered by the scope of a single rapid-deployment solution. The experience with rapid-deployment solutions projects in recent years clearly shows that most customers implement more than one solution at the same time in one project. A nice example for this is introduced in Chapter 3, Section 3.3. The case describes why and how Rainbow Chicken Limited in South Africa has applied the assemble-to-order approach with SAP ERP.

Definition   The approach of combining multiple rapid-deployment solutions together with engineered services and customer-project-specific tasks not covered by a rapid-deployment solution or engineered service is called *assemble-to-order*. Instead of composing a project structure and content from scratch, it is assembled together out of pre-defined pieces that are given by the rapid-deployment solution. Simply put, the key assets of an implementation project, the pre-configuration content in the development systems, SAP Solution Manager content for solution implementation and documentation, and the project structure, i.e., the WBS of the project, has to be assembled out of the different individual parts of the rapid-deployment solution that are the basis for the project.

WBS merge   The individual WBS from the individual rapid-deployment solutions are merged together into the single project WBS. The individual business processes are also merged and integrated. The combined business-process description is made available via SAP Solution Manager content. Finally, the pre-configuration content in the business systems has to be merged as well.

Pre-assembled solutions   If pre-assembled rapid-deployment solutions are used, the pre-assembly of the configuration content is already performed and delivered with the software and sample data in one installable image. In this case, the related combined WBS and the related solution-manager content is also pre-combined (we'll discuss pre-assembled solutions in Section 2.4).

The right structure, modularity, and compatibility of the underlying assets in the rapid-deployment solution are the fundamental enabler of the assemble-to-order approach. If these assets are structured in the right way, according to the requirements and needs of real projects, the assembly of the individual elements to a complete project structure can be easily accomplished by the project teams. The rapid-deployment solutions content has evolved in recent years to provide this basis.

2.4   Pre-Assembled Rapid-Deployment Solutions and the Cloud

The concept of pre-assembled rapid-deployment solutions combines the concept of rapid-deployment solutions, the assemble-to-order approach, and a new delivery mechanism. The new delivery mechanism uses virtualization and cloud technologies.

New delivery mechanism

It is given by the delivery of a combined image that contains the underlying software (and all the required support packages and patches) plus the related pre-configuration content and matching sample data into a single installable image. This image can be provided in a cloud environment or installed at the customer site within hours. This provides a running system with best-practices processes configured, as well as sample data. It is ready for demo and evaluation, and it provides a basis for a fit/gap analysis between the SAP Best Practices and the intended customer project scope.

Combined image

In the following sections, we'll define the approach in more detail in Section 2.4.1, shed some light on key usage scenarios in Section 2.4.2, and discuss the impact of pre-assembled rapid-deployment solutions in Section 2.4.3.

2.4.1   Definition of a Pre-Assembled Rapid-Deployment Solution

In principal, a pre-assembled rapid-deployment solution is an additional delivery vehicle for a set of rapid-deployment solutions combined according to the assemble-to-order approach, delivered via system images.

Content
Consequently, it consists of:

- The combined content of multiple rapid-deployment solutions according to the assemble-to-order approach.
- A best-practice system landscape to run the functional scope of the combined rapid-deployment solutions.

Image/integration
For each physical system that is part of the system landscape, an installable image is provided that contains the complete required software stack plus the related configuration settings and sample data in one step. The configuration settings already provide the integration with the other physical systems that are part of the combined landscape for the pre-assembled rapid-deployment solutions. Thus, the combination of the system images in the overall landscape provides running end-to-end business processes with sample data out of the box within hours. This can be achieved by combining virtualization techniques with SAP technology.

Scope of image
This approach accelerates the software installation and best-practices provisioning phase at the beginning of a project. It enables the project to start with a running system and to base a fit/gap analysis on concrete system experiences that draw on best business practices. The installable image representing the pre-assembled rapid-deployment solution will be installed on top of the base operating system. Figure 2.11 illustrates the scope of a pre-assembled rapid-deployment solution installation image.

Multi-system landscape
Multiple rapid-deployment solutions combined together usually means that an integrated system landscape comprised of different systems, i.e., servers, is required. The combination of SAP ERP with SAP CRM, SAP NetWeaver BW on SAP HANA, and mobile application capabilities, for example, requires a multisystem landscape. A pre-assembled rapid-deployment solution therefore delivers a virtualized, pre-integrated system landscape including the appropriate pre-configuration content for this system landscape.

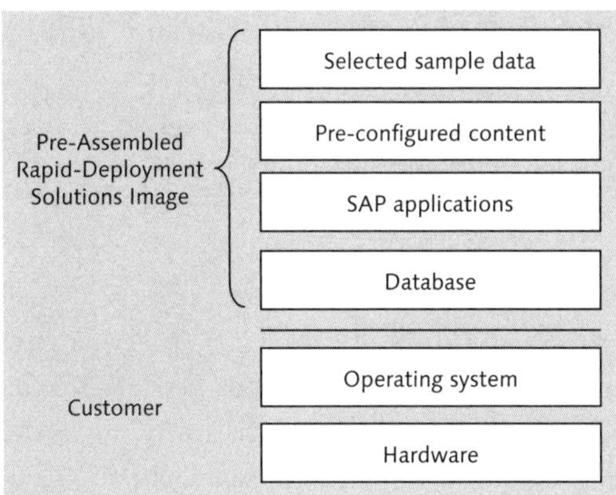

Figure 2.11 Content of a Pre-Assembled Rapid-Deployment Solution Image

Each system in the virtualized landscape is installed using a pre-assembled rapid-deployment solution image as depicted in Figure 2.12.

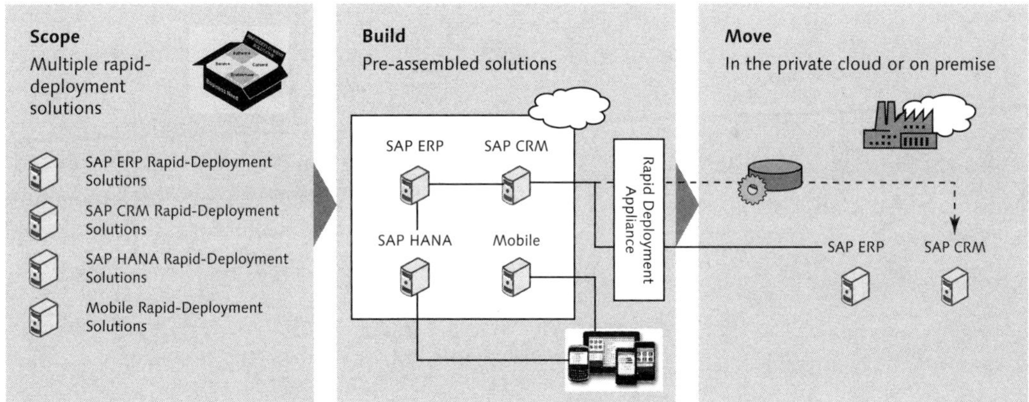

Figure 2.12 Example System Landscape of Pre-Assembled Rapid-Deployment Solution

This figure shows an example of the landscape contained in the Enterprise Foundation Extended pre-assembled rapid-deployment solution that combines the core SAP ERP foundation processes with mobile scenarios and the SAP HANA database.

2.4.2 Usage Scenarios of Pre-Assembled Rapid-Deployment Solutions

The concept of pre-assembled rapid-deployment solutions can be used in several scenarios, which we illustrate in the following subsections.

Demo

Pre-assembled rapid-deployment solutions are used to provide demo environments for prospects and customers to showcase SAP Best Practice processes. These demo systems are provided in the cloud, and access to these public demo environments can be provided within hours. This enables an easy access to a tangible demonstration of the business benefits of SAP's integrated business solutions.

Test Drive

Pilot configuration

With a test drive based on pre-assembled rapid-deployment solutions, customers can use the pre-integrated landscape with the pre-assembled rapid-deployment solution that matches as closely as possible to the intended project scope in order to experience SAP Best Practices in a system. The test drive is provided in a private cloud environment and thus enables the customer to perform pilot configuration activities. The customer can also upload their own master data into this environment in order to check out the SAP Best Practice processes that master data.

Therefore the test drive can be used as a tool to determine the final project scope and to perform a fit/gap analysis for a customer implementation project.

Project Jump-Start

Basis for project

A pre-assembled rapid-deployment solution can also be used to provide the basis for an implementation project. The SAP Best Practice scope—matching as closely as possible to the intended scope of the customer project—is provided as a pre-assembled rapid-deployment solution. It appears as a set of integrated system images for each physical system that is required for the project scope, and provides the basis for the development system landscape for the project.

The project jump-start can be deployed in the cloud or on-premise at the customer site.

2.4.3 Impact of Pre-Assembled Rapid-Deployment Solutions on Project Setup and Timeline

Following the project jump-start approach, the overall split between project deliverables and SAP deliverables changes compared to the traditional design-based project approach. This impacts the timeline of the project as shown in Figure 2.13 (you can also find more details about timelines by reading the customer use cases in Chapter 3).

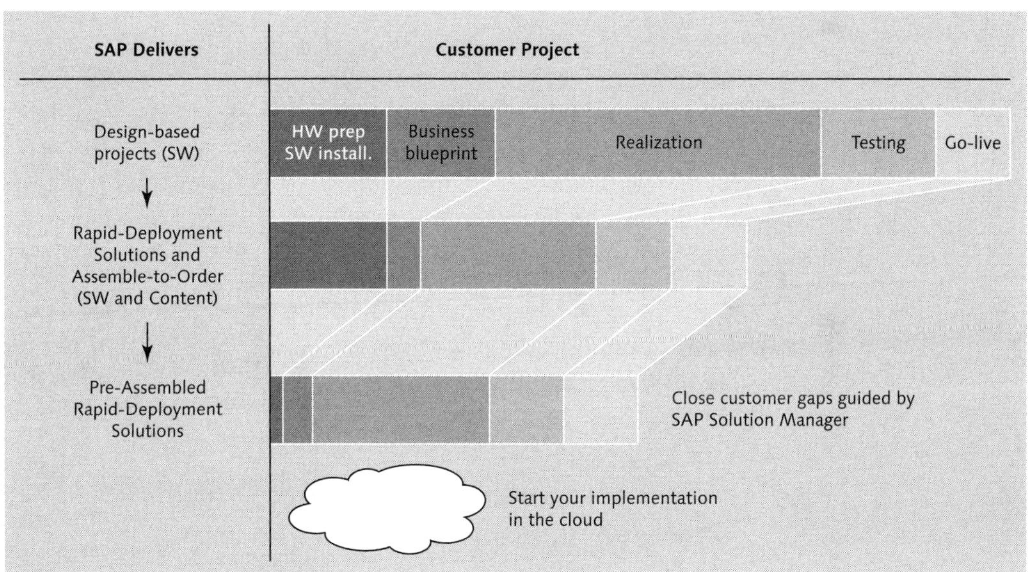

Figure 2.13 Pre-Assembled Rapid-Deployment Solutions

Following the design-based project approach, the first step after checking hardware and software requirements is an (often extensive) business blueprinting phase. In this phase, the business requirements are defined. Next, these business requirements are mapped to the software and potential gaps are identified. After that the project realization, i.e., the manual configuration according to the business requirements, takes place.

Design-based project

Rapid-deployment solution & assemble-to-order approach

The next evolution step is the *rapid-deployment solution and assemble-to-order approach*. The consumer still has to perform the hardware and software installation, or the customer hires a consultant to perform the installation. The next step is the provisioning of the SAP Best Practices content matching the project scope as closely as possible. Building on SAP Best Practices greatly reduces the implementation duration, effort, and project risk.

Pre-assembled rapid-deployment solutions

Pre-assembled rapid-deployment solutions assembling different solutions together in terms of the related rapid-deployment solution packages and software products becomes an SAP deliverable that SAP provides before the project starts—as an additional delivery channel for these solutions.

The pre-assembled rapid-deployment solution can be made available to customers in the cloud—especially in the SAP HANA Enterprise Cloud. This allows for a project jump-start and the immediate opportunity to discover SAP Best Practices for the project scope in a running system with sample data. The project can directly start in the cloud environment regardless of hardware availability at the customer site.

Another option is the on-premise installation of pre-assembled rapid-deployment solutions if the customer prefers to implement and run the SAP environment in their own data center.

2.5 Use-Cases and Delivery Options for Rapid-Deployment Solutions

When an individual solution comes into play at the customer site, there are different starting points and scenarios depending on whether customers have already introduced SAP-based business processes into their enterprise, and to what extent.

Delivery options

In general, when implementing rapid-deployment solutions in customer landscapes, three major use-cases and respective delivery options can be distinguished:

- **New business processes**
  Introduction of new or additional business processes, e.g., new processes/scenarios vs. extension of existing (implemented) processes/scenarios.

- **Infrastructure enhancements**
  Adding new infrastructure elements like a mobile platform to the customer's business solution.

- **Database migration**
  Migrating the underlying database, such as from a traditional relational database to an in-memory database like SAP HANA.

Rapid deployment of SAP solutions comes with three different implementation approaches with different degrees of automation:

Implementation approaches

1. **Pre-assembled rapid-deployment solutions**
   This approach is the most automated, where the software, the pre-configuration, and sample data are installed from a single image within hours as a jump-start for a project.

2. **Automated deployment of pre-configuration data**
   In this case, the software is installed independently, but the required pre-configuration data is loaded into the system automatically according to the project scope.

3. **Manual deployment of pre-configuration data**
   If the automated approach is not feasible, perhaps because the rapid-deployment solution should be deployed on top of an already existing configuration, the pre-configuration data can be added manually into the system. To support this step, each rapid-deployment solution contains a detailed configuration guide that gives step-by-step descriptions for which configuration settings have to be set to which value and why. Using this approach, potential conflicts between the existing configuration and the rapid-deployment solution configuration can be detected and resolved.

In the following sections, we will map out the aforementioned use-cases and explain which implementation approaches are best for the individual use cases.

2.5.1   New Business Processes

In the following sections, we'll detail a couple of cases where new business processes are involved. This includes a totally new implementation, or adding a new component or solution into an existing SAP landscape.

Case 1: Net New Implementation, "Greenfield"

New customers/renovations
This scenario is relevant for customers that are either new to SAP applications or are investing in renovation of their current landscape. Whenever new solution configuration projects start from scratch, you can benefit in many ways from an engineered approach, such as those based on best practices, right from the beginning.

The individual rapid-deployment solutions are designed to work as modules. When combined, these modules complement each other and serve as baseline for growth scenarios along further best business practices, building up and using further rapid-deployment solution as business needs dictate.

The implementation can be highly automated, either via the pre-configuration content or even pre-assembled by SAP as a rapid-deployment solution. The pre-assembled version is of particular interest when several packages are to be adopted simultaneously. In that case, SAP will pre-build the integration between the various modules. This allows the on-site approach to be even more flexible for sequential implementations of multiple rapid-deployment solutions over a longer period.

Build/grow customer landscape
Figure 2.13 outlines how rapid-deployment solutions can be utilized to build and grow a customer landscape of business processes. It starts with the SAP ERP baseline and illustrates how further modules can be added, allowing the customer to take advantage of the savings and benefits of the pre-configured approach.

The dashed boxes in Figure 2.14 and the following figures indicate new components added in a project, the solid boxes indicate components that are already part of the customer landscape before project starts.

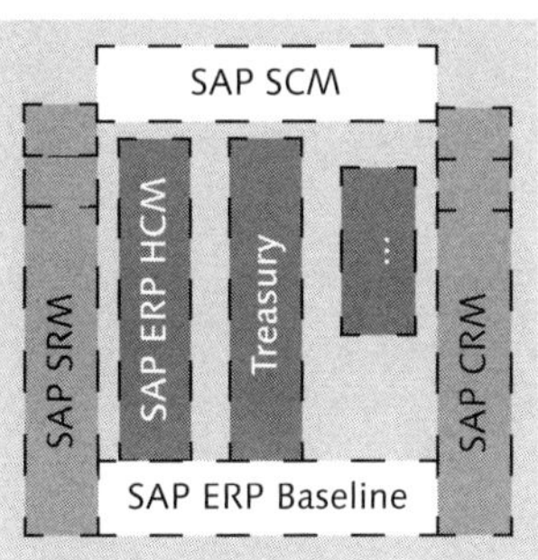

Figure 2.14 Net New Implementation, "Greenfield"

Case 2: Add New SAP Business Suite Component to an Existing Landscape

As the customer business grows and has to meet new demands from internal process owners or customers, the rapid-deployment solutions approach can simplify the adoption and introduction of new business processes to current landscapes.

Pre-assembled rapid-deployment solutions are still possible to enhance current landscapes, as long as they are focused on highly independent applications, such as new SAP Business Suite powered by SAP HANA components.

Even though the rapid-deployment solutions packages are pre-assembled and delivered to the deployment site, there is still work to be performed to complete the deployment. Final integration into the customer landscape has still to be done as an on-site project task. The size of this integration effort is determined by the type of pre-assembled order—as there are multiple pre-assemblies available, and the list is growing.

Another variant of the existing landscape deployment could be the integration with the cloud where rapid-deployment solutions especially support establishing the connectivity between business processes running in hybrid scenarios (on-premise integration with the cloud). Cloud

In Figure 2.15 we assume a customer already has the SAP ERP baseline implemented and now adds SAP CRM based on respective rapid-deployment solutions.

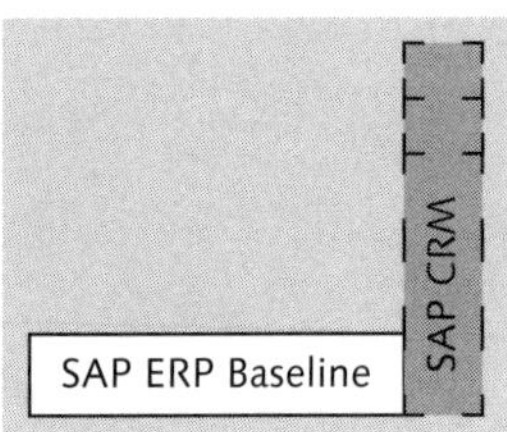

Figure 2.15 Add New SAP Business Suite Component to Existing Landscape

Case 3: Add New Solution into Customer Existing Landscapes, e.g., Customer-Configured System

SAP is often asked to add a new solution into an existing landscape. This means that the rapid-deployment solution is deployed with a previously configured system. SAP finds that these two variations fit most such scenarios: Solutions with disjointed configuration space, and solutions with overlapping configuration space. We explain these in the following subsections.

Solutions with Disjointed Configuration Space

Landscape + new scenario

With rapid-deployment solutions, new business scenarios can be introduced into existing landscapes. Automated configuration is still possible, as long as the configuration spaces of existing processes and enhancements are sufficiently disjointed. This means that there are only a limited number of integration points between current and new business processes. In these cases, the implementation tools delivered with a rapid-deployment solution provide flexibility for adjusting dependencies on typical master data, such as charts of accounts or cost centers.

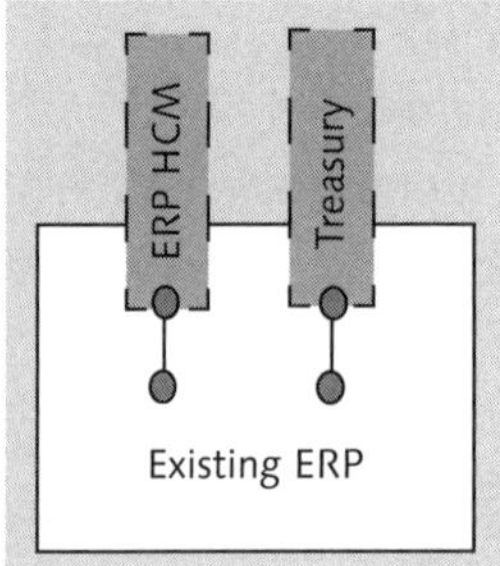

Figure 2.16 Solutions with Disjointed Configuration Space

Even with the implementation tools, manual fine-tuning is still needed as part of a dedicated project on an existing customer landscape.

Figure 2.16 depicts an SAP ERP baseline to which extensions in human capital management and treasury are added. Notice the disjointed configuration space.

Extensions

Solutions with Overlapping Configuration Space

Often, existing content in the customer's system will overlap with the new deployment. Even if new solutions are integrated into an already configured solution area, customers can still benefit from rapid-deployment solutions because, in addition to the automated implementation files, the package contains detailed configuration guides describing all settings to be done.

Depending on the level of overlap of existing, customer-configured content and the pre-configured content coming with the new rapid-deployment solution, the automated procedure might not be recommended. But customers can still use the guides to configure the landscape following the target picture, based on the described best practices.

Overlap

The ratio of benefits versus the effort to adopt increases when multiple packages are added, such as commodity and risk management and commodity procurement to existing SAP ERP and treasury, for example. Although there might be a large overlap of the existing configurations when deploying the new, additional rapid-deployment solutions best practices, the overlap only needs to be addressed once by the deployment team.

Automation will be helpful in certain cases, but the SAP Best Practices will serve as accelerators in all implementation projects. For example, take an existing treasury solution deployment. It can be enhanced with the new SAP solution for Commodity Risk Management, which is based on best practices from the available SAP Commodity Risk Management rapid-deployment solution. However, there can be overlaps. For example, the account definition rules for commodities can interfere with existing rules for financial transactions, like money markets or foreign-exchange rules received from the treasury module. Overlaps such as these need to be carefully investigated during the deployment planning—

Best practices as accelerators

before implementation—to avoid damages to configurations that already exist in the customer landscape.

Automation will be helpful in select cases only, but best practices still serve as accelerators in the individual implementation projects.

Figure 2.17 outlines a customer scenario where SAP ERP and treasury are already implemented and configured. Adding the SAP Commodity Risk Management rapid-deployment solution and the SAP Commodity Procurement rapid-deployment solution to this landscape requires manual effort, although configuration guides delivered with rapid-deployment solutions can be utilized.

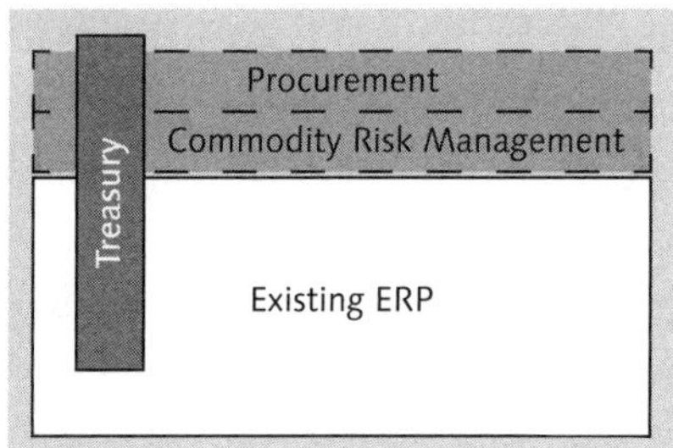

Figure 2.17 Solutions with Overlapping Configuration Space

2.5.2 Infrastructure Enhancements

If a customer is enhancing the technical infrastructure of the solution (e.g., by adding a mobile platform), and thereby extending the existing business processes with additional capabilities we talk about the *infrastructure enhancement* scenario. In this scenario, customers are in the process of a strategic transformation evaluating a new platform with an SAP ERP backend system. Say, for example, that the SAP ERP customer considers using the SAP Mobile Platform. In this use case, the SAP Mobile Platform rapid-deployment solution is ideal for a customer that is using mobility solutions to their competitiveness. Because of the predefined scope and deployment methodology, the standardized rapid-deployment solution approach allows the customer to quickly get a running system in their specific landscape based on SAP's best practices in mobile platform deployments, especially within a landscape that includes SAP ERP. The customer can check, in great detail, which additional benefits are included in the package, and determine if there is additional scope needed for their desired use case.

By reviewing the scope and identifying possible gaps, decision-makers can provide more effective input to the deployment team as part of the project planning. The customer can get a much more accurate assessment of the specific deployment—including costs and schedule—and make an informed decision to deploy the package or build upon the experience and choose other service options in the solution that provides a more customized go-live at the end of the project. Additionally, the rapid-deployment solution approach will allow the customer to have a safer and more predictable transformation to a mobile platform, largely due to the known scope, deployment methodology, costs, and schedule.

Review scope/gaps

As shown in Figure 2.18, a customer builds up a mobile infrastructure that connects to an existing SAP ERP backend.

SAP ERP + mobile

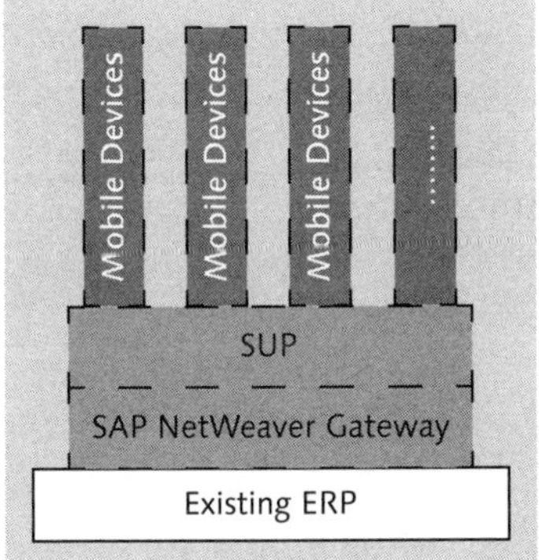

Figure 2.18 Infrastructure (Mobile Platform and Mobile Applications)

2.5.3 Database Migration

Database migration describes the technical switch from one existing database to another. Therefore, the database migration applies to customers who are currently running their SAP Business Suite application on a traditional relational database and chose to move it to SAP HANA, for example. These customers are looking for a fast, predictable, reliable, and ideally risk-free transition process.

Run on SAP HANA

This is where the SAP Rapid Deployment solutions comes into play with best-practices knowledge, standardized processes, and the latest in tool development for database migration when customers switch their SAP Business Suite to run on the power of SAP HANA. Besides the mandatory steps of updating the current application to the latest release, the preparation of the SAP HANA target landscape and the database migration itself, of course, are two major topics that are also covered via the rapid-deployment solution.

Source system preparation

One is preparation of the source system(s) before the export of the relational database management system (RDBMS). This includes the extensive manual work that is normally needed during the preparation of the source system before the export of the RDBMS, as well as post processing after the import into the SAP HANA database.

Minimal system downtime

The second is that the business downtime of the SAP Business Suite system needs to be minimized to have as little impact on operational business as possible. Both topics are now automated through rapid-deployment solution database migration packages to an extent that was not available in the past. The rapid-deployment solution eliminates the error-prone manual steps and enables the database migration team with new scenarios to minimize business downtime.

Figure 2.19 shows a migration scenario from any database to SAP HANA.

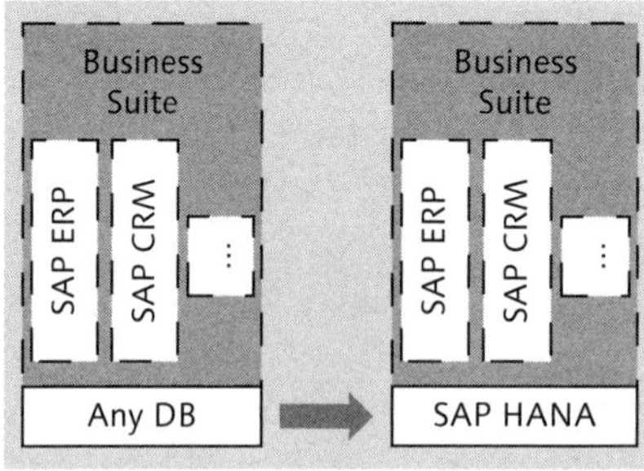

Figure 2.19 Database Migration to SAP HANA

2.5.4 Evaluation of Use-Cases and Delivery Options for Rapid-Deployment Solutions

The discussed use cases can be evaluated with regard to the recommended delivery option and to the degree where customers can benefit from the automated configuration and pre-assembled, personalized appliance. This summary is depicted in Table 2.1.

Cluster	Scenario	Recommended Delivery Options			Comment
		Manual Configuration	Automated Configuation	Pre-Assembled Solutions	
New business process	Greenfield	--	Yes	Yes	
	Add new component	--	Yes	Yes	Integration to be done on-site
	Add new solution (separate config)	--	Yes	--	Rapid-deployment solution tools allow flexible adjustments, manual fine-tuning as needed
	Add new solution (same config)	Yes	Yes	--	Depends on individual analysis
Infrastructure (mobile scenario)		--	Yes	Preconfiguration available	--	Relevant in context when connecting to business processes
Database migration		--	Yes	Yes	--	Validate

Table 2.1 Evaluation of Customer Use Cases

Depending on the starting point, current landscape, and business needs, customers can benefit from rapid-deployment solutions in various ways. We discussed how these solutions can be leveraged to achieve a faster time-to-value in different customer use-cases, be it the implementation of new or additional business processes, or the introduction of mobile infrastructure or database migration. Clearly, the respective cases can be combined to produce results that were unachievable before, such as adding mobile infrastructure to different business-process landscapes.

2.6 The Simplified Rapid-Deployment Solution Experience

This section will go into greater detail on the new implementation paradigm called the "Simplified Rapid-Deployment Solution Experience," which we briefly introduced in Chapter 1. This approach defines the next level of the rapid-deployment solution approach. It builds and extends on rapid-deployment solution concepts and further simplifies them.

End-to-end methodology The Simplified Rapid-Deployment Solution Experience defines an end-to-end methodology for the deployment of SAP solutions. As depicted in Figure 2.20, it covers the exploration of SAP solutions based on industry value maps, the selection of a project scope based on the elements of the industry value maps, the deployment of the solution based on rapid-deployment solutions, and the transition into the "Run" phase and continuous operations and improvement.

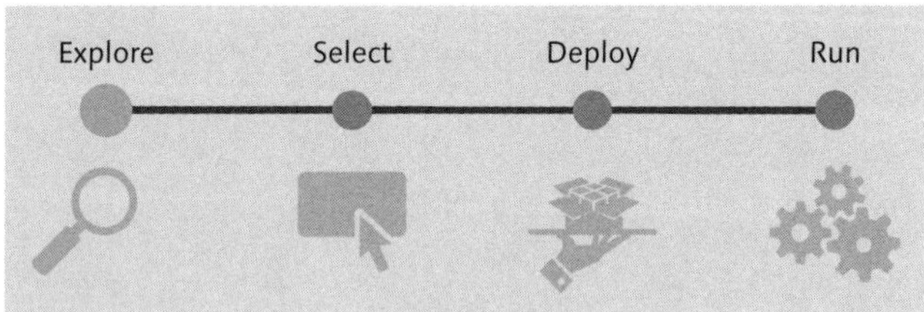

Figure 2.20 Simplified Rapid-Deployment Solution Experience

The key paradigms behind the approach are:

▸ Link best practices with the go-to-market structure of SAP solutions following the SAP Corporate Taxonomy; make SAP Best Practices an integral part of the solution.

- All projects are based on SAP Best Practices/SAP Rapid Deployment solutions. The scope of a project is described by the set of best practices that match as closely as possible to the customer scope and the remaining delta between the best practices and the customer scope. This represents a new blueprinting approach. Blueprinting is based on SAP Best Practices, instead of starting with a blank sheet of paper and processing re-engineering exercise from scratch.

- Provide a demo/test-drive system with the relevant selected SAP Best Practices in the cloud within days or even hours. The fit/gap analysis of SAP Best Practices versus customer scope is performed with a running system with sample data, not as a theoretical exercise.

- Starting point for the development system is a pre-assembled rapid-deployment solution tailored to customer needs. Ideally the development system evolves based on the test-drive used for fit/gap analysis.

- The implementation project is performed in an agile and iterative fashion. The results of the fit/gap analysis feed the backlog of the implementation project. This approach is integrated in SAP'S implementation methodology Accelerated SAP (ASAP) (see Chapter 5).

The four key phases in a nutshell:

- **Explore**
  Find the right solution for a business challenge. Structured browsing through the portfolio of SAP and the ecosystem.

  Outcome: Leaves the customer with an idea of the offerings provided for their business challenges.

- **Select**
  Define the scope for an implementation project. Map the business challenges to concrete rapid-deployment solutions that address these business challenges.

  Outcome: Scoping report that maps the business requirements to the set of rapid-deployment solutions and software products that address these requirements.

- **Deploy**
  Implement the solution based on SAP Best Practices. Start the project with a live system in the cloud that already contains the pre-configured SAP Best Practices and sample data. Perform a fit/gap analysis

based on the experience in the live system. Perform an agile and iterative implementation project to resolve the gaps.

Outcome: Production landscape based on best practices tailored to the individual needs of the customer.

▸ **Run**
Enable smooth transition into the operations phase by providing appropriate content for solution documentation and business process monitoring in the best practices and ensure refinement during the deploy phase.

Outcome: Smooth operations and a system landscape that is easy to maintain and support.

The following subsections will introduce the different phases of the experience.

2.6.1   Explore

The key objective of the Explore phase is to identify the SAP solution that is most suitable for a given business challenge. This can be performed by using customer self-service tools on the Internet to browse through the solution offering provided by SAP and partners. We briefly discuss these tools in the following subsections (you can also find more information on how to use them in Chapter 5).

Industry Value Map

The solution offering is structured around the 25 industries addressed by SAP and its partners. Each industry provides an industry value map (see Figure 2.21 for an example of the industry value map for high tech).

Transparent ecosystem

Via the industry value map, the offering of SAP and its ecosystem will be made transparent in an easy to consume fashion. Business challenges and its solutions are described in the language of the industry. Following the structure provided by the industry value map, the user can drill into the details of the solutions and learn more about business drivers, benefits, and the way how business challenges are addressed by SAP solutions.

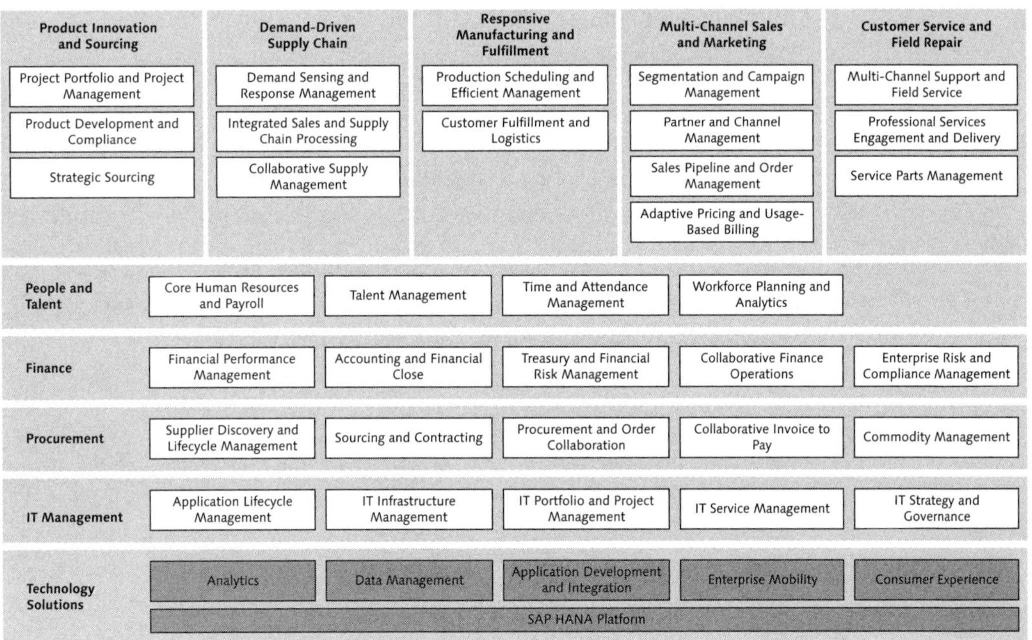

Figure 2.21 Industry Value Map for High-Tech

Rapid-deployment solutions, the documentation of the related SAP Best Practice processes, the SAP software products that are part of the solution, and the related software license materials are also included and linked to the relevant pages within the industry value maps.

Industry value maps are structured around the key business priorities relevant for the industry (e.g., Multichannel Sales and Marketing—the grey boxes on the map). Within these business priorities, the reader can drill down into the business challenges and find more detailed information, e.g., *Segmentation and Campaign Management*.

Business priorities

The red boxes refer to solutions that cover technology foundation aspects such as *Analytics* or *Enterprise Mobility* in the context of the selected industry.

A reader of an industry value map can fully examine the end-to-end solution and learn about the details, including the value proposition and roads to implement the solution and unlock its value.

SAP Solution Explorer

Industry value maps are made available via a web application called SAP Solution Explorer. It is publicly available on the Internet at *www.sap.com/solutionexplorer*. SAP Solution Explorer allows you to browse through the value maps and to drill down into the descriptions of the business challenges and solutions at different levels of granularity.

Single point of entry SAP Solution Explorer serves as the single point of entry to browse and experience the entire solution portfolio of SAP and the ecosystem. The Simplified Rapid-Deployment Solution Experience starts here, with the first step of matching business challenges and requirements to SAP solutions.

This leads directly into the next phase of the experience — the Scope phase.

2.6.2 Scope

The key objective of the Scope phase is to identify a concrete project scope to realize the solutions that have been identified during the Explore phase.

Step 1: Bookmark Solutions Based on the Industry Value Map

As a first step in this phase, the user can bookmark certain solutions while browsing through the industry value maps. Using this approach, a scope for an intended initiative or project can be captured based on the elements in the industry value map.

SAP Solution Configurator The extension of SAP Solution Explorer, the SAP Solution Configurator, maps the selected scope from the industry value maps on the business processes from SAP Best Practices. This step is the transformation from business challenges into business best practices that address these challenges.

Figure 2.22 shows the user selection of SAP solution capabilities on the left hand side. For Lead Management, the view is extended, showing related SAP Best Practices processes such as Lead Management (Mobile) or Interactive Reporting with SAP HANA. Process descriptions and more detailed information on how to configure these processes are accessible from here. Individual best-practice processes can be selected or deselected to fine-tune the scope of the planned implementation initiative.

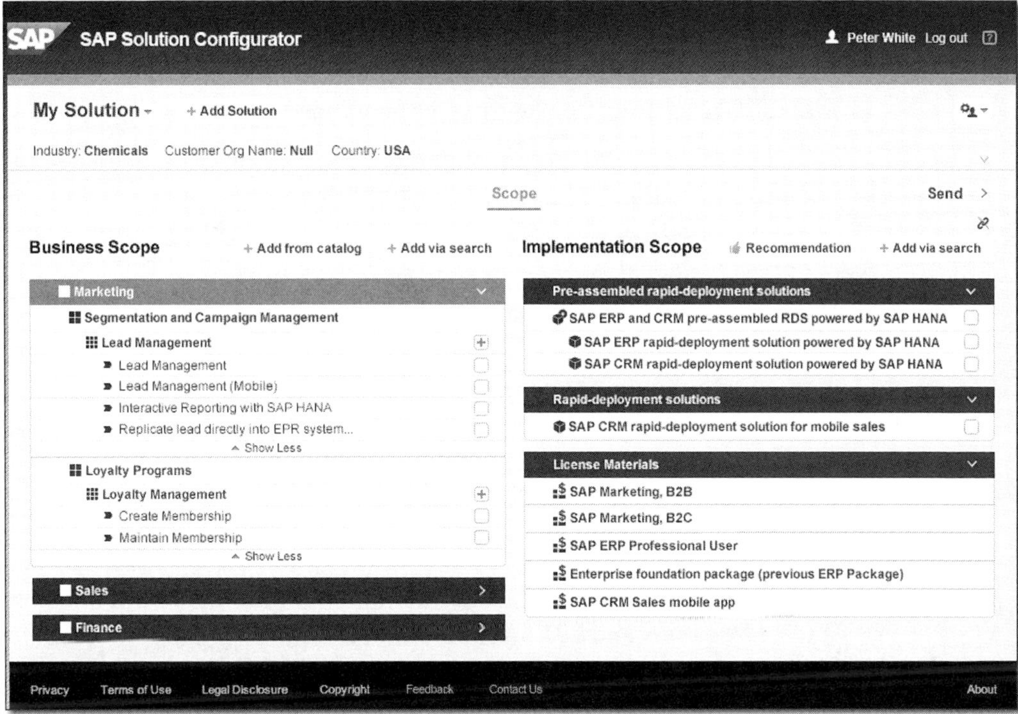

Figure 2.22 Project Scope in SAP Solution Configurator

The right-hand side of the SAP Solution Configurator in Figure 2.22 shows the optimal set of rapid-deployment solutions that contain the selected business processes, together with the products that have to be installed and the software licenses that are required to run the solution. It provides a comprehensive bill of material of packages, software, and software licenses for the project, and therefore provides an optimal basis for more detailed project planning.

Based on the set of selected business processes, the SAP Solution Configurator recommends the best-fitting rapid-deployment solution. In this case, it's the SAP ERP and SAP CRM pre-assembled rapid-deployment solutions powered by SAP HANA. This pre-assembled rapid-deployment solution is a pre-integrated combination of the rapid-deployment solutions listed below the pre-assembled rapid-deployment solution. The SAP CRM rapid-deployment solution for mobile sales will have to be applied on top, because the Lead Management (Mobile) business process was selected.

Step 2: Test-Drive the Solution in the Cloud

In the next step, the user can request access to a test-drive system in the cloud that will provide the underlying software together with the pre-configuration content and sample data for the SAP Best Practice processes included in the related rapid-deployment solution. This test-drive can be made available within hours and provides a jump-start for the following Deploy phase.

Map implementation project

The Scope phase is the key phase in the experience, where business requirements are mapped to a scope of an implementation project based on rapid-deployment solutions that contain pre-configuration content for SAP Best Practice processes.

This mechanism is crucial for the new implementation paradigm that avoids an intensive blueprinting process. The business processes contained in the rapid-deployment solutions provide the baseline of the blueprint.

Usually the scope determined by the SAP Solution Configurator is not the final scope for the implementation project, but provides a very solid base for the detailed discussion around the scope and puts rapid-deployment solutions and SAP Best Practices on the agenda. Consequently, the SAP Solution Configurator allows the user to share the defined solutions scope with others (e.g., implementation partners, SAP representatives, or other colleagues inside the company). It therefore provides a platform for collaboration around the project scope with all relevant stakeholders.

Key output of this step is the determination of the best-fitting pre-assembled rapid-deployment solution for the intended scope. This pre-assembled solution can be made available as a test-drive in a private cloud environment within days. The more detailed project scoping is now performed based on the test-drive. A real-life system with configured SAP Best Practice processes, a pre-defined model company, and sample data is provided as a starting point of the project.

Now the transition from the scope phase into the Deploy phase of the solution is seamless. Proof of concepts can already be performed based on the test-drive system. The implementation can actually start in certain areas, while other areas are still under discussion regarding the detailed solution scope.

At the end of the Scope phase, the implementation project scope is fixed to a degree that allows the setup of a contract for the execution of an implementation project.

2.6.3 Deploy

The objective of the Deploy phase is the actual implementation of the solution, i.e., the execution of the implementation project until go-live.

As we've already explained, one of the key elements of the Simplified Rapid-Deployment Solution Experience is the seamless transition between scope and deploy phase. A running system containing the SAP Best Practice processes, including sample data that mirrors the customer's intended scope as closely as possible, is available at the beginning of the deploy phase, at the very latest.

The key paradigm is that the implementation project starts with SAP Best Practices and pre-configured systems. The to-be processes of the customer will not be defined from scratch, but based on the Best Practices or as delta to the Best Practices.

This delta is identified at the beginning of the project based on the pre-configured system in a fit/gap analysis. The output of the fit/gap analysis is part of the backlog for the implementation project. The implementation project will address the resolution of the gaps determined in the fit/gap analysis in an agile and iterative fashion.

Figure 2.23 summarizes the approach.

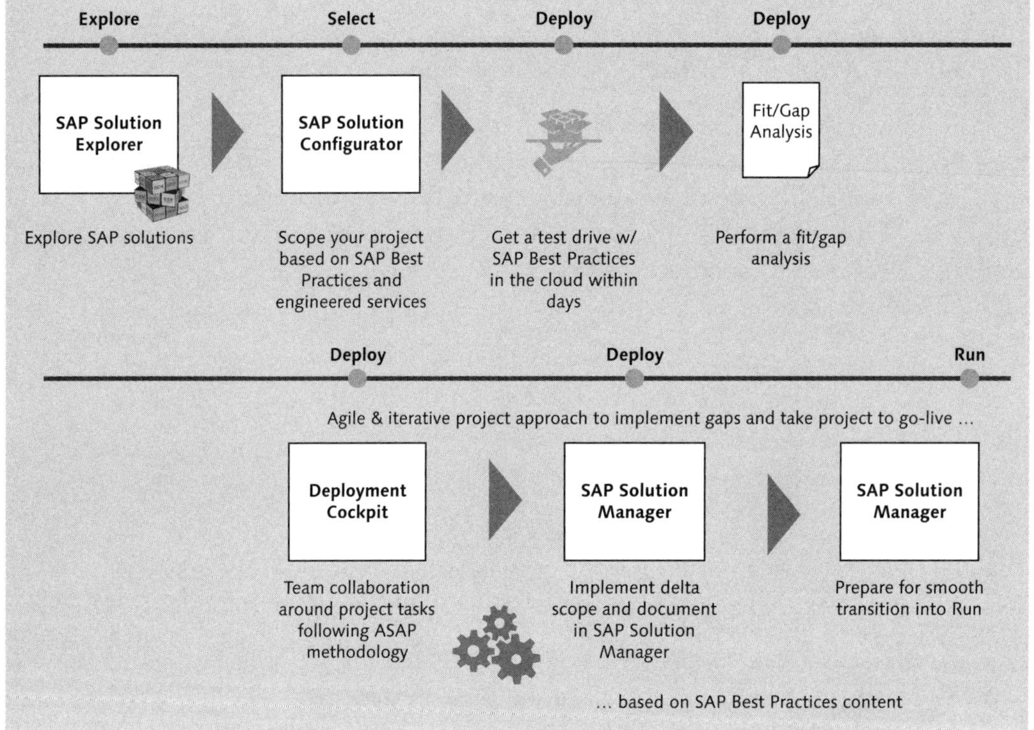

Figure 2.23 Overview on the Simplified Implementation Experience

The Deploy phase of the experience is executed using a standardized and engineered approach. As outlined in Section 2.3, each rapid-deployment solution comes with related services assets. The core asset among the services assets is the work breakdown structure (WBS). The WBS describes the different tasks that have to be executed in the project in order to take the rapid-deployment solution implementation to go-live.

Via this very standardized and engineered approach, risks in the project are minimized and a highly predictable outcome related to project duration and overall cost can be achieved.

Rapid Deployment Cockpit

To manage the project, a web-based tool—the Rapid-Deployment Cockpit—is offered. It is accessible from the Internet, and project teams use it to collaborate around the project tasks. Team members from SAP, partners, and the customer jointly use this tool.

Team members can be associated with tasks, and project members can jointly maintain the concrete WBS for an individual project. See Figure 2.24 for an example of the SAP CRM rapid-deployment solution WBS within the Rapid Deployment Cockpit. For more details around the cockpit see Chapter 5, Section 5.4.1.

Project collaboration

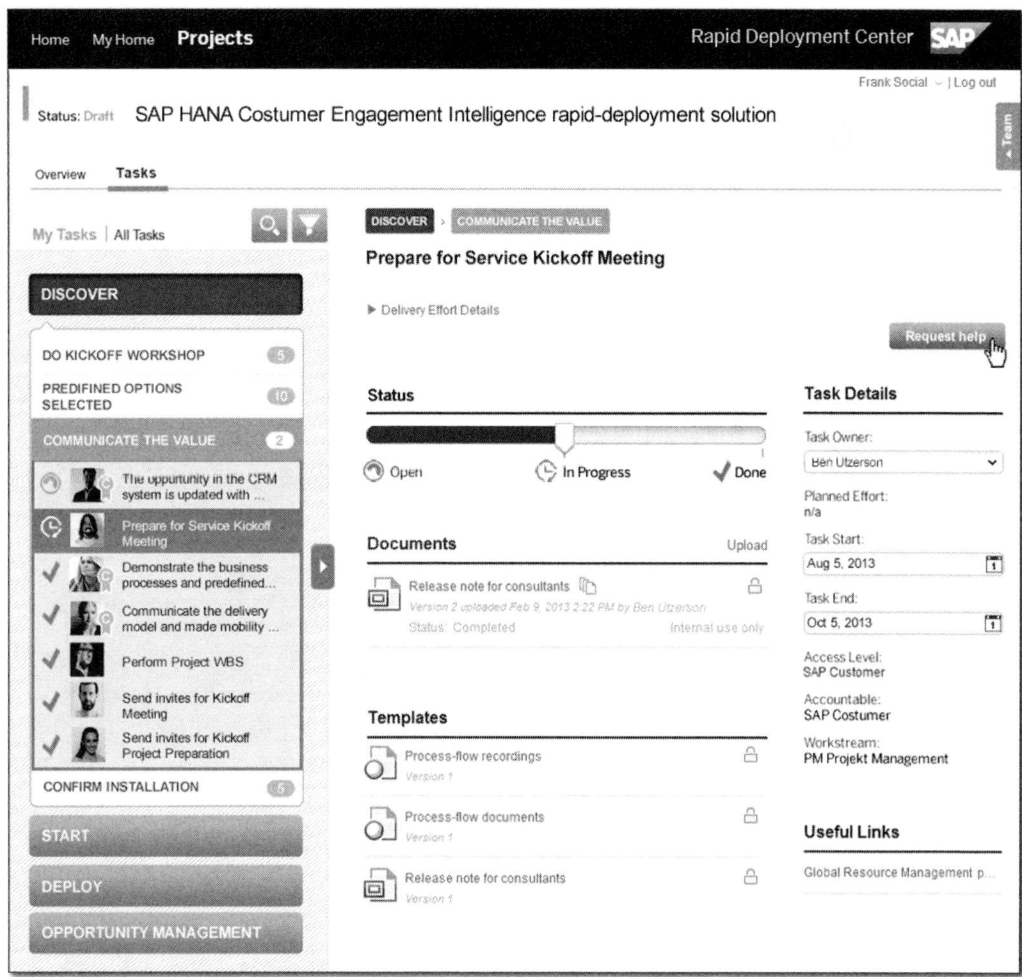

Figure 2.24 Work Breakdown Structure in the Rapid Deployment Cockpit

SAP Solution Manager

SAP Solution Manager is SAP's central tool to execute the system configuration and to document the system and process landscape of a customer solution. The Simplified Rapid-Deployment Solution Experience approach is therefore tightly integrated with SAP Solution Manager. Each rapid-deployment solution comes with the related SAP Solution Manager content. Each business process contained in a rapid-deployment solution is available in SAP Solution Manager, as well as related tabs like general documentation, configuration, test cases, business functions, etc. By this, project teams also get a jump start for SAP Solution Manager content. See Figure 2.25 for a look into the content for the SAP CRM rapid-deployment solution.

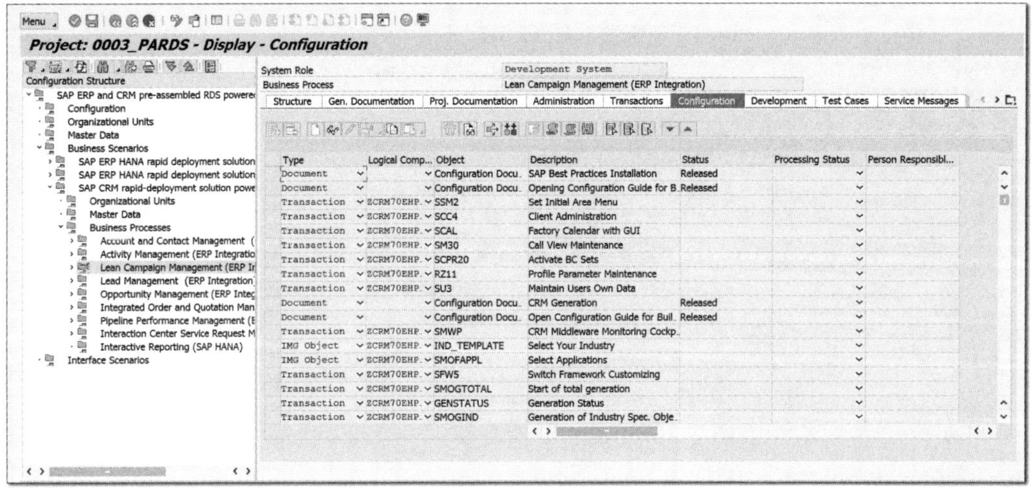

Figure 2.25 Solution Manager Content for the SAP CRM Rapid-Deployment Solution

While executing the gaps in backlog, project teams will refine the prefilled documentation in SAP Solution Manager, change test scripts accordingly, etc. This mechanism reduces the effort to provide a proper documentation of the customer solution and ensures the basis for a smooth handover to the run phase. In order to accelerate that even further, pre-assembled rapid-deployment solutions also provide predefined key performance indicators and monitoring objects that are linked to best-practice processes in order to jump-start the configuration of business process monitoring with in SAP Solution Manager. For a more in-depth discussion around SAP Solution Manager as part of the Simplified Rapid-Deployment Solution Experience, see Chapter 5, Section 5.4.2.

It is trivial, but still important to note that the content through all these phases from industry value maps to business process monitoring in SAP Solution Manager is integrated and consistent. For the rapid-deployment solutions, it has been ensured that the business processes linked with the solutions in the industry value maps are the same business processes contained in the pre-configuration content of the rapid-deployment solution, the SAP Solution Manager configuration templates, and the business process monitoring in SAP Solution Manager. This consistency is an important driver to simplify the overall experience.

Deployment Options

The Simplified Rapid-Deployment Solution Experience offers different options on how to deploy the solution. The default option is initial deployment in the cloud, which accelerates access to a system containing SAP Best Practices content as pre-assembled rapid-deployment solutions. For SAP HANA-based solutions, the default environment will be the SAP HANA Enterprise Cloud. This offering is especially tailored for hosting projects and also the production environment, and ideally supports the outlined approach. SAP HANA Enterprise Cloud and the Simplified Rapid-Deployment Solution Experience go hand-in-hand. Pre-assembled rapid-deployment solutions can also be provided for on-premise installation. For some selected scenarios an installable image that contains the software stack, the pre-configuration content and the sample data is available. It will be shipped on Blu-Ray DVD as a self-installable media.

SAP HANA Enterprise Cloud

2.6.4 Run

The Deploy phase ends with the go-live of the solution. The Simplified Rapid-Deployment Solution Experience and the content provided with the solution ensures a smooth handover from Deploy to Run.

The close integration with SAP Solution Manager and the specific content provided supports this transition. The pre-defined SAP Solution Manager content for the rapid-deployment solution provides the project team with a jump-start in the project for SAP Solution Manager content as well. This provides the basis for the solution documentation in SAP Solution Manager.

The documentation of the customer solution and the monitoring of the business processes, in turn, provide the basis for ensuring the operations of the solution following the "Run SAP like a Factory" approach. For a more detailed discussion on the "Run" services provided, see Section 6.3.

2.7 Services Complementing Rapid Deployment

As outlined in Section 2.2, the implementation services are an integral part of rapid-deployment solutions. In this section, we will briefly introduce additional services that complement the offering and are usually bundled together with rapid-deployment solution implementation services.

Bundles services In the context of rapid deployment, the following service types are of particular interest for bundling:

- **SAP rapid-deployment solutions cloud services**
  These services provide access to implementations for demo, test-drive, or project-jump-start purposes in the cloud. Pre-assembled rapid-deployment solutions can be hosted in a shared or a private cloud environment for customers to enable the discovery of SAP Best Practices and the SAP solution based on a running system or a rapid project start as introduced in Section 2.4.

- **Pre-assembly service**
  While specific, pre-defined combinations of rapid-deployment solutions are pre-built and available "off the shelf," the pre-assembly service provides a customer individual assembly of selected solutions that match as closely as possible to the intended project scope.

- **Engineered services**

  Besides the rapid-deployment solution implementation services that are tied to the business scope of a rapid-deployment solution, a rich set of additional engineered services are offered, e.g., to perform software installation, assessment services, or data migration. These engineered services follow the same paradigm as rapid-deployment solution implementation services and can be combined with the solution following the assemble-to-order approach.

- **Enablement services**

  Enablement services cover offerings to enable various target groups to leverage the SAP solution. This includes the rich portfolio of education services for end-users or consultants, and ramp-up knowledge transfer for new solutions or solution enhancements.

- **Operation services**

  In order to support customers in running, operating, and enhancing the SAP solution, SAP Active Global Support offers a wide range of services, like the Innovation Control Center and the Operations Control Center approach.

Chapter 6 will provide a more detailed discussion on these services.

2.8   The Role of SAP Partners in the New Implementation Paradigm

Today's market demand for implementation services and content cannot be fulfilled by SAP alone. Therefore, SAP Partners play a very important role in the rapid deployment of SAP solutions.

As already introduced in Section 2.2, SAP Partners are key for the SAP Business All-in-One offering for a focused go-to-market and the provisioning of implementation services. They usually combine their own extensions of the SAP solution portfolio with the core SAP solution implementation services and content. Partners also extend the SAP Best Practices content by adding their own Best Practice packages that are compatible with and extend the Best Practices content base.

Unique solution extensions

Generally speaking, partners can contribute to the new implementation paradigm in two ways:

- **Providing the SAP Business All-in-One or rapid-deployment solutions implementation service for specific packages**
  Usually the partner will also adapt the methodology to add their own expertise of the solution to integrate its own extensions of the SAP solution package.

- **Providing their own Business All-in-One or rapid-deployment solutions packages to package the partner-specific experience**
  In this case—called partner-led rapid-deployment solutions—the partner develops their own content following the SAP Best Practice methodology. Hundreds of partner-led solutions exist today and are listed on the SAP EcoHub.

> **Note**
>
> Chapter 7 provides more insight into the Rapid Deployment Partner Program.

2.9   Benefits

Deploying SAP solutions the rapid-deployment way provides customers with a wide range of benefits. These range from hard time and cost savings and reduced project risk on the one hand, to increased solution value and digestibility for the business on the other.

Less time and money
- **Reduced implementation time and cost**
  Based on best practices, the blueprinting phase can be reduced dramatically. Pre-configuration and implementation accelerator content provides significant savings during realization and testing phases. Customers often experience at least 40 percent time and effort reduction compared to a traditional project of similar scope. Using the pre-assembled rapid-deployment solutions method, these savings can be even greater. The shorter time to start is illustrated in the deploy and run phases where best practices are applied in a rapid-deployment solution (see Figure 2.26).

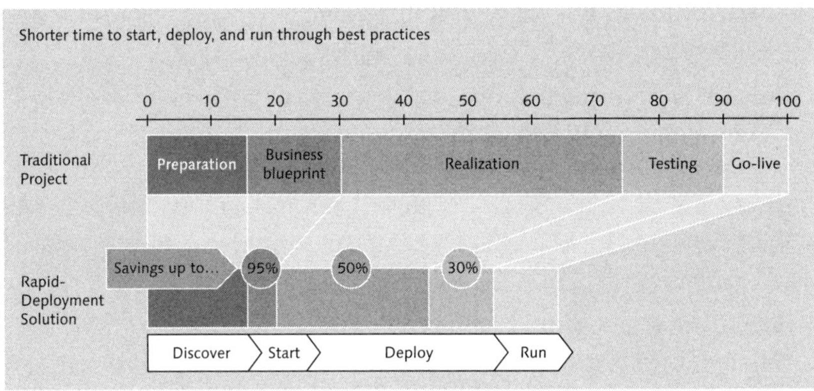

Figure 2.26 Shorter Time to Start, Deploy, and Run through Best Practices

▶ **Higher predictability and lower risk**

Risks for project failure, scope-, time-, and cost-creep are significantly reduced by targeting clear and proven best-practice scope, combined with corresponding pre-configuration, tools, and methods for deployment success like service project plans and step-by-step implementation guides—and, not least, the fixed-price service offerings related to it. All stakeholders immediately know what the project delivers, how long it takes, and what it costs.

▶ **More scalable service ecosystem**

Skilled and experienced consultants are particularly hard to find for very specialized and very new solutions. Rapid-deployment solutions scale this rare knowledge and thereby enable a much broader range of consultants for these topics.

▶ **Better business alignment, better scope**

Using a rapid-deployment solution's pre-defined best-practice scope as a starting point, it becomes much easier for business stakeholders to understand how the solution looks, where the "standard" fits, and where to change or expand on top. For many processes, implementing the standard may not only be more cost- and time-effective, but it also provides an even better business value than what an individual company would have designed, given that best practices often reflect the experience and lessons learnt through many, many implementations by comparable companies. It becomes easier for companies to make smart decisions on where to stick with best practices and where

Lower risk

Business alignment

to go for their own ones—and to be able to put the right focus and resources on these.

▸ **More standardized solution, lower total cost of ownership**
Ultimately, a rapid-deployment solutions-based approach will often lead customers to stay closer to the standard, resulting in better maintainability and extendibility of their solution—and, typically, significant reduction in related operating costs and the overall total cost of ownership.

▸ **Step-by-step adoption path at the pace of the business**
An important aspect of best practices is not only information on how to best configure a business process, but also guidelines on finding the right chunk-size scope—not too small, and not too big—to implement in one project phase. This helps customers develop their modular adoption roadmap, step by step. Respectively, change management with each step along the way becomes easier, too.

Figure 2.27 shows how to get from a customer's high-level business requirements to a rapid-deployment solution-based adoption roadmap to enable the required end-to-end solution.

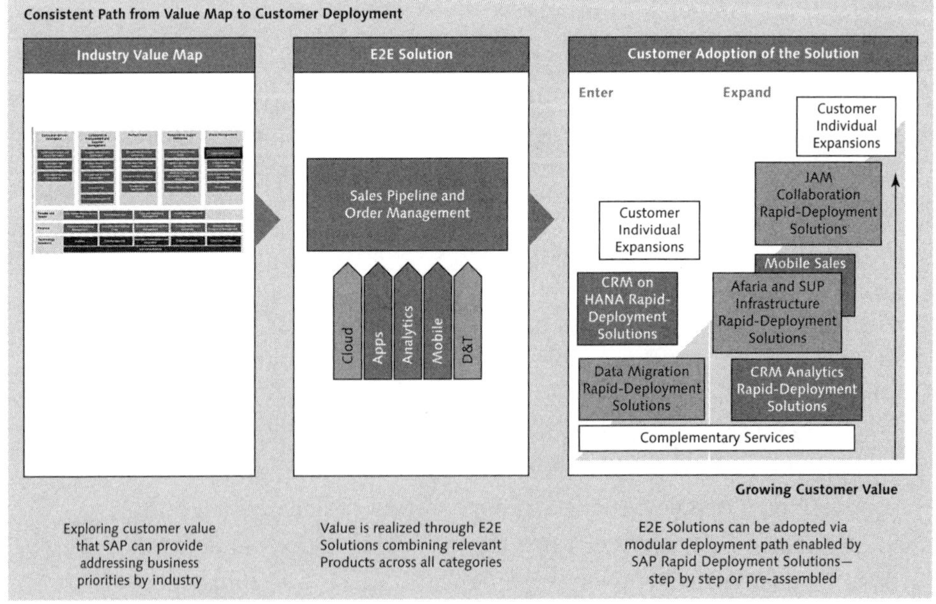

Figure 2.27 Model for Moving from Customer Requirements to Solution

2.10 Summary

In this chapter, we introduced the concepts of the new implementation paradigm. We discussed the overall foundation of SAP Best Practices that's provided to the market in two flavors: as SAP Business All-in-One for small and medium businesses and as SAP Rapid-Deployment solutions for enterprises.

The assemble-to-order approach was outlined that combines multiple rapid-deployment solutions and engineered services together to form a comprehensive customer project scope.

Based on this approach, pre-assembled rapid-deployment solutions provide the delivery of those as installable images that include the required software stack, the activated pre-configuration content, and the related sample data. This pre-assembled rapid-deployment solution serves as the starting point for the project. The best practice can be experienced in the system and a fit/gap analysis is the basis for the backlog of the implementation project. Extensive blueprinting phases are avoided by building on pre-assembled best practices as a starting point.

The Simplified Rapid-Deployment Solution Experience wraps all these concepts and approaches up in an integrated end-to-end experience from exploring the capabilities of SAP solutions to operating a solution that addresses the business challenges. Complementary services and partner involvement concerning these concepts have also been discussed.

As such, this chapter provides the overview on the key concepts detailed in the subsequent chapters. The next chapter offers some insight in how these concepts are adopted in real-life practice. We will provide insight into value cases that demonstrate the benefit the value of the new implementation paradigm based on customer projects.

The value of SAP Rapid Deployment solutions is best explained through tangible deployment case studies. This chapter provides examples of various types of SAP solutions, ranging from the SAP core solutions to innovations that include SAP HANA, mobility, and assemble-to-order.

3   Value Case Studies around the Rapid Deployment of SAP Solutions

The new implementation paradigm at SAP has many tangible examples that demonstrate the success of this deployment innovation. In this chapter, we'll explore several different, concrete case studies that involve real SAP customers that show you how SAP's rapid-deployment methodology reduces time-to-value, risks, and costs in different industries and in different scenarios.

3.1   Database Migration to SAP NetWeaver BW Powered by SAP HANA

Solution Showcase

Migrating a three-tiered landscape from SAP NetWeaver Business Warehouse to SAP NetWeaver BW on SAP HANA in 12 weeks.

Database migration describes the technical switch from one existing database to another one. Therefore the database migration applies, for example, to customers who are currently running their SAP NetWeaver BW application on a traditional relational database and chose to move it to SAP HANA as the underlying database. These customers are looking for a fast, predictable, reliable, and ideally risk-free transition process.

This is where SAP Rapid Deployment solutions come into play with SAP Best Practices knowledge, standardized processes, and the latest in tool development for database migration when customers switch their SAP NetWeaver BW to run on the power of SAP HANA. Besides the mandatory steps of updating the current application to the latest release, the preparation of the SAP HANA target landscape and the database migration itself, of course, are two major topics that are also covered via the rapid-deployment solution.

Prepare source system

One of these topics is preparation of the source system(s) before the export of the relational database management system (RDBMS). This includes the extensive manual work that is normally needed during the preparation of the source system before the export of the RDBMS, as well as the post-processing after the import into the SAP HANA database. The second is that the business downtime of the SAP NetWeaver BW system needs to be minimized to have as little impact on operational business as possible. Both topics are now automated through SAP Rapid Deployment solution database migration packages to an extent that was not available in the past. The rapid-deployment solution eliminates the error-prone manual steps and enables the database-migration team with new scenarios to minimize the business downtime.

So, the rapid database migration of SAP NetWeaver BW to SAP HANA enables customers to replace the actual underlying relational database of their SAP NetWeaver BW system with SAP HANA as a database (see Figure 3.1). This solution supports the migration of an existing SAP NetWeaver Business Warehouse installation to the SAP HANA database system without disruption of the existing BW content, and it provides an end-to-end solution to meet all necessary prerequisites. This new implementation approach was provided with SAP's rapid-deployment solutions, which leverage out-of-the-box accelerators and predefined scope to help accelerate your adoption of SAP HANA to supercharge your SAP NetWeaver BW. The simplified process eliminates any migration guesswork and uncertainties regarding realization timeline, due to automation of steps as well as planning security due to standardization of the approach.

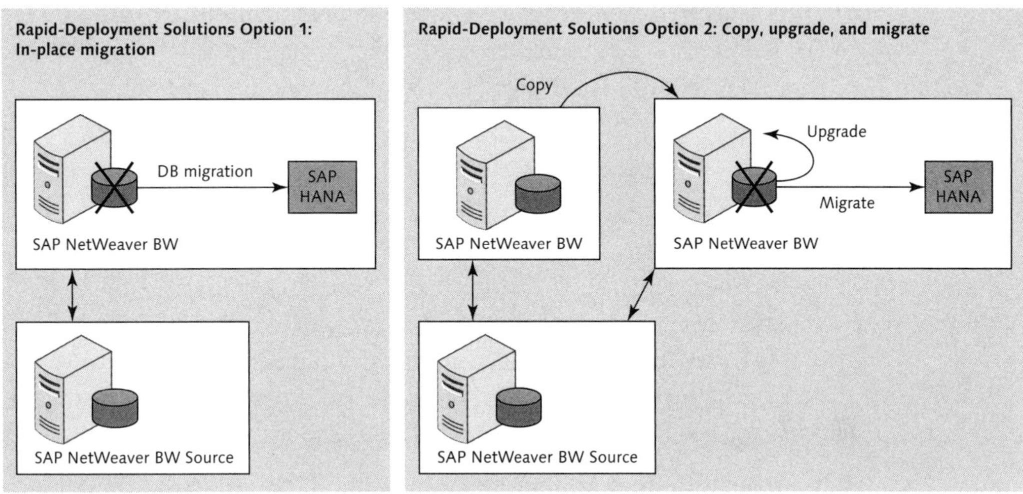

Figure 3.1 Different Scenarios and Migration Options are Covered by this SAP Rapid Deployment Solution

3.1.1 Background

The value case-study customer is in the chemical industry, producing paint with over 15,000 employees and 30 manufacturing facilities in 15 countries, and subsidiaries in 30 countries worldwide. The customer delivers chemical products to various industries, like the construction or automotive industry, with revenue of more than 1.75 billion Euro.

Due to competition amongst a large number of paint manufacturers, severe product homogeneity, over-supplied mid- and low-level products, and in addition because the production of paint is unique depending on customer requirements, paint manufacturers need more accurate, standardized, and real-time information on order execution, stock status, and cost control. Manufacturers must realize the need for effective management in production, purchasing, sales, and other processes.

Market competition

Facing such fierce market competition, the customer's executives have realized that it is a must for success to build a perfect SAP NetWeaver BW reporting system that offers faster response to market and smarter decision-making. As early as 2004, the customer started to implement its old SAP NetWeaver BW reporting system and connected it with SAP ERP, CRM, SRM, and other business systems, only to find that many

Simple decision-making

problems have been caused with the increasing requirements for real-time reporting due to maturing customer groups, diversifying channels, and the business department's growing demand for reports.

As-is issues

Relevant statistics show that the old SAP NetWeaver BW system covers more than 150 modules and over 250 reports. With this system, it takes over 12 hours to update 203 assignments and 25 processing chains every night, and even three to four days to complete the monthly financial settlement. In this case, the slow processes of data extraction and validation became the key factors that restricted the timeliness of SAP NetWeaver BW reporting. Therefore, the old SAP NetWeaver BW system was in dire need of optimization and update to support quicker reaction to changes in market conditions and faster decision-making.

SAP is recognized by the customer as the leader in enterprise management software and the only one that can provide an integrated and standard software platform throughout the supply chain, with many best-practice use cases in the international chemical industry. Furthermore, by making use of the rich documentation and knowledge pool embedded in SAP Rapid Deployment solutions, the customer expects that its IT staff could quickly learn SAP HANA-related new technology, and the internal IT skills and management level could be improved.

Smooth migration

A smooth migration without disturbing existing users was the first consideration of the customer when selecting solutions. The old SAP NetWeaver BW system was first implemented in 2004, but the company realized that their system couldn't keep up with the rapid development of business because of its problems (e.g., aging and substandard system modules, low patch versions, etc.). Therefore, it was decided to adopt SAP NetWeaver BW on SAP HANA to realize a seamless connection with existing systems and lay a solid foundation for the future.

Based on massive, detailed, and complete real-time information, SAP HANA would allow the company to analyze its business operations, to explore and analyze all transactions and analysis data, to provide a flexible view of analysis information to users immediately, and to easily integrate external data into its analysis models. Also, the easy-to-use modeling environment can be integrated with all enterprise data, providing standard interfaces for existing applications, operation systems, and other business application systems. In a word, SAP HANA, as a complete real-time analysis solution, can help the customer to gain profits as fast as possible.

After the decision was taken to go with SAP NetWeaver BW powered by SAP HANA to improve reporting performance in order to accelerate responsiveness across all business functions, the rapid-deployment solution was chosen to migrate away from the current landscape without reimplementation, no disruption of existing scenarios, and with minimal business downtime.

Solution-Deployment Planning

The first step was to analyze the current customer situation in order to come to an end-to-end deployment offering depending on the customer needs. Using the qualification questionnaire, it was directly possible to qualify the customer for the rapid-reployment solution, and it turned out that a technical upgrade was needed on top of the database migration. Afterwards, with the scoping questionnaire, the complete rapid-deployment solution was adjusted to the customer situation, and due to the availability of predefined sizing options, the offering was available in an instant. The decision to go with the "two systems" scenario was also taken at that point in time, due to the necessary upgrade and the business downtime restrictions of the customer.

Compared to the traditional database migration, which is realized by a heterogeneous system copy alone and which is also offered as an SAP Rapid Deployment solutions scenario, this second scenario incorporated the latest in SAP tool development to use a copy of the original SAP NetWeaver BW system so that all work could be conducted on that second system. In the meantime, the customer could continue to work with the existing SAP NetWeaver BW system until the project work on the copy was finished. During the initial setup of the project and the tool preparations, the quick guide was of great help for the customer and the project team to fulfill the technical prerequisites and project setup.

Deployment

System copy

To meet customer requirements and reduce downtime in the production landscape, the deployment team used one of the recommended migration paths from SAP NetWeaver BW to SAP HANA in this case, which comprises a system copy of the existing SAP NetWeaver BW system (see Figure 3.2). The system-copy procedure of SAP NetWeaver BW systems and landscapes is complex for a number of reasons, however. There are a large number of configuration settings (such as connections and delta-queue handling for data loading) and system-copy scenarios of SAP NetWeaver BW (each with different landscape aspects), for example, that have to be handled as part of every system copy. This is necessary, regardless of whether the system copy is part of the migration to SAP HANA, or if regular-system copies of the SAP NetWeaver BW landscape are performed.

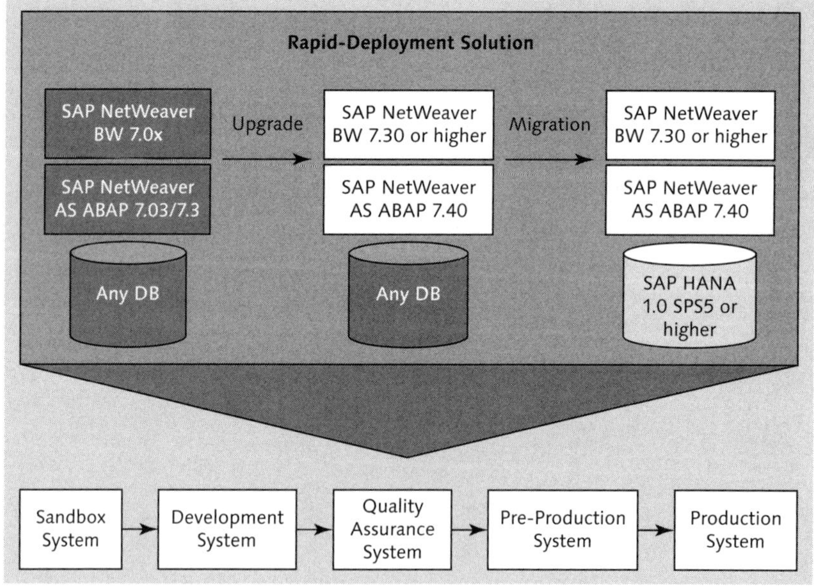

Figure 3.2 A Typical Sequence in a Database Migration Project

Post-copy

For the SAP NetWeaver BW Post Copy Automation tool (SAP NetWeaver BW PCA is part of SAP NetWeaver Landscape Virtualization Management), preconfigured "task lists" are offered and used by the ABAP task manager for lifecycle management automation. This also enabled the customer's SAP NetWeaver BW system powered by SAP HANA to "go productive" with the parallel operation of their existing production system, both connected to the same back-end systems. As in this case study, this two system scenario is achieved using a special and unique automated solution for delta-queue cloning and synchronization on the production systems. Using the post-copy automation for SAP NetWeaver BW (BW PCA) in the migration process from SAP NetWeaver BW to SAP NetWeaver BW on SAP HANA, this process was shortened by weeks and became easier, faster, and more reliable.

With the use of the configuration guide that covers all necessary steps in detail on how to set up and use the BW PCA in an optimal way, the project success was ensured.

3.1.2 Results

The project covered a three-tier landscape (PRD, QAS, and DEV) where the productive system had an uncompressed source database size of less than five TB. Including two test migrations on top of the three systems that were migrated, five migrations were conducted in total. That was all achieved in an overall project runtime of just 12 weeks and an effective business downtime for the productive landscape of just a few hours.

Landscape and migrations

Utilizing the standardized SAP Rapid Deployment solutions approach with SAP best practice guidelines, accelerators, and tool support, a project could even be completed in as little as 10 weeks depending on the customer's situation and migration scenario.

During the implementation of the project, the customer highly praised the incomparable strengths of SAP NetWeaver BW on SAP HANA. From the perspective of report performance, a user can quickly access all reports on SAP NetWeaver BW without BWA, get timely insight into the latest information via the real-time copy function, realize more simulations, accelerate planning processes, directly upload reports to SAP HANA at a high speed, work on a relatively smaller databases without data indexing, aggregation, statistics or DBA maintenance, and employ flexible and simple modeling functions. All these benefits enable developers to work more efficiently and effectively on SAP HANA and help up-skill internal team members to gain more skills.

Project phases

The project covered three phases, including the build up of a POC environment of SAP NetWeaver BW on SAP HANA, upgrade of the system hardware, and implementation of SAP NetWeaver BW on HANA. All three phases aimed to realize goals to centralize storage of hardware, increase storage speed, leave scalable space for future business demand growth, and of course to fully migrate their existing SAP NetWeaver BW system to SAP HANA with the possibility of parallel running the new system and the legacy system.

Simplified solution deployment

Thanks to SAP Rapid Deployment solutions, SAP NetWeaver BW powered by SAP HANA went live within the project timeline in just 10 weeks. During the migration project, the productive SAP NetWeaver BW system was even brought online within just eight weeks. During the full-cycle management of the project, covering project commencement, pre-inspection, project preparation and implementation, system replication, subsequent tuning, and final completion, SAP Rapid Deployment solutions simplified solution deployment through easy-to-use modules, templates and tools, promoted user adoption through guidelines and training materials, provided proven guidance documents for all operations, reduced risks by maximizing the implementation of predictability through fixed scope and prices, and shortened the project cycle.

Taking advantage of the flexible and multi-functional memory application devices of SAP HANA, the customer has accelerated its diversified businesses and refined channels, and pushed forward the strategic goals to completely support business demand and future development by analyzing all transaction data from various sources, generating different types of reports based on user groups and conference requirements, pushing analysis information through flexible views, and enabling executives to have real-time access to business reports to make more reliable and faster business decisions.

In close collaboration with the customer, SAP always thought of knowledge transfer as its key goal, by fully utilizing the world's best practices and rich knowledge bases of SAP Rapid Deployment solutions, the customer has further developed its internal management team and created an excellent, professional IT team.

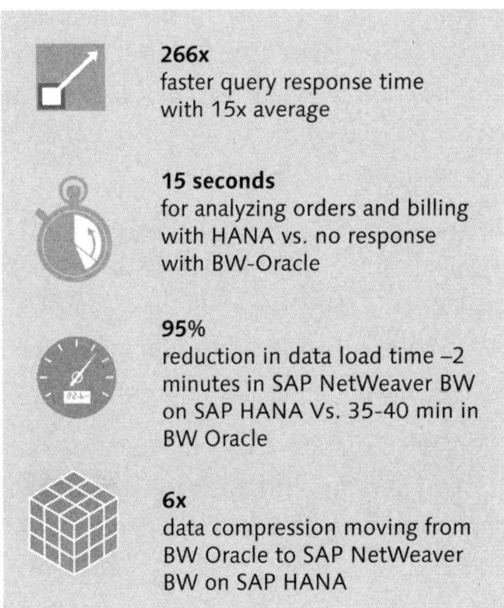

Figure 3.3 Benefits and Improvements for the Customer of this Specific Value Case for Database Migration

3.2 Data Migration to the SAP Business Suite Powered by SAP HANA

Solution Showcase

Migrating a customer's non-SAP ERP system data to SAP ERP powered by SAP HANA with the SAP Rapid Data Migration rapid-deployment solutions package.

Data migration is a major task and key for a successful SAP Business Suite powered by SAP HANA implementation. SAP Rapid Data Migration enables you to migrate the organization's data, ensuring that data can be trusted by the users and is ready for business-process execution within the new application.

SAP's portfolio in the area of Enterprise Information Management (EIM) and business intelligence (BI) is the foundation upon which the data migration approach as a rapid-deployment solution package was built.

The SAP Rapid Deployment solutions methodology in the SAP Rapid Data Migration package provides core content that creates one very smooth, simple, predictable data migration tool that has the capability to help deployment teams address many types of data migration scenarios around SAP Business Suite powered by SAP HANA.

Pre-delivered templates
First, there are pre-delivered templates and content that transform the SAP Data Services data integration platform into a strong and easy-to-use migration engine. This engine comes with built-in functionality to extract and profile any legacy data directly from and on the source system.

In addition, there is a new tool for value mapping called Migration Services, plus packaged SAP BusinessObjects Web Intelligence reports that deliver insight on the overall process and show data-quality issues to the deployment team at an early stage.

The SAP Rapid Deployment solutions tools and the out-of-the-box data migration content are designed by SAP's experts to help the consultant successfully run an effective data migration. In the following sections, you'll see an example of how an SAP customer used Rapid Data Migration to migrate ERP data to an SAP system.

3.2.1 Background

The customer is a large enterprise company running a non-SAP ERP system and currently deploying SAP ERP powered by SAP HANA. This customer's last big implementation project was one that set the stage for using SAP Rapid Deployment solutions: the previous project team underestimated the efforts needed to perform a data migration, and the initial data quality of the new system made it basically unusable for the end users. Early on, that team learned that data migration, if insufficiently planned or poorly executed, represents a significant threat to on-time, on-budget completion of IT projects. Poor data quality can bring business to a standstill even after several months since go-live. With these data migration experiences in mind, they discovered an answer to their technical and project management challenges with SAP Rapid Deployment solutions. They connected with the business value within the package and, trusting the SAP experts, decided to rely on

SAP's approach to help them produce a data migration success on their SAP HANA project. The team achieved success when they implemented the new SAP HANA-powered box with the Rapid Data Migration approach.

The key business objects to be migrated were:

Key objects for migration

- Characteristics
- Class
- Activity Type
- Activity Price
- Cost Centers
- Profit Centers
- Customer Master
- Vendor Master
- Work Center
- Material Master
- Inspection Plan
- Bill of Materials
- Service Master
- Routing
- SD Pricing
- Inventory Balances
- Accounts Payable/Receivable
- Functional Location
- Cost Center Groups
- Standard Hierarchy
- Source List
- Fixed Assets
- Organizational Management
- Initial Employee Conversion
- Current Employee Conversion

- Personnel Administration
- Benefits
- Payroll
- Contracts
- Sales Order
- Purchase Order
- Internal Order
- Open Deliveries

3.2.2 Deployment

Data integration/quality

SAP Data Services is an ETL tool (extract, transform, load) that combines data integration and data quality functionality into one software product. This tool is the foundation for the SAP Rapid Data Migration content that consists of projects, jobs, data flows, data validations, and pre-delivered routines for the migration tasks.

SAP Data Services highlights

Highlights of SAP Data Services are:

- Direct connection to one or more source systems.
- Ability to start with the data mapping and validation process even before the SAP customizing has been finalized in the target system.
- Reusable and easy-to-use drag-and-drop mapping.
- Visualization of the entire data flow, from source to target.
- Reusable validation routines to minimize own coding.
- Built-in data cleansing steps.
- Validation of the legacy data against the SAP check tables—without actually loading any data.
- A better and tighter integration with SAP Business Suite by leveraging standard SAP interfaces.

Solution-Deployment Planning

The deployment planning involves using the contents of the SAP Rapid Deployment solutions package. Technically, the Rapid Data Migration package includes the software, SAP Data Services, and the SAP Business-Objects BI platform, as well as the best-practices content. This includes:

- Data migration templates for SAP Data Services.

- Migration Services: a tool used for the value mapping.

- SAP BusinessObjects Web Intelligence reports for monitoring and reporting.

- Content for the reconciliation between the source and the target system.

The content follows SAP's Best Practices for data migration. The deployment team made their project plans using this methodology across the following steps (also see Figure 3.4):

1. Analyze and profile the data from the source system(s).

2. Extract the data from the source system.

3. Cleanse the data records to achieve a high data quality.

4. Validate the data against the target business context (i.e., the business rules of the target system, such as checking to identify if there are specific fields required or if the country codes are correct).

5. Load the data into the target SAP system.

6. Reconcile the data between the target system and the source system.

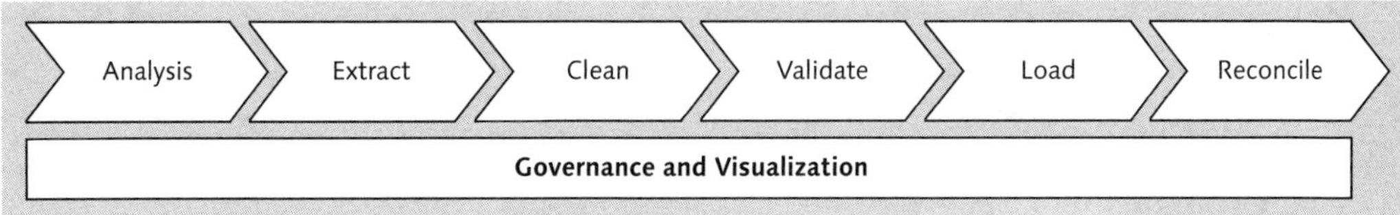

Figure 3.4 Methodology of SAP Rapid Data Migration

Deployment

When the team moved into the deployment and realization phase of the data migration project, they used the pre-defined content for SAP Data Services, which included metadata of the SAP Business Suite on SAP HANA target environment. It also contained validation routines to ensure high data quality. With this, the team found that the ETL tool became the perfect fit for a data migration to SAP Business Suite on SAP HANA while the tool is sitting in the middle between the legacy source and the SAP target side.

Adapter framework

Using an adapter framework, as shown in Figure 3.5, the deployment team employed SAP Data Services to connect via different interfaces to multiple source systems, such as relational databases, Excel sheets, and flat files. Although they were working toward a deadline, the tools within the SAP Rapid Deployment solutions package helped them reach their target goals quicker and more efficiently.

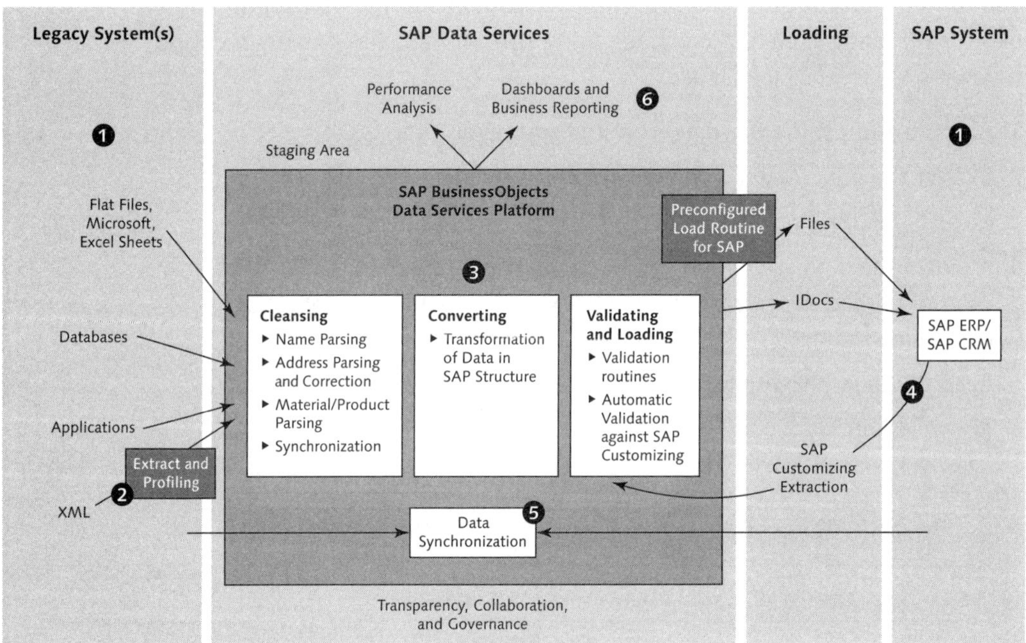

Figure 3.5 Architecture of the Rapid Data Migration Solution

Logical data migration flow

The architecture is sequential and follows a logical data migration flow of activities. Here are more details about the architecture of the Rapid Data Migration solution according to the numbers in Figure 3.5:

1. **Source and target systems**

   This is where the deployment teams first look at the target environment and legacy data environment. When using the Rapid Data

Migration for the SAP Business Suite on SAP HANA content, the environment is always an SAP Business Suite powered by SAP HANA application, typically including the SAP Rapid Deployment solutions Suite on SAP HANA package. The source environment can be any non-SAP environment, from connectivity to databases, applications, flat files, or XML.

2. **Extract and profile**

   The staging area is provided using SAP Data Services. In this staging area, deployment teams extract and profile data from the source systems. The profiling of data is a critical step, as it provides insight into the state of the data in the existing source systems. The deployment team could check for patterns across the data. For example, in the U.S., ZIP codes are five digits plus an optional four-digit numerical code. A data-profiling exercise can determine how many unique ZIP codes you have and how often the ZIP+4 extension is used across the source systems or to determine inactive data in the system, such as vendors that did not have purchase orders in the last couple of years. Another example is to know the pattern of country designations. For example, for Germany the terms Germany, DE, or Deutschland could be used in the source system.

3. **Cleanse, transform, and validate**

   The next step in the data migration includes updating the data so that it meets specific patterns, transforming the data according to rules, and validating data against the SAP business context. The customer in this case study used SAP Rapid Deployment solutions to combine two fields into one, as well as split fields, update the data within a field to match certain rules (for example, telephone number formats), and validate data against required fields and lookup values from the SAP business context and configuration.

4. **Extraction of SAP configuration data**

   As part of an SAP implementation, SAP is configured with many values such as plants, material types and groups, and sales territories. Mapping of the source data normally requires mapping fields that comply with the SAP configuration. The extraction of SAP configuration data takes the settings in the SAP system so that the source data can conform to the required format in the target system. This customer's team was able to automate those configuration activities with the rapid-deployment solutions content and the Migration Services tool that is specific to rapid-deployment solutions, and save time and resources during the migration.

5. **Reconciliation**

Reconciliation looks at what was actually loaded versus what was expected to be loaded. The deployment team used reconciliation to proof the successful migration.

6. **Reporting and dashboards**

Throughout the process, dashboards are available for people involved with the project to know the status of the migration. This customer's team was able to avoid project confusion and continuously have the latest information about their data migration project status and data validation results. Additionally, the migration starts the process of data quality expectations and governance around data management, which helped this team easily transition to an ongoing data governance use case.

Figure 3.6 shows the Rapid Data Migration content in use. It has been deployed to the customer's SAP Data Services software and the consultants have a structured view to the different data migration objects and their tasks.

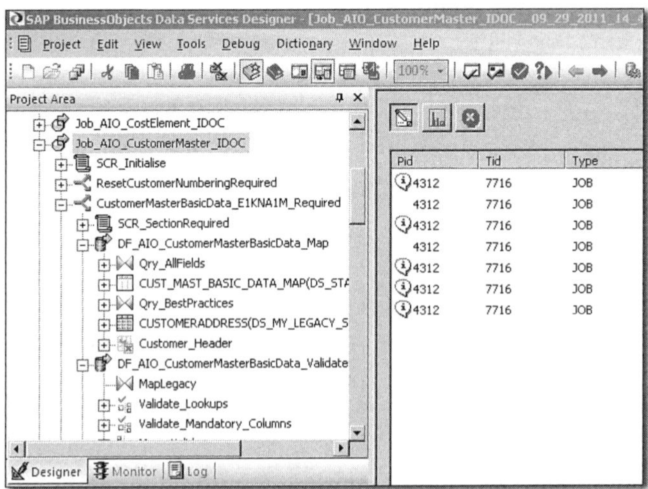

Figure 3.6 Sample Rapid Deployment Solutions Content for Migration of Customer Master Data in SAP Data Services

3.2.3 Results

This case study explained how efficiently the deployment team migrated legacy data into a new SAP Business Suite powered by SAP HANA with the rich content of the Rapid Data Migration package which can turn a generic ETL tool into a powerful engine and ease the job of migrating data. The example demonstrated the new approach, where the data quality and data validation are shown to be key to ensuring a smooth go-live with the migrated data.

The key learning points were:

Key points

- Data migration, if insufficiently planned or poorly executed, represents a significant threat to on-time, on-budget completion of IT projects (implementations, mergers and acquisitions, technology migrations).

- SAP Rapid Data Migration is the best solution for any data migration to an SAP system because its base, SAP Data Services, is a leading data-quality and data-integration tool.

- By combining data-integration software, rapid data migration content, and fixed-price/fixed-scope starter services, customers can have confidence that their data migration projects will be completed on time and in budget.

3.3 Rapid Deployment of SAP ERP with SAP ERP Rapid Deployment Solutions and the Assemble-to-Order Approach

> **Solution Showcase**
>
> Rapid deployment of SAP ERP with an end-to-end services approach to reduce the deployment cycle by four months.

This case explains the deployment of an SAP ERP solution in a consumer packaged goods company in Africa that chose an SAP end-to-end services approach and deployed the SAP ERP solution in their organization in 32 weeks.

Minimize modifications

At Rainbow Chicken Limited, IT plays a fundamental role in supporting the company's vision and strategy. Selecting an integrated IT platform of SAP ERP solution is all about ensuring that IT investments deliver maximum business benefit. Rainbow wanted to implement an SAP ERP solution that was based on a standard template. The key requirement for the deployment strategy was to minimize the amount of modifications and changes to the standard SAP solution in order to accelerate the deployment and make the operation of the solution simple and cost-effective.

Rainbow was implementing a new SAP ERP solution in their business to achieve the above goals. The customer IT organization had a number of team members with previous experience from traditional deployment of SAP solutions in another organization.

Cost effective

The business team and IT organization were specifically looking for a cost-effective approach that would deploy the SAP ERP functionality in their business, rapidly, while minimizing the modifications of the standard functionality. Although the customer considered alternatives, the final choice was to go with an SAP end-to-end services approach using the assemble-to-order deployment strategy to leverage the standard package as a baseline for deployment, and implement any enhancements on top of the existing functionality.

3.3.1   Background

Rainbow Chicken Limited is South Africa's largest processor and marketer of chicken. Rainbow is a fully integrated broiler producer that breeds and rears its own livestock, which it feeds from its own feed mills; processes, distributes, and markets fresh, frozen, value-added, and further-processed chicken. Rainbow operates in the local retail, wholesale and food-service channels with four brands: Rainbow, Farmer Brown, Rainbow Simply Chicken, and Rainbow Food Solutions. It also produces a variety of dealer-owned brands for a number of retailers and wholesalers.

The company delivers over four million products to their customers every week, which requires a highly sophisticated, integrated IT system with lower total cost of ownership than the system that was being replaced. Management found that the SAP ERP solution supported those business goals. Additionally, the IT organization favored a solution that could be deployed quickly and cost-efficiently, while supporting their business needs.

3.3.2 Solution-Deployment Planning

The customer went through an extensive evaluation period, during which they asked SAP to demonstrate the delivery capability to the company. The customer reviewed the solution against their detailed business requirements, studying how the standard SAP ERP best-practice package, which is actually the foundation of the SAP Rapid Deployment solutions, met those requirements. Upon confirmation that the standard solution had a good level of fit to those customer needs, the customer and SAP services deployment team agreed on a deployment strategy, based on a lightweight version of ASAP methodology that supported the assemble-to-order deployment strategy.

The key reason for selecting the assemble-to-order approach for the customer team was its innovative nature in re-using standard best practices. The main savings come from the fact that the solution design starts with running an already integrated solution instead of an initial requirements collection. After the best practices were made known to the business owners, the requirements were defined as delta scoping during which the team confirms solution fit and performs design for the solution gaps and solution enhancements. This ensured that the solution works right from the beginning and is integrated strongly, reducing the project risks.

A customer IT manager stated, "SAP would not have won the services deal had it not been for the assemble-to-order approach." The assemble-to-order approach and SAP ERP rapid-deployment solution were the dealmakers for SAP Services and a big part of SAP signing a group software deal as well.

The solution that has been used as the baseline build at Rainbow is the SAP ERP rapid-deployment solutions package, specifically the manufacturing variant that offers complete coverage of the ERP capabilities for finance, controlling, manufacturing, etc. Figure 3.7 shows the key components of this package—from finance management, through manufacturing, to logistics—which include the software, services, content, and enablement.

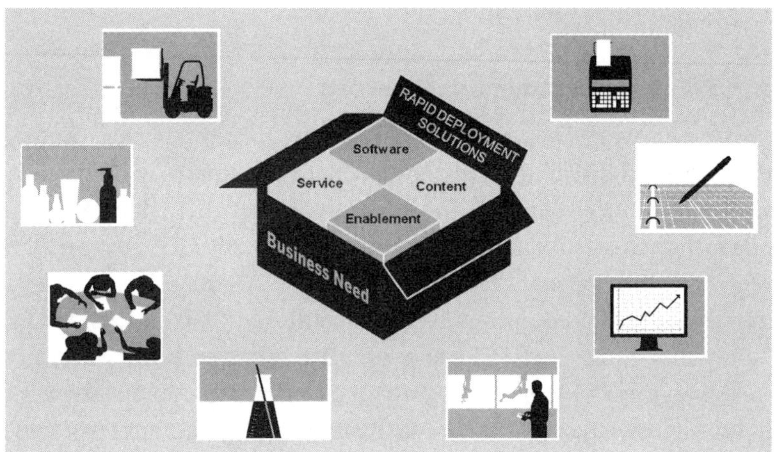

Figure 3.7 SAP ERP Rapid Deployment Solution Scope

3.3.3 Deployment

After an extensive solution-exploration phase, the customer conducted the SAP ERP deployment with a rapid-deployment solution and assemble-to-order approach. They did this with leading SAP implementation providers, and selected SAP services for deployment of the solution. The key points for selection of SAP services were the innovative deployment strategy that SAP presented with the assemble-to-order approach that leveraged standard ERP functionality based on ERP best practices. The price point that SAP was able to achieve through this approach, while delivering standard functionality, matched the customer business processes and needs, and set the stage for the end-to-end services around an SAP ERP rapid-deployment solution implementation.

The customer started the deployment project with the SAP ERP rapid-deployment solution for manufacturing best-practice content. They used the solution to guide their focus in Rainbow's scope validation workshops. During these workshops, the deployment team went through a detailed validation of requirements and fit of the business processes. At the end of the scope validation, the team increased the scope and proceeded to the realization of the solution gaps. Using best practices as a starting point does not limit the flexibility of the final solution. It is just a very effective way to come to a working final solution.

Figure 3.8 shows the recommended approach to the scope-validation workshops as it is defined in the assemble-to-order version of the ASAP implementation methodology.

Validation workshops

The validation workshops start with setting the reference value and boundaries to guide the discussion. Then the team starts the delta-scoping workshop, during which the team demonstrates the standard functionality of the package to the key users and solicits feedback on fit. For any gap that is identified, the team captures the delta requirement on a high level and marks it for follow-up in scoping workshop B.

During the Rainbow delta-scoping workshop B, the project team (together with key users) worked on the design of the solution related to gaps identified in the earlier workshops. This way, the team stayed focused on reviewing the fit of the entire package before getting into detailed design discussions. The outcome of this exercise was a delta-scope document that captured the fit and details the solution for all known gaps.

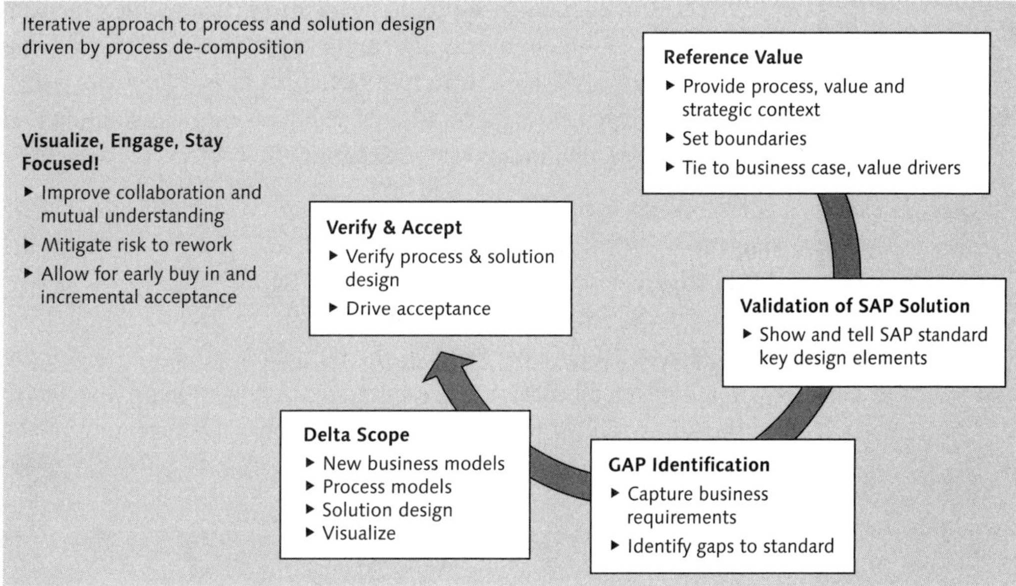

Figure 3.8 Scope Validation Workshop Flow

The scope-validation workshops helped the Rainbow IT organization and project team win the business users over. This was accomplished because the team was able to demonstrate processes with recognizable roles and outcomes that the business users valued. The SAP ERP rapid-deployment solution standard best practices content worked well together and provided integrated scenarios that the customer team could identify with in the context of their business needs. This helped the deployment team to minimize the time and effort spent to identify the gaps and understand the effort needed to close them.

The SAP ERP rapid-deployment solution package is by its nature an assemble-to-order package, as it allows for a significant amount of configuration as part of the standard package, plus the capability of the ERP solution to be configured or extended to fit customer needs where the standard package functionality does not meet the requirements. The deployment approach for the assemble-to-order solutions reflects this in the way the deployment is structured into phases that emphasize the solution validation and further enhancements of the standard functionality during the realization phase.

The realization phase of the Rainbow project focused on the build and test of the identified gaps. The project team also managed the organization change, development of training, and production of end-user documentation in similar fashion as in traditional projects. The major acceleration was achieved through re-use of a standard pre-built solution and by focusing on the delta requirements during the project.

Organizational change management
The project team focused strongly on execution of organizational change management (OCM) activities during the course of the project. With the rapid deployment of a solution in an organization, it is critical to perform rapid OCM activities. It was critical for the project success to integrate OCM activities in every step of the implementation journey. Rainbow used dedicated business representatives that were hand-selected to drive the key activities in the project and support the execution of the organizational changes in the business.

3.3.4   Results

This SAP ERP customer team related the re-use of the SAP ERP best practices as the primary vehicle that enabled the company to reduce the ERP deployment project from 12 months to eight months. A four-month savings multiplied across an entire deployment team, and the customer resources that supported that team, was a substantial savings to the customer. The Rainbow customer team underlined the above statement by saying that the cost efficiency the SAP Services team helped them gain through a best-practice system was a big win for them.

Being able to use the pre-built SAP Rapid Deployment solutions packages to significantly accelerate the ERP project produced tangible savings in time and investment, especially in the initial setup of the baseline solution. They accomplished these savings without sacrificing on requirements.

SAP Services was able to help the deployment team to accelerate the implementation while still staying focused on the customer requirements, so that the core business requirements were not compromised. The team was able to simplify the work on the delta requirements and stay focused on the customer's unique processes and practices, then implement the difference as a delta on top of the standard functionality provided by the package.

The Rainbow Chicken Limited implementation project innovation and success was recognized during the SAPPHIRE 2012 event in Madrid with two SAP Quality Awards–Gold in the category of Medium Implementation and Silver in the Innovation category. You can learn more about SAP Quality Awards at *http://www.sap.com/corporate-en/our-company/quality-awards*.

For more information about execution of assemble-to-order projects, we recommend you review the guidance in the ASAP methodology that is available to customers and partners on SAP Service Marketplace (*http://service.sap.com/asap*) and in SAP Solution Manager.

3.4   Deploying SAP CRM with SAP HANA

Solution Showcase

How SAP CRM on SAP HANA deployment helped DFB–the German Football governing agency—to improve the customer experience of millions of game-goers, improve sales, and use SAP CRM, mobility, and SAP HANA to elevate their marketing campaigns to new levels.

This case study is about SAP CRM on SAP HANA, an SAP Rapid Deployment solution implemented by DFB, the German national football association, governing body of football. A founding member of FIFA and UEFA, the DFB has jurisdiction on the German football (soccer) league system and is in charge of the men's and women's national teams. It is the world's biggest sports federation with 6.8 million members in Germany. It is headquartered in Frankfurt, with 26 regional offices all over Germany.

3.4.1   Background

Marketing DFB implemented the SAP CRM on SAP HANA rapid-deployment solutions for their ticketing system, focused on the marketing. They have a large customer base of 6.8 million; however, they had a challenge in retrieving the right customer data at the right time, since the customer data was kept in multiple systems. There was no central place to extract the overview of the customer information. If a customer had an issue with ticketing, and if they called the switchboard to gather all the relevant information about that specific customer, it was an uphill task. It was very time-consuming and involved a lot of manual work to extract the customer data. The manual process caused errors, slowed down business transactions, and frustrated customers.

Inefficiencies in as-is Another challenge DFB faced was that there was no interaction, connection, or collaboration between the sales and finance departments. Both teams were forced to operate in silos with separate systems, and it compromised each team's efficiency and productivity.

DFB dealt with several external service providers that took care of their business processes and supported DFB customers directly. DFB management aimed to streamline and optimize the data-sharing process by bringing the service-provider information in-house and also by better integrating with the external service providers to serve their customers.

These business challenges led DFB to conduct an evaluation with an external partner and create a roadmap to improve and solve their customer-related inefficiencies. They completed the evaluation in six months.

DFB wanted to start with an enterprise system that could meet the business requirements of today, and scale and grow gracefully with the business. They identified a quick-installation system with the rapid-deployment version of SAP's CRM solution. The SAP Rapid Deployment solutions preconfigured approach was preferred, because it offered a way to achieve quick time-to-value, and allowed DFB to leverage the packaged best practices and enablement material that is packaged with the rapid-deployment solutions. It was decided to start the SAP CRM implementation with the marketing focus (see Figure 3.9).

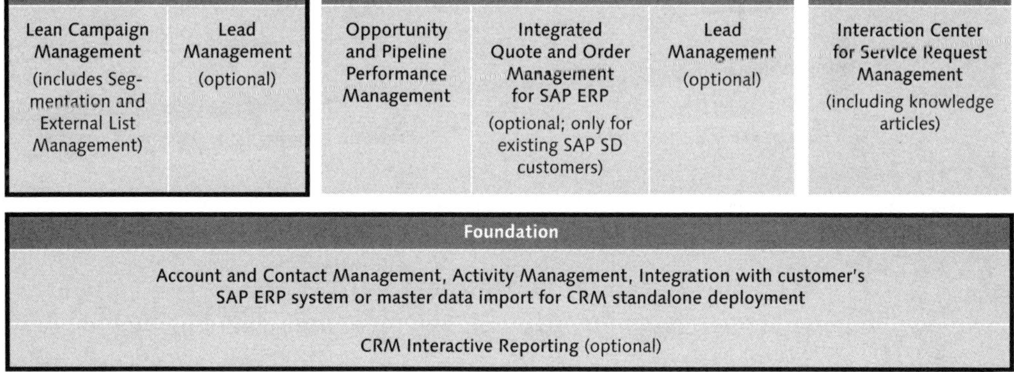

Figure 3.9 The Scope of the DFB Deployment Included the SAP CRM Rapid-Deployment Solution with SAP HANA

3.4.2 Deployment

DFB decided to use the rapid-deployment methodology and made full use of the step-by-step guide to keep the project on track, within scope and within the timelines (see Figure 3.10). The step-by step guide provides a logical progression of steps for each phase of the deployment, as shown in the figure. It also provides various relevant accelerators to help kick start the tasks so that the project team members do not need to start from scratch. This helped to keep the project moving forward and accomplish DFB's marketing goals.

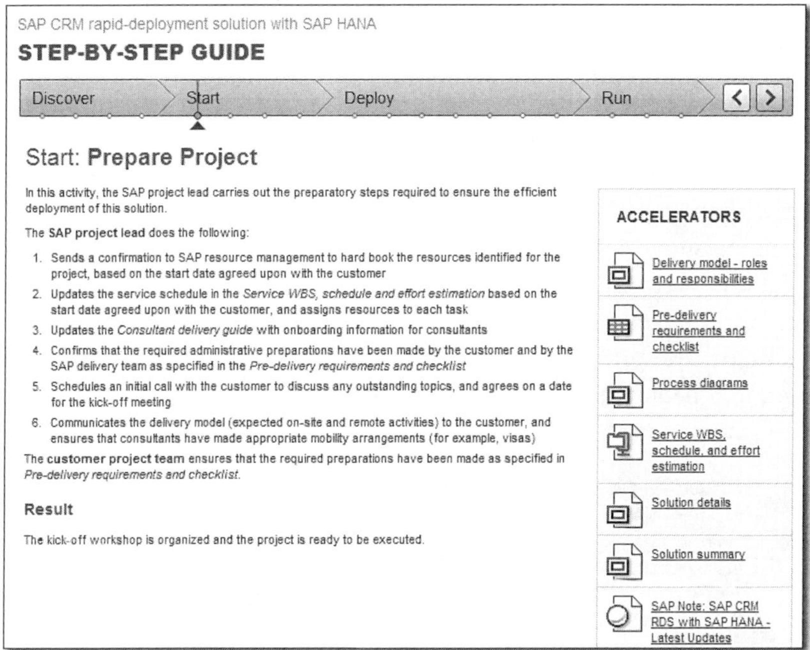

Figure 3.10 Step-by-Step Guide for SAP CRM Rapid-Deployment Solution with SAP HANA

Solution-Deployment Planning

Standard methodology/ accelerators

The result of the previous analysis to select the right enterprise system and the rapid-deployment approach was very helpful to keep the planning phase simple. During the planning phase, it was decided to leverage the standard methodology and accelerators as much as possible. The accelerators, such as solution-scope document and scoping questionnaire, met this requirement and helped the deployment-planning team to understand the needed timeframes within the solution deployment. It was crucial to implement and personalize the solution in the fastest possible way to meet the immediate business requirement to execute a campaign for the upcoming women's soccer world cup—the next high-priority marketing campaign.

The DFB IT team was very lean, overall four people, and they were very vigilant in identifying and allocating the right business resources with the right skills and capacity to the critical deployment activities before the deployment project started.

With a preconfigured solution and a clear roadmap laid out by the SAP services organization, DFB was able to implement the SAP CRM application in about three months. As time is money with ticket sales, this team knew the clock was ticking.

Deployment

The deployment phase executed the plan to leverage the SAP Rapid Deployment solutions methodology and accelerators. The overall implementation process was simplified and deployment was very fast using the predefined solution scope for the SAP CRM Marketing subcomponent.

The initial foundation scope from the SAP Rapid Deployment solution was realized by the deployment team, easily, with no road blocks. One of the consultants was able to deploy and personalize the marketing scenario within a very short time frame: 28 hours.

The DFB team tested the solution thoroughly using the test scripts delivered with SAP Rapid Deployment solutions content. The knowledge transfer went smoothly, since the team members assigned to conduct knowledge transfer were already part of the project team. The project communications were sent out at all the major milestones of the project and it kept all the parties informed and engaged.

The first marketing campaign was run 15 days after go-live; DFB's new SAP CRM marketing system performed flawlessly, supporting ticket sales for the DFB Women's Cup final in Cologne, Germany.

The SAP Rapid Deployment solutions approach is quick, but a lot of work goes in this implementation to make it successful. Key lessons from this project are as follows:

- It is critical that employees and deployment team members who are involved in the deployment have the right capacity and right skill set to support the project in addition to their daily duties.

- Communication is very important with all the stakeholders, project team members and users, as it kept everyone informed and engaged in the project activities.

- Celebrate the quick wins to motivate the team and keep the momentum going. Keep the project landscape simple. DFB successfully managed these factors in their project.

3.4.3 Results

The lean and dedicated team from DFB and SAP took the project live in 90 days. The first campaign was run immediately after go-live. This campaign was for the event to be held in Cologne. They were able to monitor the campaign, run reports, and actually had a direct contact with their customer base for the first time. They were able to personalize the campaign for the fans. This empowered DFB to take their customer relationship to the next level and achieve new customer service and relationship-building that could be measured in terms of behaviors and revenue.

Customer-specific offers
With all its customer information in a centralized database, DFB was able to create customer-specific offers that were integrated with sales. It delivered a personalized promotional material to more than 8,700 fans. The personalized emails were opened by 37 percent of the fans and 47 percent of those fans clicked through to the DFB ticketing site.

This campaign helped DFB connect with their customers, making the event more exciting, manageable, and successful. The tangible result was measurable with increased sales and revenue. It was a proud moment for the DFB team.

"With SAP CRM on HANA, it's the first time for us that we are able to do marketing campaigns by ourselves. We can now serve fans through digital channels and improve customer loyalty with offers that meet their needs. By using SAP HANA Enterprise Cloud, our processes will be much more efficient," said Daniel Gutermuth, Program Manager at DFB.

DFB feels it has established a good partnership with SAP. "I'm glad that SAP is our partner and I think this partnership will last a long time," said Gutermuth. DFB's vision is to have its core SAP applications and SAP event-ticketing software all integrated and running using SAP HANA enterprise-cloud service. "In five years I hope we still have one of the best national football teams in the world," said Gutermuth. "And that we are able to offer our customers a completely integrated customer journey that is linked to our back-office systems."

With SAP on the DFB team, football in Germany is poised for a winning future.

3.5 Combining SAP Rapid Deployment Solutions with an Incremental Rollout Strategy to Integrate Disconnected CRM Systems

Solution Showcase

Common sales platform rolled out to 18 countries and 2,000 users, integrated into the company's ERP system.

This case study provides an overview of how VWR deployed SAP CRM, including the marketing, sales, and service functionalities, to 18 country locations with multiple local systems. VWR International is a global leader in the distribution of research laboratory products. They distribute over 1,200,000 items to more than 250,000 customers in North America and Europe, with sales in excess of $4.1 billion in 2012.

VWR was challenged with complex business requirements and disconnected local systems that reduced visibility into customer information, and thus reduced collaboration mechanisms for sales-team members. The local systems were not cross-validated or standardized. VWR struggled for more than a year trying to find the right CRM software, including CRM implementations approaches, in terms of scope, time, and budget. It hadn't been for lack of trying, it was due to the fact that the business case was too big. It never got past the planning stage due to the perceived risk involved in launching one of those big, scary CRM implementations.

After having wrestled with what to do and how to deploy a CRM system, the VWR team discovered SAP's CRM rapid-deployment solution approach. The solution provided an alternate approach to focus on the specific business priorities and reduce the risk. This approach would allow the rollout in stages, and would allow the company to stop studying and start using a best-practices CRM system. This case study shows how leveraging the rapid-deployment methodology provided VWR with an option to realize quick time-to-value, within weeks as opposed to a big-bang, traditional project-implementation approach that could take up to a year or more.

Modular construction

The SAP Rapid Deployment solutions approach and the strong value prop of the SAP CRM package made the needed innovations easy to consume based on best practices and pre-configured solutions. The solution is modularly constructed, thus consumption is simple. VWR found the SAP CRM solution to really help them find a way to deploy a far-reaching, extensive CRM system quickly and with best practices designed into the deployment to achieve a high level of customer satisfaction in a matter of weeks.

This case study takes you through the customer's journey using SAP Rapid Deployment solutions to solve their CRM business issues around marketing, service, and sales, especially during the quotation processes.

3.5.1　Background

Localized, disconnected systems

VWR wanted a cost-effective, fast, and competitive CRM offering to address business challenges of localized, disconnected systems. There was no visibility in the customer information, and there was no standard structure to get accurate and timely information before customer visits. This also made the quotation process long and arduous. VWR found that SAP Rapid Deployment solutions met the need for an efficient and effective solution. For example, the average CRM rapid-deployment solution deploys in weeks and provides an average of 40% time-savings compared to the traditional on-premises implementation.

Fixed-scope style was a good starting point to meet the needs of the user community, and it allowed them to implement the scope using the content best practices and enablement material that was bundled as part of the SAP Rapid Deployment solutions package.

Fixed-scope style

In this particular case, VWR had been working on the CRM project for years, and when they discovered the SAP Rapid Deployment solutions approach they adopted the deployment methodology and instantly took control of the project. VWR was able to complete the deployment and roll out for the first country in four months. As if this were not enough of an achievement, it provided a single system and single source of truth for their customer data, improved collaboration amongst the sales teams, and product specialization in a matter of weeks. In fact, this customer had been missing core CRM capabilities such as providing accurate, consistent, and timely quotes to their customers, which the new solution brought with it in terms of standard scope and content.

So, VWR called up their SAP account executive to ask if he could help them come up with a detailed proposal. Two days later they were having calls with SAP CRM experts and an SAP Rapid Deployment solutions architect to analyze their requirements. They were able to pin down the main requirements and decided on an on-site workshop to create a customized roadmap for their CRM journey. During the workshop, the knowledgeable SAP architect helped the team come up with a phase roadmap, including multiple CRM solution capabilities. It was decided to begin with a simultaneous implementation of the CRM rapid-deployment solution for Sales, Marketing, and Service, illustrated in Figure 3.11.

In the second phase they would leverage the implemented marketing functionality as well as using SAP CRM as a service hotline for handling service requests from customer side. As a third step, they would then add a mobility platform, again heavily leveraging SAP Rapid Deployment solutions backend capabilities to show the relevant information out of CRM on mobile devices.

Marketing		Sales			Service
Lean Campaign Management (includes Segmentation and External List Management)	Lead Management (optional)	Opportunity and Pipeline Performance Management	Integrated Quote and Order Management for SAP ERP (optional; only for existing SAP SD customers)	Lead Management (optional)	Interaction Center for Service Request Management (including knowledge articles)
Foundation					
Account and Contact Management, Activity Management, Integration with customer's SAP ERP system or master data import for CRM standalone deployment					
CRM Interactive Reporting (optional)					

Figure 3.11 Scope of the VWR Deployment

Incremental approach This incremental approach (see Figure 3.12) is a major benefit of SAP Rapid Deployment solutions. Each solution delivers value to the business within a quarter, not a year, and as customers start this path, they can develop roadmaps aligned to business needs, bringing efficiency and value gains that drive the organization forward, unlocking new innovations.

Figure 3.12 Example of Incremental Approach Leveraging Rapid-Deployment Solutions

SAP CRM was integrated with an ERP quotation management functionality, which helped define the complete business process to make a strong business case. It showed a break-even, based on greater effectiveness in the sales force and a much better grip on quotation processes, which they were struggling with historically. As a result, the large numbers of quote process users were all working in a single system.

The entire project was a success for the IT organization and for the business stakeholders. It provided a centralized, best-practice-based approach, which turned out to be effective and contributed towards the overall business goal.

3.5.2 Deployment

The deployment phase of the project was very critical and overall it went well. The best approach to build the common deployment strategy was to agree and build on the already agreed-upon scope of the SAP CRM rapid-deployment solution. After a test drive of the system, additional requirements like mobility were identified by the users. These requirements were then included in the project pipeline to be implemented in the following phases. This approached helped the project to manage scope effectively and stay within the planned timeline.

Solution-Deployment Planning

Discovery of the right solution is critical before start of the project. A detailed breakdown of the functionality that is required by the business should be mapped to the functionality that is included in the rapid-deployment solution, to ensure there are no surprises later.

An SAP account executive pointed VWR to the portfolio of SAP CRM rapid-deployment solutions, offerings with fixed-price, fixed-scope, and fixed-schedule deployments that apparently expedited the implementation of SAP software considerably while deploying SAP's CRM best-practices content. The SAP CRM package would be a very good fit for them from a functionality perspective, at least for the first phase.

VWR was very savvy in assigning dedicated resources very early in the project for continuity, quality, and successful delivery of the project.

The project team used a step-by-step guide to get a clearer picture of the project and the requirements of the project team to adopt the standard SAP Rapid Deployment solutions process.

It was then decided to select this approach and execute the fixed scope and price project even though an area was discovered where the standard functionality would not cover the required business scenario.

Implementation

SAP was able to provide a pre-assembled rapid-deployment solution for VWR to kick off the project. Based on their previous experience in implementing SAP CRM, the most influential "multipliers," i.e., opinion leaders in the field, were identified together with sales leadership, and they were integrated into the project team along with SAP consulting resources.

Standard step-by-step approach

The standard step-by-step approach helped to accelerate the project deployment. It provided the starting point at every stage of the project, so that the team did not have to start from scratch. For example, at the start of the project, the standard project plan was leveraged and it was modified only to accommodate the timelines and resources, while most of the other tasks remained unchanged.

Best-practices processes were already configured and documented, operational documentations were available to use.

The systems landscape was set up by the IT team of VWR. They followed the best-practice guides to do so. The consulting team was put in place to work collaboratively with the customer team. The consulting team leveraged the step-by-step guide to execute the project; for example, leveraging the checklist, project plan templates, and test plan templates.

The SAP pre-configured system was validated by the customer team and very limited changes were made to the system. As a result, the standard test scripts could be used without many changes, thus saving time.

The solution was demoed to stakeholders to show that the initial scope was met successfully. The team then successfully executed the knowledge transfer to the customer team.

Run

Business gaps that could not be delivered during the project were identified and incorporated in the roadmap to take the project to next level.
Feedback was collected from users to build the roadmap.

One vocal member of the business team voiced concerns about the
search functionality and brought up some ideas for additional reporting.
Fortunately, the project manager was able to defend the scope with full
backup of the sponsors based on the detailed information that was
shared during the preparation phase. The features were added to the
backlog of the future roadmap.

The SAP consulting team worked with the customer team to support the
initial go-live. The customer team was responsible for the ongoing support.

On go-live weekend for the initial country, the SAP CRM rapid-deployment solution approach proved very effective at reminding the team of
every little step necessary to bring an SAP CRM system up and live. Even
the initial download and connection to the live SAP ERP system went
smoothly.

Over the next months, an additional 17 countries were taken live.

Key Drivers for Success

The overall CRM implementation success could be attributed to the following:

- There was strong management support and sponsorship for the
  project.
- Dedicated team members were assigned to work on the project.
- The project leadership was very strong and effective.
- The collaboration with between the business and IT was very robust,
  and as a result there was close alignment.
- A standardized template was created for roll out to the rest of Europe,
  the Middle East, and Africa. Using this repeatable process was both
  efficient and effective.

- The close collaboration between the SAP consulting team and customer team was also a very strong suite; as a result the teams worked together like a well-oiled machine.

- Streamline communication about the objective and scope of the project is critical to manage expectations and help adoption.

3.5.3 Results

The VWR implementation was successfully completed to serve 18 countries and 2,000 users in a short time span. The VWR sales team is accessing information in an organized fashion and getting accurate and timely information to serve their customers. Studiously following the SAP Rapid Deployment solutions methodology and approach helped to keep the project on time.

Malika, the sales director for Europe and business lead for the SAP CRM project, said: "With the rapid-deployment solution approach, the project went very fast and in a structured approach."

In summary, the major point for success was to agree with the business on the methodology and approach and use the predefined steps of the step-by-step guide strictly and without compromises. That starts with one of the first steps to communicate the scope and find out the percentage of coverage between customer needs and the scope of the best practices of the package.

3.6 Assemble-to-Order Deployment of SAP ERP

> **Solution Showcase**
>
> Japan Display deployed SAP ERP for manufacturing and SAP ERP subsidiary rollout rapid-deployment solution using an assemble-to-order (A2O) approach.

Japan Display, Inc. (JDI), the world's largest manufacturer of small and medium-sized liquid-crystal displays, decided on the SAP Rapid Deployment solutions for SAP ERP to drive business-process standardization in its headquarters, as well as in its foreign subsidiaries. Rolled out in less than six months, using a cloud-based quick start, the solution supports JDI in achieving sustained operational excellence and profitable growth.

3.6.1 Background

Japan Display was founded in 2011, when Sony, Toshiba, and Hitachi merged their display divisions to achieve economies of scale. When three of the world's leading makers of displays join forces, you can expect the outcome to be big. From the first day of business operations, JDI has expanded its turf as the world's largest maker of small and medium-sized monitors.

Drawing on cutting-edge technologies from the three integrating companies, JDI manufactures high-quality LCDs for a wide range of applications. These include smartphones, other mobile devices, consumer products, automotive electronics, medical devices, and industrial equipment. At the forefront of research and development for next-generation display technology, JDI pioneers technologies such as organic light-emitting diode (OLED) panels.

Headquartered in Tokyo, JDI employs some 6,200 people. In addition to Japan, the company operates in China, Germany, Hong Kong, Singapore, South Korea, Taiwan, the United Kingdom, and the United States.

Changing lifestyles and new ways of doing business are spurring rapid growth in multiple technologies. These range from wireless devices, intelligent automotive electronics, and consumer products like digital cameras, to industrial technology. All of these technologies have one thing in common: They are creating an increasing demand for high-quality small and medium-sized displays in the global marketplace.

JDI is committed to capitalizing on this growth in demand through superior products—designed, developed, and delivered ahead of competitive offerings. The company's ultra-light media tablet (ULMT) display technology for the increasingly popular tablet PC is a case in point.

SAP ERP is a vital part of the framework that enables JDI to tune its business processes to the changing needs of the marketplace. Today, JDI is the world's number one player in its line of business. What's more, JDI is in an excellent position to further expand its market share.

3.6.2 Deployment

Before their merger, the display divisions of Sony, Toshiba, and Hitachi were looking for the "right" ERP application for JDI. Above all, the application was expected to enable and support common processes across multiple JDI sites in various countries. This key requirement called for a software vendor with a strong global presence. JDI was also looking for the right methodology for bringing this application to bear within a very short time frame.

Solution-Deployment Planning

JDI's requirements quickly reduced the number of contenders to a short list. SAP was selected for its ability to demonstrate that the rapid-deployment solution SAP ERP for manufacturing and SAP ERP subsidiary rollout provided the right fit for JDI. This decision was further reinforced by Hitachi's long-standing relationship of trust and collaboration with SAP.

Cloud-based quick start
To get the software up and running quickly and accelerate its time-to-value, JDI turned to the SAP Services organization to provide a cloud-based quick start. This service combines preassembled software and content, hosting in a private cloud environment, and logistics services to move the software to its final infrastructure before it goes live.

Action

Using a cloud-based quick start, SAP Services provided preassembled software—configured, tested, and preloaded with content specific to JDI's needs.

This predefined content was instrumental to the smooth deployment of SAP ERP rapid deployment solutions at JDI. Next, SAP Services moved the software—complete with the predefined content—to a private, secure cloud. It remained hosted in the cloud for just over a week while the infrastructure for local installation was finalized. During this time, JDI could access the preconfigured software from the cloud in a virtual "sandbox" to see it in action and fine-tune it using real-life data.

SAP Services then transferred the solution from the cloud to the local data center at JDI headquarters. The entire project—including the preassembly of content, cloud-based provisioning, fine-tuning, and local installation—was completed in only four months. Classroom training sessions helped ensure a smooth start for approximately 300 business users at JDI headquarters.

Within another two months, a single instance of SAP ERP was rolled out at the overseas sales organizations in China, Germany, Hong Kong, Singapore, South Korea, Taiwan, the United Kingdom, and the United States. This rollout brought more than 100 business users on board. All eight sales organizations switched to production mode within two weeks, enabling JDI to complete its quarterly closing settlement on schedule.

3.6.3 Results

Today, the business units of JDI rely on SAP ERP to drive standardized business processes. These include customer-facing activities such as order processing, delivery, invoicing, and order-to-cash, as well as inventory management, purchasing, and finance.

Standardized business processes

Experts from SAP services helped JDI to strike the right balance between local requirements and standardization. "Initially, the challenge for JDI was in convincing our overseas business units that standardized processes would make life easier for them, too," notes Tomotaka Yano, senior general manager of information systems at JDI. "Running the same consistent processes on a shared-application platform enables us to communicate in a common language."

The rapid deployment of SAP ERP at JDI has strengthened the ties between the company's IT organization and its business units. While the IT organization has deepened its understanding of the specific business needs in each country, the business units are aware of the benefits of process standardization. When it comes to expanding business operations or integrating additional sites, the business units at JDI rely on the corporate IT organization as their trusted advisor.

Fast time-to-value

The cloud technology to accelerate the start to the project was instrumental to the fast time-to-value of SAP ERP at JDI. Big yet nimble, JDI was able to rapidly achieve operational excellence across its globally distributed business units. Robust business processes, standardized through SAP ERP, support JDI in consistently delivering on the expectations of its customers.

At the same time, process standardization delivers synergies that help JDI keep a tab on costs. For example, shared sourcing enables JDI to boost purchasing efficiency and reduce purchasing costs by an attractive margin.

Standardized business processes support the company in cost-effectively embracing change and also contribute to its bottom line. The global reach of the sales organizations at JDI helps the company make the most of windows of opportunity in the marketplace.

Future Plans

JDI is committed to providing its customers with the best-quality products in the shortest lead time in the marketplace, i.e., the optimal customer experience. To deliver on this commitment, JDI is currently investigating ways of integrating unstructured data with SAP ERP to support its business processes. This unstructured data includes customer orders received via email as well as market information. Yano trusts that this integration will help the company further streamline its processes and expand its market.

3.7 Telco Accelerates Billing Project Using a Rapid-Deployment Solution

Solution Showcase

A mobile service provider deployed the SAP Billing and Revenue Innovation Management rapid-deployment solution; accelerating their blueprint and reducing the total project implementation time for a new billing system.

The introduction of a new telecommunications billing system usually takes a long time, depending on the size, the complexity, and the demand of the operator. Even the blueprinting phase, which is used to define the required configuration or customization of the solution, is usually a significant financial and resourcing investment.

With a rapid-deployment solution from SAP that includes best practices and content, months can be shaved off the time it takes to do the initial solution blueprinting and customization, leading to significant time and cost savings. Instead of investing the deployment team's efforts in the initial set-up and configuration of the solution, a complete end-to-end system is consistently delivered through the SAP Billing and Revenue Innovation Management rapid-deployment solution. This offers a core foundation, created by SAP experts in CRM and billing management processes, which are common across a wide range of business types and sizes.

At the front-end of the deployment project, and immediately after the SAP Rapid Deployment solution is deployed, the customer can start blueprinting based on a set of common, fully configured and well-documented telecommunications processes by matching the customer's demands against the pre-configured best practices, and identifying the project requirements that may be supplementary to standard-delivered SAP Rapid Deployment solution content. This helps deployment teams to quickly advance through the first phase of setting the foundation, before moving rapidly into the second phase of configuration and customization. This innovative approach allows business and IT stakeholders to touch and feel what the final solution will more or less look like, instead of doing months of theoretical documentation and analysis. It also allows stakeholders to quickly get to an appropriate comfort level with the new solution concepts so that design decisions for the implementation can be made in a more efficient and timely manner.

3.7.1 Background

The customer in the case described here was a new entrant in the telecommunications market, just starting a new mobile services business. So they needed a complete new set of systems to support their initial service launch, but open and flexible enough for their future growth ambitions.

Greenfield

Being either a greenfield (as in this case) or a well-established communications service provider (CSP), these types of customers need to implement a next generation CRM and billing business support system to support the launch of new, innovative, and often complex multi-sided revenue models. Considering the hyper-competitive telecommunications market, it is expected that the solution will not only allow the deployment of new complex services in days instead of months so that the CSP can keep on the cutting-edge of its market, but that the implementation of the solution itself will be vastly accelerated to get a quick return on investment.

In this case, the CSP billing department analyzed competitive offerings from a number of vendors and finally decided to select the SAP Billing for Telecommunications solution as their flexible and future-proof billing solution. They assured themselves that it covered existing scenarios, and was open and configurable to easily support new products and business models.

SAP demo cloud landscape

One important decision driver for the CSP to select the SAP solution was that during the decision-making process they could see the complete solution pre-configured in the SAP demo cloud landscape using the SAP Billing and Revenue Innovation Management rapid-deployment solution as the basis for the content. Note that the SAP Billing for Telecommunications solution and the SAP Billing and Revenue Innovation Management solution leverage the same product sets under the hood and the SAP Rapid Deployment solution is common for both.

In addition to being able to investigate the solution by themselves during the evaluation phase, the CSP discovered that the SAP solution could also be deployed in its own landscape in a matter of weeks with the same configuration content as the demo, and that it could even be personalized to integrate with the customer's existing SAP ERP environment. The personalization of the rapid-deployment solution covers aspects like organizational structure, as well SAP ERP master data and configuration items like chart of account, G/L accounts, tax codes, and currency. This was a major asset to accelerate the detailed business blueprint and the subsequent implementation.

The business and IT stakeholders within the CSP understood that the value of the rapid-deployment solution was instrumental to delivering on the SAP promise of best-in-class, low total cost of integration (TCI), and quick time-to-value.

3.7.2 Deployment

The following sections provide more details about the rapid-deployment solution by first explaining what the CSP had to decide upon in the planning phase and how the actual deployment was done in the CSP's prepared system landscape.

Solution-Deployment Planning

The SAP Billing and Revenue Innovation Management rapid-deployment solution provides a preconfigured baseline of end-to-end processes along with the required product master data to run the processes without any further configuration or master-data creation work.

In the planning phase, the main task for the CSP was to decide which scenarios to deploy (either post-paid or prepaid billing scenarios, or even both) and to plan the availability of the system landscape where the solution would be deployed.

Based on the included business process documentation, the customer had the ability to start early on, and the deployment team was able to meet the business demand with the pre-configured processes and use them to further accelerate the implementation project.

Deployment

The deployment of the SAP Billing and Revenue Innovation Management rapid-deployment solution is completely done using a specific deployment tool provided by SAP. Since the solution spans three SAP applications and packages (SAP CRM, SAP Convergent Charging, and SAP ERP), there were two instances of the deployment tool required—

one instance in the SAP CRM system and one instance in the SAP ERP system.

Consultant profiles
Two different consultant profiles were involved: technical and application consultants. Before starting the deployment, a set of technical steps and checks were executed in the system by a technical consultant. Those were mainly to check if all required technical components are installed with the correct version, to activate the business functions, to set up the system users (for RFC connections and for activation of content), and to perform specific settings on the J2EE server. In addition, the integration points to the finance general ledger (FI-GL) system of the CSP were defined (e.g., company code, chart of account, currency, and more) and transferred as personalization activities to the deployment tool.

All tasks during the solution activation and deployment were done by application consultants. Automated checks were made throughout the full deployment to ensure the consultants had correctly performed the configuration steps within the three systems in the right sequence, and with clear guidelines to keep the project timeline on track. For those configuration parts that were not automated, the project team followed the detailed configuration guides provided in the rapid-deployment solution package.

An experienced SAP CRM application consultant, who was new to the SAP Rapid Deployment solutions concept, mentioned after the deployment that "in all projects, we always reserve a few days of technical consulting support—say, for example, for the CRM middleware or other technical parts. Surprisingly, we did not use any of these allocated support days here." This is just one example where the deployment of the SAP Billing and Revenue Innovation Management rapid-deployment solution allowed a reduction of the CSP's initially allocated consulting budget.

Process testing
The last step of the deployment was process testing. By following the business process description, the deployment team ran a series of tests on the complete end-to-end processes. Since all previous deployment steps did not cause any problems, the project team decided to include CSP employees—including those who were already named in the blueprinting phase as candidates—to participate in testing. Once all

processes delivered by the rapid-deployment solution were successfully tested, the project proved to be a highly efficient and substantially short blueprinting and final-implementation phase.

Even though the rapid-deployment solution played a big role in delivering such a quick, successful, and affordable implementation, there were behavioral factors that played into the success. Overall, the deployment went well because the project team and the customer worked well to manage mutual expectations, in particular with respect to what the rapid-deployment solution was being used for and what was required to be added on top of it. Clarification of expectations was key for the deployment team to identify the foundational content of the rapid-deployment solution and how to leverage what was there before moving onto further configuration and customization in the second phase. CSPs compete with each other on the basis of their different service offerings, pricing, and bundles, and this of course leads to some variability in telecommunications processes between CSPs and a lot of variation when it comes to pricing, packages, and other master data. Customer-specific project work is therefore always required on top of standard SAP Rapid Deployment solutions content, before being able to go live. In addition, it is worth mentioning that, while the project team was new to the tools and concepts used with rapid-deployment solutions, they secured a successful deployment by carefully following the guidelines and description delivered with the solution, in particular avoiding missing any steps or going sideways when following any manual configuration procedures.

By using a rapid-deployment solution as an accelerator for this project, they achieved their ambitious goal to launch their new business only seven months after starting the project. Further extension of services and offerings provided by the CSP is planned and will be realized on subsequent phases.

3.7.3 Summary

The SAP Billing and Revenue Innovation Management rapid-deployment solution allows project teams to quickly set up a baseline configuration as a basis for proof-of-concepts, to facilitate design discussions during business blueprint phases and overall to drive an efficient implementation of the solution. As shown by this concrete CSP use-case, the savings in time, resources, and the lowered project risk is substantial.

3.8 Consumer Products Company Deploys SAP Demand Planning in Weeks

Solution Showcase

SAP Demand Planning rapid-deployment solution at a German mid-size consumer products manufacturer.

This case study shows how an SAP customer's discrete manufacturing organization benefitted from SAP Supply Chain Management rapid-deployment solutions to increase efficiency and reduce supply-chain costs. See what the best practices are in terms of the deployed SCM solution, as well as deployment methodology.

3.8.1 Background

Deployment teams might ask: How can a firm increase their accuracy in demand-planning figures to improve service levels, lower inventory, and increase reliability to the purchasing departments? These were the challenges that a mid-size German consumer products company, faced before starting to implement the SAP Demand Planning rapid-deployment solution.

The management wanted to optimize demand-planning and focus on reducing the planning effort and expense. They sought a solution to provide better input for production and purchasing—especially when looking at inventory demand related to seasonal items.

The purchasing behavior of certain product lines was well known, but especially for articles showing sporadic sales patterns, the company wanted precise information that required intensive monitoring. The company management expected their software support to make the demand planners' work much easier and more accurate. So, the solution had to be able to differentiate between products with steady sales on a regular basis (which the system could forecast fairly independently) and those products which have a seasonal or even sporadic buying behavior, where the solution should apply mathematical models (which serve as a suggestion for the planner only and which require manual adjustments in almost all cases).

3.8.2　Deployment

The company was able to deploy SAP Supply Chain Management rapid-deployment solutions and achieve substantial improvements with the core content of the solution package. The rapid-deployment methodology that the deployment team used consisted of an integrated start, deploy, and run phase to align all stakeholders on a predefined best-practice scope which could be deployed quickly, and then effectively handed over to productive usage.

The following sections describe how the customer deployed quickly to realize unequalled time-to-value in the organization.

Solution-Deployment Planning

Deployment planning is always first with SAP's uniform rapid-deployment methodology. Therefore, the project start and kickoff of SAP SCM rapid-deployment solutions is always conducted in a similar way.

The project teams, consisting of service providers as well as customer representatives from both business as well as the IT department usually meet at one place to review and discuss the detailed project scope along the predefined scope of the solution, which serves as a template during the quick blueprinting phase.

In the kickoff workshop, the process documentations are shared and the future solution is made visual through a demo or use of sandbox systems that help to streamline discussions to detail the scope and avoid non-value-adding fundamental documentation and re-invention of existing processes.

Collaboration

In a short time horizon, both customers were able to scope the solution so that all stakeholders agreed and all requirements were specified at a level of detail that the implementation could be conducted without having to go back and fill in missing requirement descriptions.

In a rapid-deployment package, scope requirements and definition is supported through the standard documents that are part of the solution, such as qualification and scoping questionnaires, as well as kick-off presentation templates and other materials. This methodology allows the deployment team and customer to visualize the scope and content of the rapid-deployment solutions.

Deployment

Since the result of the planning phase is so clear and leaves almost no questions open, the deployment can be conducted very effectively. Usually the majority of the configuration work is conducted remotely and the communication is limited to a weekly status call of two hours, as well as individual sessions talking about results of configuration items or tackling some minor open points that were left out in the scoping workshop before. That is what this customer did, too.

During the deployment, the consulting team used the summer holiday, where the employees of the client went on vacation and the client's premises were closed down for two weeks, to do the majority of the consulting effort. The process owners simply went on holiday and were presented with the suggested solution for acceptance testing when they came back. This can only work if the scope of the solution is crystal clear.

With a rapid-deployment solution, consultants—as with all rapid-deployment solutions—were supported with project accelerators that helped when configuring the system with highly repetitive tasks, especially those that require no deep knowledge. In addition, each solution comes with a detailed how-to guide describing each step in the configuration so that the expected system behavior is created. The concept allows centralizing certain configuration tasks and leveraging knowledge hubs where specialized consultants can work on similar projects in parallel. The team used those guides precisely to deploy the rapid-deployment solutions.

The solution-deployment concept maximizes and benefits from the learning curve of the consultants so that specialization can happen and there is no need to always learn all the details of a solution; instead, participants can leverage experts on-demand and on a global level. This allows consultants to work proficiently through the deployment, from customer to customer.

3.8.3 Results

After the SAP Rapid Deployment solutions package was deployed, the customer in the case study achieved measurable improvements. The German consumer-products company profits from a more efficient supply chain with reliable and solid forecast data. Having implemented this solution, the company could successfully reduce the number of rush orders and rush notices, minimize excess production quantities and inventories, and now can more easily execute planning for each individual sold-to-party.

- The average planning accuracy at each ship-from location had been 40 percent to 55 percent.

- The planning accuracy has risen by an average of 20 percent to 30 percent—a stupendous improvement.

3.9 Deploying Integrated Supply Chain Solutions Rapidly

Solution Showcase

Deployment of multiple SAP SCM rapid-deployment solution packages to accelerate supply chain time-to-value.

This case study shows how Bonfiglioli, a component manufacturer in the Mobile & Wind Energy sector, benefitted from the SAP Supply Chain Management rapid-deployment solution to increase efficiency and reduce costs in their supply chain. We'll explain the best practices in terms of the deployed solution, as well as deployment methodology.

3.9.1 Background

Bonfiglioli is a midsize Italian industrial component manufacturer. Before implementing a rapid-deployment solution, they had a manually-based planning process that used MS Excel, subsequently only achieved low visibility on planning data, while experiencing the pain of inaccurate and improperly allocated products and scattered planning environments.

Single planning platform

Before the implementation of the SAP Demand Planning rapid-deployment solution, the different departments of that component manufacturer were weakly connected, with different targets, speaking different planning languages, and acting in inconsistent ways. The solution therefore had to provide a single planning platform and join these dislocated pieces of information into a comprehensive communication system within the planning organization. To connect and enhance the company's planning capabilities, the deployment teams developed a new process based on a single environment that supports them in the entry door of the extended supply chain: the demand planning process (see Figure 3.13).

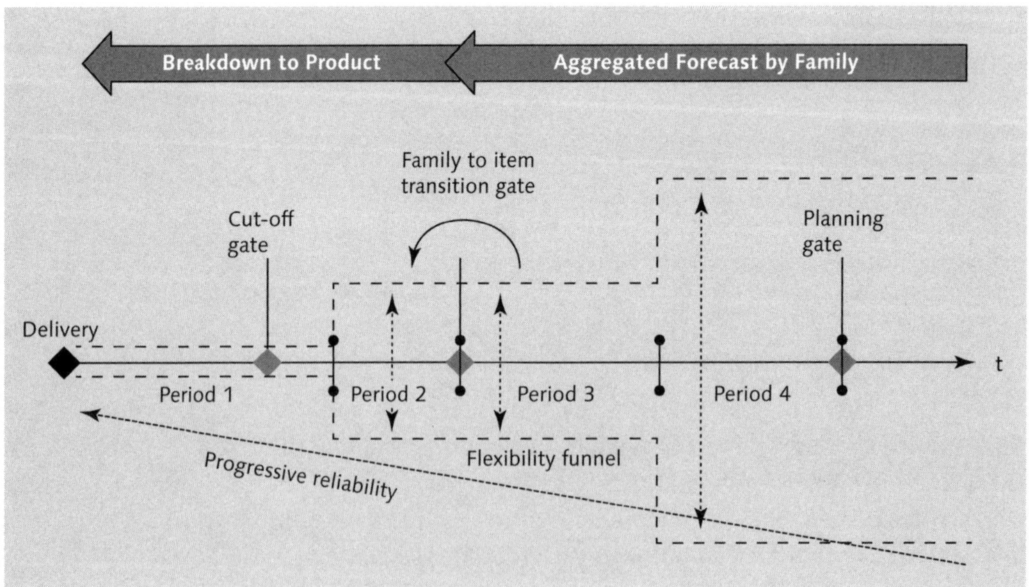

Figure 3.13 Demand Planning Process

3.9.2 Deployment

Bonfiglioli deployed the SAP Supply Chain Management rapid-deployment solution to achieve substantial improvements with the core content of the solution package.

The following sections describe how Bonfiglioli deployed the SAP Demand Planning solution quickly, to realize unequalled time-to-value in the organization.

Solution-Deployment Planning

The customer was able to go live with two rapid-deployment solutions; namely the SAP Demand Planning rapid-deployment solution and the SAP Global Available to Promise rapid-deployment solution combined in a single project in as little as 17 work weeks. The preparation involved an enhanced collaboration facilitated by a single project location where all—the business team and the IT team from Bonfiglioli, as well as the APO consultants from the service providers were located. They installed a project portal to share documentation effectively and established a simplified governance model that has been designed to keep any decisional process as simple as possible.

Two solutions

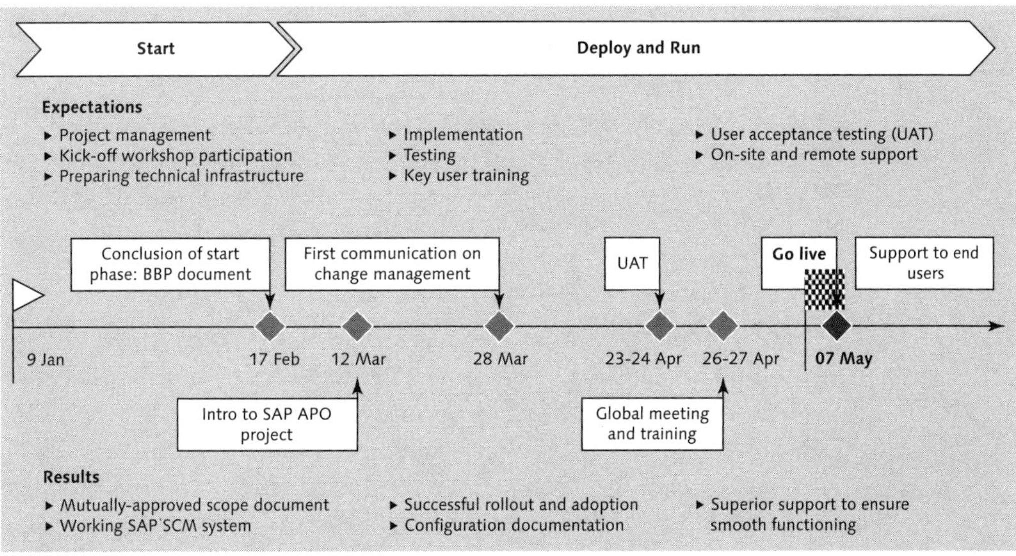

Figure 3.14 Simplified Governance Model

Deployment

The solution deployment concept maximizes and benefits from the learning curve of the consultants so that specialization can happen and there is no need to always learn all the details of a solution but leverage experts on demand and on a global level. This allows consultants to work proficiently through the deployment, from customer to customer.

Test environment A key element of the success of the project was the fact that master and transactional data completeness and consistency was verified in the test environment upfront in order to avoid issues during integration of production environments later down the road. Furthermore, due to the fact that the process testing is quite complex and crucial, the timing in the project plan allowed for some buffer so unexpected issues could be solved without putting the overall project timelines at risk. This applies as well to the planned time for the handover. In the rapid-deployment approach, it was fundamental to fix the business needs at the requirement stage and postpone all additional low and medium priority requirements to a second implementation wave. This prescriptive approach to solution implementation helped to avoid unnecessary discussions and helped the team to focus on the core of the implementation. The lean project structure was supporting this and was fundamental to achieve the short timelines of the implementation project: the project team had the authority to solve issues without any bureaucracy if the go-live date or project costs are not going to be affected.

Finally, there is a strong commitment from the stakeholders to the end user and a sound communication plan, helping the team focus on the key success factors that must be kept in mind during each phase of the project.

3.9.3 Results

After the rapid-deployment solution package was deployed, Bonfiglioli reduced planning activities by around 70%, for example, by facilitating loading and storing massive volumes of planning data. They significantly lowered their planning errors due to quota allocation misalignments by 100%. The company now makes use of planning KPIs and alerts to improve the reliability of the master plan, leading to a more accurate forecast and a more stable plan. They also reduced the response time to evaluate changes required to the demand plan by 50%. Ultimately, the company managed to reduce the number of systems used for planning from four to one and can now even profit from the optimized system synchronization, because the SAP solution facilitates the exchange of planning and sales data between SAP ERP and SAP APO seamlessly.

Proven to be successful, this new centralized and standardized model for planning, which provides increased higher transparency and on demand availability of planning data, is in the process of being rolled out as the to-go solution to other plants within the company, at the time this book went to press.

3.10 Integrating Multiresource Scheduling into SAP ERP and Plant Maintenance

Solution Showcase

SAP Multiresource Scheduling rapid-deployment solution deployment.

Customer Case Study: Manufacturer, paper

By deploying SAP's SAP Multiresource Scheduling rapid-deployment solution throughout their manufacturing facilities, a large producer and exporter of paper in Brazil was able to improve the efficiency and agility of its resources-planning process and generate savings in excess of R$500,000 per year.

3.10.1 Background

With 114 years of history and 16 plants, this customer is a large producer and exporter of paper in Brazil. They also have sales offices in eight states, a branch in the United States, and a logistics distributor in Europe. The company is organized into four business units—forestry, paper, corrugated cardboard, and industrial sacks. This customer believes that productivity coupled with quality of its products and excellence of its customer relations ensures superior business results.

Additionally, they values conservation of natural resources and commitment to sustainability and made these two objectives a cornerstone to their daily operations.

Modernize planning and scheduling

To deal with this complex scenario, which increasingly requires accurate and fast planning, they needed to modernize planning and scheduling procedures for maintenance activities. The company had used SAP ERP with a Plant Maintenance (PM) component since 1999, and in 2013 decided to invest in solutions that optimized the use of IT to give more flexibility to the planning and scheduling of maintenance resources.

In 2012, the company launched a study to evaluate several alternatives to improve the process of planning and scheduling their maintenance activities. The result of that study and the evaluation of several options was the decision to deploy the SAP Multiresource Scheduling rapid-deployment solution to further enhance planning and scheduling of maintenance activities. The company opted for a rapid-deployment solution to accelerate the adoption of the new software.

Why SAP Rapid Deployment Solutions?

Since SAP ERP was adopted nearly 15 years ago, the customer has been relying on the PM component in its daily operations. PM was the component with the most users in the company's 16 plants. Since then, they have consistently performed all required maintenance and updates to the PM component. In 2012, it decided to assess what could be done in terms of IT evolution to improve its processes of planning and programming maintenance activities, which led to the adoption of the SAP Multiresource Scheduling rapid-deployment solution.

One area of concern was the fact that there were no SAP Partners familiar with this particular planning and scheduling solution in Brazil for the customer to rely on to support the project. To overcome the situation, SAP recommended SAP Rapid Deployment solutions, as it encapsulates the necessary best-practices content and would consequently minimize the need for customization. In early 2013, they decided to embark on the project of deploying the SAP Multiresource Scheduling rapid-deployment solution together with the SAP consulting organization.

3.10.2 Deployment

A full deployment of the SAP Multiresources Scheduling rapid-deployment solution was initiated with integration to the HR and PM components in accordance with SAP's best business practices as recommended by the SAP consulting organization.

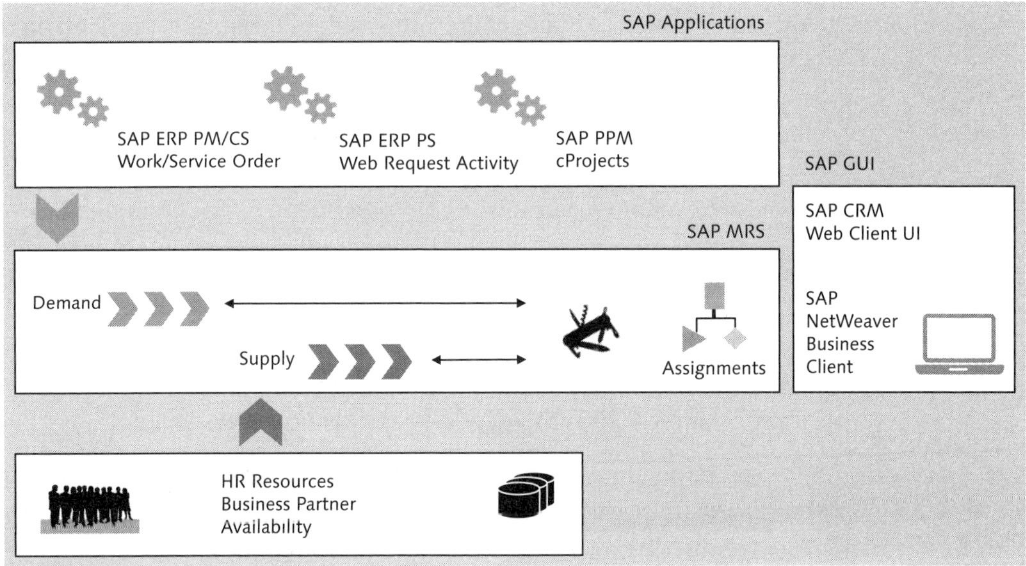

Figure 3.15 SAP Multiresource Scheduling Rapid-Deployment Solution Architecture Overview

The SAP Multiresource Scheduling rapid-deployment solution introduces quick essential steps to achieve the next level in preventive maintenance and immediate repair processes in enterprise asset management:

Steps

▶ Planning, scheduling, and dispatching service personnel.

▶ Configurable setup of a user-friendly scheduling process with graphical planning board.

▶ Improved service quality supported through advanced qualification and skill management of technicians for assignments.

Solution-Deployment Planning

In February of 2013, the customer and SAP's project teams started to define the solution based on the customer's requirements and SAP's recommended best business practices. Their high-level requirements were that the system should resolve all resource availability constraints (people, qualification, tools, and machines) with full integration with the SAP ERP system. Although the proposed solution met most of their requirements and supported most of their business processes, there was some concern regarding completing all integration requirements within the five-month projected duration of the solution.

Deployment

Following the configuration of the SAP Multiresource Scheduling rapid-deployment solution based on the guidelines and the customer's requirements, the solution was deployed throughout the customer's manufacturing facilities, and 60 professional planners, responsible for approximately 1,200 employees, started using the system.

Automated

The solution automates the planning of hundreds of service orders per month, ensuring that all of them are treated according to their priority and considering all constraints such as employee availabilities, vacations, and other important parameters. The system determines by priority which activities will be performed, which employees will be allocated to each activity, and what material will be used.

3.10.3 Results

Time/cost savings

Despite the complexity of human resources and plant maintenance integration, the SAP Rapid Deployment solutions implementation was so effective that the five-month project was completed in only three months. And thanks to this extremely fast deployment, the company saved the cost of its on-the-project resources and gained all associated benefits faster. Since the solution has been in use, the customer improved its productivity and was able to eliminate most errors associated with the previous manual processes.

Although it is hard to quantify these financial gains, they estimate the increased productivity, and the time gained due to process automation, improved schedules, better information, and errors elimination to be approximately R$500,000 per year. In addition, the planning group, which spent a good part of their working hours printing and retyping data, can now devote their time to more important issues, such as strategic planning.

Business benefits include:

Business benefits

- Shorter time to ROI.
- Faster introduction of process-optimizing resource-planning tool.
- Automated scheduling and efficient planning.
- Higher quality of repair work through improved qualification matching.
- Ability to view, analyze, and interpret order data for better decision-making.
- Reduced operation downtime.
- Improved technician productivity.

Beyond this current initiative, the customer is planning new projects that will extend the availability and intelligence of the information generated by the Multiresource Scheduling rapid-deployment solution:

Solution extension

- First is a project using SAP Mobile Platform to extend the availability and speed of propagation of the information generated by the main project. Once scheduling activities from SAP Multiresource Scheduling solution are optimized, they will pilot the SAP Mobile Platform project. The integration of the mobility platform is being performed in parallel to the main project and should come into operation before the end of 2013.
- Following the completion of the SAP Mobile Platform project, the customer will implement SAP BusinessObjects Asset Analytics solution, also an SAP Rapid Deployment solution. This new initiative will provide more intelligence (via dashboards) of the information generated by SAP Multiresource Scheduling and propagated by the mobile platform.

3.11   Assemble-to-Order Finance on SAP HANA

Solution Showcase

Deployment of multiple SAP HANA rapid-deployment solutions packages to accelerate SAP HANA time-to-value.

The area of finance is one of the core business processes in SAP ERP, used by the highest number of customers. In fact, SAP ERP is almost synonymous with finance, general or material ledger, and controlling applications. Moreover, this area is known for high volumes of data where the adoption of SAP HANA is high. Therefore, when the most critical use-cases for SAP HANA were identified for deployment, finance was one of the first areas to be included.

ConAgra is one of the largest food-production enterprises with over $12 billion USD in annual sales. They are long-term SAP customers and were one of the early customers who implemented SAP HANA. Their first step was to target their financial close and reporting, although there was a much larger overall roadmap.

Since there are multiple modules under finance and most customer cases involve more than one, as it was for ConAgra, it was an obvious use-case for assemble-to-order SAP Rapid Deployment solutions.

3.11.1   Background

Financial data usually has very large data volumes across multiple modules like general ledger (GL) or Controlling and Profitability Analysis (CO-PA). Most of these customers have their historical data in SAP NetWeaver Business Warehouse for enterprise reporting. With the transaction records ranging from a few hundred million to billions, even SAP NetWeaver BW reporting faces performance issues and data-volume limitations. Moreover, the reports are only accurate to the last data load.

Secondly, businesses incrementally create millions of records per quarter in the SAP ERP system in the main tables: BSEG and FLEXGLA. Real-time operational reporting on this from the SAP ERP system slows the system down and each transaction can take 20-30 minutes. For ConAgra, some of these queries timed-out before yielding any result.

Finally, for the IT teams within companies there are a multitude of requirements coming from each direction, and developing reports could take as much as three weeks to six months, resulting in frustrated business-users and over-burdened IT teams.

Any project undertaken to address all these issues would be a complex one. For ConAgra, many problems were resolved in a period of weeks using more than one rapid-deployment solution from the finance cluster of solutions. These are end-to-end solutions designed by the SAP Rapid Deployment solutions team to be deployed in an efficient and cost-effective manner.

Finance Cluster of Rapid-Deployment Solutions

SAP developed multiple rapid-deployment solutions based on SAP HANA specifically targeted towards the finance components. All of the following packages were included in the finance SAP HANA cluster to provide an end-to-end solution to the customer that addressed acceleration of business processes, real-time reporting and advanced analysis:

End-to-end solution

- ► SAP HANA ERP rapid-deployment solution for accelerated profitability analysis (also known as CO-PA accelerator)—merged in finance and controlling (FICO) accelerator in May 2013 SAP Rapid Deployment solutions release.
- ► SAP HANA ERP solution accelerated for FICO accelerator.
- ► SAP HANA ERP Operational Reporting rapid-deployment solution.
- ► SAP HANA Net Margin Analysis rapid-deployment solution.

As ConAgra was an early adopter of SAP HANA—adopting it even before the last package SAP HANA Net Margin Analysis was released!— they wanted to leverage SAP HANA for one of their key IT goals for the company: to accelerate business processes. These were their IT goals in the area of finance:

IT goals

- Improved performance of financial and controlling transactions and business processes.

- Faster close and analysis of actuals through reducing job-processing time (CO-PA, material ledger, GL, and associated analytics).

- Capabilities for faster data integration and faster consolidations of SAP and non-SAP data.

- Financial accounting opportunity to re-engineer and simplify financial-close process.

- Foundation to build real-time operational reporting and analytics.

Accelerators They selected two SAP Rapid Deployment solutions packages—the CO-PA and the FI-CO accelerators–as their first steps towards those goals. In their own words: "Accelerators utilize the power of SAP HANA to improve the performance of existing functionality of SAP Business Suite applications dramatically in small, well-defined areas that bring immediate value to customers."

Accelerators were specifically designed to be delivered within weeks and with very low risk to the existing production environment, as they are a side-by-side deployment of SAP HANA. This makes the packages very efficient and low-risk, ideal for driving adoption of a new technology like SAP HANA.

In an accelerator, the transaction data is replicated to SAP HANA using the SAP Landscape Transformation (SLT) software. SLT is a trigger-based replication so that any change in the transaction record triggers an update in the data in SAP HANA simultaneously. When standard finance transaction codes like KE24 and KE30 are initiated in SAP ERP, they are optimized to run on SAP HANA with the results being returned to the SAP ERP GUI. Therefore, the process is completely transparent to the business-user except for results being returned in seconds instead of minutes! In addition, there is a simple switch to turn the SAP HANA option off and run it locally, making the ultimate low-risk, proof-of-concept for showcasing the strength of SAP HANA (see Figure 3.16).

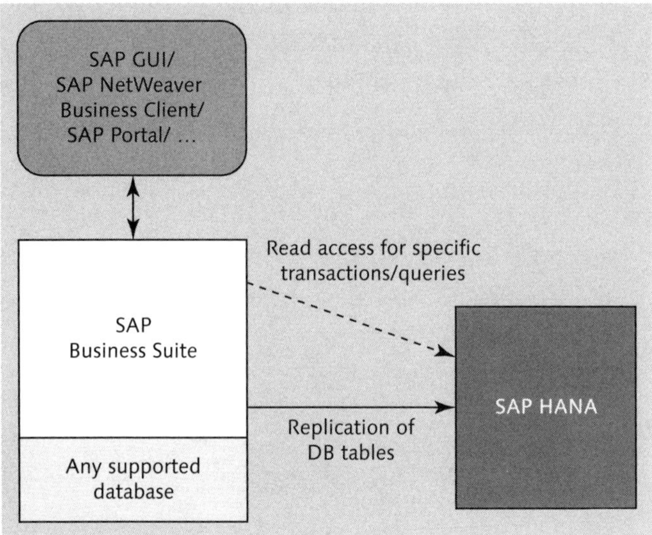

Figure 3.16 High-Level Architecture and Data Flow for a Side-by-Side Accelerator Configuration

3.11.2 Solution-Deployment Planning

As with all SAP Rapid Deployment solutions, the accelerator packages also include detailed project plans and other collateral for project kick-off and delivery. In this case, ConAgra did not have an SAP HANA landscape set up and therefore the project had two phases planned. The duration and detailed tasks included in each phase are listed in the following subsections.

PHASE 1: Landscape Setup

For net-new SAP HANA customers such as this one, the SAP Rapid Deployment solutions package includes best-practices in the form of a pre-delivery checklist. This list includes system-landscape check because SAP HANA upgrades are being released frequently, and nearly every environment has to be updated with the notes and service packs to leverage the latest bug-fixes and functionality. This avoids issues later into the project and saves precious time and resources trying to resolve errors addressed by a note or upgrade. Since ConAgra had to implement and set up SAP HANA, this service, which is not part of the standard SAP

Pre-delivery checklist

Rapid Deployment solutions, was the first step. The SAP Rapid Deployment solutions team realized after the first few deployments that this was the first best-practice step in planning to avoid delays and issues.

Duration: Three weeks.

Teams involved: Basis, data warehouse, security, storage, HP, and SAP.

Tasks:

- Connectivity of pre-built SAP HANA with SLT server, SAP HANA server, and DB install.
- SAP HANA Studio install and configuration.
- Security setup.
- Create schema and test connections between ECC, SLT, and SAP HANA.
- Production initial load-tuning activities (index in ECC tables, setting up parallelism, etc.).

The preparatory phase to set up the production and non-production landscape with SAP HANA and SLT servers was a pre-requisite for the standard SAP Rapid Deployment solutions. There is an engineered service that enables this phase and the SAP Rapid Deployment solutions team provides the information for this.

PHASE 2: Rapid Deployment of Accelerators

Parallel implementations

Both packages were to be started in parallel. It has been one of our most successful implementations.

Part I CO-PA Accelerator
Duration: Four weeks.

- Start: Three days. Project preparation.
- Project kickoff.
- Check connection.

Deploy: 2.5 weeks

- Activate solution: three OSS Notes.

- Configuration: CO-PA solution.
- Data replication.
- Testing.
- Knowledge transfer.
- Migration.

Run: One week.

Part II FICO Accelerator
Duration: Eight weeks (ideal 12 weeks).

Start: Two weeks.

- Project management.
- Project kickoff.
- Scope validation.
- Sign off.

Deploy: Four weeks.

- Activate Solution: 30-plus OSS Notes implementation.
- Table replication.
- Configuration.
- Regression and performance testing.
- Knowledge transfer and technical training.
- Migration to other systems.

Run: Two weeks.

- End-user training.
- Go-live.
- Stabilization.

3.11.3　Deployment

The deployment was done in a three-tier landscape of development, test, and production, where the SAP Rapid Deployment solutions team led the first phase, the SAP and ConAgra IT teams shared the second

Three-tier landscape

phase, and the final cutover to production was led by the customer with support from the SAP Rapid Deployment solutions team. The step-by-step approach, starting with system checks and using well-defined and tested implementation or configuration guides, accelerated the project.

The data involved in each of the packages were as follows:

- CO-PA: 10 tables, 180 million records.
- FI-CO: 30 tables, two billion records.

After initial internal evaluation, the customer chose HP servers due to their maturity. The pre-requisite first phase of landscape set-up was completed before the rapid-deployment solutions began. The security set-up and the connections to the back-end systems were also tested in this phase.

The deployment of the CO-PA accelerator went smoothly and was delivered within four weeks without any changes to existing documented steps. The FI-CO accelerator was started in parallel and has some changes due their source system configuration and was completed in eight weeks. The main cause of success was immense support from the SAP Rapid Deployment solutions team, which also had access to the development teams.

3.11.4 Results

The result of the multiple accelerator deployment is listed in Table 3.1.

Rapid-Deployment Package	CO-PA Accelerator	FI-CO Accelerator
Compression achieved	6:1	8:1
Time for replication	8 hours	48 to 52 hours

Table 3.1 Results of the Deployment of Two Finance Accelerator Rapid-Deployment Solutions

Rapid-Deployment Package	CO-PA Accelerator	FI-CO Accelerator
Business benefits	▶ Significant performance improvement in CO-PA transactions Example: KE30 was reduced from 10 minutes to 4 seconds, KE24 from 15 minutes to 2 seconds! ▶ Capability to run real-time reports ▶ Reduced time for CO-PA and financial reconciliation	▶ Easy access to FI, CO, and material ledger transactions during period close ▶ Estimated 200 hours/month saved in period end closing ▶ Enhanced transaction codes for operational reports for cost centers, new GL and internal orders ▶ Ability to run real-time reports
RDS success	▶ Faster delivery of solutions in weeks ▶ Well-defined scope with predictable cost and no surprises ▶ Faster response from SAP to address Issues ▶ Independent of other RDS and single transaction to control security in ECC to enable/disable HANA ▶ Very few technical changes to ECC to activate CO-PA solution ▶ Very limited or no change management process implemented	▶ Faster delivery of solutions including preconfigured software and implementation services in weeks ▶ Well-defined scope with predictable cost ▶ Faster response from SAP to address issues through the life cycle of the project ▶ Users will not see any changes when using standard transactions ▶ Simple process ECC to enable/disable SAP HANA

Table 3.1 Results of the Deployment of Two Finance Accelerator Rapid-Deployment Solutions (Cont.)

The customer attributed the success of the project to faster delivery of the SAP Rapid Deployment solutions, the well-defined scope with predictable cost, and faster response from SAP to address issues.

As one of the earliest projects on SAP HANA, there were also lessons learned from the customer as well as the service delivery team feedback. All of these were incorporated into the future versions of the packages.

In each of these cases, the value provided by the solution is not just the implementation guides or the content, but the training and enablement of SAP HANA and best practices for modeling and reporting on it. The new technology makes it difficult for customers to find the expertise in their IT teams. Multiple implementations of the SAP Rapid Deployment solutions packages (over 70 at the time this is being written!) have created a depth of expertise on how to develop the most efficient and fastest reports on SAP HANA. The knowledge transfer of this skill done as part of the SAP Rapid Deployment solutions delivery has been invaluable to customers who have taken it to the next stage by creating all their custom reports far beyond the standard list in a period of weeks.

Lessons learned | The customer and services feedback project have been incorporated into future implementations as the packages are continuously improved as the services feedback is rolled into it. These results found:

- It is important to check on the system landscape, including implementation of all the notes, as that is usually not included as part of the SAP Rapid Deployment solutions.

- Since each customer uses some of finance modules, the two accelerators were combined into one package with the option of selecting any of the modules: Finance, General Ledger (new and classic), Material Ledger, Controlling, Production Cost, and CO-PA.

- The initial loads should be scheduled during weekends to minimize disruption, and performance tuning of the systems should also be completed prior to loading data.

- Business-user engagement scheduled should be checked, especially for financial projects, as they are not available during company financial close.

- The extensive support from SAP teams as well as SAP development communities was used for resolving many of the technical issues.

3.12 SAP Business Intelligence Adoption Rapid-Deployment Solution

Solution Showcase

The BI Adoption rapid-deployment solution provides data visualization to gain better business insight.

Customers that have investments in SAP NetWeaver BW often use tools provided by SAP to visualize the information in the form of dashboards and reports. Customers often face the challenge of choosing the right type of visualization that correctly represents the information in the right format. The right visualization helps them to make informed decisions from the insights that they get from these data visualizations. SAP released a Business Intelligence (BI) Adoption rapid-deployment solution that helped customers to simplify the consumption of visualization tools by providing sample content and best practices that help them to make informed choices. Rust-Oleum is one such customer that has made investments in BI that includes SAP NetWeaver BW and various BI tools. They used the content of this solution to universally adopt the best practices across their enterprise. What was their vision and how did they benefit from this solution? Read ahead to see how Rust-Oleum was able to extend their investments in BI.

Rust-Oleum recognized that BI is all about providing the right data at the right time to the right people using the right visualization, so that they can make the right decisions. The BI Adoption rapid-deployment solution comes in as an end-to-end solution. It caters to a BI customer with a menu choice from starters to desserts. This means that the package starts off with helping the customer install the BI platform and get connected to the source systems. This is backed up by the service offering that helps implement the basic tool and content delivered in this package.

Next, it comes with content for all LOBs, namely executive reporting, sales, purchasing, inventory, finance, and data analytics. The content is built in an architecture where it can be consumed both on desktop and mobile devices.

The data analytics piece comes in as a game-changer for SAP NetWeaver BW customers and addresses the pain points that are common issues, namely data trust, data latency, and data discovery. The BI Adoption rapid-deployment solution package comes with data reconciliation, data availability, and data lineage tools to help alleviate this adoption issue with users.

Finally it comes with best practices to help the customer pick the right tool to help them create the right reporting job, from analytical to operational reporting.

Criteria for Rust-Oleum

- Quick time-to-value–investments in BI must generate value to the business in a short period of time.
- Understand different reporting types to provide the right visualization.

SAP Rapid Deployment solution scope at Rust-Oleum:

- Demonstrate ability to create feature-rich reports that provide better insights into the data.
- Produce multi-platform compatible reports: desktop and mobile.
- Create identified reporting area for POC–Purchasing.
- Provide vendor analysis and purchasing dashboard reports.
- Reconcile SAP ERP data with reporting data.

3.12.1 Background

Customers like Rust-Oleum were looking for a strategic approach for leveraging investments in BI software. This SAP Rapid Deployment solution addressed this specific issue and provided a clear direction on implementing BI tools in the right manner by helping them to identify the right tool for the right job.

The package comes with rich pre-configured content that demonstrates the power to differentiate between self-service reporting (vs.) dashboards and apps (vs.) reporting, and helps pick the agile tool for the right purpose.

The package helps in two dimensions, namely:

- ▶ Pick the right tool for the right job.
- ▶ Pick the right tool for the right user.

By providing a structure for implementation, this approach also reduced the uncertainty from the implementation.

3.12.2 Deployment

Reports samples were implemented. The customer implemented the Purchasing Volume dashboard along with the PO value by month mobile reports. To reconcile the date back to the SAP ERP system, the purchase order data reconciliation report was implemented.

Desktop Version

Prior to implementing this SAP Rapid Deployment solutions package, the key challenge faced by the customer was that it was a manual process to obtain the vendor and contract information. Also, the right visualization along with rankings of vendors was not possible. After implementing the purchasing-volume dashboard (see Figure 3.17), the customer was able to get a clear picture of the top vendors, their performance, and accurate contract information, along with the best-performing materials.

Another big value to customers that came from this rapid-deployment solution was to get the analytics capabilities on mobile devices (see Figure 3.18). Customers were able to consume the analytics content on the mobile device by using the BI app available on the mobile app stores. This helped the management to not only get quick insights on business-related information like vendors and contracts; but the same content was accessible anytime, anywhere, and on any device.

Figure 3.17 Purchasing Volume Dashboard

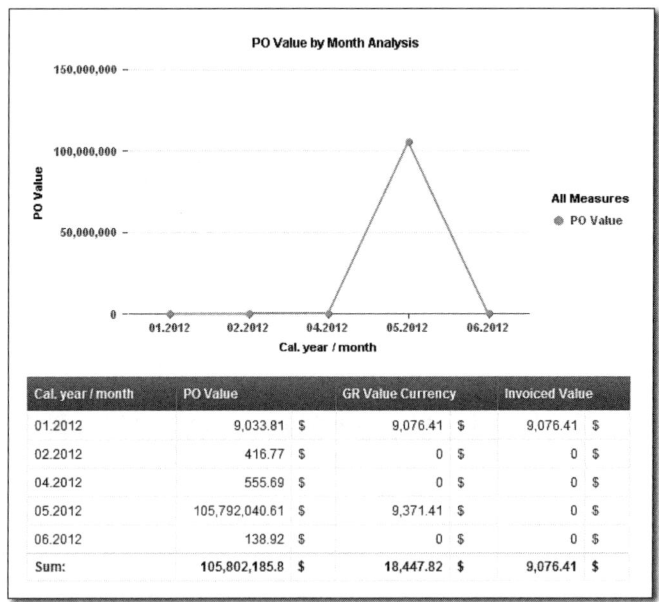

Figure 3.18 Mobile Version PO Value by Month Mobile Report

Once the dashboard was implemented, another big challenge was to trust the data. Prior to this SAP Rapid Deployment solution, this was a manual task. Customers would dump data out of the transactional system and perform manual validations. After implementing this solution and the corresponding purchase-order reconciliation report, the success was instant, because of the fact that the single reports brought in data from SAP ERP and SAP NetWeaver BW and instantly showed that all the data was accurate and, if differences were seen, the same was identified on the purchasing-document level to take instant action (see Figure 3.19).

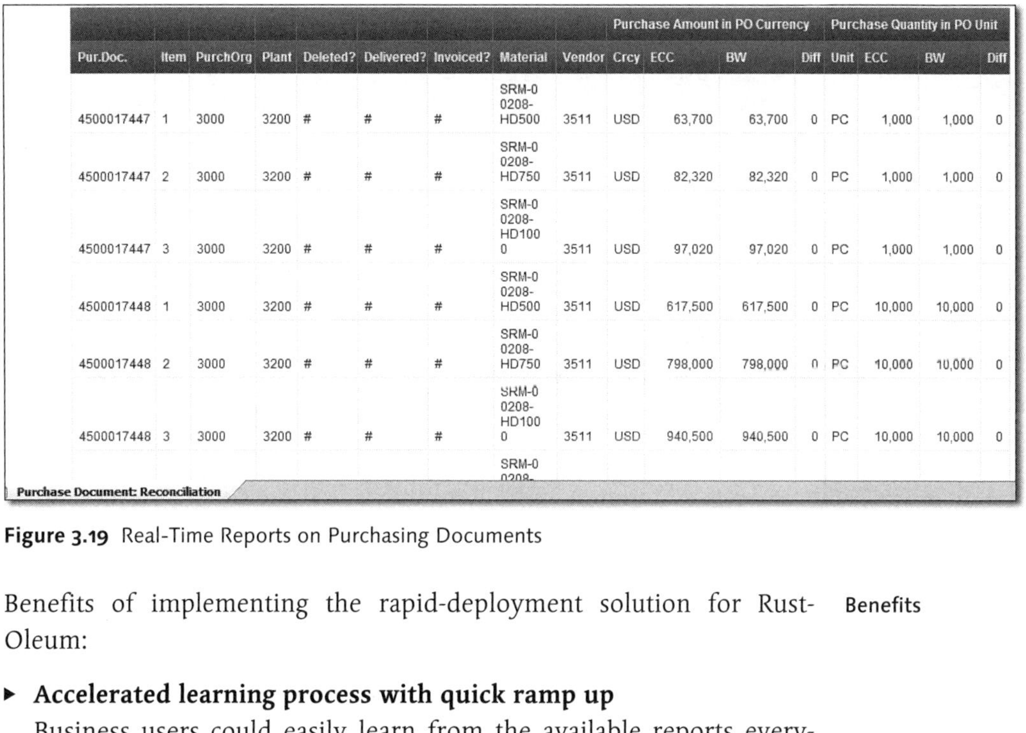

Pur.Doc.	Item	PurchOrg	Plant	Deleted?	Delivered?	Invoiced?	Material	Vendor	Crcy	Purchase Amount in PO Currency			Unit	Purchase Quantity in PO Unit		
										ECC	BW	Diff		ECC	BW	Diff
4500017447	1	3000	3200	#	#	#	SRM-0 0208-HD500	3511	USD	63,700	63,700	0	PC	1,000	1,000	0
4500017447	2	3000	3200	#	#	#	SRM-0 0208-HD750	3511	USD	82,320	82,320	0	PC	1,000	1,000	0
4500017447	3	3000	3200	#	#	#	SRM-0 0208-HD1000	3511	USD	97,020	97,020	0	PC	1,000	1,000	0
4500017448	1	3000	3200	#	#	#	SRM-0 0208-HD500	3511	USD	617,500	617,500	0	PC	10,000	10,000	0
4500017448	2	3000	3200	#	#	#	SRM-0 0208-HD750	3511	USD	798,000	798,000	0	PC	10,000	10,000	0
4500017448	3	3000	3200	#	#	#	SRM-0 0208-HD1000	3511	USD	940,500	940,500	0	PC	10,000	10,000	0
							SRM-0 0208-									

Purchase Document: Reconciliation

Figure 3.19 Real-Time Reports on Purchasing Documents

Benefits of implementing the rapid-deployment solution for Rust-Oleum:

Benefits

▸ **Accelerated learning process with quick ramp up**
Business users could easily learn from the available reports everything about their business in a manner that allowed them to make important decisions.

▸ **Better data visualization with SAP BusinessObjects reporting tools**
All the investments that Rust-Oleum had made in BI tools could be now leveraged across the business, and business had a variety of ways to visualize data points.

- **Use standard content to explore new functional areas**

  Rust-Oleum was using the standard content provided by SAP for its reporting needs. However, the reporting tools that came with the SAP NetWeaver BW were very technical in nature and required the end-user to have technical skills. Given that the business end users had little technical expertise, it was not very well-adopted. The new reporting tools changed that and provided a simplified user-experience so that business users had a flexible way to analyze complex data stored in multi-dimensional formats. The SAP Rapid Deployment solutions team used the standard content.

- **Use existing SAP NetWeaver BW queries to build new SAP BusinessObjects reports**

  The IT department of Rust-Oleum had built a number of queries in the past to get insights into specific business situations, but it was also leveraging queries that were part of the SAP NetWeaver BW content. By using standard queries delivered by SAP, the SAP Rapid Deployment solutions did not require any additional work from the customer's IT department.

- **Self-service data reconciliation**

  One of the major advantages that the package offered to the customer is to help resolve one of the major issues around data reconciliation. Once they had the purchasing dashboard available, it was pretty difficult to ensure that the data was correct. The purchase-order reconciliation report helped match the open purchase orders in the SAP NetWeaver BW system back to the SAP ERP system. This allowed the business users to trust the data and they were able to confidently take actions from the dashboard.

The following summarized the benefits of the SAP Rapid Deployment solutions package for the customer:

- Enhanced BI 4.0 business analytics on SAP NetWeaver BW/BW on SAP HANA: WebI, SAP Crystal Reports, Analysis Workspace, SAP Design Studio, Information Space, SAP BusinessObjects Dashboards (swf, html5).

- More track on analytics data: Data reconciliation and data availability.

- All reports were easily made available for a mobile device.

- Faster deployment of BI 4.0 on SAP NetWeaver BW content by following an easy-to-use, step-by-step guide.

Additionally the BI Adoption rapid-deployment solutions best practice guide (how to make the right choice of BI) is a huge benefit for the customer. It provided:

- Solution architecture with BI 4.0 (BI on SAP NetWeaver BW, BI on SAP ERP, SAP BusinessObjects BI), how to choose (advantage and applicability for each solution).

- How to choose visualization reporting tools according to each user role and the business area's requirement.

- Reporting tools for different usage (self-service, dashboard and app, reporting): Dashboards, WebI, SAP Crystal Reports, Information Space, Analysis Workspace, Design Studio, SAP Lumira (Visual Intelligence), Predictive Analysis:

  - According to each business-user role
  - According to each business area's specific requirements

Would you like to test-drive some of the content that is delivered in this solution? Use the link below or use the QR code reader available on your iPad or other mobile device to directly access a click-through demo of the solution.

http://demo.tdc.sap.com/SpeedDemo/bb7f9081fe31005d

3.13   Enterprise Performance Management

Solution Showcase

SAP's Business Planning and Consolidation approach with rapid-deployment solutions deploys in weeks and enables the organization to achieve time-to-value quickly.

SAP positions Enterprise Performance Management (EPM) solutions to enable customers to monitor, capture, and analyze historical and forward-looking financial and operational results. SAP is a leader in the Enterprise Performance Management solution area, and a key to SAP's success in the market is simplifying the deployment of EPM solutions across complex organizations.

End-to-end financial planning and consolidation process

Enterprise Performance Management incorporates a wide array of financial business processes, and the ultimate leader in the market will help customers manage enterprise performance with the highest rate of return on investment in EPM solutions. This case study explains the customer value proposition for SAP's rapid-deployment solutions in the Enterprise Performance Management arena. SAP's rapid-deployment solutions cover the end-to-end financial planning and consolidation process, allows customers to save on implementation costs, helps customers take advantage of best practices, boosts the customer's rate of return on investment on investment in software, and helps customers realize the vision of SAP's flagship Enterprise Performance Management product.

3.13.1 Background

SAP Business Planning and Consolidation

SAP's top-selling Enterprise Performance Management solution is SAP Business Planning and Consolidation. SAP Business Planning and Consolidation handles both planning and consolidation within one SAP software solution (SAP customers often expand on SAP Business Planning and Consolidation to include reporting and analytics). The unique combination of planning, consolidations, and reporting—using one software solution—provides SAP a very compelling advantage over its main software competition. As a contrast in offerings, a competitor would need to offer and sell two or more unique solutions in order to compete with the capabilities of SAP Business Planning and Consolidation.

But, executing on the unified vision of SAP Business Planning and Consolidation has often proven difficult in the field. Why? Customers often deploy planning and consolidation projects using unique timelines, unique consulting organizations, and variable employee-groups in the company. As a result, pockets in the same company often use a non-SAP Business Planning and Consolidation solution for planning and/or consolidation, despite the fact the SAP Business Planning and Consolidation solution is in place in other areas of the company. Even if SAP Business

Planning and Consolidation is deployed for planning and/or consolidation at the same company, the maintenance and user experience in each solution is different for the reasons noted previously.

The truth is the vision of SAP Business Planning and Consolidation ("unified platform for planning and consolidation") has sometimes been difficult to realize at a single customer, despite the absolute competitive advantage of offering one solution (SAP Business Planning and Consolidation) for major EPM activities.

3.13.2 Deployment

To help SAP take advantage of the unified vision of SAP Business Planning and Consolidation, SAP believed that rapid-deployment solutions could help realize the SAP Business Planning and Consolidation vision. SAP's rapid-deployment team took a look at the most common SAP Business Planning and Consolidation deployment scenario at SAP customers. These scenarios became the basis for three key rapid-deployment solutions in the Enterprise Performance Management space. These rapid-deployment solutions took advantage of SAP Business Planning and Consolidation capabilities in planning and consolidation, leveraging a single SAP solution, SAP Business Planning and Consolidation.

To understand what to build in the rapid-deployment space, SAP first looked at SAP Business Planning and Consolidation's most common customer: SAP Enterprise Resource Planning (ERP) customers. To understand this, be aware that SAP Business Planning and Consolidation is data-source-neutral and is marketed and sold to a very wide array of ERP and non-ERP customers. But, SAP Business Planning and Consolidation's largest customer segment is SAP's own ERP customers. To address the largest SAP Business Planning and Consolidation customer segment, SAP built and released rapid-deployment solutions for both planning and consolidations to appeal directly to SAP ERP customers. This means key items like integration to SAP ERP would be handled "out-of-the-box".

Second, SAP looked at the most common deployment scenarios. The most common planning scenario at SAP customers is detailed, shorter-term profit and loss and/or balance sheet planning. Another common

Common deployment scenarios

planning scenario is high-level, long-term strategic financial planning. The most common consolidation scenario is the monthly financial close and disclosure management process.

As a result, SAP has released three key rapid-deployment solutions into the market using SAP Business Planning and Consolidation:

- Planning
  - SAP G/L Financial Planning rapid-deployment solution
  - SAP Strategic Financial Planning rapid-deployment solution
- Consolidation
  - SAP Financial Close and Disclosure Management rapid-deployment solution

These three solutions enable an SAP ERP customer to realize a single SAP solution (SAP Business Planning and Consolidation) for detailed planning, strategic financial planning, and consolidations. Through a carefully crafted assemble-to-order strategy, customers can now deploy two or more of these solutions and take advantage of shared technology, look-and-feel, and processes.

Solution-Deployment Planning

Flexibility with solutions

A key selling point of the three current SAP Business Planning and Consolidation-based rapid-deployment solutions is that they can be deployed on their own, in a phased-approach, or all at the same time. Through SAP's stringent assemble-to-order directive, the rapid-deployment solutions are available as individual offerings and also can be combined in any combination at a single customer. This offers customers flexibility and helps customers manage projects based on their own needs rather than based on solution restrictions.

For example, if a customer wants to deploy SAP Strategic Financial Planning rapid-deployment solution this year, but SAP Financial Close and Disclosure Management rapid-deployment solution next year, that will work. But, if a customer wants to only deploy SAP G/L Financial Planning rapid-deployment solution, that scenario will work, too. Of course, another customer may wish to deploy all three SAP Business Planning and Consolidation-based rapid-deployment solutions at the same time.

Each rapid-deployment solution has a unique return on investment (ROI), but SAP believes a customer can increase the ROI on an investment in SAP Business Planning and Consolidation by deploying two or more SAP Business Planning and Consolidation rapid-deployment solutions because of the assemble-to-order capabilities.

Deployment

As consultants and customers begin to deploy the SAP Business Planning and Consolidation-based rapid-deployment solutions, the deployment models will vary but the advantages of using a unified platform for planning and consolidation will become very evident. As noted above, the capabilities of SAP Business Planning and Consolidation make some of this possible, but the use of rapid-deployment solutions that can be deployed individually, over time, or all at once really help.

Examples

For a net new SAP Business Planning and Consolidation customer, the customer trains the user on the front-end SAP Business Planning and Consolidation Excel tool, called the EPM Add-in for Excel. If a customer deploys SAP Business Planning and Consolidation or only one SAP Business Planning and Consolidation rapid-deployment solution, the customer can train users on one front-end tool. If the customer later deploys one of the other SAP Business Planning and Consolidation-based rapid-deployment tools, the users will already be familiar with the front-end and should need little or no additional training. The coordination across the SAP Business Planning and Consolidation-based rapid-deployment solutions will help, too, as the common template naming conventions and look and fell will make the user experience much easier as they move from business processes (e.g. planning vs. consolidation) within SAP Business Planning and Consolidation.

As a second example, if a customer wishes to deploy the G/L Financial Planning rapid-deployment solution first, the SAP NetWeaver BW team will help setup and deploy some back-end BW content in order to integrate data from SAP ERP into SAP Business Planning and Consolidation. If the customer later chooses to deploy the Financial Close and Disclosure Management rapid-deployment solution, the BW content deployed earlier will be shared for usage with the consolidation rapid-deployment solution.

3.13.3 Results

To understand the value of leveraging rapid-deployment solutions and assemble-to-order in achieving the vision of a unified model under SAP Business Planning and Consolidation, we can break down the "value" equation into three unique buckets. We can look at the value proposition of SAP Business Planning and Consolidation stand alone. We can then look at the value of any single SAP Business Planning and Consolidation-based rapid-deployment solution stand alone. Finally, we can look at the value of combining two or more SAP Business Planning and Consolidation-based rapid-deployment solutions as one customer.

The value of SAP Business Planning and Consolidation solution:

- Single Excel-based front-end tool for input, reporting, and analysis
- Single web-based front-end tool for administration
- Single security framework for both planning and consolidation
- Standard set of report and input form templates

The value of single SAP Business Planning and Consolidation-based rapid-deployment solutions:

- Pre-built, purpose-built SAP Business Planning and Consolidation model for planning or consolidation
- Pre-configured data integration to the SAP ERP system
    - Pre-defined front-end load process
    - Pre-defined transformation files
    - Pre-defined conversion files
    - Pre-built master data load process
    - Pre-built transaction data load (delta and full)
    - ECC reconciliation process and template

- Pre-built templates
  - Purpose-built reports
  - Purpose-built input forms

The value of assemble-to-order (e.g. two or more SAP Business Planning and Consolidation-based rapid-deployment solutions at same customer):

- SAP Business Planning and Consolidation model
  - Shared dimensions and naming conventions
- SAP Business Planning and Consolidation data integration
  - Common data integration process for both planning and consolidation
    - Shared data integration object behind both planning and consolidation (e.g. single deployment leads to time savings during implementation)
    - Common process to import master data and transaction across SAP Business Planning and Consolidation -based rapid-deployment solution models
    - Common process to transform and convert data from SAP Business Planning and Consolidation-front end
  - Pre-build integration between SAP G/L Financial Planning rapid-deployment solution and SAP Strategic Financial Planning rapid-deployment solution
- Templates
  - Common look and feel for SAP Business Planning and Consolidation -based rapid-deployment solution templates
  - Common naming convention for SAP Business Planning and Consolidation -based rapid-deployment solution templates
  - Documentation, including assemble-to-order process documentation across multiple rapid-deployment solutions
  - Common set of configuration guides
  - Common set of business process documentation

The combination of SAP Business Planning and Consolidation + rapid-deployment solutions + assemble-to-order lead to a higher return on investment for an investment in SAP Business Planning and Consolidation.

Why?

Customers buy a single SAP solution: SAP Business Planning and Consolidation. Customers can then deploy rapid-deployment content to help speed up the delivery of planning and consolidation models. This content can then be deployed in any order or all at one time. Finally, the rapid-deployment solution contains a coordinated set of business process documentation. As a result, the customer can train users on one solution and roll-out unique planning and consolidation solutions using a common approach.

3.14   Mobile Apps and Infrastructure

<table>
<tr><td>**Solution Showcase**</td></tr>
<tr><td>SAP Mobile Apps and Infrastructure rapid-deployment solution.</td></tr>
</table>

Accelerate ROI

Even the most conservative companies are starting to look into using the new upcoming mobile solutions. With the advances in mobile technology, companies find it easier to find adequate business cases with a quick return on investment (ROI). There are several factors that are accelerating the demand of mobile solutions:

▶ High-performing mobile devices are now affordable (robustness, touchscreen, large displays, etc.).

▶ Wide use of mobile devices especially in "in-field" environment. Companies allow strategies involving bring-your-own-device (BYOD) into the corporate environment.

▶ Enhance the end-user experience for normal day-to-day activities so that mobile devices become an extension of corporate environment and support employees.

▶ Wireless data transfers are more affordable and at an acceptably high speed.

▸ The availability of mobile platforms allows one to manage many devices with heterogeneous technologies efficiently.

Today customers are asking, "How quickly and how easily can we connect our SAP ERP system to a wide variety of mobile devices with a high data security level?" Due to the fact that a connection to a mobile device can be (technically) easily accomplished, customers are achieving high business value with small and simple business processes, which are frequently used.

3.14.1 Background

The demand for mobile solutions is overwhelming. SAP addresses this need by involving and enabling trusted partners to deliver high-quality implementation solutions. The partner eco-system is a very important part of the SAP Rapid Deployment solutions strategy.

SAP Partners

The SAP qualified partner is a large provider of enterprise applications and managed-service solutions in Johannesburg, South Africa.

One of the first customers in South Africa to implement the Mobile Apps and Infrastructure rapid-deployment solution was an SAP customer in the mining sector. The customer invested into mobility simply in order to stay at the forefront of innovative business processes. In any case, the most important tangible reason for the management of the customer is to enhance its business continuity in general. Any idle time— for example, waiting for a management approval—is to be minimized. Nevertheless it is crucial that management is on-site with their customers as long as possible. Business continuity is ensured by using mobile apps that allow management to provide approvals via mobile devices in an easy, user-friendly way.

3.14.2 Solution-Deployment Planning

The SAP partner states that the SAP Rapid Deployment solution was a real door-opener to get the customer involved. The customer, as well as the implementation partner, had not yet implemented SAP Mobile Apps on the SAP Sybase Unwired Platform. The confidence for a successful project was higher just by knowing about the existence of SAP Rapid Deployment solutions.

The SAP partner, when asked about the above, simply stated: "The [SAP Rapid Deployment solutions] made it much easier to follow through the project."

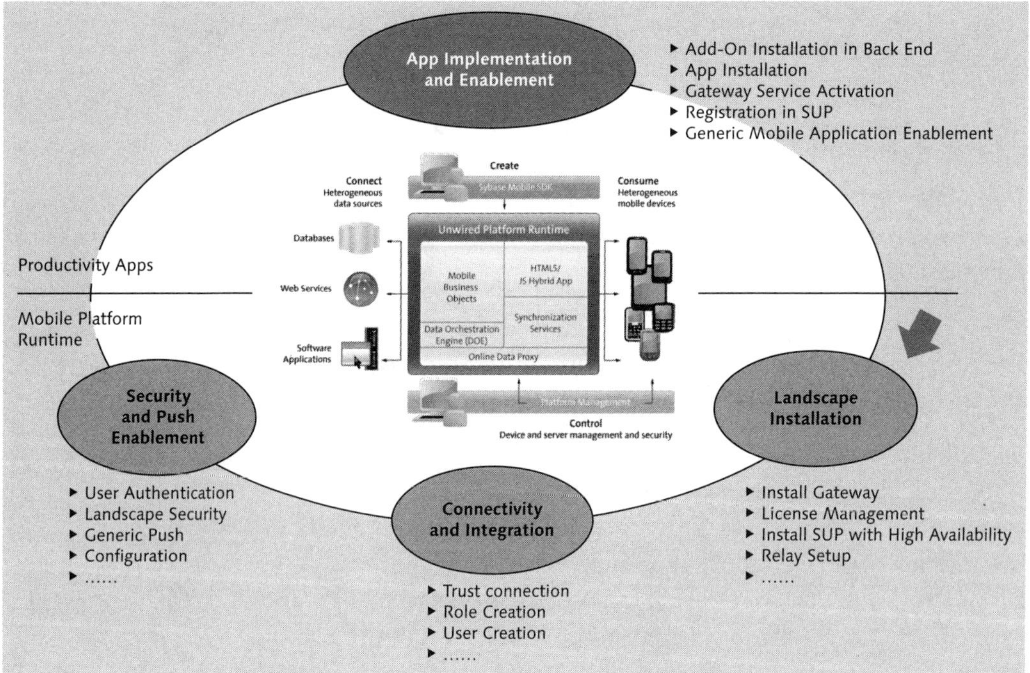

Figure 3.20 Scope of Services Provided within the SAP Rapid Deployment Solutions

The project kick-off was done mid-December 2012. The plan had taken two weeks of Christmas vacation into account, so that after eight weeks of implementation time on the project the final end-user testing by the customer was performed in the middle of February 2013.

On the 15th of March, the successful sign-off of the Mobile Apps and Infrastructure rapid-deployment solution was realized. The SAP partner was able to offer a competitive fixed-price project. In total, two consultants and five employees from the customer were involved in the project. The proposal time for the customer was the standard eight-week time period, which was then pushed to fit into only five weeks.

3.14.3 Deployment

As in many other implementation projects, the SAP Rapid Deployment solutions scope (see Figure 3.20) was flanked with additional customer-specific mobile apps.

Nine out of 10 mobile apps were SAP-standard mobile apps available and ready to implement. One mobile app was developed according to the customer's own specifications.

The following mobile apps were implemented:

1. SAP Cart Approval mobile app
2. SAP HR Approvals mobile app
3. SAP Leave Request mobile app
4. SAP ERP Order Status mobile app
5. SAP Sales Order Notification mobile app
6. SAP Financial Fact Sheet mobile app
7. SAP Material Availability mobile app
8. Purchase requisitions approvals packaged in a hybrid web container
9. SAP BusinessObjects Mobile and BusinessObjects Explorer
10. SAP Ent Int-Travel ReceiptCapture MobApp customer specific mobile app

The modular approach allowed the customer to run complimentary mobile SAP Rapid Deployment solutions implementations, like the SAP Afaria rapid-deployment solution and the SAP Mobile Platform rapid-deployment solution.

The SAP Sybase Unwired Platform was the most integral part of the customer's strategy to move into mobility. The typical connectivity to the SAP gateway server, as well as an SAP Relay server in front of the firewall was part of the SAP Rapid Deployment solutions scope to be deployed. Additionally, the complementary Afaria rapid-deployment solution was bundled into the project and was executed in parallel by tying into the mobile apps and Infrastructure rapid-deployment solution.

The customer was convinced that for a large part of the implementation project, the fixed scope offered by the solution was sufficient. The customer understood how this approach reduces the implementation time and therefore reduces the risk through the fixed-scope offering.

An interruption to the progress of the project that had not been anticipated was to load the correct licenses onto the provisioned servers. After two weeks the issue was resolved, so that the implementation could begin. This procedure itself does not form part of the scope of the SAP Rapid Deployment solutions, as every customer has its own system landscape.

At the time of the implementation, the latest version of the SAP Sybase Unwired Platform 2.1.3 was used together with SAP Gateway 2.0 and a standalone SAP Relay server. The customer implemented only on a single-tiered landscape.

3.14.4 Results

The Mobile Apps and Infrastructure rapid-deployment solution consists of over 200 documents referred to as "content accelerators," as these documents accelerate the implementation time. An SAP rapid-deployment solution usually not only contains documentation, but also automation procedures. In the case of Mobile Apps and Infrastructure rapid-deployment solution, only very few automated implementation steps can be delivered.

Nevertheless, how did the documentation help?

Fixed scope Due to the nature of the solution, the fixed scope allows to prepare a big portion of the project documentation in advance. This advantage was intensively used by the SAP partner.

The SAP partner enthusiastically commented: "We followed the SAP Rapid Deployment solutions logic down to the T!"

The deployment team re-used the kick-off presentation for the project initiation at the customer's site. It is advantageous that the kick-off presentation document is provided by SAP Rapid Deployment solutions as a Microsoft PowerPoint presentation, so that they could easily edit and adapt the presentation for the specific customer.

As in any software implementation project, it is recommended to check the read-me document for any latest updates to this version. In SAP Rapid Deployment solutions, this is provided in a specific SAP Note and in the quick guide, which was a great help during the implementation.

Each mobile app that is part of SAP Rapid Deployment solutions has its own qualification questionnaire and was used to leverage the experience of many previous projects on what is needed from start to finish to ensure a successful implementation. The customer and the SAP partner answered the prequalification questionnaire as well as the pre-prerequisites matrix to determine what was in scope and what was out of scope to ensure that the customer requirements were met and set the stage for the deployment.

The partner was using the SAP Rapid Deployment solutions documentation from SAP Mobile Apps and Infrastructure Version 3. Many parts of the accelerators were used and of course amended to fit even better to the individual project.

Once the customer had chosen the mobile app to implement, each mobile app had an individual business process document (BPD). This showcases the out-of-the box business processes that lie behind the mobile app. Due to the fixed scope, the implementation team could re-use these documents, and handed them over as project documentation and even as training documentation for the end-user. Associated with the BPDs are the configuration guides, which were followed step by step so that the implementation project could follow a clear path forward and potentially estimate more precisely the progress made and the future effort needed. Together this increased the overall confidence in the project. Naturally the configuration guides deployed within the project were re-used as project documentation at hand-over to the customer.

The SAP Rapid Deployment solutions approach and process certainly assists in rapid SAP implementations for mobility. The condensed project methodology start, deploy, and run assisted the team in delivering a successful project.

3.15   SAP HANA Enterprise Cloud

In 2013, SAP introduced the SAP HANA Enterprise Cloud, a new cloud-based service from SAP combining the power of real-time with the simplicity of the cloud. The SAP HANA Enterprise Cloud is an instance hosted in SAP's enterprise-class managed cloud environment. Powered by the breakthrough SAP HANA Cloud Platform, it supports mission-critical applications such as SAP Business Suite and SAP NetWeaver BW or custom SAP HANA applications. SAP HANA Enterprise Cloud offers cloud elasticity, making it a scalable choice for large enterprises.

The SAP HANA Enterprise Cloud is a fast time-to-value option for enterprise customers who want to implement SAP HANA quickly. This case study shows how a global company began the production migration on a Friday and had the business running on SAP HANA by Monday.

3.15.1   Background

This customer is a multi-billion dollar company operating on a global basis, and the first SAP customer to go live with SAP ERP in the SAP HANA Enterprise Cloud. From an IT perspective, they thought they might need SAP HANA resources and expertise. Not so. The beauty of SAP HANA Enterprise Cloud is that it's provided. It's a managed service. That fit precisely with the customer's business goals.

3.15.2   Deployment

The foundation of great deployment efforts are based on planning and a skilled deployment team. The customer depended on SAP's expertise with SAP HANA to guide them through the adoption of SAP solutions through the SAP HANA Enterprise Cloud. They chose to deploy SAP ERP 6.0, and run it from Sales and Distribution to Materials Management. In other words, they wanted to run the full stack.

Noteworthy is the speed of the implementation once it was under way. The team began the actual production migration on a late Friday. SAP and the customer had the migration completed on Sunday and it was literally business as usual on Monday.

Solution-Deployment Planning

As part of the planning phase, the customer's deployment team developed detailed project plans and divided the project into two scenarios (see Table 3.2). Each scenario has its own set of objectives while having some common objectives for the overall SAP HANA Enterprise Cloud.

Scenario	Scenario Objectives
SAP ERP on SAP HANA as Managed Service in SAP HANA Enterprise Cloud	Compare performance of SAP ERP on SAP HANA on a cloud infrastructure to current ERP/SQL Server cloud implementation: ▶ Transaction response times on known lengthy standard SAP transactions (batch and OLTP) ▶ Stress testing on "simulated month-end" close
SAP NetWeaver BW on SAP HANA as Managed Service in SAP HANA Enterprise Cloud	Compare performance of SAP NetWeaver BW on SAP HANA on a cloud infrastructure to the current BW/BO cloud implementation and to the original on-premise implementation, including: ▶ SAP NetWeaver BW BW query response times on select reports ▶ SAP NetWeaver BW BW batch data loading times

Table 3.2 The First SAP HANA Enterprise Cloud Customer Used Scenarios and Scenario Objectives to Plan the Deployment

The deployment planning effort brought the team to form specific objectives. Those defined for the SAP Enterprise Cloud included the ability to demonstrate the cost and customer experience advantage of the SAP HANA Enterprise Cloud deployment:

▶ Optimized, consolidated SAP IT landscape for improved performance.

▶ Centralized, consolidated data in the cloud for ease of data migration.

▸ Centralized, consolidated application landscape for ease of patching and upgrading, as well as new app introduction.

▸ Shared application and database infrastructure for more cost-effective, optimized dev/test, backup/restore, disaster recovery and high availability.

▸ Managed hardware and software infrastructure for reduced enterprise IT burden.

Once the objectives were clearly established, execution plans were developed. At a high level, both scenarios required migration of the SAP application from a traditional database to SAP HANA database based on SAP Enterprise Cloud.

Action

The entire SAP ERP on SAP HANA migration was accomplished in three weeks, including an extensive testing for all development, testing, and production landscapes. Migration steps (see Figure 3.21) involved system copy, EHP upgrade, and database migration for each tier system in the landscape such as development, quality, and production.

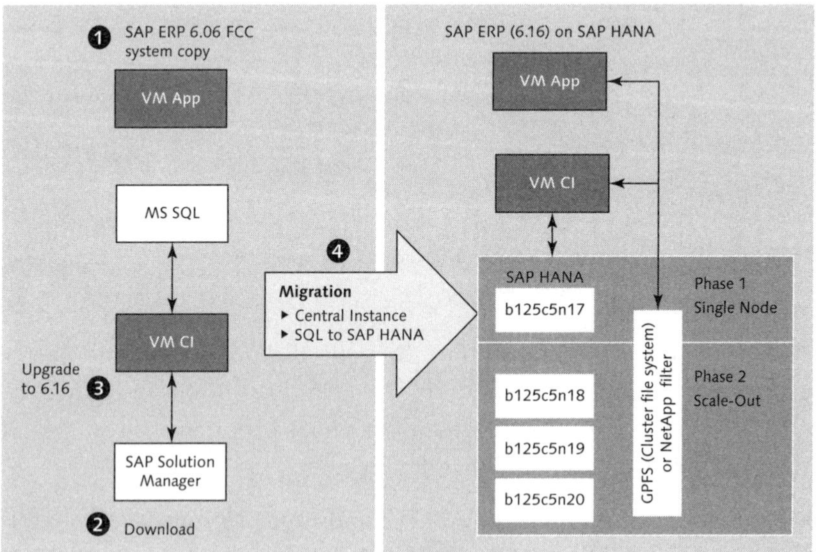

Figure 3.21 Migration Steps for SAP ERP on SAP HANA

All the planning, preparation, and practice resulted in a successful migration over a weekend for the production instance.

After the migration from SAP ERP to SAP ERP on SAP HANA was performed, the deployment team conducted three phases of testing. Table 3.3 describes the three phases and the types of testing that was performed after migration.

Testing Phase	Activities
Testing I: Functional Test	▸ Compare performance of top 30 transactions in SAP SD, PP, QM, FI, CO, and MM components ▸ Execute transactions 3x on SAP HANA and on MS SQL system
Testing II: User Test	▸ End users: 12 ▸ Tested 184 key transactions, reports, background jobs, batch jobs and test scripts ▸ Across SAP FI, CO, MM, SD, HR components (SAP HANA only)
Testing III: User Stress Test	▸ Month-end close live stress test ▸ 75+ FCC users, 3 sessions each ▸ 2000+ transactions executed ▸ 320+ month-end and daily business transactions ▸ Typical 3-4 day workload compressed into 3 hours ▸ All main SAP ERP functional areas tested (FI, HR, MM, SD)

Table 3.3 Three Phases of Testing on the Deployment

The entire SAP NetWeaver BW on SAP HANA migration was accomplished in two weeks including the system copy, database migration, performance testing, and functional testing for all the landscapes such development, testing, and production. The migration steps are illustrated in Figure 3.22.

The following three phases of testing were performed after migration from SAP NetWeaver BW 7.3 to SAP NetWeaver BW powered by SAP HANA. This covered functional, load performance, and scalability for the customer (see Table 3.4).

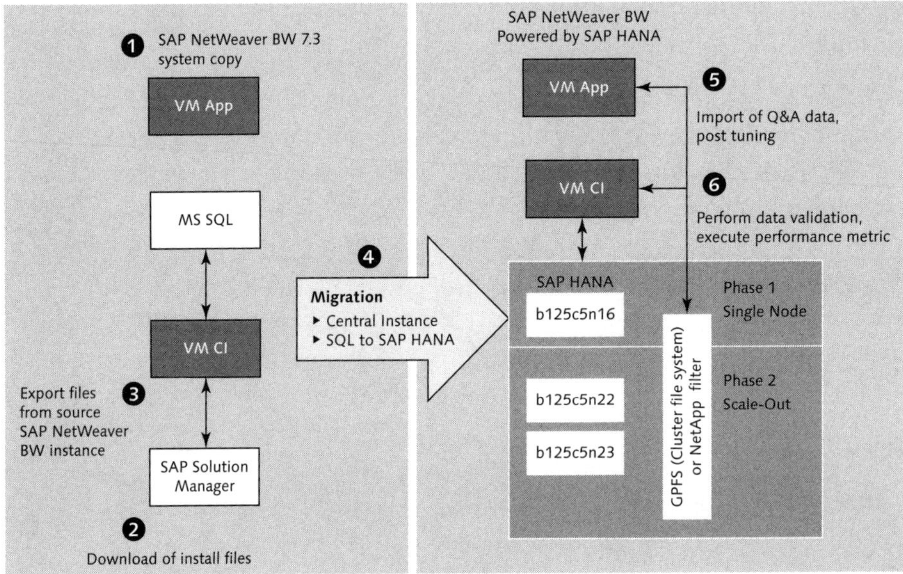

Figure 3.22 Migration Steps for SAP NetWeaver BW on SAP HANA

Testing Phase	Activities
Phase I: Functional Test	▶ Performance test top 10 customer queries (5 most frequently used, 5 longest running) ▶ Executed queries serially, multiple times both on SAP HANA and SQL server systems ▶ Before/after SAP HANA opt. of key InfoProviders ▶ Validated DM response time
Phase II: Load Performance Test	▶ Executed single data load process ▶ Before/after optimizing DSO & InfoCube ▶ Validated load & activation times
Phase III: Validate Scale	▶ Scheduled and ran 30 CATT3) jobs in parallel, simulating 30 concurrent users executing the same set of queries

Table 3.4 Migration from SAP NetWeaver BW to SAP NetWeaver BW on SAP HANA

These tests required focus and planning to accomplish in a short time. The deployment team credits detailed planning, engaging users early on for validation, and expert support on SAP HANA Enterprise Cloud as a managed service as important factors that led to the successful production migration over a single weekend.

3.15.3 Results

The customer reports that SAP HANA allows the organization to look at customers and get answers they could really not get before. After the SAP HANA Enterprise Cloud deployment, the organization could more quickly get information with regard to supply chain. This is enabling extended throughout the supply chain—both from the solution provider and then the end users. At a minimum, the customer's management could have decision-making information a day earlier, and could take a look from the highest level, asking why certain sales groups performed, or business areas achieved, certain results. And users were able to respond with answers, such as, "Well, I was able to run accounts payable faster. I could close the books faster."

The customer was able to run batch jobs in real time. This change allowed management to consider: What would we do with that time?

Management also noted that SAP HANA Enterprise Cloud allowed the workforce to move from transactional to analytical. An employee's day is no longer spent running transactions, but it is spent taking the results of those transactions and using that to a business advantage. This, in turn, allows them to run the business faster and transform the use of their employee knowledge and skill base in new and net more powerful ways.

3.16 Case Study for a Rapid-Deployment Solution Implementation of SAP Fiori

Solution Showcase

A utility company uses SAP Fiori mobile apps and rapid-deployment solutions to make them more competitive, faster.

In today's fast-paced world where time is money, it is becoming more and more critical that applications are available anywhere, anytime. It is becoming not just an enabler but a differentiator. Response times in certain industries portrays a professionally run organization that is in control of their operational process.

Mobile changes the way we operate in an industrial ecosystem because it creates untethered users and customers allowing flexibility while allowing convenience.

Reducing the need to lug around the traditional laptop, with mobile applications there is no reason not to enable 24/7 ability at areas outside the traditional working place. Examples of this include at an airport while waiting for the plane to take you to that business meeting, at a business lunch where critical up to date data is a key requirement.

That said, technology convergence is another key topic where mobile plays a part, many technological systems need to evolve to performing similar tasks. How is it that we integrate voice, data, and video as synergistic shared resources?

As technologies converge it is critical to ensure that applications operate over multiple devices seamlessly. There is sometimes a contradiction in delivery because a lot more effort is spent ensuring that applications are device independent.

3.16.1 Background

The customer is a utility company that generates approximately 95% of the electricity used in South Africa and approximately 45% of the electricity used in Africa. They generate, transmit, and distribute electricity to industrial, mining, commercial, agricultural, and residential customers and redistributors.

Native mobility applications
The mobile project started in February 2013 with a Proof of Concept for Native Application rapid-deployment solution covering three native mobility applications, Leave Request, Leave Approval, and Cart Approval.

The native mobility applications were completed at the end of May 2013. The applications were developed and it seemed to be difficult to provide customer specific enhancements. It was seen that the Native Cart approval application did not meet their requirements and a change request was raised to replace the Cart Approval with Travel Expense approval.

Beginning in June 2013, the customer was informed about a new SAP product called SAP Fiori. These benefits on the new SAP Fiori applications were very high. For example the user could now use a portal, where applications could be accessed seamlessly. SAP Fiori also released the requirement for specific applications developed for specific devices, allowed to run on many devices that can run HTML5.

As the mobile applications based on the native development was ending by the year 2013. The customer took the decision to go with the new SAP Fiori applications.

The SAP Afaria product can be used for the mobile device management it was not needed anymore to enable the application set up itself. Instead, the use of a portal was promoted.

3.16.2 Solution-Deployment Planning

The SAP Fiori project kicked off on the 13th of June, 2013, and had a proposed end date of the 25th of July, 2013, a six week implementation. There is no way they would have been able to even attempt an implementation like this without an rapid-deployment solution enabler.

In the six weeks the deployment team implemented SAP Fiori in the development and quality assurance environment. Due to the protracted timeline, the customer agreed to bypass the pre-production environment and allow the team to manage the implementation into production.

The deployment team picked up 32 defects with the build being related to the display of warning messages. They managed to get the software to a release state in the six weeks but on request to go live, they were delayed with a requirement to authenticate Active Directory.

SAP ABAP stacks does not allow a Point-to-Point authentication against an LDAP Provider (i.e. AD, Novell, etc.). To have this functionality implemented, the intermediate component needs to be put into place to

Point-to-Point authentication

allow for this integration. The team decided to use the portal as that intermediate component.

Utilizing the SAP NetWeaver Portal as a SAP SSO2 Token Provider, the deployment team gave the customer added benefit in utilizing existing infrastructure. You can setup single-sign on between two SAP systems seamlessly. The SAP NetWeaver Portal does have the capability to generate this token if authenticated successfully.

SAP NetWeaver Portal

Currently the SAP NetWeaver Portal has been implemented for making use of ESS and MSS scenarios, and therefore is already available within the customer's topology.

It is understood that a more sustainable Identity and Access Management solution (IDM) solution will be required in their environment.

3.16.3 Deployment

The project had to wait for the Portal Authentication work to be completed.

The product was deployed across the entire group IT business unit. This comprises about 800 users in total.

The only anticipated deployment complexity is the 3G enablement which involves a third-party vendor.

3.16.4 Results

Having run rapid-deployment solutions in the past, a new presentation layer was found exceptionally easy to use and easy to understand. The accelerators were at the customer's fingertips and split by project phase.

Documents

Due to the strict rapid-deployment solutions framework, customers do not need to request documents outside of the project scope.

The sales documentation was constructive and very easy to use. It provided an easy to use reference to explain the benefits of a rapid-deployment solutions project and the SAP Fiori overview. Over the duration of the project, the company adapted the content provided in the sales overview documents as an introductory overview for sponsors meeting, training and support overviews, in fact any session where we were introducing SAP Fiori for the first time.

The overall infrastructure documentation is generic in nature, which is correct per the rapid-deployment solution structure, and therefore it is critical to customize this to the customer environment. It implies that you need to have an understanding of a typical mobile infrastructure set up.

Once the project team was established and the project kickoff session held by using the already existing documentation and we had ensured that the required infrastructure was in place, the customer's team moved to ensure that the prerequisites were fulfilled. The documents are easy to use, as the prerequisites are split into SAP NetWeaver, SAP Fiori application, or both together. It was important to have a session with the customer to ensure that the document and the deliverables are understood in detail.

A service of SAP to verify the implementation plan and then progressing to the configuration. The configuration guides were clear to use, but at the time did not contain enough detail and interaction with the RIG (Regional Implementation Group) teams ensured we were always presented with the most up to date information.

One of the most critical documents was the SAP business process document, as this allowed very quick identification as to potential gaps. Several existing customer modifications in the environment the application followed the backend better that the native applications and were easier to implement.

It is critical to identify front end UI changes to be done as these may pose potential customization points.

The training guides were instrumental in providing structure, but you shouldn't underestimate the work that goes into this documentation. Whilst this team provided key user training, it was important to keep an eye on knowledge transfer as in this environment, the SAP NetWeaver Gateway server was an additional component and it may be necessary to spend some time to get a true owner for this.

The test scenarios were basic and the team found it better to rely on the customer test cases as they were more comprehensive. During this task, the team isolated the 242 customer test cases. The test cases require an environment where data has been set up. Always ensure that the data is set up and that the back end environment is operational prior to starting the testing. We picked up some errors that were evident on the back end and not as such an SAP Fiori issue.

The team found a few areas that need some additional work:

- **Fiori roadmap**
  The customer wants an understanding as to the future direction. While the rapid-deployment solution documentation provided an indication as to the future roadmap, it didn't seemed to be clear and congruent.

- **Browser settings**
  The team had an issue on the project obtaining a clearer understanding as to the HTML 5 browsers supported as well as the link between device and phone.

3.17 Winning the Ratings War with SAP Personnel Administration and Organization Management Rapid-Deployment Solution

Solution Showcase

SAP Personnel Administration and Organization Management rapid-deployment solution for Hindi general entertainment television channels.

Many organizations today are revisiting their processes and IT platforms for human capital management. Challenged by cost pressure on one side and the increasing global competition for talent on the other, HR leaders have to establish effective people-development processes while simultaneously increasing efficiency in administrative functions. Consolidation of global HR systems, decentralization of tasks via self-services for managers and employees, and centralization of functions in shared service centers are common transformational steps to increase efficiency.

Cloud solutions are increasingly in focus, particularly when it comes to talent-management solutions. They offer quick access to innovative business tools—while minimizing costs for hardware, development, and maintenance, and reducing reliance on IT. The hybrid approach at SAP maximizes these benefits and leverages your on-premise investments. Packaged integration services help you take advantage of this hybrid solution.

Hybrid approach

SAP offers a wide range of solutions to help you transform your business by automating and aligning your HR processes with your business objectives. These solutions are provided on-premise and on-demand, and where necessary, adapted to local requirements. A broad range of rapid-deployment solutions, illustrated in Figure 3.23, make up a comprehensive roadmap to help you implement a state-of-the-art human capital management solution, step-by-step, at your own pace.

Automate and align HR processes

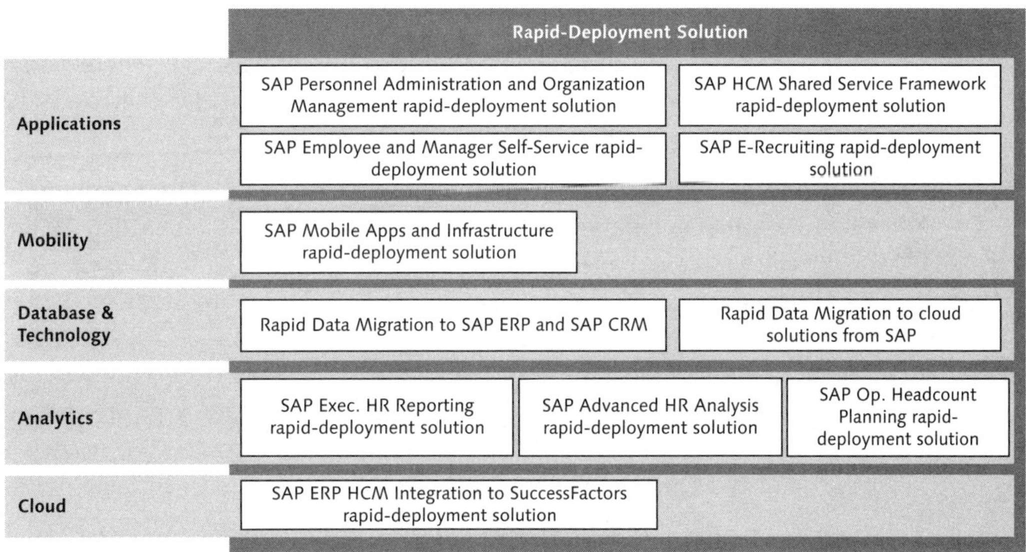

Figure 3.23 Rapid-Deployment Solutions for SAP HCM Solutions

The customer use-case demonstrates the implementation of personnel administration and organization management, as well as SAP Interactive Forms software by Adobe.

3.17.1 Background

The television industry in India is booming. To succeed on the small screen, broadcasters need compelling content to engage their audience while running their business operations with speed and efficiency. Leading broadcast channel Multi Screen Media Pvt. Ltd. deployed SAP software and configured SAP Interactive Forms software by Adobe to help win the ratings war.

Multi Screen Media Pvt. Ltd. is one of India's leading Hindi general entertainment television channels. It occupies a pivotal position in the country's booming television business, which is more than twice the size of India's Bollywood film industry.

Since its launch in October 1995, Multi Screen Media has consistently made innovations in its content lineup and created highly popular new content across the genres. Complementing its new TV content with a mix of high-profile events and Bollywood blockbusters, it uses unique and imaginative programming and exciting formats. The general entertainment channel reaches more than 42 million households across India and more than 300 million households globally.

Automate business-management processes
As television ownership grew rapidly across India and competition in the general entertainment category of television intensified, Multi Screen Media management decided to automate its business-management processes. "Multi Screen Media's legacy business processes required significant manual intervention," explains Sagar Kunte, assistant vice president in the systems group. "There were disparate systems, multiple owners, and no centralized data. Reporting was spreadsheet-based, time-consuming, and inaccurate in some cases. We needed a solid and reliable software backbone."

As a first step to streamlining its business processes and providing business executives with access to accurate and current business data, Multi Screen Media deployed the SAP ERP application. The company then turned its attention to automating its human capital management processes, delivering self-service functionality and enhancing collaboration with suppliers and customers.

3.17.2 Deployment

Seeking help from ITC Infotech India Ltd., Multi Screen Media deployed the SAP ERP Human Capital Management rapid-deployment solution for personnel administration and organization management to streamline its HR processes. The ITC team configured core HR functionality to standardize employee administration, performance management, and reporting.

Next, ITC worked with the HR team to streamline HR forms–based communication. Having selected SAP Interactive Forms software by Adobe, the HR team defined core areas for employee and manager self-service functionality, such as key responsibility areas, behaviors, skills, and organizational values. ITC then designed and integrated the forms with the SAP software landscape.

Streamline communication

The entire deployment was undertaken within just three months, and training was conducted through self-learning activities at the employee level.

3.17.3 Results

With the new software in place, all employee-related data at Multi Screen Media now resides on one platform, and the company is benefitting from standardized HR reporting. Using SAP Interactive Forms, employees can now manage their information and complete performance-management processes at their own pace. Managers benefit from automated task-processing. The electronic forms are automatically generated, prepopulated with the most current information that resides in the SAP solution. When new data is submitted via the forms, the SAP business software is dynamically updated.

Employee data on one platform

The key benefits obtained with the deployment of the SAP Personnel Administration and Organization Management rapid-deployment solution are highlighted in Figure 3.24.

75% – 80%	75%	60%
Faster to produce HR reports	Faster cycle time for HR processes	Less time required for training

Figure 3.24 Key Benefits for Customer with SAP Personnel Administration and Organization Management Rapid-Deployment Solution

Customer satisfaction is evident in some of the customers' statements about the deployment of the solution:

"The solution has automated processes and improved efficiency, which complements our growth strategy," says CIO Ajay Meher. "…The use of the interactive forms also helps us meet our sustainability objectives."

"The implementation of the SAP rapid-deployment solution and SAP Interactive Forms has lifted employee satisfaction levels," comments S. Srivatsan, assistant vice president of HR at Multi Screen Media. "The need for multiple data entry has been eliminated, while employees and managers are benefiting from a much simplified performance-management process."

"The forms have helped minimize transactional HR requests, allowing the HR team to focus on more strategic matters. The transactional activities on the HR front will be further reduced with the IT team's plan to use interactive forms to enable employees to manage their income tax declarations," adds Srivatsan. "For instance, every taxpayer in India is eligible for certain tax rebates if they make investments, deposits, or home loan repayments, and so on. "

"We're configuring the form so that employees can manage this information," explains Kunte. "This will further reduce the need for the HR team to perform transactional HR requests."

How can you achieve consistency between the different parts of a rapid-deployment solution? How can you make sure multiple packages fit together to enable the assemble-to-order approach? Well-defined architecture concepts for the content of rapid-deployment solutions are a key part of the answer.

4   Content Architecture: Foundation of SAP Rapid Deployment Solutions

As outlined in Chapter 2, Section 2.1, a core part of SAP Rapid Deployment solutions are a set of documents that enable project teams to learn about the business best practices, and to implement these practices in an SAP system efficiently by following a standardized and engineered approach. In addition, a rapid-deployment solution also contains a set of configuration settings that exactly matches some of the documents (the configuration guides) and can be deployed automatically to the system.

Simply speaking, large parts of a rapid-deployment solution involve a knowledge management tool for consulting teams at SAP and SAP Partners that sell and deploy SAP solutions. A rapid-deployment solution or an SAP Business All-in-One package comes with a well-defined set of knowledge documents. It presents this knowledge in a structured and standardized fashion. The key objective of this standardization is acceleration of the project-team enablement (so if you know one rapid-deployment solution, you understand the structure of every rapid-deployment solution) and to support the assemble-to-order approach where multiple rapid-deployment solutions are combined in order to cover the scope of a customer initiative.

To meet these objectives, the knowledge documents that make up a rapid-deployment solution have to be clearly structured, built according to standard templates, and they have to be consistent in themselves and

Knowledge management

with documents from other rapid-deployment solutions that cover related aspects. A key challenge is that within one solution, multiple knowledge documents talk about the same aspect from different viewpoints.

Scope items
For example, different elements of the business scope of a rapid-deployment solution—called "scope items"—are described in different documents from a different angle for different target groups. The business overview highlights the business value of a scope item and is used during the sales phase. The configuration guide describes how the businesses processes of the scope item are implemented in the software for the consultant in the project. The work breakdown structure (WBS) addresses the tasks that are required in the project to realize the scope item for the project manager.

The concepts behind the scenes that enable this structure, standardization, and consistency are called *content architecture*. Roughly speaking, content architecture describes the structure and the semantic relationships between the content of the knowledge documents. In this chapter we will explain the general concepts of SAP's content architecture and their application to the domain of SAP Rapid Deployment solutions.

Section 4.1 introduces the general concept of content architecture for knowledge documents in general. This concept is applied across SAP's solution lifecycle for a variety of different domains.

After introducing the general concept, Section 4.2 describes how the general concept of content architecture is applied to rapid-deployment solutions. The focus of this section is on the domain of rapid-deployment solutions, while Section 4.3 describes how this domain integrates with other related domains.

Section 4.4 provides a deep-dive into the content architecture aspects of the assemble-to-order approach.

Let's get started.

4.1 Content Architecture Defined

SAP's definition of content architecture follows the approach outlined by Cleve Gibbon. Content architecture is a set of guiding principles, techniques, and best practices for effective content management. Process design, content modeling, and user-experience definition help to build out a content architecture that communicates a shared understanding of "how" content should be managed and published.

In the context of the rapid deployment of SAP solutions, the content strategy is defined by the objectives of the rapid-deployment solutions as outlined in Chapter 2. Content management is defined by the processes and tools used for content creation and consumption. These tools will be introduced in Chapter 5.

In the following sections, we'll introduce the business value of content architecture, followed by a description of the objectives. We'll then focus on the key concepts of content architecture before we provide an example in Section 4.1.4. This discussion ends with a deep dive into concepts around managing the various assets types that are part of the content architecture in SAP using an asset type inventory.

4.1.1 Business Value of Content Architecture

The key value of content architecture is consistency—a crucial aspect of knowledge assets quality—and the ability to provide this consistency and the provisioning of multiple knowledge assets for multiple target groups at reasonable costs. This is done by enabling structured re-use as a basic principle, while creating knowledge assets. The goal of content architecture is to provide a framework to the field of knowledge assets around SAP's solutions and products. The goal is to get to a systematic and structured management of knowledge assets, to enable consistency of information across knowledge assets, knowledge capturing, and sharing where applicable.

Without a structured content architecture in place, the same semantic content is usually created, maintained, and independently put into different systems multiple times. Knowledge assets are hardly shared across units. Without the guiding principles of content architecture, this will lead to loss of information, low quality, inconsistency, customer confusion, employee frustration, and high cost.

The example in Figure 4.1 shows that a bunch of documents are created during a lifecycle of a product dealing with similar content. This content doesn't necessarily need to be identical, but the documents should at least build on each other and be consistent. Available information should be reused and harvested along the value chain.

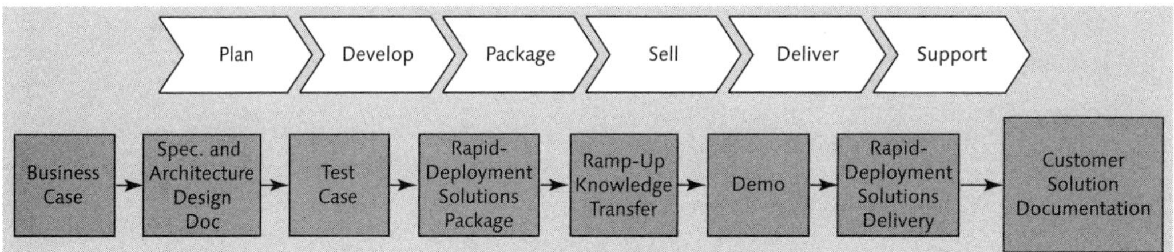

Figure 4.1 Content Architecture along the Value Chain

Content architecture enables managers, employees, customers, and partners to work efficiently, and it provides them with the knowledge they need according to their task. People also better understand what purpose they're providing information for, and where it is used. Customers and other knowledge-assets users are provided with more consistent assets across the various levels of details, e.g., for a rapid-deployment solution.

4.1.2 Objectives of Content Architecture

Content architecture defines the structural backbone for managed asset-creation at SAP. The key objectives of content architecture at SAP are:

- Achieve a common understanding on what content is dealing with (entity types and asset types) by definition of a meta model and an asset type inventory.

- Harmonize content across business units including the corporate taxonomy (structuring) by content coaching and governance.

- Achieve transparency about process or infrastructure issues due to collection of processes including data flows, infrastructure information, harmonized roles across the company, etc.

4.1.3 Key Concepts of Content Architecture

The content architecture describes the entity types and their relationships (ontology) as well as the asset types that exist for SAP, the processes in which these types are created, maintained, and distributed, the bill of materials in which they are relevant, and the taxonomies used to classify the content of these entities. Besides this, concepts for re-use, integration, and infrastructure improvements are provided (see Figure 4.2).

Ontology

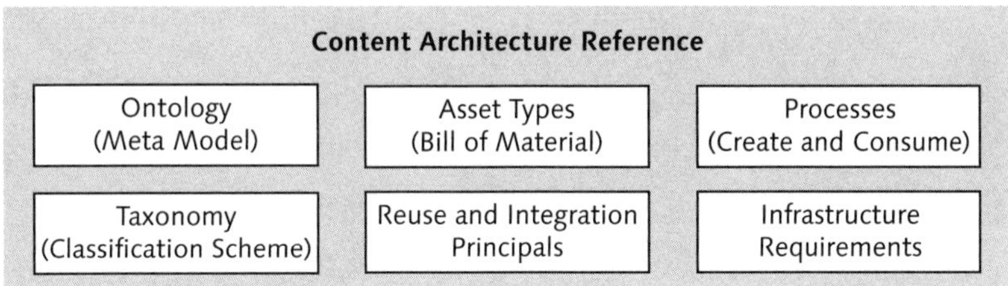

Figure 4.2 Content Architecture Reference

The content architecture therefore serves as backbone for an appropriate knowledge management infrastructure, content management, and information architecture.

Content modeling is an effective way to reach out for a common understanding, harmonization, and reuse of structured content. There are two parts of content modeling—the ontology and the taxonomy of SAP content:

Content modeling

- *Ontology* describes a thing (a housecat lives in a house, chases mice…)
- *Taxonomy* is a classification of things (a cat is a house pet, is a…)

Both need to be done. The ontology ensures a common understanding of the content SAP deals with (entity types) and the taxonomy ensures harmonized structures e.g., when presenting the content to end-users.

In information science, ontology formally represents knowledge as a set of concepts within a domain, and the relationships between pairs of concepts. It can be used to model a domain and to support reasoning about concepts. The ontology of the SAP content architecture is represented by a meta model. It is defined by a unified modeling language model.

SAP's meta model

The meta model in SAP is structured into different areas like business consulting, positioning, or software licensing. An overview on these areas is provided in Figure 4.3.

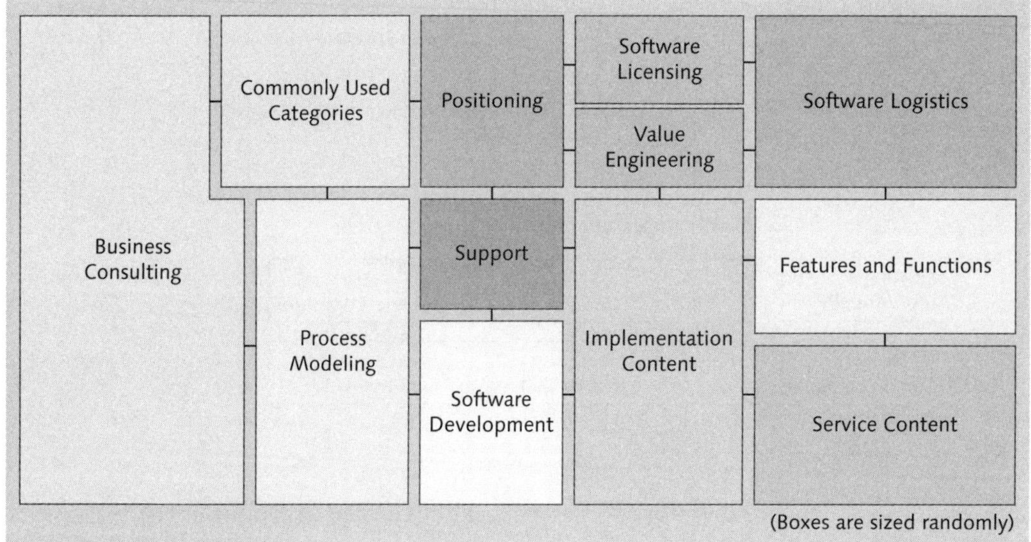

Figure 4.3 Areas of the Meta Model of the SAP Content Architecture

Figure 4.4 shows the complete, high-level meta model of the SAP content architecture.

It's important to acknowledge that you can't understand the relationships of things without understanding the actual things you are relating. Therefore it is imperative that a central, well-managed taxonomy be developed, rolled out, and standardized across the company for all aspects, such as people, locations, industries, audiences, and processes.

Bills of materials of knowledge assets

To achieve this, a company will use a *bill of materials* (BOM) in the SAP system, which describes which asset types have to be provided in which way to fulfill a specific task, e.g., to deliver a rapid-deployment solution. The set of asset types across all bill of materials of knowledge assets is captured in the asset type inventory (ATI, you can find additional information in Section 4.1.5). Reuse and integration principles ensure that content is not created or replicated wherever possible. Infrastructure requirements support these concepts.

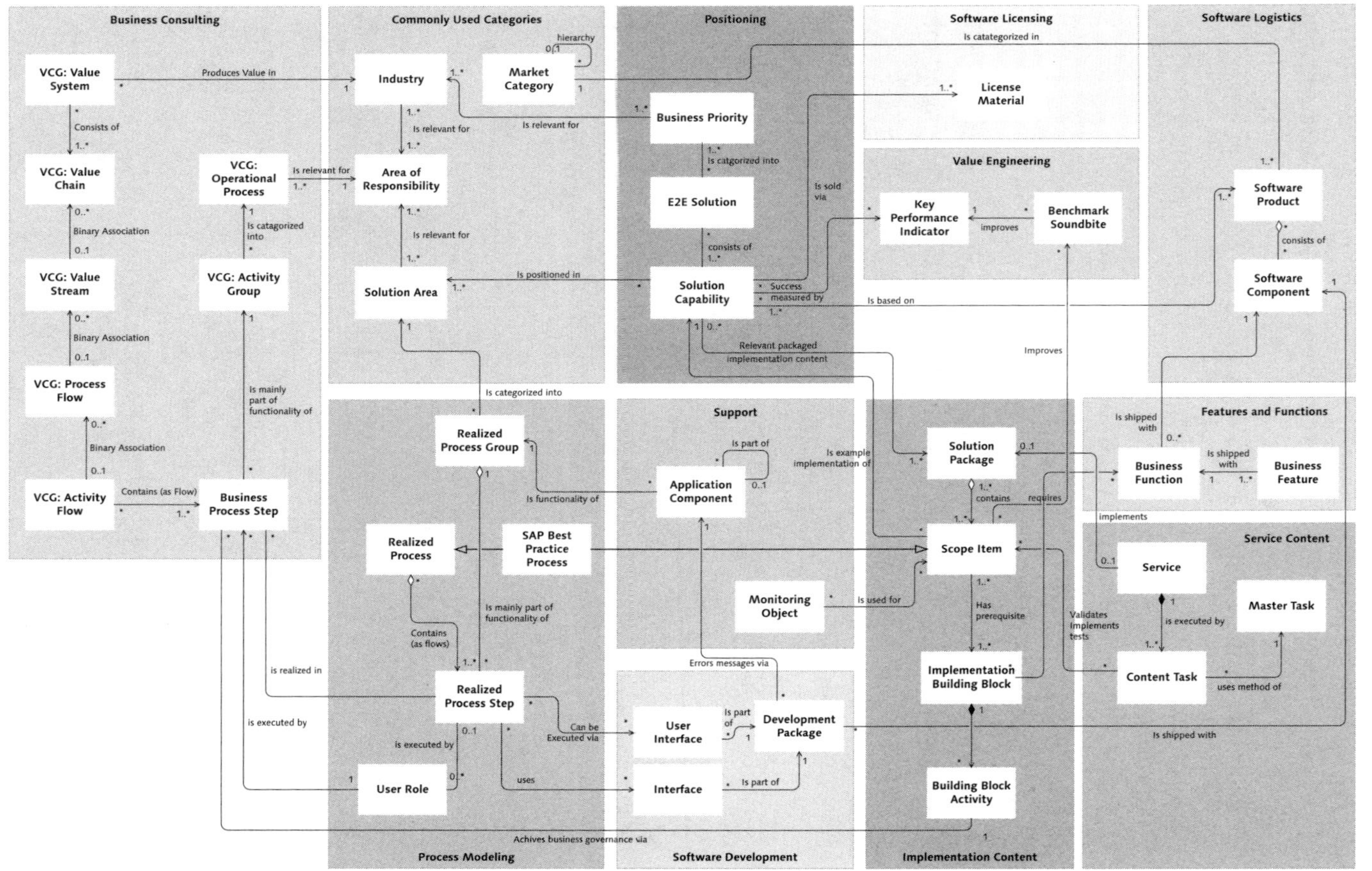

Figure 4.4 Overview on the SAP Content Architecture Meta Model

Processes describe how content is created, maintained, and distributed, which is of importance to understand which groups in SAP are responsible for which content, and how this content is used within SAP. It also gives insight about quality assurance, e.g. via governance processes.

A content architecture is only complete and only ready for execution if the related processes are defined, documented, agreed-upon by all stakeholders and executed in the related organizations.

4.1.4   Content Architecture Example

At this point, let's have a look what content architecture means more concretely, along a simple example from the rapid-deployment solutions context. Figure 4.5 provides a visualization of the example.

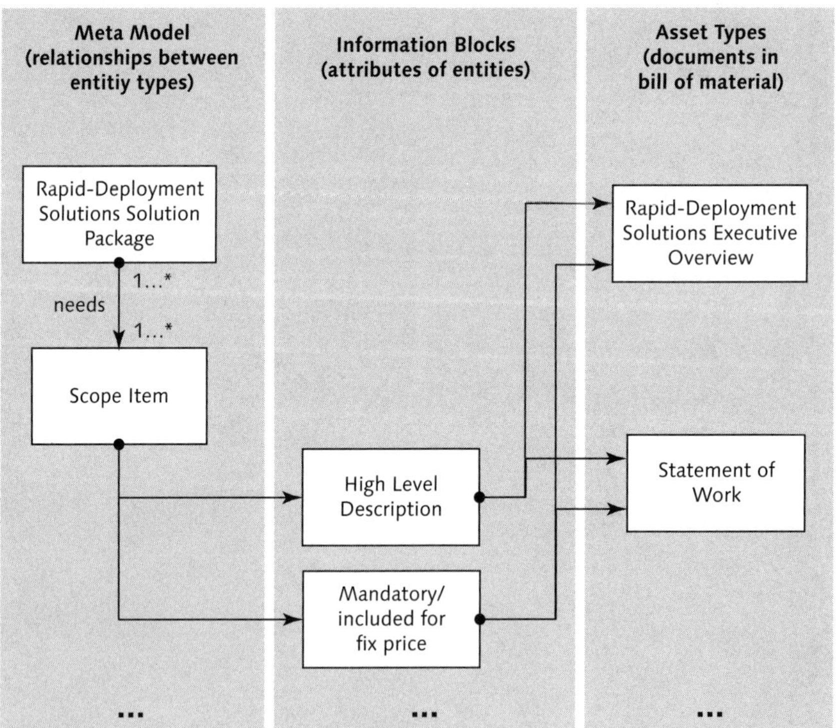

Figure 4.5 Simplified Example for Content Architecture in the Rapid-Deployment Solutions Domain

A rapid-deployment solution package consists of several scope items. In the ontology of the SAP content architecture, rapid-deployment solutions packages and scope items represent entities. There is a many-to-many relationship between these entities, because a rapid-deployment solutions package can contain multiple scope items and a single scope item can be part of multiple rapid-deployment solutions packages, because a certain base piece of business scope like "sell from stock" might be relevant in multiple industries, and thus in multiple rapid-deployment solutions, for example.

Scope items

A scope item has certain attributes, like the high-level description or the information whether the scope item is mandatory (included in the fixed-price consulting offer) or optional (not included in the fixed price).

Different documents (knowledge assets) that are part of the rapid-deployment solution use information that is linked to the entity scope items. The documents are structured and written for certain—different—target groups, such as customers, services sales representatives, bid managers, or technical consultants. All need information about scope items, but in different flavors or levels of detail. Thus, the redundancy of information within the assets in the bill of material of a rapid-deployment solution is a feature and not a failure. Not a failure, that is, if the redundancy is managed and it is made sure that the redundant information is always the same in all the different assets of a rapid-deployment solution.

Knowledge assets

In our little example, it is vital that the high-level description of a scope item or the mandatory/optional information is exactly the same in all assets within a rapid-deployment solution, e.g., in the rapid-deployment solution executive overview, in the WBS, and the statement of work that represents the legally binding addendum to the service contract for the fixed price. Imagine a customer who finds in the executive overview that a certain scope item is listed as "included in fixed price" and the scope of work provided later as part of the contract excludes that same piece. Additional confusion can be created if the high-level description differs.

To avoid any confusion in the scope of the project, the content architecture defines the entity types, their information elements, relationships, and the decomposition of assets as shown in Figure 4.5.

4.1.5   The Asset Type Inventory (ATI)

The asset type inventory (ATI) describes which types of assets are to be provided or used in the context of an entity type. While this sounds simple at first sight, it is actually not in a large enterprise. The base assumption is that assets are produced to describe a specific topic. The asset type inventory is defined by information regarding what the asset types are, and to which entity types they belong on an abstract level. Figure 4.6 illustrates this relationship based on same examples. The entity types are given by the products. Entities are concrete products like "washing machine" or "electric iron." *Asset types* represent classes of documents that talk about different aspects of the entity types for different purposes or target groups, like pricing guidelines of user manuals.

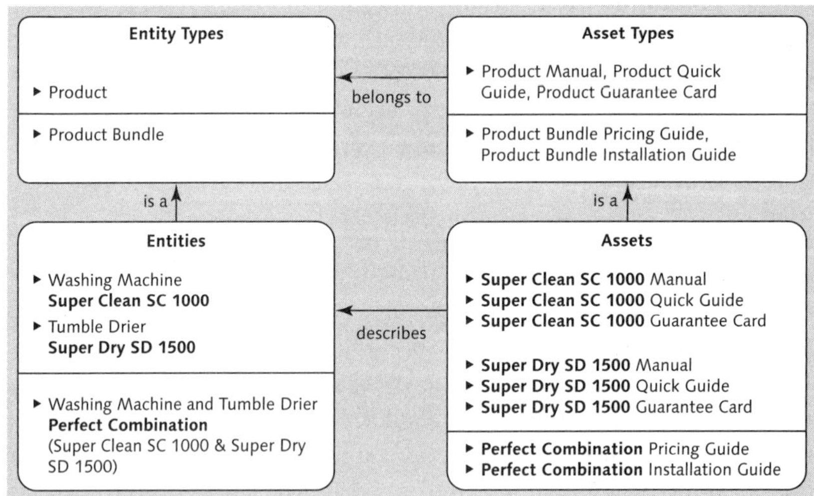

Figure 4.6 Relation of Assets and Entities

Assets -> topic
The information in the ATI is very limited, for the purpose of keeping it simple and maintainable. It is usually context- and even format-independent.

Content architecture doesn't only look at the high-level assignment, but also at the insights of an asset type. Of course, a detailed analysis and defragmentation cannot be reached for all asset types that exist in SAP, but it can be done for focus asset types.

Asset harmonization shall be done whenever two asset types in the asset type inventory seem to be very similar, but might be developed by different author groups. It must be checked if there is a re-use potential to save costs, or at least if the used templates are compliant, to ensure a smooth user experience. To do so, the assets are analyzed by checking the chapters and content in the asset types.

Asset type defragmentation is the detailed analysis and guidance about the content of an asset type. The asset type is defragmented into its (reuse) building blocks. It is checked to see the source (raw input) for a building block, which could be one or many attributes at an entity type (see Figure 4.7).

Defragmentation

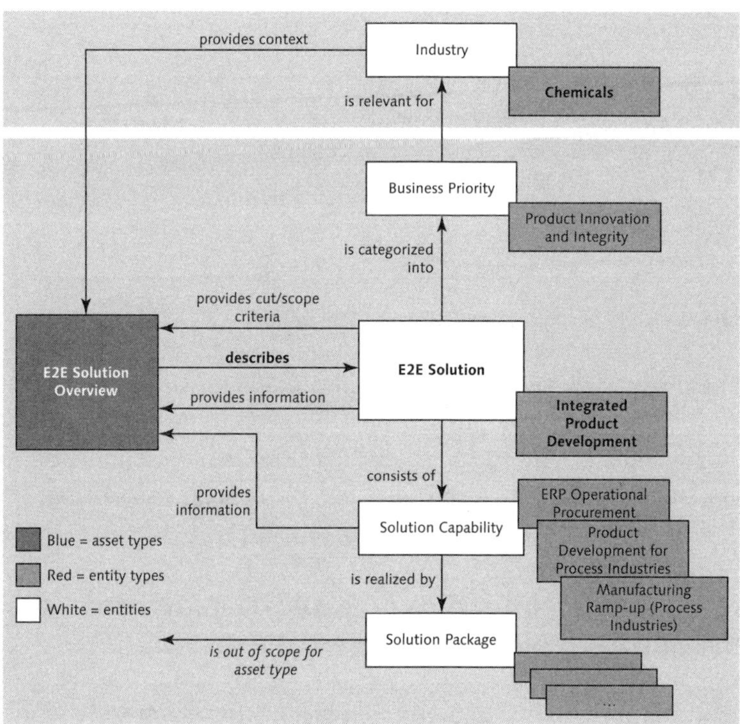

Figure 4.7 Asset Type Defragmentation (Simplified)

In addition, it demonstrates how much information is to be provided for a specific asset type. Example: If you find a document called "XY Overview," you do not expect a detailed description of everything ... but how far should the author describe things and how can we ensure that authors have the same opinion about the scope? All this is done by asset type defragmentation.

Consumer Satisfaction

Sometimes SAP will find that their consumers don't have required asset types. ATI will allow for the identification and closing of these gaps. It will also make evident that certain information is missing for a specific context (see Figure 4.8).

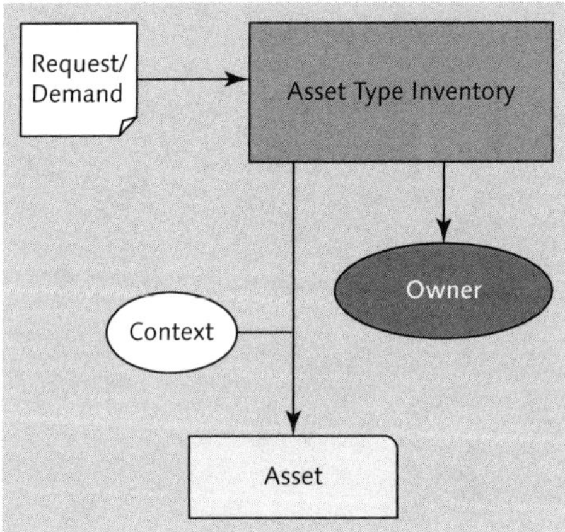

Figure 4.8 Asset Type Inventory and Consumer Satisfaction

It shall be possible to collect the gaps and provide missing information as soon as possible. The topic can be addressed, either to an entity owner for whom specific additional information is required, or to the asset type owner if only the assets for a specific context are missing.

4.2 Content Architecture of Rapid-Deployment Solutions

This section introduces the content architecture for the area of rapid-deployment solutions. We will provide an overview on the key entity types, their relationships (the meta model) and the key definitions of these entity types. After that we will provide an overview of the complete list of assets that are associated with a rapid-deployment solution package—the bill of material—and how the assets are linked with the key entities.

4.2.1　Meta Model

Figure 4.9 provides an overview on the meta model of the rapid-deployment solution area. A rapid-deployment solution package is comprised of one or multiple *scope items*. A scope item describes a well-defined piece of implementation scope. For applications that support business processes like SAP CRM or SAP ERP, a scope item is given by an SAP Best Practice process. Scope items can be contained in multiple rapid-deployment solutions.

Each scope item refers to one or many *implementation building blocks*. An implementation building block refers to the actual configuration settings or master data that is required to implement a scope item.

Implementation building blocks

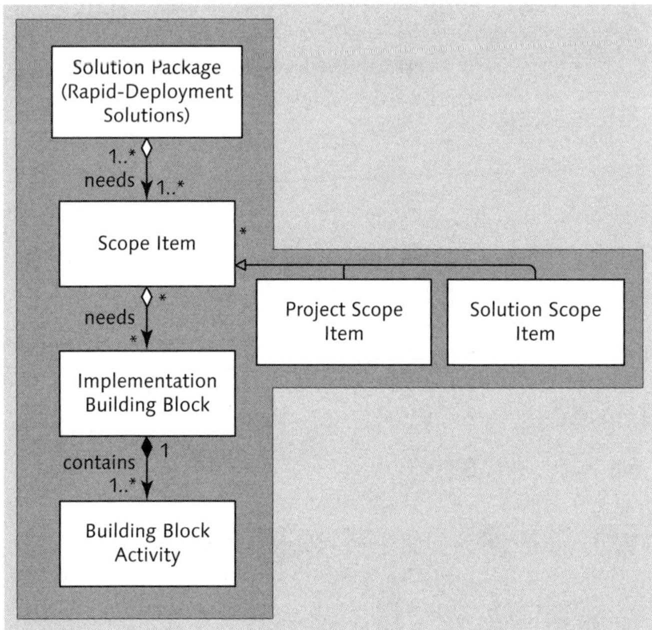

Figure 4.9　High-Level Meta Model of a Rapid-Deployment Solution

An implementation building block describes a procedure a consultant is executing during an implementation project, while a scope item describes a procedure a customer user is executing on a productive system. One or more implementation building blocks are required to implement a scope item. Most rapid-deployment solution packages are delivered with automated configuration content. In this case, an implementation building block is not only a document on how to configure the system, but a set of configuration settings that can be loaded into the system automatically.

The individual configuration settings within an implementation building block are called *building block activities*.

4.2.2 Key Entity Type Definitions

In the following subsections, we'll describe and define the key entity types introduced in the last section, as well as provide examples.

Scope Item

Best practice implementation

Definition
A scope item represents a best-practice implementation choice for a customer. It includes all content required to implement that choice.

Key Properties

- Scope items are functional, reusable entities of a rapid-deployment solution, i.e., they can be reused by one or many rapid-deployment solutions in the context of assemble-to-order.

- Scope items aggregate core enablement content (e.g., scope-item description), implementation content (i.e., a set of implementation building blocks) and service content (e.g., scope-item-specific tasks).

- Scope items support implementation of processes (SAP Best Practice process), analytics (packaged reporting scope item), infrastructure components (packaged infrastructure scope item). Via a set of assigned implementation building blocks, this functionality is confined as a pre-thought configuration (e.g., based on a best practice).

Categories of Scope items

We are distinguishing the following two kinds of scope items:

1. Solution scope item:

   ▸ **Description**: Solution scope items are activities that are typically executed by a customer on a productive SAP system. In most cases a solution scope item refers to a business process.

   ▸ **Examples**: opportunity management, SAP account intelligence, CRM interactive reporting

2. Project scope item

   ▸ **Description**: A project scope item comprises service tasks that have to be selected as one part of the project scope (all or nothing). As such, project scope items are reusable prerequisites for different solution scope items.

   ▸ **Examples**: Data migration for HCM/OM, HCM installation, generic project management

Implementation Building Block

> **Definition**
>
> An implementation building block is a self-contained group of building block activities dealing with the implementation of settings like system settings, configuration, master data, etc.

Examples:

▸ C20 — CRM Transaction Types — Basic Settings

▸ C10 — CRM Central Master Data

▸ C07 — CRM Web Client UI for Sales

Building Block Activity

> **Definition**
>
> A building block activity is a single step in an implementation building block that needs to be executed in the given sequence in order to activate the building block (no "optional" activities are permitted).

Step execution Building block activities can be enabled for automated execution and/or manual execution. They refer to documentation (in general: paragraph in Configuration Guide) and may comprise all activities required during an implementation project (system set-up, configuration settings, master data settings, etc.)

According to the technical content authoring, building block activities are separated as much as possible between a stable, framework-related part (e.g., object enabled for automated execution like eCATT, BC-Set etc.) and the more specific, content-related part (settings, associated as parameter value set). Thus, during an implementation project, content structure and settings can be adapted without adapting the structure of the implementation building block itself.

Figure 4.10 shows an example for a building block activity (C10 – CRM Central Master Data).

▼ C10		CRM Central Master Data	
• OPEN CONFIG GUIDE FOR BB C10	MANU	Open Configuration Guide for Building ...	
▼ 🗀 PERSONALIZATION OF MASTER DATA		Personalization of Master Data	
• /SMBCRM0/BP_0009_C10	ECAT	Personalization of Business Partners	
• /SMBCRM0/COMMPR01_0001_C10	ECAT	Personalization of Products	
▼ 🗀 DEFINING NUMBER RANGES - COMPETITORS		Defining Number Ranges - Competitors	
• /SMBCRM0/BUCF_0008_C10	ECAT	Defining Number Ranges - Competitors	
▶ 🗀 DEFINING GROUPINGS - COMPETITORS		Defining Groupings - Competitors	
▶ 🗀 CREATING COMPETITORS		Creating Competitors	
▶ 🗀 DETERMINING PRICING PROCEDURES		Determining Pricing Procedures	

Figure 4.10 Building Block Activity "CRM Central Master Data"

4.2.3 Rapid-Deployment Solution Bill of Materials

Assets combination This section lists the different assets that together make up a rapid-deployment solution. For simplicity, we list the master bill of material. Individual rapid-deployment solutions may deliver differently—in particular, there is a tailored bill of material for Industry & Line of Business rapid-deployment solutions and other tailored bill of material for Analytics and Technology rapid-deployment solutions, respectively.

Clusters The rapid-deployment solutions bill of materials is divided into four major parts called *clusters*. A cluster usually consists of multiple deliverable groups. Each deliverable group consists of multiple knowledge assets, in this context called "deliverables."

The rapid-deployment solution's BOM shown in the following four tables is a subset of the asset type inventory introduced in Section 4.1.3. Some of the documents in the BOM are—depending on their nature— only available for SAP Partners or for SAP consulting and not for customers.

The software cluster shown in Table 4.1 describes the required software products (what has to be installed) and software licenses (what has to be purchased) for the individual rapid-deployment solution.

Software cluster

Cluster	Deliverable Group	Deliverable	Description
Software			
	Software and software licenses		
		License material numbers	A definition of the exact licenses that a customer receives as part of the solution.

Table 4.1 Master BOM of a Rapid-Deployment Solution—Software Cluster

The implementation content cluster shown in Table 4.2 lists all the documents, scripts, and data files that support the project teams in describing and implementing the business scope of the rapid-deployment solution.

Implementation content cluster

Cluster	Deliverable Group	Deliverable	Description
Implementation content			
	Manual configuration		
		Building-block configuration guides	A document describing in detail how to configure the system manually.
		Building-block descriptions	A description of the content and functions covered by the building block.
		Content library	A single webpage that lists the building block ID numbers and the building block titles.

Table 4.2 Master BOM of a Rapid-Deployment Solution Implementation Content Cluster

Cluster	Deliverable Group	Deliverable	Description
		Manual activation and configuration page	A generated page that groups together information about manual activation and configuration.
		Prerequisites matrix	A spreadsheet that lists the required building blocks and their implementation sequence.
	Master data		
		Master data overview	A table to quickly understand the sample master data shipped in the package.
		Master data procedures	A document that describes how to create master data, supported by the preconfigured content.
		Organizational data overview	A table to quickly understand the organization model data shipped in the package and how it relates to the software.
	Preconfiguration		
		Activation content	All content that is used to activate a solution in a customer's landscape. The exact technology used depends on the solution.
		Automated activation page	A generated page that groups together information about activation with solution builder for SAP Best Practices.
		Forms overview	A list of forms and their technical names.

Table 4.2 Master BOM of a Rapid-Deployment Solution Implementation Content Cluster (Cont.)

Cluster	Deliverable Group	Deliverable	Description
		Online reference system for a rapid-deployment solution	A preconfigured system for support and for evaluating the solution.
		Solution scope file	A definition of the solution scope as an XML file that is used to activate preconfiguration in the target system with SAP Best Practices solution builder.
	Solution installation		
		Quick guide for package implementation	A procedure to implement the complete package scope after the technical landscape has been defined according to the software requirements.
		SAP Note	A compilation of additional information or corrections for the installation and documentation of the solution.
		Software requirements	A table that lists all software required to implement and run the solution.
	Solution scope		
		Business process documentation page	A generated page that groups together information about the business processes in the solution.
		Function list	A list of the transactions in the scope.

Table 4.2 Master BOM of a Rapid-Deployment Solution Implementation Content Cluster (Cont.)

Cluster	Deliverable Group	Deliverable	Description
		Process diagrams	A presentation that contains diagrams to describe the sequence of steps in each scope item in the solution.
		Release note for consultants	A document to describe changes to the solution, in relation to an earlier solution.
		Scope-item descriptions	A document describing the business context and process flow of each business process or key feature.
Template in SAP Solution Manager			
		SAP Solution Manager template	A container for the implementation content for one or more solutions in an area.
		SAP Solution Manager template description	A list of the solutions that are in the template, and any dependencies within each solution.
Training materials			
		Business process documentation	A detailed procedure that describes each business process as it is realized in the software.

Table 4.2 Master BOM of a Rapid-Deployment Solution Implementation Content Cluster (Cont.)

Services cluster The services cluster shown in Table 4.3 focusses on the accelerators for the project teams to provide the (fix price) implementation service for the rapid-deployment solution, the project methodology, and the service definition/scope description.

Cluster	Deliverable Group	Deliverable	Description
Service			
	Project accelerators		
		Consultant delivery guide	A presentation to get started with the implementation of the solution, clarifying SAP and customer activities.
		Pre-delivery requirements and checklist	A list that is used to confirm that the required preparations have been made by the customer and by the SAP delivery team.
		Qualification questionnaire	A set of questions to help the prospect to decide if the solution is suitable for them.
		Scope document	A definition of the package, used to understand the agreed scope and as the basis for handling changes to it.
		Scoping questionnaire and options list	A questionnaire used in workshops to capture data about the customer's business processes and reporting, to be used for the implementation.
		Statement of work	A document that describes the work that SAP delivers in an implementation project for the solution, and also any aspects that a customer must honor.
		Test plans and scripts	A set of tests to be performed on the implemented solution as part of the standard services.

Table 4.3 Master BOM of a Rapid-Deployment Solutions Services Cluster

Cluster	Deliverable Group	Deliverable	Description
		WBS, schedule, and effort estimation	A decomposition of the work to be done by the project team to complete the project objectives.
	Project methodology		
		Step-by-step guide	A standardized sequence of activities for the rapid deployment of the solution, with assets to support these activities.
		Step-by-step guide (service enablement)	A standardized sequence of activities for the rapid deployment of the solution, with assets to support these activities. Includes service-enablement assets.
	Service definition		
		Master service description	A document that defines the fixed-price services for the solution.
		Service one-page slide	An at-a-glance overview of the solution and service, tailored for sales roles.
		Portfolio overview session	A short set of slides covering business case information, and delivered approximately six weeks prior to RTC as part of an overall portfolio session.
		Sales guide	An overview of the solution, with all relevant information required to sell it.
		Sales one-pager	An at-a-glance overview of the solution and service, tailored for sales roles.

Table 4.3 Master BOM of a Rapid-Deployment Solutions Services Cluster (Cont.)

Finally, the core enablement cluster shown in Table 4.4 contains the documents that support customers, partners, and SAP sales representatives in understanding the content of the rapid-deployment solution and selling the solution.

Core Enablement cluster

Cluster	Deliverable Group	Deliverable	Description
Core enablement			
	Discover the solution		
		Production demo including storyboard	An online demo, created as a "role" in the demo landscape.
		Scope-item recordings	A simulation of each or selected business process or capability in a solution.
		Solution details	A detailed presentation that covers the scope of the solution and the service.
		Solution profile	A detailed definition of a solution and its scope items, using a standardized, modular, and reusable structure.
		Solution summary	An overview presentation that covers the scope of the solution and the service, and business benefits.
	Sell the solution		
		Knowledge-transfer sessions	A recording that covers the scope of the solution and includes a possibility for self-assessment.
		Portfolio overview session	A short set of slides covering business case information, and delivered approximately six weeks prior to RTC, as part of an overall portfolio session.

Table 4.4 Master BOM of a Rapid-Deployment Solution Core Enablement Cluster

Cluster	Deliverable Group	Deliverable	Description
		Sales guide	An overview of the solution, with all relevant information required to sell it.
		Sales one-pager	An at-a-glance overview of the solution and service, tailored for sales roles.

Table 4.4 Master BOM of a Rapid-Deployment Solution Core Enablement Cluster

4.2.4 Layered Architecture of Implementation Building Blocks

The implementation building blocks introduced in Section 4.2.1 are organized following a layered approach as depicted in Figure 4.11 for SAP ERP. They are defined according to content architecture principles by incremental design and forming content layers. For other products like SAP SRM or Transportation Management, it looks similar. You can see that we defined "layers" (groups of building blocks) which are the common prerequisite for all kinds of processes (all processes have a least the core layer as prerequisite).

Incremental content design

The incremental content design helps to avoid any kind of content redundancies. This helps avoid making the same settings on different levels of the architecture. A specific configuration setting should be unique within this architecture. This incremental design is arranged from generic to specific in order to assure a close integration between all content of the content architecture.

Layers

Within a specific architecture (for a product version) we have different layers: Layers simplify and speed up the assembly of a building block. Layers are formed by building blocks that represent the common prerequisite for a group of more complex building blocks and can be regarded as building blocks by themselves.

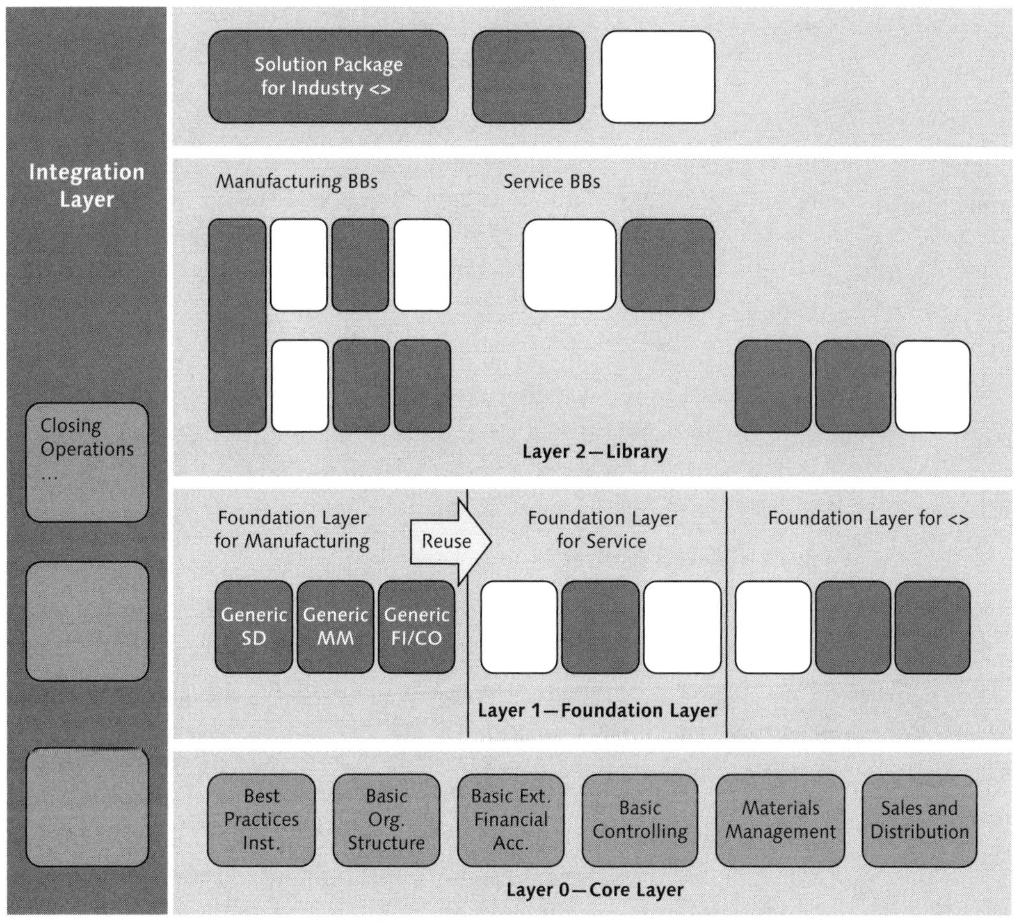

Figure 4.11 Layered Content Architecture of Implementation Building Blocks

While defining layers, you have to find the balance and compromise between:

▶ Settings in generic building blocks, which might not be relevant for at least some of the more specific building blocks on a higher level.

▶ Ease of use and handling of layer constructions.

All processes or scope items contain all required building blocks of subordinate layers and building blocks with specific settings.

4.3   Rapid-Deployment Solution Domain in the Context of SAP Taxonomy

As outlined in Chapter 2, it is essential for the Simplified Rapid-Deployment Experience that the rapid-deployment solution content is connected with the content of the other domains such as solutions go-to-market content, the SAP software products, i.e., the installable units, and the software license materials that are required for use of the underlying software of a rapid-deployment solution. The content architecture defines how the different pieces fit together.

In this section we will first introduce how the other areas are linked with the rapid-deployment solutions meta model shown in previously Figure 4.9 and will also define the key connected entities in detail.

4.3.1   Meta Model

Figure 4.12 shows how the rapid-deployment solutions entities relate to the solutions go-to-market, products, and license entities.

Solution capability Each scope item of a rapid-deployment solutions package is related to a solution capability. A solution capability describes a certain functional scope of a solution. It is the core element of content displayed in the SAP Solution Explorer (see Figure 2.22 in Chapter 2 for an example of a solution capability in SAP Solution Explorer). This link between the solution capability in the solutions go-to-market content and the scope item in the implementation content is the key relationship that is used by the SAP Solution Configurator in order to determine the recommendation of SAP Best Practice processes or implementation content in general for a certain solution scope that has been defined based on selected solution capabilities from an industry value map (see Chapter 2, Section 2.3).

An industry value map is composed out of business priorities, which are composed out of end-to-end solutions. As stated in Section 2.3, end-to-end solutions combine several interconnected solution capabilities

Rapid-deployment solutions refer to the underlying software product versions that have to be installed to realize the solution. They also reference the software licenses that a customer has to purchase to execute the underlying software scope.

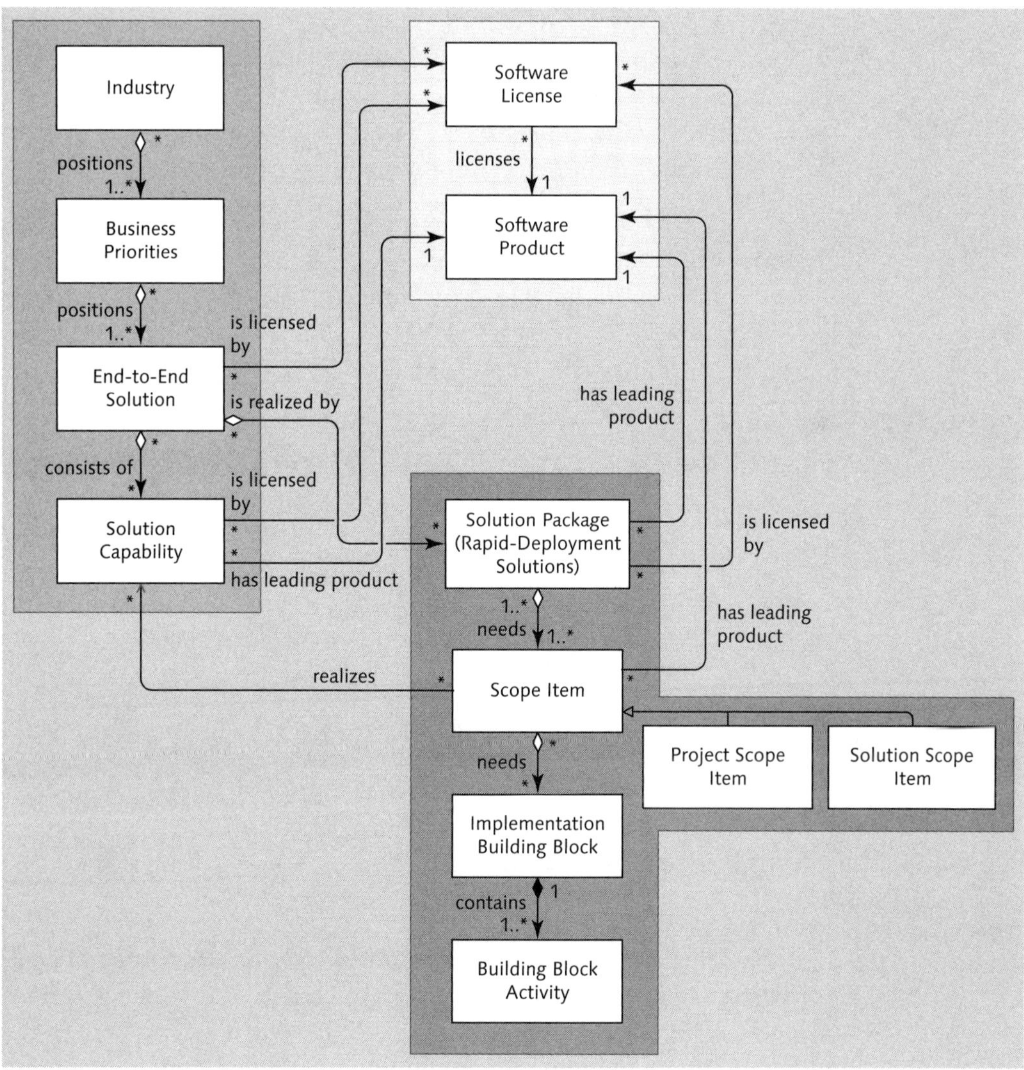

Figure 4.12 Meta Model Excerpt of a Rapid-Deployment Solution and its Key Related Areas

4.3.2 Definition of Key Entities

In this section we will provide the definitions of the new entities of the meta model shown in Figure 4.12.

Business Priority

A business priority is a thought leadership topic, or an area that the management team of a company cares about. It is used as a go-to-market and positioning instrument to sketch out to SAP customers the priority topics that SAP identifies and supports in a certain *industry* or *area of responsibility*.

Combined in an industry value map, several business priorities tell the story of the industry's value chain. Strategic business priorities are very closely connected to strategic high-level outcomes like revenue, profit, cost, asset utilization, market share, growth, risk, compliance, liquidity, brand value, or customer satisfaction.

> **Definition**
>
> A business priority is a collection of solutions addressing an industry priority topic. It highlights SAP's competitive advantage by demonstrating their ability to provide a solution addressing a thought-leadership topic via a combination of several of its end-to-end solutions.

Description

Ideally, a business priority spans across multiple areas of responsibility, and SAP's ability to provide this is one of the company's key differentiators in the market.

Strategic vs. supporting business priorities

We distinguish between strategic business priorities and supporting/enabling business priorities.

- Strategic business priorities are industry-specific. Their cut and naming is defined by a certain industry. In certain cases, business priorities might be shared between similar industries, but this is not the norm. In value maps, strategic business priorities are visualized vertically.

- Supporting/enabling business priorities are used throughout industries. They are defined for supporting areas of responsibility, such as human resources or finance. Their content and naming can differ slightly from industry to industry, but overall they match. In value maps, supporting/enabling business priorities are visualized horizontally.

Example

The value map for consumer products contains five strategic and two supporting/enabling business priorities as outlined in Figure 4.13.

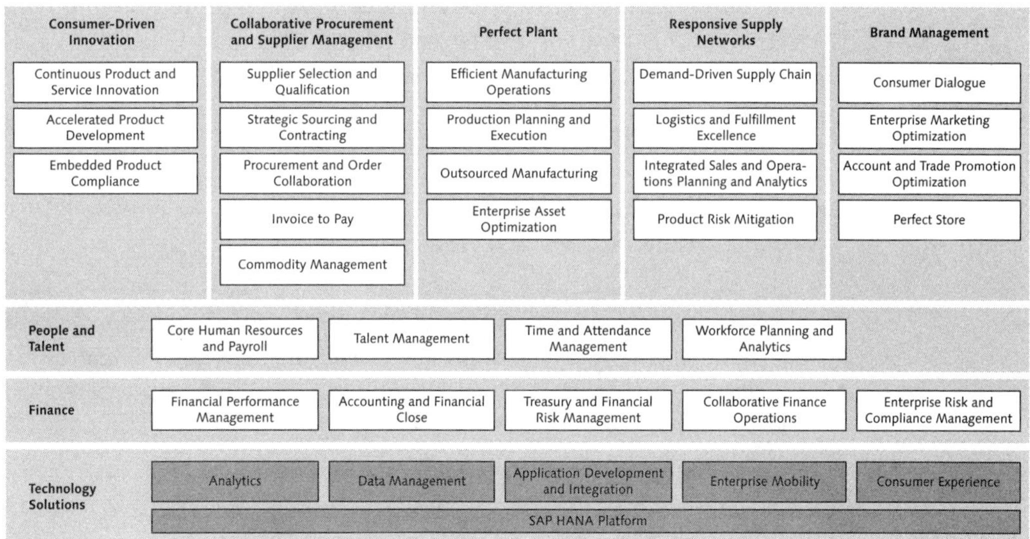

Figure 4.13 Example Industry Value Map: Consumer Products

Strategic business priorities include:

▶ Consumer-driven innovation

▶ Collaborative procurement and supplier management

▶ Perfect plant

▶ Responsive supply networks

▶ Brand management

Supporting/enabling business priorities include:

▶ People and talent (defined by human resources area of responsibility HR and refined for the industry)

▶ Finance (defined by area of responsibility FIN and refined for the industry)

End-to-End Solution

Business and technology

An end-to-end solution is an integrated end-to-end business and technology scope for one or more industries. It contributes strategically to a business priority of an industry's value chain. It is relevant for the customer, value-creating, and implementable via multiple solution capabilities.

It is used as a go-to-market and positioning instrument that allows SAP to sketch out the end-to-end business and technology scope that the company identifies and supports via its products. It is positioned mostly within a certain industry and via a certain business priority.

> **Definition**
>
> An end-to-end solution is a predefined combination of solution capabilities working together to realize a broad functional scope addressing business challenges, typically across areas of responsibility.

Examples

Figure 4.14 shows the Promotion Optimization end-to-end solution in SAP Solution Explorer.

93 solutions

The consumer products industry knows 93 end-to-end solutions, amongst them:

▶ Operational Risk Management

▶ Commodity Management

▶ Continuous Product and Service Innovation

▶ Embedded Product Compliance

▶ Multichannel Marketing Management (B2B/B2C)s

Solution Capability

Functional decomposition

The corporate taxonomy defines a hierarchy of capabilities, i.e., a functional decomposition that is used as the structure for the catalog of all SAP's solutions. On the third level of this function decomposition, the concrete solutions are represented by solution capabilities, each describing SAP's realization of a low-level business capability. For customers, they are key for finding out which part of the SAP offering is relevant to them as a starting point for implementation projects.

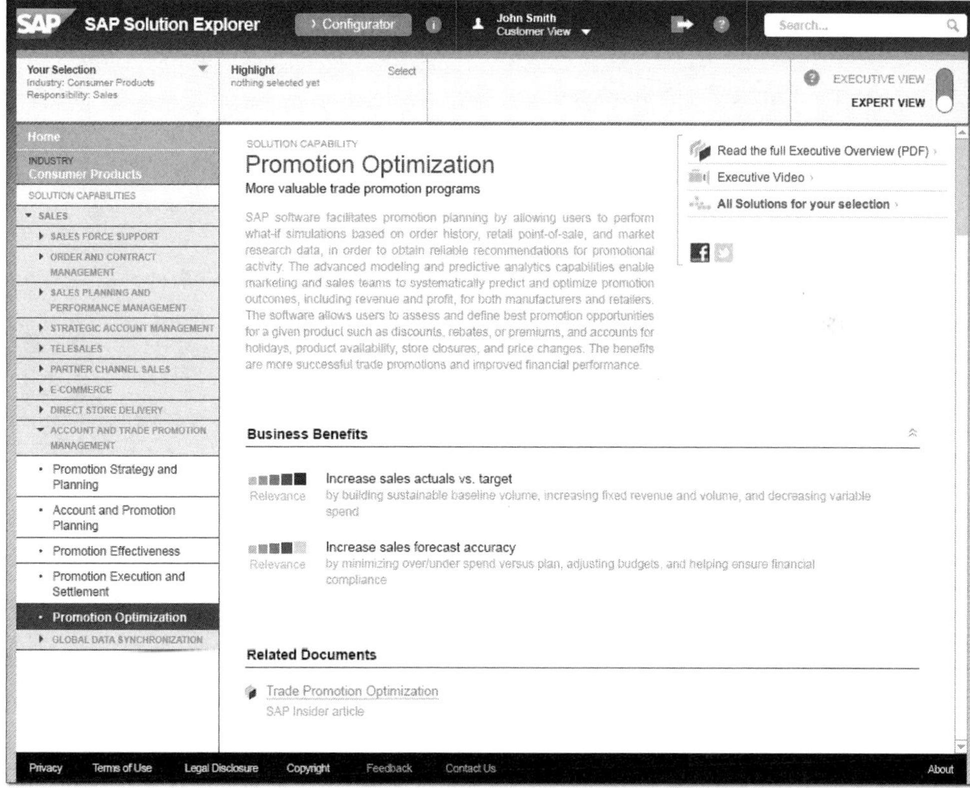

Figure 4.14 Example for End-to-End Solution: Promotion Optimization

<table><tr><td>**Definition**</td></tr><tr><td>A solution capability is a product-specific realization and deployment alternative, which offers a focused functional scope to address a specific business challenge within an area of responsibility.</td></tr></table>

Examples

Following are a few examples of solution capabilities:

- Development and Handover of Workforce Action Plans
- Accounts Payable (SAP ERP)

- Health and Safety Management
- Lean Planning
- Perfect Order Processing (SAP ERP)
- Perfect Order Processing (SAP CRM)
- Spare Parts Management
- Physician Partner Management
- Command and Control Interoperability
- Sales and Logistics Planning
- Fulfillment for Subscriptions of Journals

Software Product Version

Definition

A software product version is a set of software component versions having a well-defined scope of functionality and made available as one release.

The software product version is the leading entity for the development, production, and delivery of the SAP software. It provides a certain scope of functionality to the customer and represents an installable unit, i.e., is an installable software package.

Software License Material

Definition

A License Material is a material master in SAP's productive system that is referenced in sales-order items when a customer buys SAP software.

The license material references the usage license that the customer has to purchase from SAP to be allowed to use the software. The software license is not identical to the product. The product references the installable unit (e.g., on DVD) that needs to be installed on a system in order to use the software.

Example

▸ 7011212: SAP Charging and Billing for Banking

▸ 7011643: SAP Multichannel Order Management

4.4 Assemble-to-Order Content Architecture Principles

In assemble-to-order software implementation projects, the project starts with pieces of already running pre-integrated solutions combined and extended to obtain the specific solution the customer needs. In contrast to usual consulting projects, assemble-to-order projects do *not* start with an extensive business blueprint, a transformation into requirements on a blank sheet of paper followed by a mapping of these requirements to features of the software application. Instead the scope of (usually) multiple rapid-deployment solutions is combined to match the scope of the customer initiative as closely as possible. We introduced this concept briefly in Chapter 2, Section 2.4.

This section will introduce the content architecture principles of the assemble-to-order approach.

The key principles in a nutshell are:

Key principles

1. The key element for assembly is the scope item. The rapid-deployment solution itself represents the go-to-market hull around a couple of scope items. The scope items—usually representing best-practice business processes—are the core, reusable elements for assembly of a customer project best-practice scope.

2. During the assembly process, the different elements of a rapid-deployment solution like pre-configuration content, scope, and business process descriptions, WBS, etc., have to be compiled from their respective parts for the individual scope items. To ease this process for the individual projects, the rapid-deployment solutions knowledge documents are primarily structured on scope item granularity.

4.4.1 Structure Content Around Scope Items

In all the phases (bid, implementation, handover to support) structuring content at the granularity of scope items provides benefits, which we'll discuss in the following subsections.

Bid Phase

In the *bid phase* of a implementation service (the bid for the implementation project—not the software) a bid manager and a solution architect compose high-level solution to the needs of the customer by using as much packaged content as possible to reduce the risk and the cost of the project. As proven by the success of SAP Business All-In-One for small and mid-size companies, the right granularity to initially discuss the needs of the customers are the scope items (= the best practice processes).

Implementation Phase

In the *implementation phase* the consultants structure their work around the solution scope items. Every scope item (process or other piece of functionality) that is part of the productive system has to be discussed with the customer key users. The process details have to be configured, the process has to be tested with master data from the customer, errors have to be corrected, and key users have to be trained, followed by the execution of the final acceptance test. The document collaboration therefore is very much about the same document (the detailed use-case description of the final functionality from user perspective = the BPD) in all those tasks. The current tasks in the WBS are a very good checklist for the project manager to ensure that he or she has not forgotten anything for the project.

Detriments Structuring projects in a different way is much less successful due to the following:

► Structuring around features and functions does not work at all, since the customer users do not understand what the final solution means for them.

- Structuring around long end-to-end process chains involves too many stakeholders at SAP and at the customer in the project, and is practically not feasible. You have to break it up in workable pieces (the scope items).

- Using full process models, which show all the potential flow possibilities the software provides, makes it incredibly hard for SAP to provide this content. Also, if it is provided for a certain area, it is hard for a customer to read and still leaves far too many options. It is much quicker to make one example as a proposal (the scope item) and provide all the details on how to use it at field- and value-level (the business-process documentation) and how to configure it at field- and value-level (the configuration guide). Customers and consultants can more quickly understand all their options if one working example is provided (rather than deriving the example out of an abstract description).

Handover to Support

The support (both from SAP and customer) needs a documented solution. This means activities that are essential to execute the implementation project (e.g., do a kick-off workshop) might be irrelevant for support, since they do not influence the productive solution. This means at a certain point in time a transformation from the project manager point of view (which tasks have to be done when—in the WBS) to the solution view (the scope item view) is needed to obtain a proper documentation for support.

Documented solution

4.4.2 Structuring Content around Scope Items

The different content elements of a rapid-deployment solution like tasks from a WBS, software license material, implementation building blocks, etc., are structured according to the granularity of scope items. Figure 4.15 shows an excerpt of a scope item map showing the relationships between the different scope items and the related pieces of knowledge documents indicated as colored dots. We'll discuss these in the following subsections.

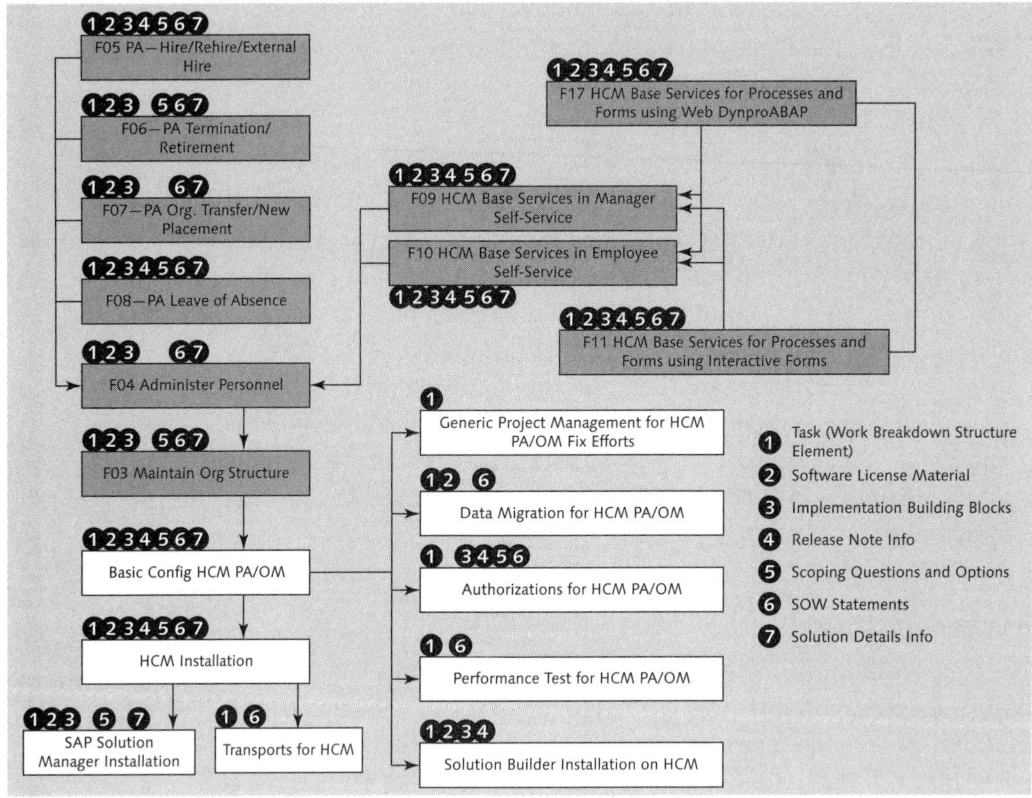

Figure 4.15 Excerpt of Scope Item Map for HCM Personnel Administration Rapid-Deployment Solution

Analyzing the Implementation Project Tasks

Content re-structure

The starting point of the content re-structuring is to bring the solution Scope items of the implementation content together with the tasks of the implementation project as documented in WBS. This means that the usual tasks, which have to do with an individual scope item (like scope clarification, implementation of the defined gaps, testing, end-user training) are defined per solution scope item and linked to it. The rest of the tasks are grouped into project scope items with the focus of what needs to be executed in the project, rather than how and when it needs to be done. The resulting project scope items are checked for duplicates across other content-production projects so that an overall consistent catalog of solution scope items and project scope items is created.

Linking Other Content to the Scope Items for Re-Use

Once the scope items are defined, the information that can be defined per scope item is split into modules per scope item and linked to the scope item. This means, for example, the detailed functional description, the corresponding scope statements for the statement of work, the information about needed license materials, the relevant scoping questions, the release information about changes compared to the last package version, and last but not least, the information about which implementation building blocks (and hence, which configuration guides) are needed to implement the scope item.

This approach ensures that in a given implementation project the relevant information can quickly be adapted to the exact solution scope of the project.

4.4.3   Creating a Network of Scope items

Assembling a customer project out of scope items requires a lot of know-how about the dependencies of the given scope items. Most of this know-how is not specific to the customer situation and therefore can be captured in advance to re-use it in every implementation project. Even though those dependencies seem to be trivial for an experienced application consultant within his or her area of expertise, they form a challenge for big projects, which cover multiple areas and in which no single person oversees the complete solution. To still be able to handle such projects, a formalized approach to capture these dependencies is needed.

So for example it might still be simple to know that setting a sell-from-stock scope item productive also requires basic stock-handling to be productive, which also includes physical inventory, since this is a legal requirement. However, that some scope items require some period end-closing scope items to be productive since they are mandatory to keep the data clean in the system, could be overseen by project teams. The scope item network helps to plan and cross-check the completeness of a customer project. It also helps to avoid missed opportunities, since it points to other scope items which are related, like the relevant reports, mobile and side panel applications, risks in access control and links to more advanced solution scope items based on specialized applications (for example, SAP Extended Warehouse Management).

We discuss the relationship types that are used in the following subsections.

Assemble-to-Order Relation

The assemble-to-order relation means that scope item A in the scope requires scope item B to have a working, productive solution. Note that this means that two scope items can be set up in a demo system completely independently from each other, but for a working business solution in the final productive system, one scope item requires the other to be active, too. So the A2O relation is not a technical relation of configuration settings, but a combined business and application logic relation for proper solution design. The A2O relation can occur between solution scope items, between project scope items, and from solution scope items to project scope items. With regard to Boolean logic, mainly two cases occur: A scope item requires all other scope items (AND) or it requires at least one of a group of other scope items. The A2O relation comes with two flavors: The integration between the scope item and the required scope item is:

1. Covered by the software or
2. Covered by the software *and* supported out-of-the-box and tested by the best practice content

This ensures the correct planning of efforts in the implementation project.

Flow Relation

The flow relation means that two scope items are integrated from a process or data-flow perspective. The flow relation can only occur between solution scope items. To avoid exploding complexity of relations, it makes the most sense to document the (weaker) flow relation only in cases where there is no (stronger) A2O relation between the two solution scope items already (no matter in which direction). With this convention, the flow relation can be read as follows: There is a process or data flow from scope item A to scope item B, but A is optional for B and vice versa.

4.5 Summary

In this chapter, we took a deep dive into the topic of content architecture, which provides the foundation for rapid-deployment solutions. After introducing content architecture in general, we discussed details of the rapid-deployment solutions content architecture and showed how the rapid-deployment solutions domain integrates into the overall picture of SAP's corporate taxonomy. A deep dive into the content architecture principles of assemble-to-order concludes this chapter.

This chapter will help you understand how to discover which solutions SAP offers; how to evaluate the solution's capabilities; how to define the scope of your implementation by mapping your business requirements to the solution's capabilities and keep track of gaps; and finally, how to actually go about rapidly implementing the solution.

5   Tools for an End-to-End Experience: From Discovery to a Running System

As you've already seen in previous chapters, customers who have benefitted from SAP Rapid Deployment solutions and the assemble-to-order approach have often leveraged the best practices contained therein as the core of their implementation. They have also implemented some additional functional scope provided by the SAP software but not covered by the scope of the rapid-deployment solutions. Since SAP expects this to be the norm, they had to find an approach to provide answers for customers to discover the overall capabilities of the SAP solutions, not just the scope covered by rapid-deployment solution best practices.

SAP has done this by providing methodology and tools for exploring, scoping, and implementing, which lead you from an overview of all SAP solutions to those areas where you can profit from rapid-deployment solutions best practices and the assemble-to-order approach. Similarly, when scoping and implementing, the tools SAP provides allow you to scope and implement capabilities that are covered by rapid-deployment solutions best practices as well as those that are not.

Exploring, scoping, and implementing

In the following sections, we'll discuss the main methodologies and tools for exploring SAP's solution offerings, for configuring the scope to be implemented, and for rapidly implementing the solution.

5.1 Exploring SAP's Solutions with SAP Solution Explorer

SAP provides solutions to your business problems by providing software and services. As technology has advanced, so have the technical possibilities for providing solutions to business challenges, which means that now many products and technologies can be leveraged together to provide compelling solutions that were not possible before. For example, a comprehensive solution to a business challenge might include the core business system, along with mobile technology and advanced in-memory analytics and/or data warehousing products. Instead of explaining what their products can do, and letting you figure out how that helps solve your business challenges, SAP has defined solutions consisting of solution capabilities that address typical business challenges. SAP explains which of their rapid-deployment solutions, products, and services can be leveraged to implement these solutions and solution capabilities.

Explore solutions

The way in which you do this is through SAP Solution Explorer, which is a public website at *www.sap.com/solutionexplorer*. This site allows you to explore SAP's complete solution offering, navigate through the value maps to discover the strategic business priorities and solutions for your industry, benefit from executive brochures, videos, and success stories, and find which solutions are available and which software products need to be implemented to provide the solution to your business challenges. It will help you find what's relevant for your industry, for your area of responsibility (such as marketing, sales, finance, etc.) and for your technology needs.

Executive view/ catalog

Figure 5.1 shows the entry page of the SAP Solution Explorer. There are two ways of accessing the solutions to your needs: you can start with the *executive view*, which enables you to navigate through the value maps, illustrating the key business priorities and strategic solutions for your area of interest, or you can browse the complete catalog of solutions SAP offers based on your selection of industry, area of responsibility, and technology or business drivers to help you improve your business.

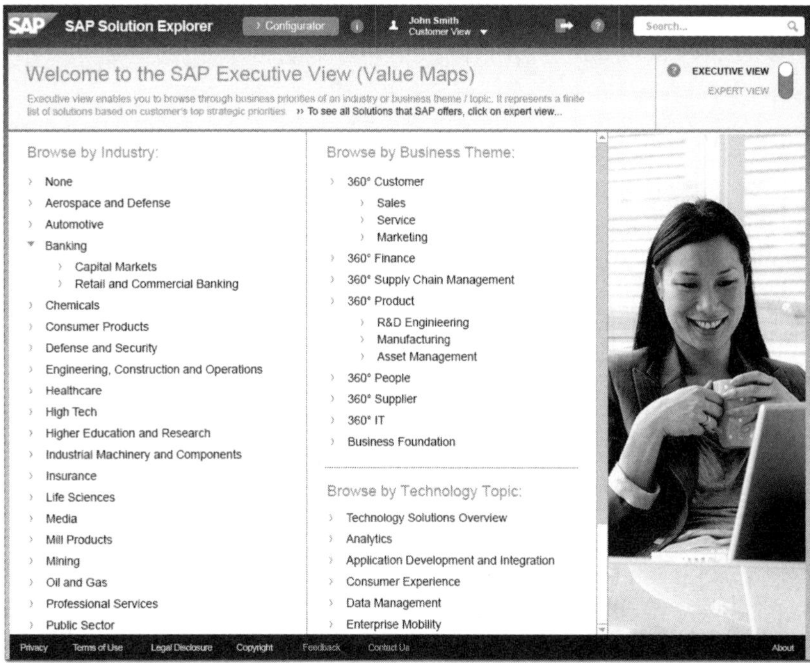

Figure 5.1 The SAP Solution Explorer Entry Page: Executive View

The next few sections give a more detailed overview of the SAP Solution Explorer:

▶ **Value maps**

Provide a business-value-oriented framework for telling a relevant, integrated solution story. They depict the most relevant business priorities (grey boxes) and solutions (blue boxes) for an industry or line of business. The value maps address challenges most companies are facing in their industry, and allow you to easily highlight innovations or drill down to more details, benefiting from a vast number of brochures, videos, customer stories, demos, and more.

▶ **Catalog of end-to-end solutions and solution capabilities**

Explains how to search, browse, and filter the catalog of end-to-end solutions and solution capabilities, and find solutions addressing selected business needs ("business drivers") or covering specific topics ("highlights"). This section also gives an overview of the kinds of information provided per solution capability, such as benefits, success stories, demos, available rapid-deployment solutions, software products, and services.

5.1.1 Value Maps

Due to SAP's close engagement with their many customers, they have a good understanding of the major challenges faced by businesses in each industry. *Value maps* highlight the areas where the biggest challenges exist for your industry, and show the most relevant end-to-end solutions provided by SAP for addressing these challenges. As Figure 5.2 shows, value maps are a simple depiction of the strategic value of SAP's solutions for industries and lines of business. They provide a framework for telling a relevant, integrated solution story.

At the value-map level, customers have access to a compelling set of executive brochures and videos. Within each value map, you can highlight specific innovations or technologies, such as mobile, cloud, and SAP HANA. By clicking on each of the boxes in the value map, you can navigate into details of the business priorities (grey boxes) or solutions (blue/green boxes).

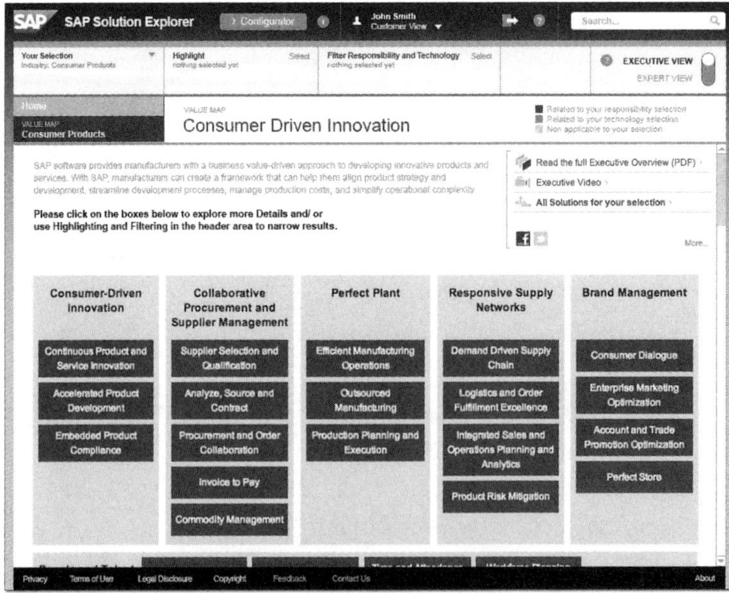

Figure 5.2 Value Map for the High-Tech Industry

Note that the value map does not show all end-to-end solutions for a given industry, but only those most relevant for the industry's current business priorities.

Figure 5.3 shows an example of selecting the end-to-end solution ACCOUNT AND TRADE PROMOTION OPTIMIZATION and then selecting the Solution Capability PROMOTION OPTIMIZATION. On the left you see where you are in the value map structure; i.e., that you are in the value map for CONSUMER PRODUCTS, the business priority BRAND MANAGEMENT, and the end-to-end solution ACCOUNT AND TRADE PROMOTION. Below this on the left you see the list of solution capabilities that are included in the end-to-end solution, and the details of the selected solution capability PROMOTION OPTIMIZATION are shown on the right. Scrolling down will give you access to all the information.

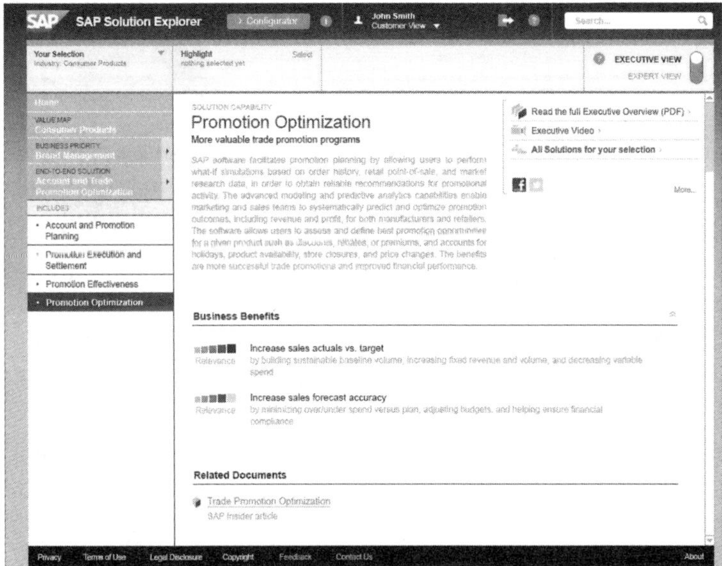

Figure 5.3 Information Regarding a Solution Capability After Drilling Down from the Value Map

5.1.2 Catalog of End-to-End Solutions and Solution Capabilities

With SAP Solution Explorer, you have access to all the solutions and solution capabilities available for your industry, area of responsibility, or for your technology needs. You have two easy ways to find what you are interested in: using search, or by browsing the catalog in the expert view. You can toggle between Executive View and Expert View on the top right of the SAP Solution Explorer entry screen. The default entry page for SAP Solution Explorer is the Executive View, as depicted in Figure 5.1. The Expert View entry page is depicted in Figure 5.4.

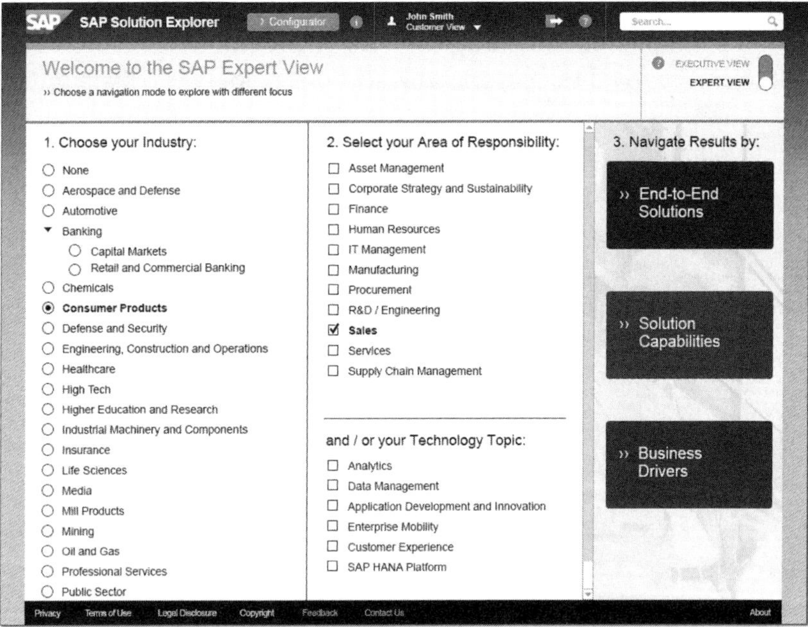

Figure 5.4 SAP Solution Explorer Entry Page: Expert View

Browse catalog

To browse the catalog, you need to select an industry, and then optionally your area of responsibility and/or the technology topic you are interested in. You can then navigate to all end-to-end solutions, directly to all solution capabilities or via business drivers, which allow you to select relevant business KPIs and then see which solution capabilities help you improve these KPIs.

> **Note**
>
> End-to-end solutions are a combination of solution capabilities that come together to solve business problems for customers, as well as support business priorities. In order to actually implement a solution, you will need to

select one or more solution capabilities. If you choose to navigate via the end-to-end solutions, and you select a solution, you will find the solution overview, customer stories, videos, demos, service offerings, and the list of solution capabilities and rapid-deployment solutions that make up the solution for you.

If you chose to navigate via the catalog of solution capabilities, you will find these grouped via responsibility and solution areas. Figure 5.5 shows a selection via the catalog of solution capabilities for the consumer products industry: on the left-hand side of the screen you can see the catalog structure, where the solution capabilities are grouped by solution areas. The details of the selected solution capability PROMOTION OPTIMIZATION are shown on the right; they are always the same, no matter which search or navigation path you used to get there.

Solution capability grouping

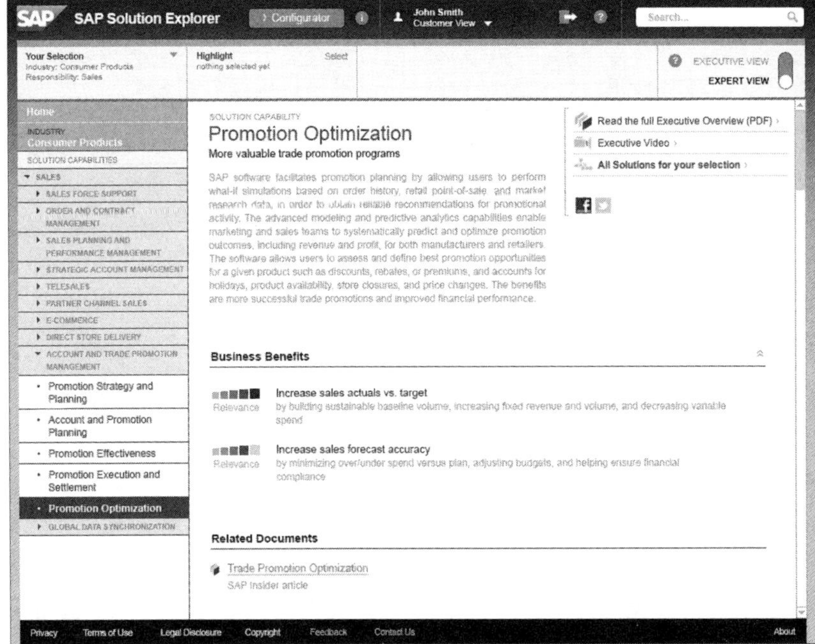

Figure 5.5 Expert View for Consumer Products via the Catalog of Solution Capabilities

Solution capability detailed information

By selecting a solution capability as shown in Figure 5.5, you will get the detailed information about the solution capability, amongst other things:

- What it provides to your business.
- The business value, depicted in the form of its relevance to typical business drivers. Examples for business drivers in sales and marketing are "Drive growth in market share" and "Increase up-selling and cross-selling."
- Related documents (brochures, videos, demos, success stories, etc.).
- Related products, i.e. a list of SAP products recommended to implement the solution.
- Related license materials.

Similarly, selecting a rapid-deployment solution will give you an overview of its benefits, related products, and what SAP provides with the whole solution.

5.2 Scoping Your Solution with the SAP Solution Configurator

The SAP Solution Configurator (Beta) allows you to scope your solution, i.e. map your business requirements to the available capabilities and services and capture gaps. We provide a simpler version for use by customers directly on the web, and a more advanced web version for SAP bid managers to help them put together assemble-to-order-based implementation project proposals together with the customer.

Document gaps

Since the SAP Solution Configurator stores your selections, you need to log on in order to access it. Your *www.sap.com* or Service Marketplace user and password can be used for this.

SME partners

Note that for partners in the small and midsize enterprise (SME) segment, we provide an SAP Solution Configurator for Business All-in-One, which allows partners to define their best-practice-based offering with their own branding. It does not cover all SAP solutions, because it has a very dedicated functionality for the SME space, and continues to be a valuable lead-generation tool in this area.

5.2.1   The SAP Solution Configurator for Customers

You enter the SAP Solution Configurator via SAP Solution Explorer, by clicking on the CONFIGURATOR button at the top of the page.

The SAP Solution Configurator gives you access to the same information about the solution offerings that is available in the SAP Solution Explorer, but allows you to select specific solution capabilities and scope items to include in the assemble-to-order implementation project, as shown in Figure 5.6. The left half of the screen shows the business scope which you have selected, using the solution capability catalog structure as used by the SAP Solution Explorer Expert View, i.e. grouping solution capabilities by responsibilities and then by solution areas. As shown in the figure, individual scope items can be selected for each solution capability.

Select capabilities/ scope items

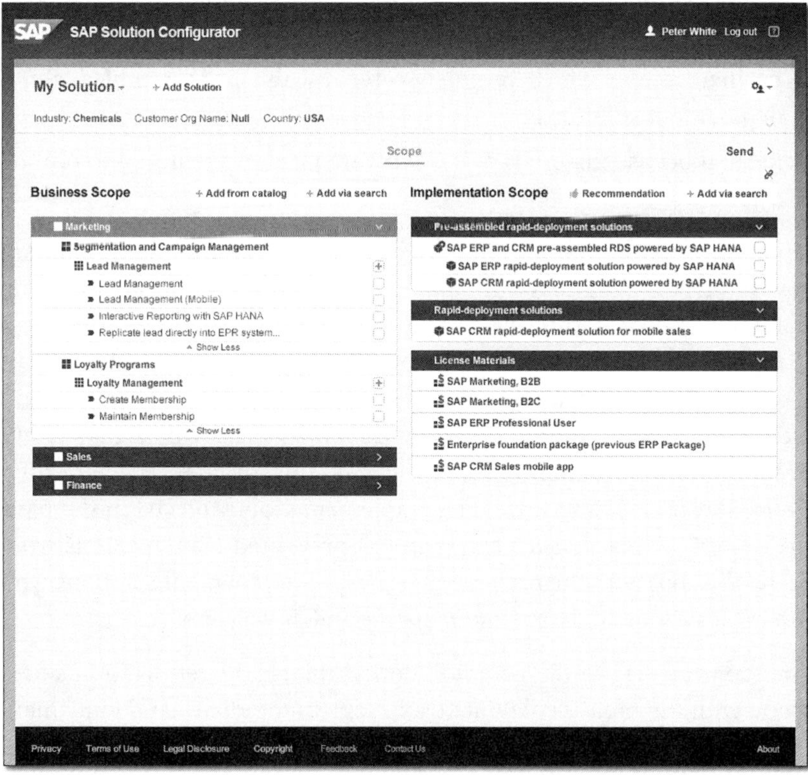

Figure 5.6 The SAP Solution Configurator for Customers

The example in the figure shows the following selection: the chosen responsibility is Marketing; below that the two solution areas Segmentation and Campaign Management and Loyalty Programs have been selected. Within Segmentation and Campaign Management, the solution capability Lead Management has been selected, and for this capability the four scope items Lead Management, Lead Management (mobile), Interactive Reporting with SAP HANA and Replicate Lead directly into ERP system have been selected.

Implementation scope

The right half of the screen shows the implementation scope required in order to implement the business scope depicted in the left half of the screen. The implementation scope consists of the following:

- Pre-assembled rapid-deployment solutions available in the SAP HANA Enterprise Cloud, which provides a test and evaluation environment at low cost for jump-starting your implementation
- Additional rapid-deployment solutions required in order to cover business scope which is not covered by the pre-assembled rapid-deployment solutions
- Related license materials of the software products required to run the solution

Reduce implementation cost/risk

Experience shows that the most effective way to reduce implementation cost and risk is to discuss the planned solution with your business stakeholders based on a running system that leverages those best practices that are closest to your requirements. Doing this significantly reduces the risk of misunderstandings—the business stakeholders can immediately see how the solution works, and identify areas where they might need changes or enhancements. Overall, this results in significantly faster, lower-cost, and lower-risk implementation projects. In the past, the cost of setting up such a system has prevented many projects from doing this, but with the pre-assembled, rapid-deployment solutions, you can get a system landscape immediately and at very low cost.

Scope items

The scope items are the common entity linking the left-hand business scope with the rapid-deployment solutions in the right-hand implementation scope: on the left you can choose the solution capabilities you need for your solution, and for each solution capability you can select which scope items you want to implement. On the right you see which pre-assembled rapid-deployment solutions and rapid-deployment solutions contain these scope items, and hence need to be used for the implementation project. Whenever you select one or more scope items in the business scope, you will see the corresponding scope items and rapid-deployment solutions highlighted in the implementation scope, so that you can more easily see how the two are related. This is depicted in Figure 5.7.

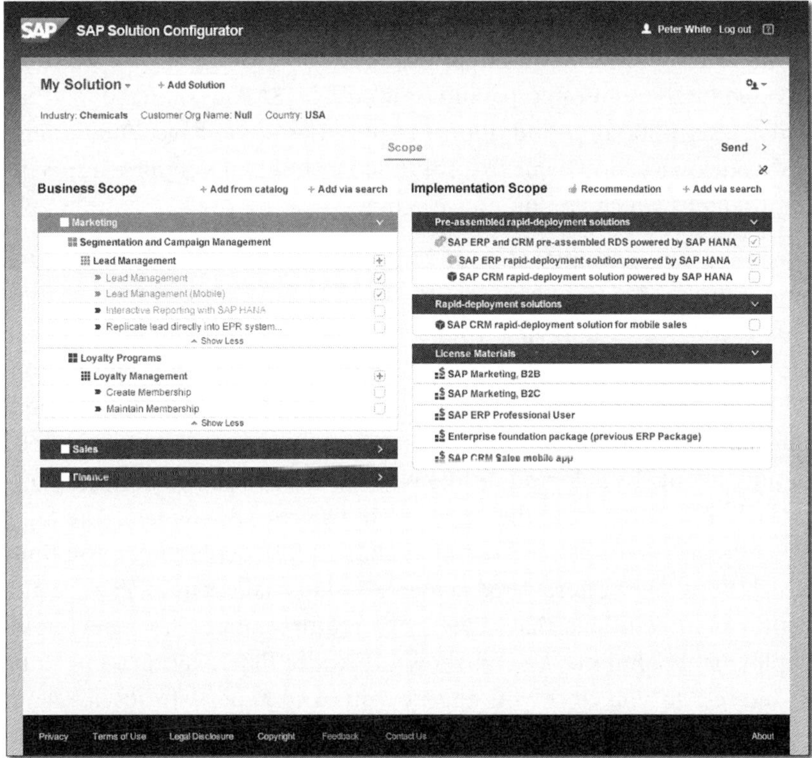

Figure 5.7 Highlighting Business Scope and Implementation Scope in the SAP Solution Configurator

To add solution capabilities and scope items to the business scope, you can either leverage a simple search over the solution capabilities and scope items by clicking on ADD VIA SEARCH, or click on ADD ITEMS FROM CATALOG, which brings you to the same solution capability catalog structure as used in the SAP Solution Explorer Expert View. Whenever you

Add capabilities/
items

add scope items to the business scope, the implementation scope will automatically be updated to include these scope items, i.e. to include the pre-assembled rapid-deployment solutions and rapid-deployment solutions which contain these scope items.

You can add scope items to the implementation scope directly via a simple search over rapid-deployment solutions, scope items, and engineered services.

Add requirement

When searching or browsing through the business scope in the configurator, you may feel that some of your requirements are not adequately covered by the solution capabilities offered by SAP. In this case, you can add a description of the additional requirements you have. You can also add your own scope items to a solution capability if you have a specific requirement which you do not see covered.

Review selection

Once you have completed your business scope definition, and added any engineered services you would like to implement to the implementation scope, you can review your selection using the same screen. Some scope items are contained in more than one rapid-deployment solution, which means that there can be occasions when more rapid-deployment solutions are listed in the implementation scope than you actually need to implement. To help you decide what to implement, click the RECOMMENDATION button on the right-hand half of the screen. The blue "thumbs up" icon appears next to those rapid-deployment solutions which best cover the selected scope, i.e. the smallest number of rapid-deployment solutions that cover your requirements. The other rapid-deployment solutions are still shown, because they may turn out to be of interest to you once you engage with SAP experts to discuss your planned scope in more detail. Figure 5.8 shows what a completed configuration looks like, including a recommended rapid-deployment solution, and in this case showing the screen for adding your own scope item to document a specific requirement which you do not see covered by the solution capability.

Contact SAP

The final step in the SAP Solution Configurator allows you to contact SAP. By clicking on SEND, you get to a screen to provide your contact details and send your configuration to SAP. You can indicate whether you would like to get a test and evaluation environment in the SAP HANA Enterprise Cloud, whether you would like to start with SAP Rapid Deployment solutions in your own data center, or whether you would like to discuss your custom solution with an SAP representative.

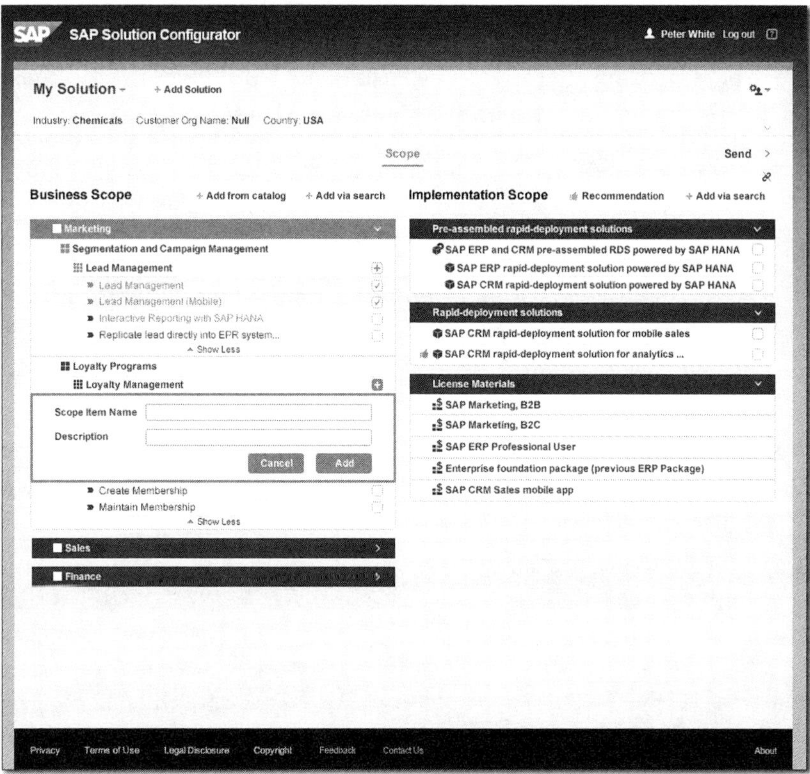

Figure 5.8 Review your Selection in the SAP Solution Configurator

This selection can serve as a starting point for a detailed discussion about the scope of the implementation project with SAP or the partner who will help you implement the solutions. For this discussion, we provide the SAP Solution Configurator for bidding teams, discussed in the next section, which allows your implementation partner to make a more detailed scope selection and gap analysis as a basis for their offer to implement the project using the assemble-to-order, rapid-deployment approach.

5.2.2 The SAP Solution Configurator for Bidding Teams

SAP has so-called "bidding teams" within global services, whose job it is to make an offer (a bid) on the cost of implementing your chosen solution. The SAP Solution Configurator for bidding teams leverages the same cloud infrastructure as the SAP Solution Explorer and SAP Solution Configurator for customers. It provides additional features that allow SAP's bidding teams to capture the customer's requirements, map them to available rapid-deployment solutions, and identify gaps.

Gaps — In the context of SAP Rapid Deployment solutions, there are two kinds of "gaps" that can be documented at a high level in the SAP Solution Configurator:

1. Features and functions supported by the underlying software, but not covered by the best-practice content; these can be implemented by consultants with good knowledge of the underlying products, but without the acceleration provided by the best-practice content.

2. Requirements that are not covered by SAP products, which require custom-specific development and/or integration with other non-SAP products.

> **Note**
>
> SAP customers who have purchased an SAP Premium Engagement support level (SAP Active Embedded Support or SAP MaxAttention) can also take advantage of the ICC (Innovation Control Center) service, which supports customers for the second type of gap by providing a recommended architecture for additional development and integration, and which leverages dashboards in SAP Solution Manager for managing the implementation. The ICC is explained in Section 6.2.

Using the SAP Solution Configurator for bidding teams, the bidding team is able to leverage aggregated effort figures from the work breakdown structure (WBS) that is provided with each rapid-deployment solution as a basis for making the project bid. They can also add new scope items and tasks to the WBS for activities related to the identified gaps. The team can define these tasks on an ad-hoc basis, or choose from a task repository filled with additional tasks based on experience from prior customer projects where the implemented scope went beyond the scope of the rapid-deployment solutions.

In other words: the bidding teams, and hence also SAP's customers, profit not only from the best-practice content provided with rapid-deployment solutions, but also from the so-called harvested content based on previous experience from selected customer projects. SAP provides the central infrastructure and tools to support both building the best-practice content for rapid-deployment solutions, and to support harvesting content from selected projects, so that they are available in the SAP Solution Configurator.

Harvested content

> **Note**
>
> Content harvesting is done by SAP global services by identifying customer implementation projects that go beyond the scope of rapid-deployment solutions in a way they consider to be worth sharing with future implementation projects. This could be the case for interesting industry-specific cases, or for functional enhancements in specific areas. The content is harvested by creating harvested scope items and task descriptions in the task repository for the relevant parts of the project. These harvested scope items and tasks follow the ASAP 8 methodology—the task repository enforces this by only allowing these scope items and tasks to be created with reference to a master template that follows the ASAP 8 methodology.

In order to help support bidding teams in accomplishing the above, the SAP Solution Configurator for bidding teams consists of two parts:

1. **Scope definition**

   A similar screen as provided by the SAP Solution Configurator for customers, but with additional features to allow a more detailed configuration.

2. **Assemble**

   A screen only for bidding teams, allowing them to assemble the work breakdown structure for the overall project.

The scope definition screen for bidding teams is shown in Figure 5.9. If a customer formulated a text for additional requirements before sending to SAP, the bidding team can see this text. Similarly, they see any customer-specific scope items which the customer created. In addition, dur-

Scope definition

ing the discussions with the customer, the bidding team can capture individual requirements, and for each such requirement assign a suitable business scope to the requirement. For example, the bidding team could capture in more detail a requirement stating that the customer needs to manage marketing campaigns, including some details on what the customer wants to achieve. Then, they can assign the suitable solution capabilities and scope items to this requirement as depicted in Figure 5.9. If they see that some aspects of the requirement are not covered by pre-defined scope items, the bidding team can manually add new scope items with a description.

Extend scope

As well as being able to manually add scope items, bidding teams can also extend the implementation scope on the right-hand side by selecting from pre-defined engineered services.

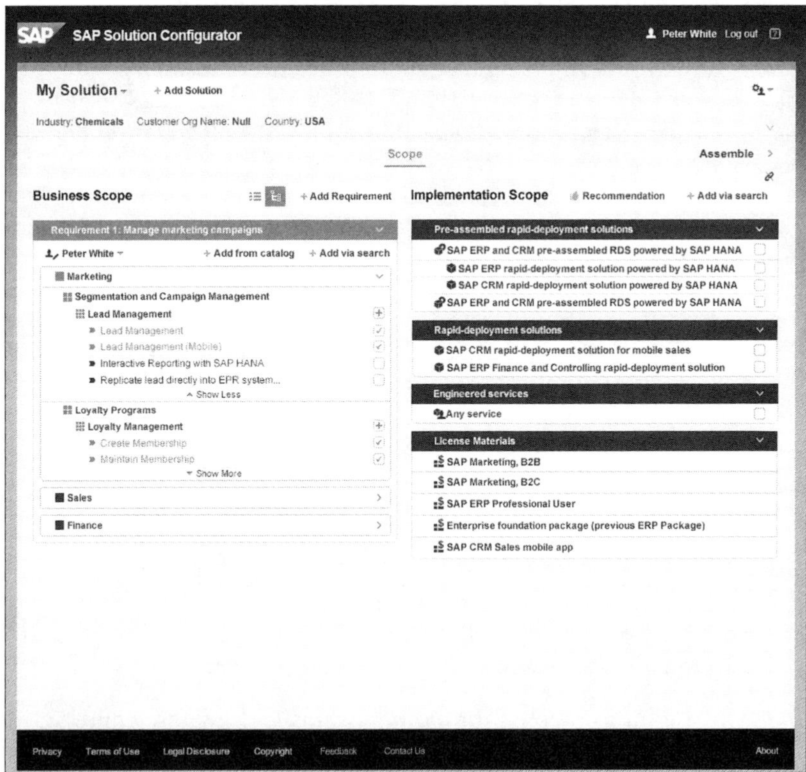

Figure 5.9 The SAP Solution Configurator for Bidding Teams: Scope Selection

Bidding team members get to the ASSEMBLE screen by selecting ASSEMBLE on the scope definition screen. The ASSEMBLE screen is depicted in Figure 5.10; it gives an overview of the effort required by SAP consultants as well as by customer project team members in order to implement the project. For SAP Rapid Deployment solutions, these efforts are not collected at scope item level, but an aggregate called *scope options* are used, which group a number of scope items together (typically those which only makes sense to be implemented together).

The scope of the pre-assembled rapid-deployment solutions, the rapid-deployment solutions, and the engineered services are completely determined by the implementation scope defined in the scope definition screen, and hence the assemble screen merely shows the efforts involved according to their WBSs. The actual assembly is done by adding design-based scope items to the project in order to cover gaps, i.e. customer requirements which are not covered by rapid-deployment services or by engineered services (see Figure 5.10).

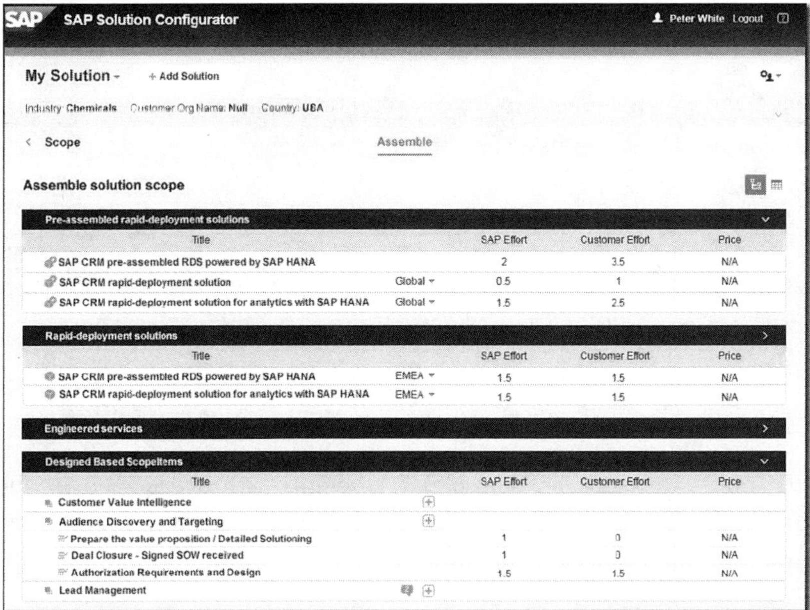

Figure 5.10 SAP Solution Configurator for Bidding Teams: Entry Screen for Assembling the Project's WBS

These can be added by searching for scope items and/or tasks in the task repository, and hence leveraging harvested content, as depicted in Figure 5.11, or they can be manually added.

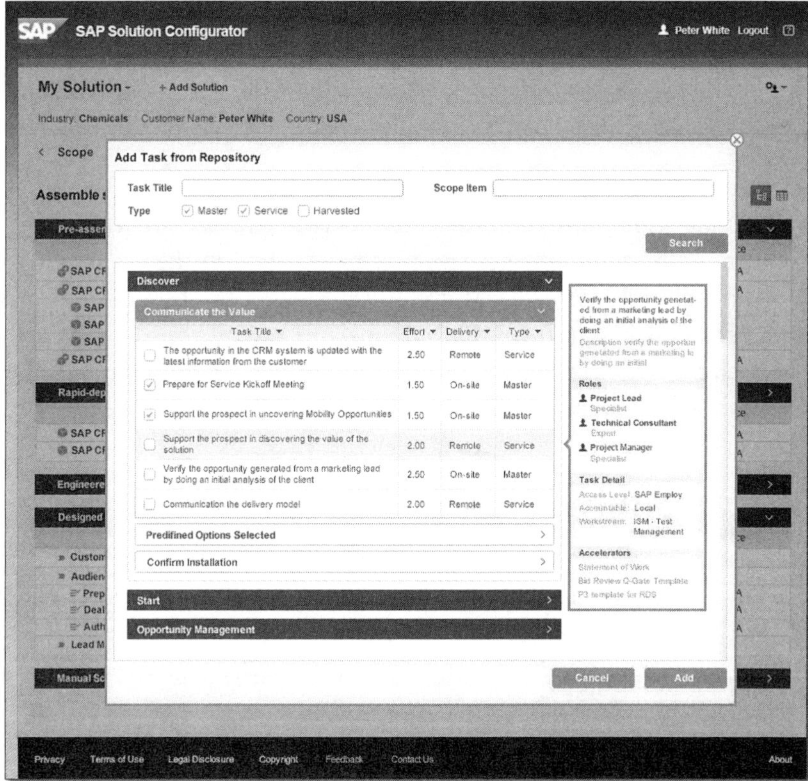

Figure 5.11 Adding Scope Items/Tasks from Task Repository to Project's WBS in SAP Solution Configurator for Bidding Teams

Bidding team members can toggle between the ASSEMBLE SOLUTION SCOPE view depicted in Figure 5.10 and an alternative view, the ASSEMBLY TABLE view, which summarizes the total effort required in the project for each rapid-deployment solution per role, for roles fulfilled by SAP, partner, and customer project members.

Roles in assembly table

Figure 5.12 shows an example of this assembly table view—the leftmost column contains the service provider (Customer or "Service Provider"; i.e., a consultant from SAP or from an implementation partner), the next columns cover the competency category (e.g., project manager, business support), the career level (e.g., specialist), deployment mode (e.g., on-site, offshore), and finally you see the total efforts for each role, in four columns: ONSITE, REMOTE, SERVICE PROVIDER, and CUSTOMER.

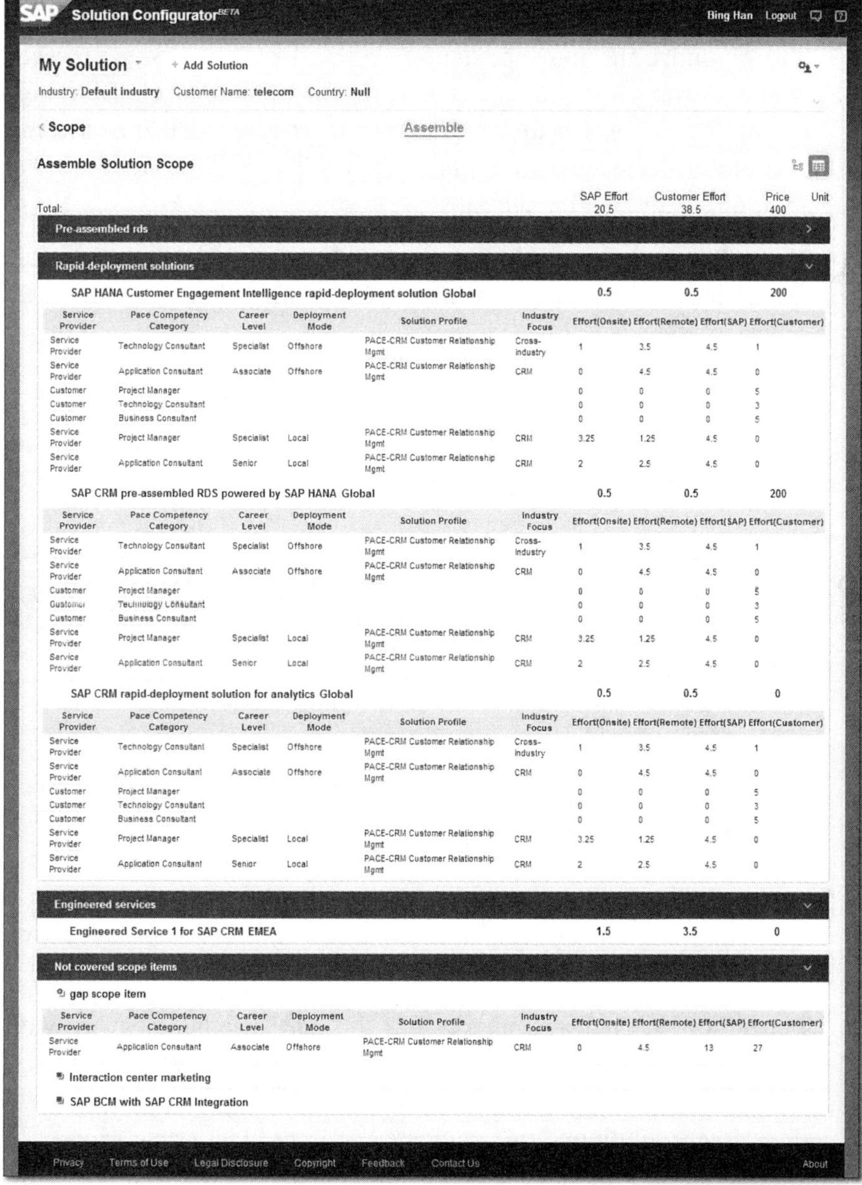

Figure 5.12 The Assembly Table View in SAP Solution Configurator for Bidding Teams

Once all the customer's requirements have been captured and mapped to scope items or gaps, the end result is a high-level, assemble-to-order-based WBS for the implementation project, which serves as the basis for the service bid. Following this approach helps the bid manager to maximize the amount of best-practice content used in the project, and therefore minimize the implementation cost and project risk for the customer. Customer requirements have been mapped to available best-practice scope items or to gaps, so that the project team that later comes in to do the implementation understands why the customer requested additional activities, i.e. the gaps.

The WBSs created by the bid managers follow the ASAP 8 methodology for efficient and effective implementation of SAP solutions, which is the subject of the next section.

5.3   ASAP Methodology for Implementing SAP Rapid Deployment Solutions

ASAP is the SAP implementation methodology that supports delivery of projects and services to SAP customers, with clear guidance to project teams on how to structure and run SAP implementation projects. In addition to guidance, it provides them with a set of templates, documents, samples, and guides that represent proven practices from thousands of successful SAP deployment projects.

The ASAP methodology has been continuously improved since it was introduced over 10 years ago. The latest version incorporates the current delivery-project innovations that arose from the use of rapid-deployment solutions, as well as from executing projects in an agile manner, using time-boxing and short iterations to quickly deliver project value to the customer.

Pre-defined models per customer | Depending on the customer's needs, the ASAP methodology provides the SAP deployment teams with pre-defined models that support delivery of a single rapid-deployment solution, delivery of multiple rapid-deployment solutions, and engineered services in an assemble-to-order project or delivery of traditional implementation projects using either an agile or a traditional approach.

SAP updates the ASAP methodology at least once a year in order to stay up to date with innovations such as rapid-deployment solutions and the assemble-to-order approach. In the next sections, we'll discuss the most recent version of ASAP (as of October 2013), and discuss its structure and methodology.

5.3.1 Overview and Benefits of ASAP 8

The latest release of the ASAP methodology (version 8) has been re-designed to better support the various lifecycles for delivery of SAP projects. The ASAP 8 framework supports both the deliverable-based view of the project that is favored by project managers, project sponsors, and leaders, and supports the view favored by consultants, key users, and project-team members—that is, the prescriptive level of tasks that detail what the team needs to do to deliver expected outcomes.

Support various lifecycles

The ASAP methodology tightly connects deliverables and prescriptive tasks in one hierarchy, the WBS. The benefits of ASAP to the SAP deployment teams are listed here:

ASAP benefits: deployment teams

- Enables consistency, reduces complexity, and increases quality by creating and delivering services on one common platform.

- Provides scalability—since ASAP has been re-designed to support all types of services delivery from solution deployments to large-scale implementations.

- Uses prescriptive and comprehensive methodology, including guided-work procedures for project teams, deliverables for project managers, and accelerators for all users.

- Incorporates innovative concepts such as agile deployment, application visualization, and cloud-based deployment.

- Uses a foundation of sound practices, such as the time-tested project quality gates for traditional and rapid-deployment solutions projects.

- Capitalizes on SAP knowledge capture and re-use by leveraging knowledge from thousands of SAP solutions implementations, and using prescriptive guides to extract knowledge related to current projects that can improve future projects.

Figure 5.13 shows the key characteristics of the ASAP methodology.

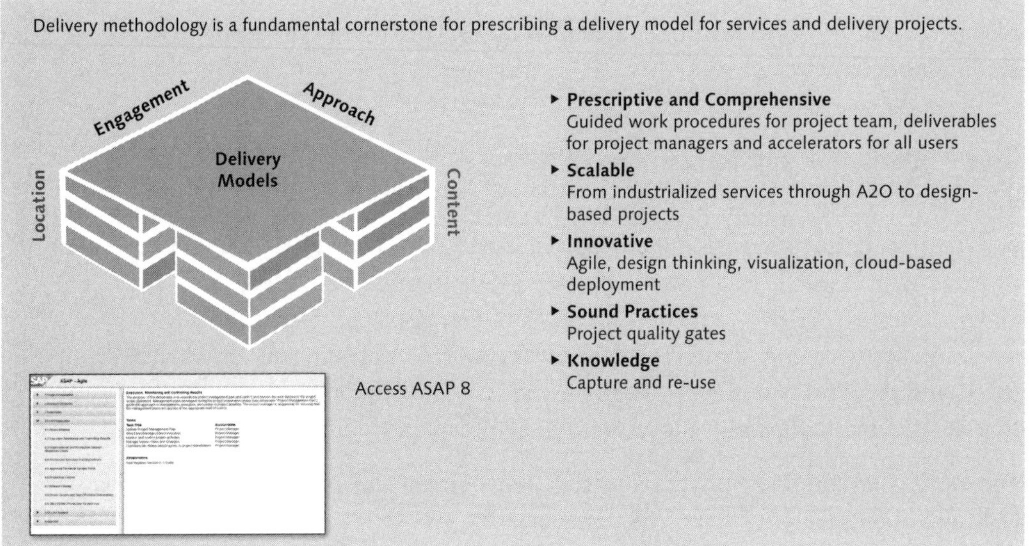

Figure 5.13 ASAP 8 Methodology: One Integrated Framework for Services and Project Delivery

5.3.2 The Taxonomy of the ASAP 8 Methodology

In order to establish a common framework for the design of projects and services, SAP fine-tuned the methodology content taxonomy in ASAP 8 to support both key target audiences of ASAP: project managers and project teams.

The ASAP methodology is delivered in a hierarchical structure that defines the structure of the project or service on the following levels (Figure 5.14):

▶ **Phases**
Six logical groups of deliverables that are delivered in a pre-defined time frame, sequenced in a specific order.

▶ **Deliverables**
The measurable outcome of work performed by the project team that contributes to the completion of project goals.

▶ **Tasks**

Activities and work performed by the project team to contribute to completion of a deliverable.

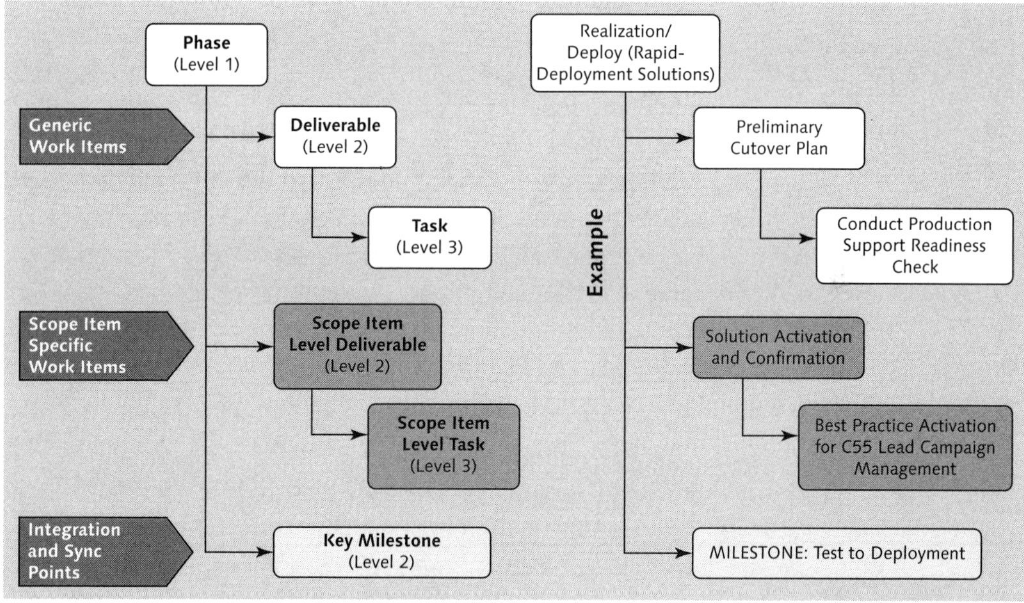

Figure 5.14 The ASAP 8 Methodology Hierarchy Structure

In addition to these hierarchical elements, the methodology contains WBS item definitions—the "what." For tasks, the hierarchy also defines the person accountable for completion of the task—the "who." Within the phases, deliverables, and tasks, the users of this hierarchy have access to accelerators—which are documents, templates, links, or tools that assist the team with completing the task—the "how." For example, in the deliverable for project scope, there is a description of the outcome template for capturing project scope and details about how to capture the project scope in a structured way.

As you will see later in Section 5.4.1, the Rapid Deployment Cockpit provides project teams with an overview of the WBS and access to the accelerators.

5.3.3 Agile Delivery with the ASAP Methodology

Agile/scrum

The ASAP methodology for implementation has been introduced in the book *Applying Real-World BPM in an SAP Environment* by Ann Rosenberg, et al. (SAP PRESS 2011). In this section, we will focus on the agile version of the ASAP methodology that brings the power and flexibility of the scrum approach to an SAP implementation. The agile approach, also known as the "scrum" approach, originated in software development. Now very popular, it has been applied successfully in other fields including implementation of packaged software. The essence of the agile approach is to avoid inefficiency by planning and executing small steps at a time, delivering tangible results with each step, gathering feedback, and then using that feedback as part of the input for the next step. This allows much faster reaction to new experiences or surprises, which every project faces, and also helps to avoid over-specifying a solution based on false assumptions.

The agile ASAP methodology for implementation is a content-rich, prescriptive methodology for efficiently, consistently, and thoroughly assisting customers with the implementation of SAP solutions across industries and environments. Built on SAP's experience in agile-implementation projects, agile ASAP provides content, tools, and best practices, for example:

- Agile project governance guide.
- Project backlog template.
- Key decisions document.
- Sprint and release planning template.
- Burn-down tracking template.

Agile ASAP is built on a solid foundation of the iterative implementation approach represented by the scrum methodology. The phases, deliverables, and tasks are designed consistently with the principles and practices from the scrum methodology.

ASAP phases for assemble-to-order

The six phases of ASAP for assemble-to-order projects (project preparation, scope validation, realization, final preparation, go-live support, and operate) and the way the methodology provides SAP deployment teams with support throughout the life cycle of an SAP solution, are highly consistent with the scrum approach. Underlying these phases is a series of value-delivery checks to make sure that the solution, as implemented, delivers the expected value. In agile ASAP, the project team has the ability to deliver the working solution in a series of short, time-boxed sprints that are grouped in one or more releases to the business. Figure 5.15 illustrates the agile ASAP approach of iterative, incremental delivery of projects.

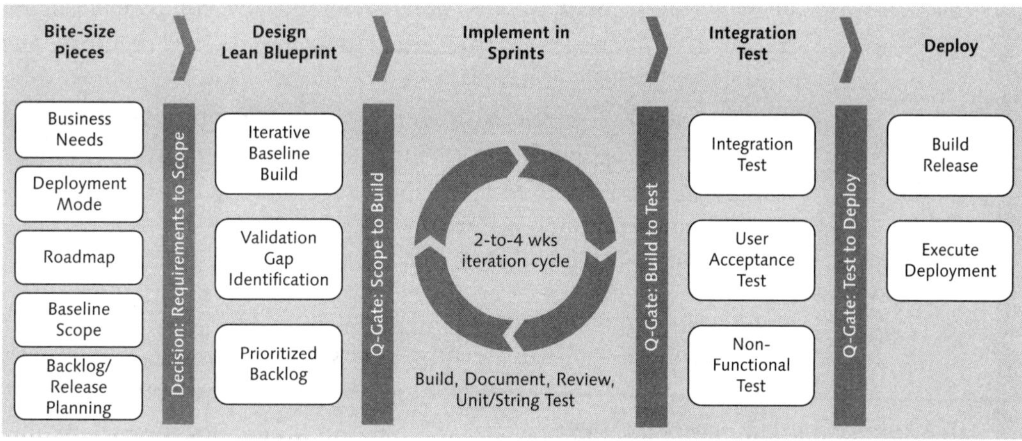

Figure 5.15 Agile ASAP Lifecycle Outline

In the first stage, the project team works closely with the product owner, who is typically one or more business users, to understand the business needs, define the project scope, and chart the implementation roadmap. These steps help clarify the expected business outcomes, so the team can better respond to business needs.

Business needs

Once the objectives and scope are well understood, the project team deploys the baseline build based on pre-built packages such as SAP Best Practice or SAP Rapid Deployment solutions. This is most easily done by using a pre-assembled rapid-deployment solution provided in the cloud. The project team uses this baseline build to demonstrate the standard functionality to business users and identify any outstanding or delta requirements not covered by the standard functionality. In situations where new requirements are identified, the project team uses application visualization techniques to document the requirement in an intuitive way.

Baseline build

Implement delta requirements

The implementation of the delta requirements is done in short, time-boxed iterations (sprints) during which the team designs the functionality, codes or configures, unit tests, and string tests the functions so they can be shown to the product owner at the end of the iteration and accepted. The team works only on a committed set of requirements in each sprint, which helps the team to focus on high-priority/high-value requirements first.

Iterations/release

The team runs through the iterations until they have completed a significant portion of functionality according to the pre-defined roadmap, and then they release the functionality to the business (upon approval from product owner). The release undergoes full-integration testing, user-acceptance testing, and non-functional tests like performance and load testing. As in traditional projects, the team simulates the cutover activities, readies the production data for the cutover, and conducts end-user training activities.

Upon release of the functionality to production, the project team continues to fulfill the remaining requirements for the next release in very much the same way as in the prior one. Figure 5.16 shows the process in a Gantt chart-like view.

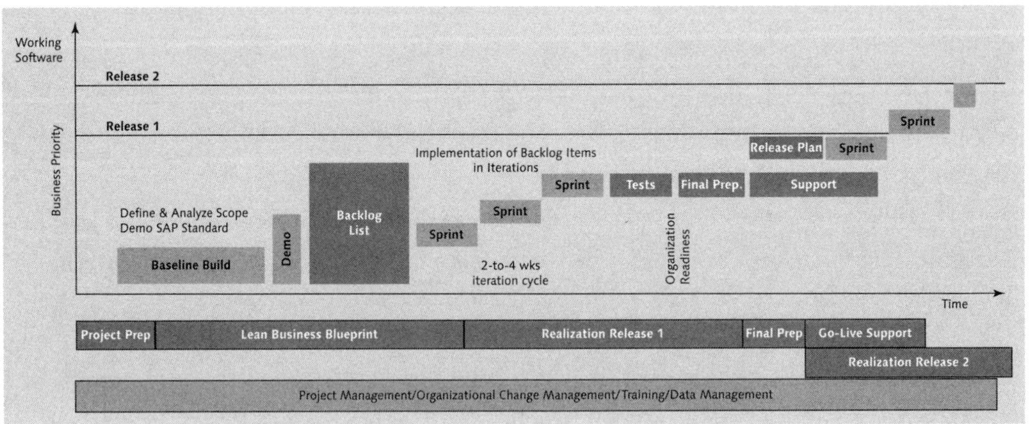

Figure 5.16 The Agile ASAP Methodology: Key Phases and Deliverables

Note that while this section provides a good overview of the ASAP methodology and agile-deployment strategies, it only scratches the surface of the capabilities and content delivered in ASAP. SAP recommends anyone interested in the ASAP and agile deployment to follow the ASAP methodology space on the SAP Community Network, which provides additional information and serves as a space for raising questions and communicating with SAP experts. You can access the ASAP methodology community via the link *http://scn.sap.com/community/asap-methodology*. SAP offers traditional and virtual-training courses for project teams that help broaden understanding of the methodology and support the project team's adoption of leading implementation practices.

5.4 Project Execution with the Rapid Deployment Cockpit, SAP Solution Manager, and Solution Builder Tool

In the past, many implementation projects suffered from a lack of communication regarding detailed scope information from the sales phase, causing confusion for the customer and resulting in higher overall implementation costs and risks. Now, the Rapid Deployment Cockpit allows a hand-over of the detailed information gathered during the sales phase, especially the information collected via the SAP Solution Configurator for bid managers in the form of a high-level, assemble-to-order-based ASAP 8 WBS for the implementation project, which is the basis of the service bid.

The Rapid Deployment Cockpit is a web-based tool supporting the detailed assembly of work breakdown structures as a starting point for the implementation of projects with a significant amount of assemble-to-order, rapid-deployment best-practice content. It also provides an intuitive, easy-to-use collaborative environment for executing the implementation project, allocating tasks to each participant, and giving participants access to the relevant documents and assets to help them with their tasks. As such, the Rapid Deployment Cockpit acts as a supplement to SAP Solution Manager.

Collaborative implementation

SAP Solution Manager 7.1 is *the* central solution for Application Lifecycle Management (ALM) and the operation of software solutions. It supports heterogeneous system environments, and it covers the entire lifecycle of a solution, from implementation and go-live to operation and

SAP Solution Manager

ongoing improvement of solutions. SAP Solution Manager 7.1 combines tools, content, and direct access to SAP to increase the reliability and stability of solutions and lower the total cost of operations (TCO).

The solution lifecycle is well explained by version three of the IT Infrastructure Library (ITIL), which describes six phases (see Figure 5.17):

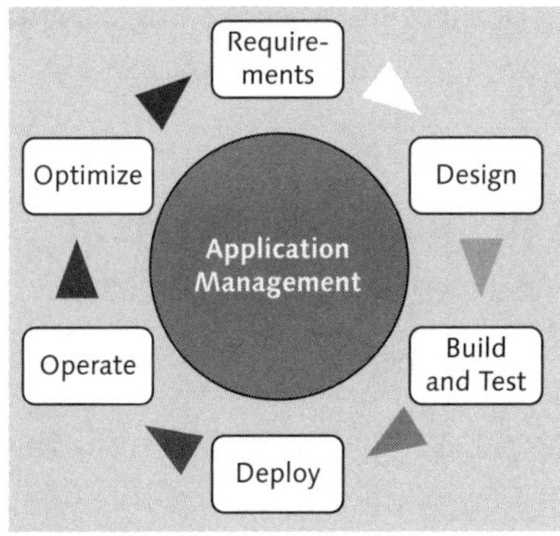

Figure 5.17 The Lifecycle of IT Solutions

▶ **Requirements**
Collect requirements for new applications or for the distribution of existing applications.

▶ **Design**
Convert requirements into detailed specifications.

▶ **Build and Test**
Configure the application and create an organizational model in accordance with the specifications.

▶ **Deploy**
Transfer changes and the organizational model into the existing live IT landscape.

▶ **Operate**
Provide IT services required for ongoing operations.

▶ **Optimize**
Analyze service-level fulfillment and perform any activities necessary to improve results.

The Solution Builder tool is an add-on to SAP systems that automates the activation of the customizing settings contained in SAP Rapid Deployment solutions. The Solution Builder tool is only recommended for cases where the SAP system has been newly installed, and therefore has not yet been configured.

The following sections give more details on how each of these three tools supports implementation projects.

5.4.1 Collaborative Project Execution with the Rapid Deployment Cockpit

As we mentioned, the Rapid Deployment Cockpit is a web-based tool supporting the collaborative implementation of projects with a significant amount of assemble-to-order, rapid-deployment best-practice content. It has two main parts: the overview sections MY HOME and PROJECTS, and the project-specific section containing the sections OVERVIEW and TASKS. The rapid-deployment best-practice content is structured in the Rapid Deployment Cockpit according to the ASAP 8 implementation methodology, so you can't go wrong: executing projects using the Rapid Deployment Cockpit guarantees that you are following the ASAP 8 methodology.

The MY HOME section gives you a complete overview of the most important information regarding your implementation projects: A list of the upcoming tasks to which you have been assigned, a list of the projects you are working on, recent messages from project members, and useful links. Clicking on the tasks or project brings you straight to the concrete project-execution page. Figure 5.18 shows an example of MY HOME. My Home

The PROJECT page gives you an overview of all projects you are working on, with direct access to these projects. SAP employees also get a simple list of other projects currently active in the Rapid Deployment Cockpit, showing the project name, customer name, and SAP project lead. Project

> **Note**
>
> SAP employees, partners, and customers can only access projects to which they have been assigned by the project's manager, thus guaranteeing project confidentiality.

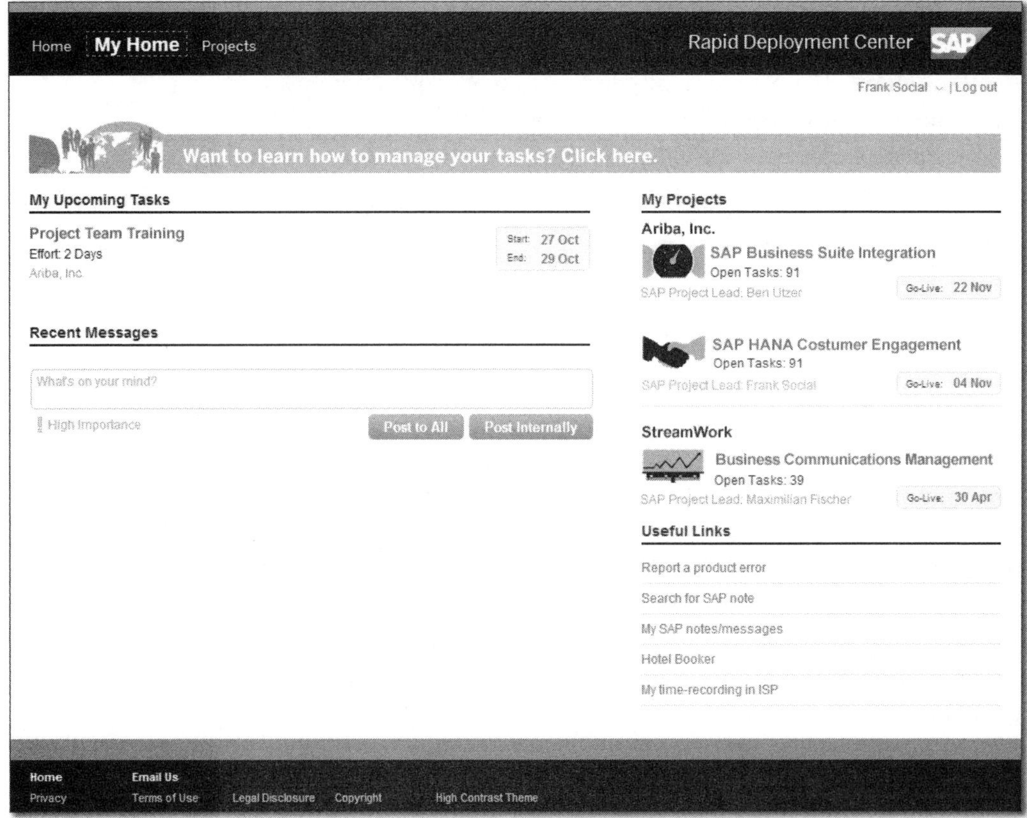

Figure 5.18 The My Home Page in the Rapid Deployment Cockpit

Overview When you select a project, you first land on the OVERVIEW page, which summarizes information about the customer—such as their address and contact information—along with project details such as the SAP project lead and customer project lead. It also shows which solutions and services are included in the project, provides a graphical depiction of the project's progress (i.e., what percentage of tasks have been completed), and gives an overview of the recent messages posted by the project team members (see Figure 5.19). A list on the right of the screen can be opened to show the project team members assigned to the project by the project lead.

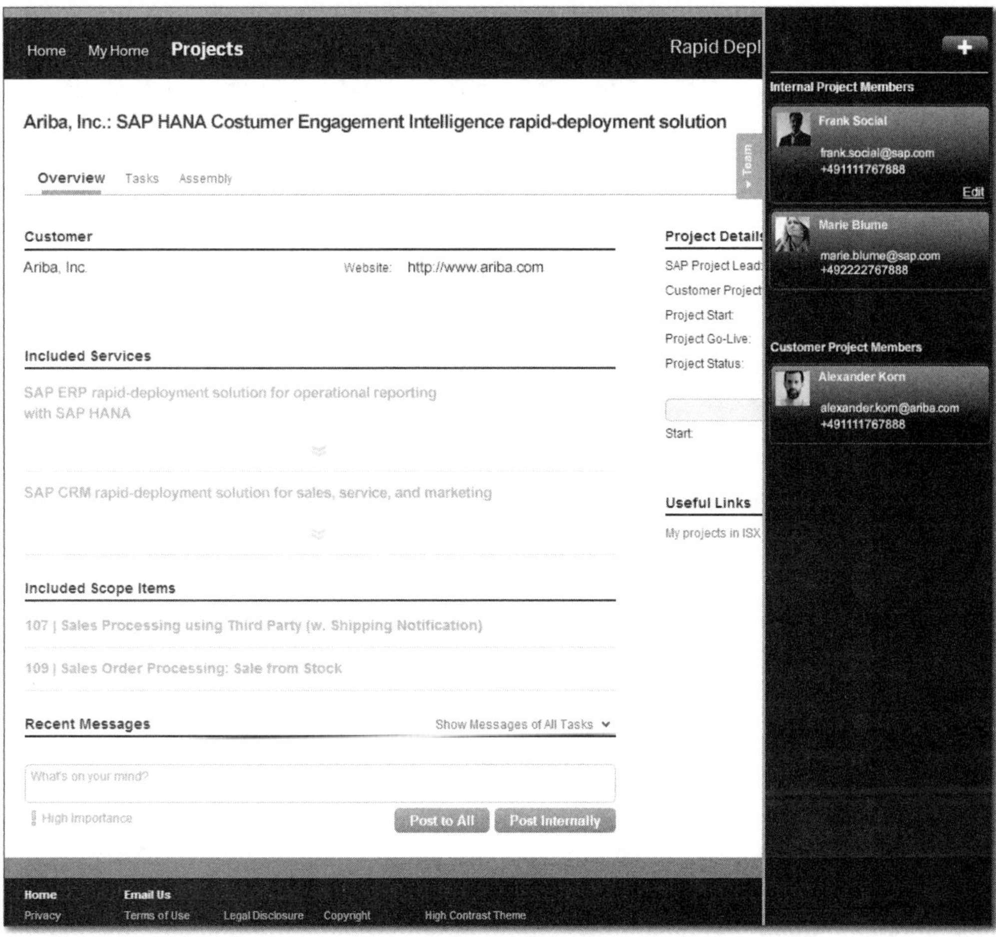

Figure 5.19 Rapid Deployment Cockpit Project Overview for a Selected Implementation Project

The ASSEMBLY page is used to assemble one single project WBS out of the WBSs provided with each rapid-deployment solution and with each engineered service. In addition to copying the tasks from each of these WBSs to the new, consolidated WBS, project leads can also assign tasks from scope items which were manually added by the bidding team in the SAP Solution Configurator. They can also manually add additional tasks, if needed. This functionality is core to be able to efficiently and effectively implement assemble-to-order projects. Figure 5.20 shows an example of the ASSEMBLY screen.

WBS assembly

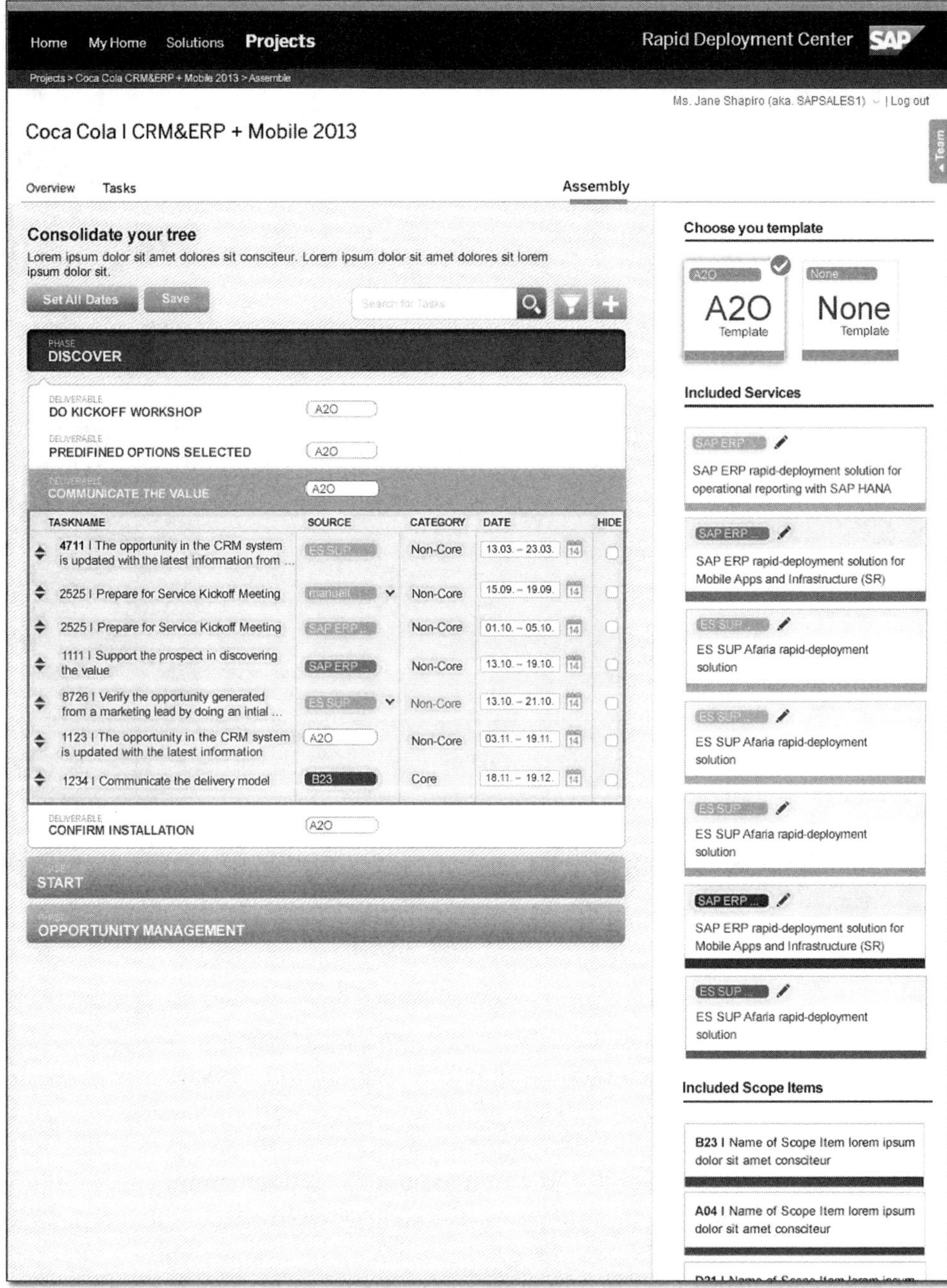

Figure 5.20 Assembling One WBS out of Multiple Rapid-Deployment Solution WBSs

The TASK page is the main page for collaborative project execution:

Task

- The project manager uses it to invite team members to the project and to assign them to tasks from the WBS.

- Team members use it to access the relevant templates and information needed to execute each task, to communicate amongst themselves, and to set the status of each task.

> **Note**
>
> You can get an overview of all tasks in the project, by selecting ALL TASKS or select only the tasks to which you have been assigned by selecting MY TASKS.

When working on a task, you not only have access to templates, you can also store the documents as a work in progress or as a final document in the Rapid Deployment Cockpit. Figure 5.21 shows an example for the task PREPARE FOR SERVICE KICKOFF MEETING which is still in progress. A document has been uploaded and its status set to *Completed*. In addition, you can see that three documents have been provided under the TEMPLATES heading in this example.

Task status

You can set the status of the task to *Open*, *In Progress*, or *Done*. Tasks which are in progress are indicated in the list on the left with a clock; completed tasks with a tick. This helps the project manager see at a glance how the project is progressing.

The message board allows you to create messages for other team members within the context of the concrete task at hand.

Finally, SAP project members are able to see additional information about the expected delivery effort required for the task, which was the basis for the service bid, by clicking on DELIVERY EFFORT DETAILS.

Clicking on the TEAM tab on the right of the TASK page shown in Figure 5.21 gives you an overview of the project team members, grouped according to whether they are customer employees, partner employees, or SAP employees (as shown in Figure 5.19). The project lead can assign people to tasks via drag and drop from the list on the right to the task on the left.

Project team

At the end of the implementation project, the documents relevant for describing the implementation, such as the configuration documentation and the process descriptions, need to be transferred to the SAP Solution Manager implementation project to ensure that they are stored for later reference during operations and maintenance. This is simply done by manually downloading the documents describing what was implemented and uploading them to SAP Solution Manager.

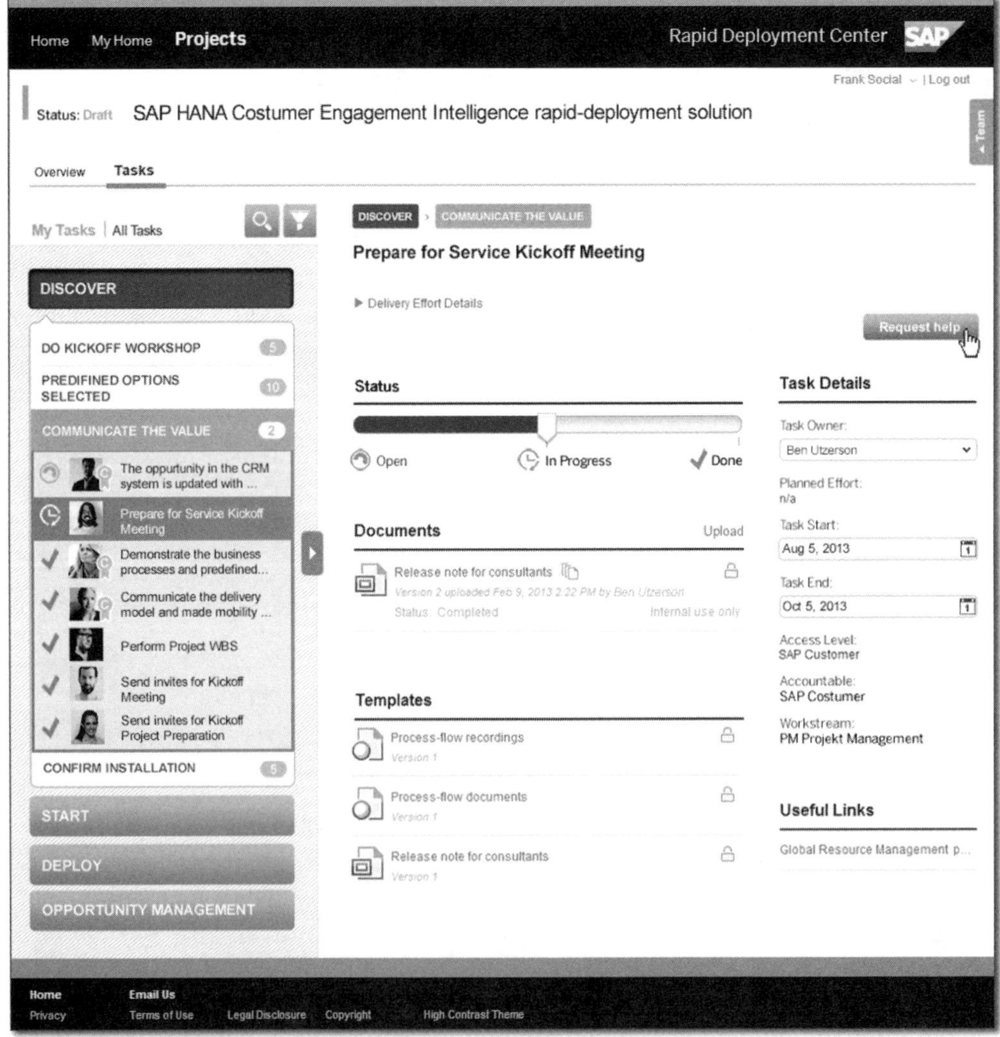

Figure 5.21 Show MY TASKS; Only Tasks Assigned to the User Are Displayed

Prior to the availability of the Rapid Deployment Cockpit, all the templates and assets related to a rapid-deployment solution were provided in the Service Marketplace in the form of a step-by-step guide for each rapid-deployment solution, which can also be viewed online or downloaded to a local PC or laptop as a self-contained .zip file, containing the assets themselves as well as links to information such as configuration guides. These step-by-step guides will continue to be available for SAP Rapid Deployment solutions for a while, and can be found at *http://service.sap.com/rds*.

5.4.2 Supporting Your Implementation with SAP Solution Manager

SAP Solution Manager 7.1 is the central solution for Application Lifecycle Management (ALM) and the operation of software solutions, and it covers the entire lifecycle of a solution. A project in SAP Solution Manager describes the grouping and organization of business, technical, and organizational tasks during the implementation of SAP software in an enterprise. In an implementation project, the project team performs tasks that are structured according to a common project plan and roadmap. In SAP Solution Manager, projects follow the ASAP methodology, starting with project preparation and completing the project in the go-live phase.

From the lifecycle perspective, a project covers the application management phases, from requirements gathering through the build and test phases. All information that you collect over the course of the project is applied in the solution at the end of the deploy phase. This includes the transfer of knowledge to the end-user by means of e-learning or the implementation of the support organization.

In order to implement SAP Rapid Deployment solutions in SAP Solution Manager 7.1, you first need to create a project using the project administration transaction. SAP provides a template for each rapid-deployment solution; you need to select the templates for each of the rapid-deployment solutions you want to implement by going to the Scope tab and adding them to your project scope. This creates a project-specific

259

copy, which you can adapt to your needs during the implementation project.

Advantages

Using SAP Solution Manager for projects has many advantages, including the following:

- Structured, systematic procedure throughout the project.
- Strict adherence to a process-centric approach, which is separate from individual applications and components, and provides a more comprehensive view of process flows in heterogeneous system landscapes.
- Centralized metadata repository for solutions, including documentation, test cases, and configuration information.
- No information loss between project phases. Once created, content is reused throughout the software lifecycle, preventing integration gaps.

From the perspective of the lifecycle, an SAP Solution Manager project covers phases from the requirements phase to the preparation of the go-live (deploy phase). The scope of a project varies and can range from large-scale projects, such as upgrade projects, to smaller changes implemented during a maintenance cycle.

Manage system landscape

When using the Rapid Deployment Cockpit for collaborative project execution while leveraging rapid-deployment solutions, SAP Solution Manager helps you to manage your system landscape, i.e. installing components, using support packages and notes, documenting customer-specific processes directly in the tool, managing your test using a test catalog, conducting end-user training, and in particular, performing the final go-live activities. Before going live, the documents in the Rapid Deployment Cockpit relevant for describing the implementation are transferred to the SAP Solution Manager project, and with go-live are transferred to the solution directory in SAP Solution Manager for later reference.

5.4.3 Activating SAP Rapid Deployment Solutions Pre-Configuration Content with the Solution Builder

When leveraging pre-assembled rapid-deployment solutions, you receive a system in SAP HANA Enterprise Cloud that already contains all the pre-configured customizing settings, and hence is ready to run.

In cases where you want to implement additional rapid-deployment solutions, or if you choose not to leverage pre-assembled rapid-deployment solutions, the Solution Builder allows you to automate the activation of the pre-configuration settings for many of the available rapid-deployment solutions.

The Solution Builder is an add-on to SAP systems that automates the activation of the pre-configuration settings contained in rapid-deployment solutions. For the largest packages, it is able to automate over 2,000 configuration activities. The SAP SRM rapid-deployment solutions for operational sourcing can be activated in 20 minutes—resulting in a system in which users can create shopping baskets (i.e., actually use the system).

Solution Builder tool

> **Note**
>
> The Solution Builder tool is only recommended for automated activation where the SAP system has been newly installed, and therefore has not yet been configured. The reason for this is that it directly updates configuration settings, which could result in existing settings being overwritten. It can also be used before activation to analyze potential conflicts between existing and pre-configuration settings.

You can either select the scope to be activated in SAP Solution Manager in the SCOPE tab, and trigger the activation via the Solution Builder tool from SAP Solution Manager, if you have configured the remote system connection between SAP Solution Manager and the Solution Builder. Alternatively, you can go into the SAP Solution Builder tool directly and select the concrete scope to be activated there, as depicted in Figure 5.22. On the left-hand side you see the scope items which you select via drag and drop to the right side.

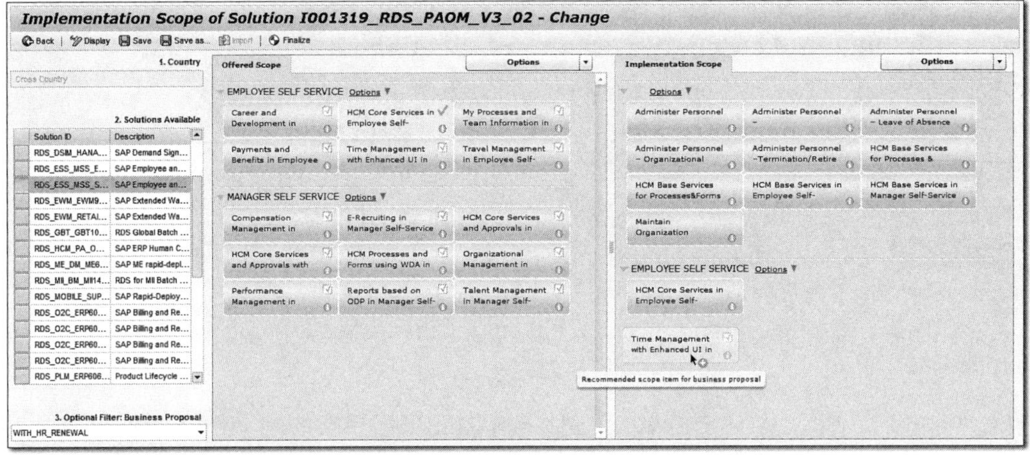

Figure 5.22 Selecting Scope to be Activated in the Solution Builder

The Solution Builder supports the automatic activation of organizational structures. Since these are highly custom-specific, a personalization feature is offered, allowing you to change the names and even IDs of the various pre-configured organizational units. This is depicted in Figure 5.23.

Activation The Solution Builder calculates which implementation building blocks are required for the selected scope, and combines them into one overall list of activities to be performed. These can be automated tasks or manual tasks. In cases where configuration activities cannot be automated, such as setting passwords for remote connections, manual tasks are defined. If the automated activation needs to stop because the next step in the activation is a manual task, the Solution Builder can notify the responsible person via email and SMS, so that that individual can perform the manual activity and then continue the activation.

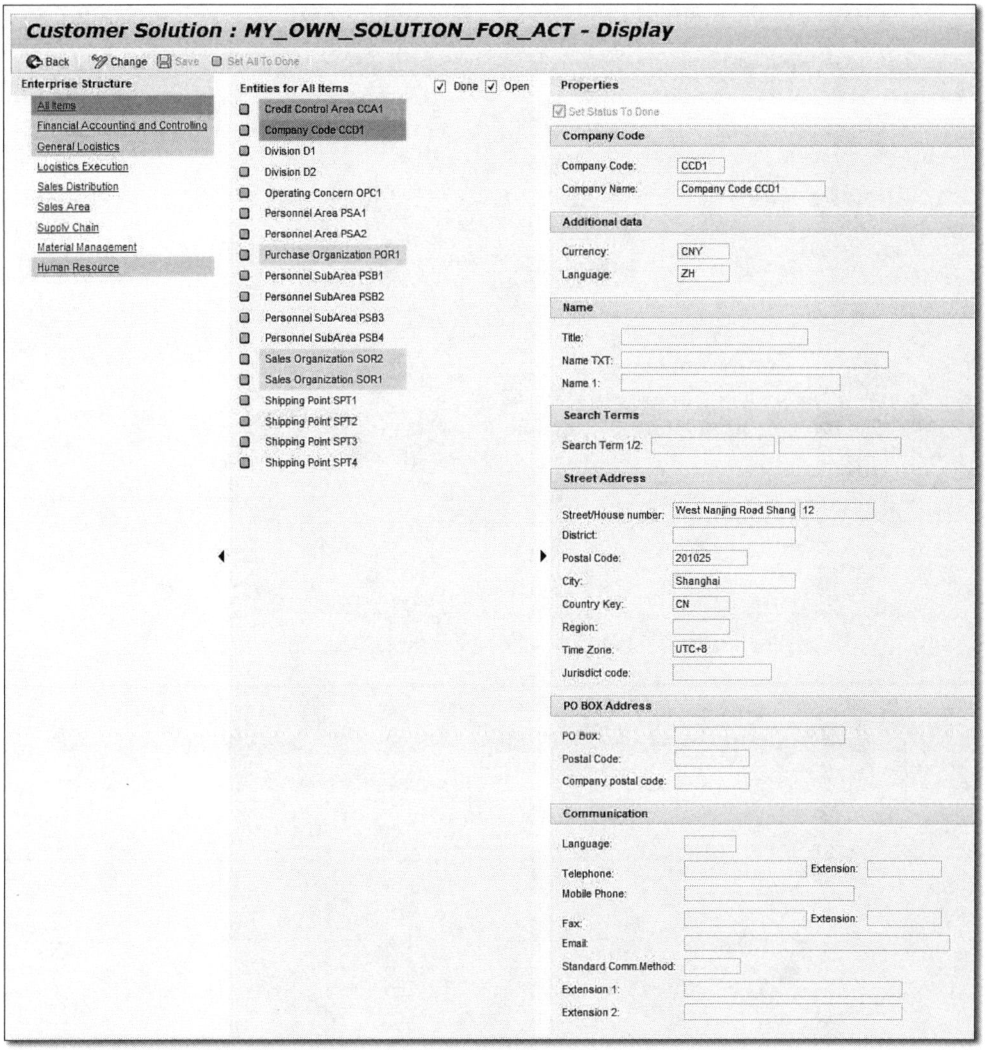

Figure 5.23 Personalizing Pre-Defined Organizational Structures in the Solution Builder

Figure 5.24 shows the activation monitor with an example where the automatic activation has stopped in order to allow you to perform a manual activity.

Figure 5.25 shows the activation log after the activation has successfully completed, i.e. after all automated and manual activities have been performed.

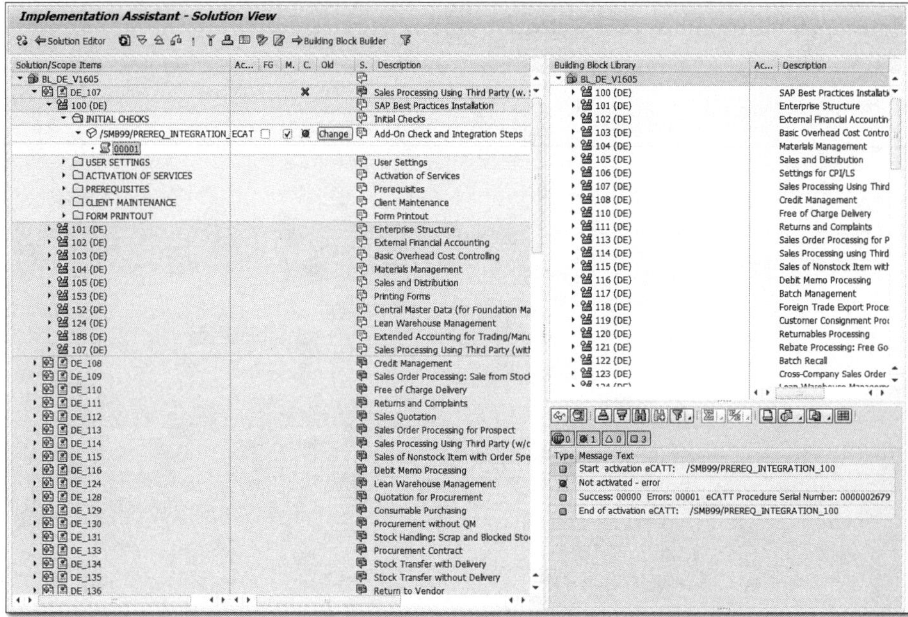

Figure 5.24 The Solution Builder Allows Manual Activities

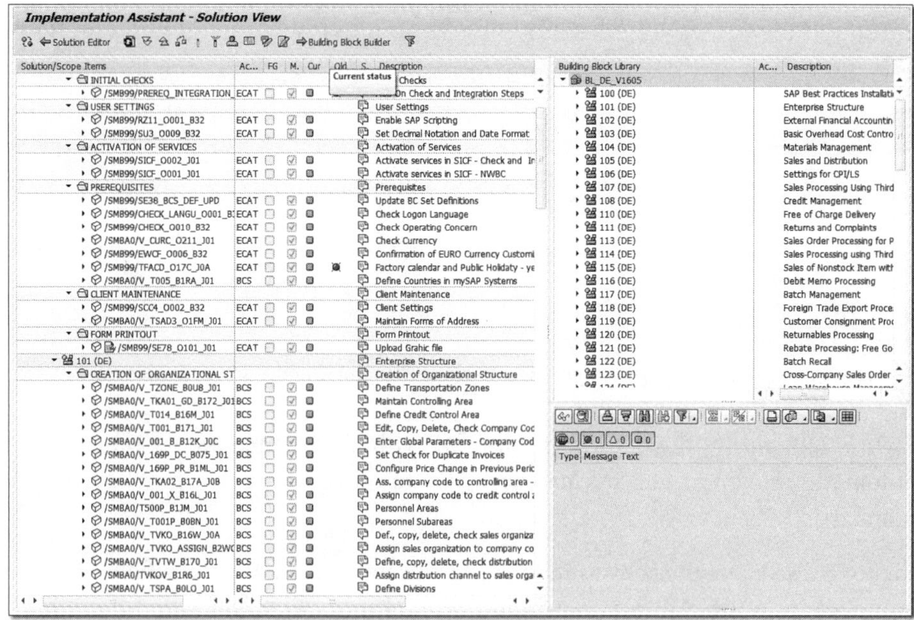

Figure 5.25 The Solution Builder Showing a Successful Activation

5.5 Operating Your Solution with SAP Solution Manager

After you have successfully completed an implementation project, the challenges you encountered during operations document the knowledge you gained during the project and keep it constantly up to date. The *solution* concept of SAP Solution Manager helps you do this. During import for production use, all of the information accumulated in your project is transferred into a solution. An SAP Solution Manager solution contains all of the information about systems, software components, and business processes (scenarios) needed in the operation and continuous optimization of your IT solution. This ensures that all information remains accessible and can be consolidated when a project is over.

A solution naturally spans a longer period of time than a project. However, the operational phase is also the phase of the lifecycle in which you create value from your investments in projects. Therefore, the integrity of your solution is the key to a successful operation.

In serving as an information source for operation, the solution differentiates between two dimensions: Horizontally, each software component that is required for the execution of the customer's business processes in accordance with the solution documentation can be administered with SAP Solution Manager processes. Vertically, every layer of the solution can also use these processes, including databases and IT assets.

Solutions in SAP Solution Manager offer the following advantages:

- ▶ All assignments are in the SAP Solution Manager project
  - ▻ Scenario and business-process structures are transferred to the solution.
  - ▻ Configuration object assignments are readily available.
  - ▻ Test cases in the structure can be used to test changes that have been made.
  - ▻ E-learning materials from projects in the solution can be reused.
  - ▻ The solution has the same system landscape as the project, so you can reuse the structure when you upgrade.

- Solution components, such as servers, systems, business processes, and scenarios are provided in a standard presentation.
  - The display of graphics and diagrams is clear.
  - You can export graphics to Microsoft Office or HTML.

From the perspective of ALM, the solution in SAP Solution Manager covers the phases from handover into operation (the deploy phase) to operation (the operate phase) to optimization (the optimize phase).

Processes Supported by SAP Solution Manager

12 processes

To cover the entire lifecycle, SAP Solution Manager offers 12 processes. These processes bundle functions in SAP Solution Manager that support you in the respective focus areas on a long-term basis:

- **Solution documentation**
  The solution documentation includes the documentation of the technical landscape as well as the business-process documentation. It forms the basis for all other functions of SAP Solution Manager. It describes a customer's SAP and non-SAP technical components, core business processes, and interfaces. The documentation also includes custom code and modification documentation, as well as links to supporting technical objects, such as transactions and programs.

- **Solution implementation**
  Solution implementation involves the identification, adaptation, and implementation of new and enhanced future-oriented business and technical scenarios. It is designed to decouple technical installation from business innovation and uses SAP Solution Manager to implement innovation within the system landscape.

- **Template management**
  Using this process, customers with SAP installations that include multiple locations can also efficiently administer their business processes over long distances. Template management is part of a global rollout approach and includes template definitions, template implementation, and template optimization.

- **Test management**
  Here you define the integration-testing requirements and test scope

based on a change-impact analysis. You can also develop automatic and manual test cases, manage the testers, and report on the test progress and test results.

▶ **Change control management**
This process offers workflow-based management of changes to improve a business or technological aspect. Integrated functions for project management, quality management, and synchronized provisioning support you in the optimal management of risks associated with the implementation of the solution and in ensuring technical and functional stability.

▶ **Technical operations**
This process includes all capabilities for monitoring, alerting, analyzing, and administering SAP solutions, and allows customers to reduce TCO by using pre-defined content and centralized tools for all aspects of SAP Solution Manager operations. It provides end-to-end reporting functionality either out of the box or as individually created by customers.

▶ **Business process operations**
This process covers the most important application-related aspects of operation. It is necessary to take these aspects into account to ensure a smooth and reliable flow of the core business processes and thus the fulfillment of the business requirements.

▶ **Application Incident Management**
This process enables centralized and common incident- and problem-message processing on multiple organization levels and offers a communication channel with all relevant stakeholders of an incident. The process includes business users, SAP experts at the customer site, SAP AG, and partner-support employees. It is integrated in all processes of SAP Solution Manager and in any SAP Business Suite solution, can be connected to a non-SAP help-desk application, and includes follow-up activities such as knowledge research, root cause analysis, and change management.

▶ **Maintenance management**
This process includes packages for software correction, from identification and provisioning to optimization of the test scope. These packages

can be optionally imported into the production environment on an automatic basis.

- **Upgrade management**
  This process includes the identification, adaptation, and implementation of new and enhanced business and technical scenarios, and it uses SAP Solution Manager to holistically and effectively manage the upgrade project end-to-end. It allows SAP customers to better understand and manage the major technical risks and challenges within an upgrade project and to make the upgrade project a non-event for the business.

- **Landscape transformation management**
  This process helps you to accelerate business and IT transformations – in case of mergers or acquisitions, for example; and to plan, analyze, organize, and implement complex business requirements using standardized transformation solutions.

- **Custom code management**
  Includes tools and methods that support you in analyzing custom code and in deciding whether individual developments can be replaced by standard software to minimize the TCO with upgrade projects, for example.

SAP Solution Manager 7.1 offers a number of improvements compared to previous versions, including state-of-the-art user interfaces, increased openness for integrating with partner products and for managing non-SAP systems, and a new monitoring infrastructure, amongst others.

> **Note**
>
> For a comprehensive introduction to SAP Solution Manager, see the book *SAP Solution Manager* by Marc Schäfer and Matthias Melich (3rd edition SAP PRESS, 2012).

An overview of SAP Solution Manager for SAP customers and partners, including the new functions offered with release 7.1, is available in the Service Marketplace at *http://service.sap.com/solutionmanager*.

5.6 Summary

Now you have seen the answers to the questions posed at the beginning of the chapter: how to find out which solutions SAP offers; how to evaluate the solution's capabilities; how to define the scope of your implementation by mapping your business requirements to the solution's capabilities, and keep track of gaps; and finally, how to actually go about rapidly implementing the solution.

SAP Solution Explorer makes it easy for you to find out which solutions SAP offers, and allows you to drill down to discover the available rapid-deployment solutions as well as the underlying products. Leveraging the pre-assembled rapid-deployment solutions in the cloud allows you to rapidly evaluate the solution's capabilities on a running system at low cost. The SAP Solution Configurator helps you define the scope of what needs to be implemented and identify gaps, and provides you with an overview of the available rapid-deployment solutions covering your required scope. The version for bidding teams provides additional functionality to help them assemble a bid based on the assemble-to-order approach. The ASAP 8 implementation methodology tightly connects the deliverables and prescriptive tasks in one hierarchy, the WBS, making it easy for implementation project managers and project team members to understand exactly what needs to be done, and when.

Actually implementing your solution is made easy with the Rapid Deployment Cockpit, SAP Solution Manager, and the Solution Builder. The Rapid Deployment Cockpit leverages the ASAP 8 based work-breakdown structure and gives each project participant access to the templates and documents they need to perform their tasks, which are delivered as part of the rapid-deployment solution best-practice content. The Solution Builder allows you to automatically activate configuration content, which is also provided as part of the rapid-deployment solution best-practice content. SAP Solution Manager manages the whole lifecycle of your system landscape. It contains all the information about systems, software components, and business processes (scenarios) needed in the operation and continuous optimization of your IT solution. The 12 processes supported by SAP Solution Manager allow you to manage your solution efficiently and sustainably.

SAP Active Global Support provides different levels of support and engagement for choice. SAP customers can select which life-time support option will best fit their individual requirements and their individual situation.

6   Support Services for the Rapid Deployment of SAP Solutions

SAP customers, partners, and deployment teams would be less efficient without key SAP services that help optimize and accelerate the performance of the deployment teams. In principal, all services allow you to control costs and minimize risks while enabling innovation and growth while taking the entire lifecycle into account. This is made possible by using proven, predictable methodologies and predefined scope that employs a best-practice, template-driven approach. The engagement format may range from consulting to support services for solution implementation and operation. It may focus on gaining the latest core knowledge and skills, or enhancing the ability to collaborate and expedite the solution deployment. In this chapter, we'll cover the following key services that SAP provides to help support the implementation and use of rapid-deployment solutions:

- Engineered services
- Services for solution implementation and operation
- Services for enablement

Let's get started.

6.1   Engineered Services

SAP Advanced Delivery Management

Technology is ever evolving, markets are continuously growing, and competition is always increasing. Software providers are tasked with the challenge of consistently offering relevant, high-quality products and support that not only help businesses keep pace with constant change, but also allow them to thrive and excel. To continue with this tradition of helping its customers adopt innovative technologies more quickly and implement software more efficiently, SAP has created a modern, cost-effective delivery approach: SAP Advanced Delivery Management.

Engineered services play an important part in SAP Advanced Delivery Management. These services are engineered effectively to enable SAP, service providers, and customers to assemble them as needed, and in so doing make projects much faster and less costly.

6.1.1   Why Engineered Service?

Routine tasks

The current Services space revolves largely around a make-to-order model. However, a large percentage of projects are currently reinventing the wheel for common tasks. Among these recurring tasks, there is no differentiation from one project to another. Instead, these tasks, which tend to be at the lower rungs of the value creation ladder, should be routinized. SAP leads this industry transformation, taking an assemble-to-order approach by engineering common services for quality and peak efficiency and creating standards and assets that enable them to be combined and applied to new projects. By doing this, we can accelerate projects and time-to-value in a dramatic way while reducing the services-to-software ratio.

Quality checks

Customers also benefit from a quality perspective. Any pre-engineered service or standard that SAP prescribes goes through rigorous quality checks. Whether a customer contracts with SAP or a certified partner for these types of services, they can expect clear, predictable outcomes. Fewer escalations, in turn, allow SAP to make a much greater investment in high-value services. Engineered services offer the following benefits:

- **Minimized implementation time and effort**
  Instead of creating everything from scratch for each project, engineered services using reusable, predefined service modules and content, such as standard accelerators.

- **Reduced cost**
  Delivery model for engineered services engages a blend of local, nearshore, and offshore resources. This provides an onsite, virtual implementation and collaboration platform that fosters more flexible and cost-efficient remote delivery. By using the delivered accelerators and available templates, implementations can be done in a matter of days or weeks, reducing the time and costs of engaging your resources in the project.

- **No surprises**
  Instead of being billed by time and material, businesses are now paying for the services and intended outcome. In many cases, you will know the effort, cost, and result of the implementation before the project starts.

- **Consistent quality**
  Engineered services are being delivered based on integrated infrastructure to assist you with project tasks such as scoping and planning, as well as the execution and monitoring of the implementation. The new approach provides you with templates, business processes and configuration guidance, test cases, and training materials to ensure your project and solution are delivered with consistent quality.

- **Faster adoption of innovation**
  When deploying SAP Rapid Deployment solutions and services involving SAP HANA and mobility, SAP Advanced Delivery Management allows you to take advantage of these innovative technologies more quickly, with faster ROI and lowered risks.

Difference between Engineered Services and SAP Rapid Deployment Solutions

SAP Rapid Deployment solutions combine preconfigured software, engineered services, and SAP Best Practice content (pre-configured content) to deliver immediate and tangible value at a predictable price—with the flexibility for future extensions. This also means that every rapid-deployment solution will by default have an engineered service component, which is based on ready-to-use content and service components for end-to-end processes with clearly defined scope, timeline, and effort. This ensures that assembly is done easier, quicker, with the better quality and lower risk of implementation issues.

6.1.2 Structure of Engineered Services

Phased, task-oriented

Engineered services can be of different types—Plan, Build, or Run services—that come without a rapid-deployment solution or the engineered services which are part of the solution. To ensure the best results, engineered services of all types are created and delivered based on the ASAP methodology. It is a phased, task-oriented methodology that streamlines implementation projects. The methodology supports project teams with templates, tools, questionnaires, and checklists, as well as guidebooks and accelerators to ensure the step-by-step and pragmatic implementation of the new SAP Solution Packages.

Predefined scope

The methodology follows a number of key phases. You won't see a business blueprint phase in most engineered services. One of the reasons for this is that all rapid-deployment solutions and engineered services have predefined scope, meaning that there is no need in doing requirements and design workshops, but customer can choose to implement full service or different variants (also called scope options) for customer situations. Table 6.1 shows an example of standard accelerators for each implementation phase, delivered with the engineered service for a rapid-deployment solution.

Every engineered service is structured based on established standards that are defined by ASAP methodology. These tasks, which tend to be at the lower rungs of the value creation ladder, are routinized and the same task can appear/be reused in many services and projects. Every task comes with templates and accelerators as well as set of attributes that prescribe how the task should be delivered. These attributes dictate the delivery mode (onsite or remote), deployment mode based on a three-tier delivery model (local, near-shore, offshore), effort that it takes to deliver the task as well as roles and responsibility.

Start	Deploy	Run
▶ Project management ▶ Kick-off workshop participation ▶ Preparing technical infrastructure	▶ Solution realization ▶ Master data load ▶ Refinement workshop and realization ▶ Knowledge transfer to key users	▶ Performance tests ▶ End-user training ▶ Sign-off solution ▶ Go-live preparation ▶ Go live ▶ Post go-live support and activities ▶ Improvements and roadmap workshop
Accelerators/Deliverables	**Accelerators/Deliverables**	**Accelerators/Deliverables**
▶ Consulting delivery guides ▶ Project schedule ▶ Work breakdown structure ▶ Service delivery model roles and responsibilities ▶ Request for consultant template ▶ Process descriptions ▶ Process flow documents ▶ Kick-off presentation ▶ Consumption guide ▶ Pre-delivery requirements and checklist	▶ Installation guide ▶ Solution documentation ▶ SAP Solution Manager content ▶ Best Practices content (preconfiguration) ▶ Configuration activities ▶ Consulting delivery guide ▶ Implementation content	▶ Test cases ▶ Deliverable acceptance forms ▶ Training materials, such as process flow recordings ▶ Go-live checklist

Table 6.1 Standard Accelerators for Each Implementation Phase

6.1.3 Delivery Approach

In contrast to a traditional, "build-to-order" delivery approach, engineered services enhance and expand the existing SAP Rapid Deployment solutions philosophy in order to provide faster time to value for

Time-to-value

customers. As we mentioned, most engineered services follow a three-tiered resource deployment structure—onsite, near-shore, and off-shore—to ensure the best availability of resources anywhere in the globe. The target is to deliver most engineered services in an automated way and remotely as much as possible. Local engagement on a country level is limited to onsite project management and solution architect related activities. A factory-based, lean delivery approach is adopted with a focus on increasing productivity via automation/repeatability. For customers, this means optimized project costs via a mix of onsite delivery and virtual delivery that offers a sustainable collaboration platform between the customer and SAP.

6.2   Services for Solution Implementation

There are many types of deployment and consulting services offered by SAP. In this section, we will explicitly elaborate on the following topics that support the SAP Rapid Deployment solutions. We'll help you understand how SAP's support programs foster innovation, from Product Support for Large Enterprises (PSLE) and SAP Enterprise Support, to premium support engagements; from Accelerated Innovation Enablement (AIE) to the Innovation Control Center (ICC).

6.2.1   Services for Solution Implementation and Operations

Innovation and technology

In a streamlined experience where you continue improving on the foundation of SAP Rapid Deployment solutions through innovation and technology, you can expect that SAP's services and support approach follows that same line. After the first insights into SAP Solution Manager, the proven "single source of truth" that serves as a technical support infrastructure (Chapter 5, Section 5.4) for SAP Rapid Deployment solutions have been shared, the current chapter takes a closer look at SAP's support programs that foster innovation and at support services built to accelerate innovation in your enterprise (Section 6.2.2).

How SAP's Support Programs Foster Innovation

SAP Enterprise Support is the universal maintenance offering for all of SAP's customers. SAP Enterprise Support aims to help customers in all phases of the software lifecycle and therefore to operate better, innovate better, and implement better through collaboration, automation, and empowerment. It is important to understand that it's independent from the chosen implementation methodology and is therefore 100 percent suitable for SAP Rapid Deployment solutions. See Figure 6.1 for a graphical representation of SAP Enterprise Support.

SAP Enterprise Support

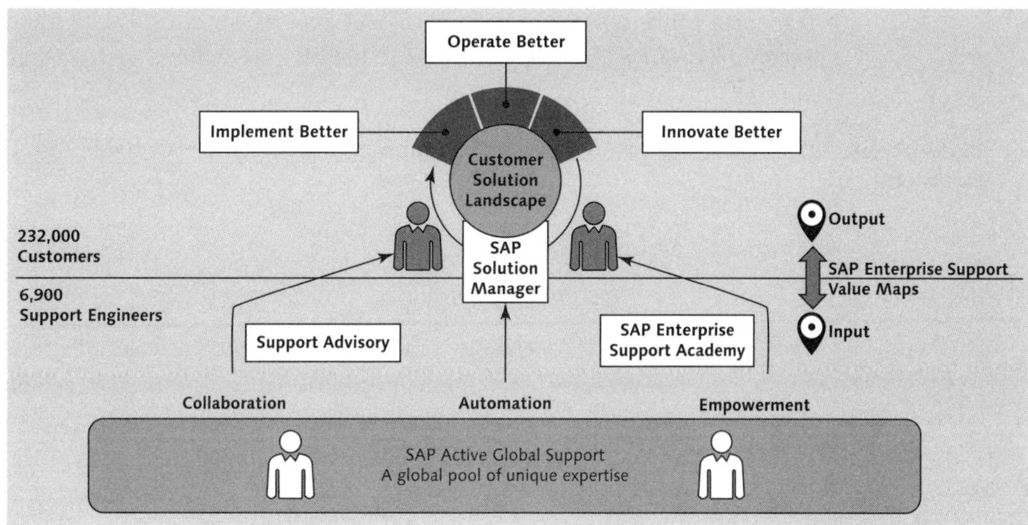

Figure 6.1 SAP Enterprise Support

It goes without saying that the different software lifecycle phases (operate, innovate, implement) are connected with each other. An efficient and effective operation is the precondition to free up resources. This is needed to efficiently evaluate innovation potential and implement it quickly to bring fast value to the business.

As SAP Support has its origin in operations, we start our journey from there and discuss how SAP support helps foster innovation via the new SAP Rapid Deployment solutions implementation paradigm. From product support for large enterprises and SAP Enterprise Support, to premium support engagements, we'll explore what these programs help

Support to foster innovation

customers do with SAP Rapid Deployment solutions in the following subsections.

Operate Better

Big solution landscapes supporting complex and fast-changing business requirements challenge today's IT departments. The starting point to mastering this challenge is to optimize the operations phase and keep housekeeping activities as automated as possible. This is why SAP Enterprise Support is continuously investing in the advancement of services, tools, and methodologies to automate what can be automated, and to provide a built-in collaboration with SAP experts for critical issues and exceptions. Once the homework is done, the innovation path can be entered.

Services, tools, methodologies

A broad range of services, tools, and methodologies are available to:

▶ Optimize performance.

▶ Monitor performance.

▶ Improve business processes in terms of business efficiency.

To enable educated decisions where investments into innovations count, full transparency is gained via additional tools (e.g., "Reversed Business Process Documentation," analyses of the current business-processes usage, and custom code tools give insights into the technical usage of solutions).

This transparency on the current system's usage gives an indicator of what is of interest for a customer, to be further evaluated and to determine if SAP HANA, for example, can be of relevance.

Innovate Better

A growing number of choices for new business functions are available that can replace custom code, as well as new choices for mobile or cloud opportunities, spark the need for an intelligent decision criteria based on what is of high relevance for the business. Essentially: How do you choose the right software that best fits the individual situation?

Transparency

We learned that transparency is a positive side effect when users operate systems according to SAP Active Global Support (AGS) best practices, delivered via SAP Enterprise Support. Technical and business key performance indicators (KPIs) are available to translate into potential business needs from an IT perspective and are the basis for future investment discussions between business and IT.

A major investment spot in SAP Enterprise Support is in how to best support SAP's customers in this decision process. The "as-is" business process, fully transparent through the previously mentioned offerings, is mapped to the "to-be" business process, which includes available innovations. This happens on a technical basis and provides as output the filtered/relevant options for the individual customer situation.

Implement Better

Once the decision is made on what to implement, several support-relevant strategy aspects need to be kept in mind. The prioritized targets are to:

Targets

- Minimize implementation costs.
- Maximize time-to-value for the business.

SAP Enterprise Support helps customers succeed in both areas.

Minimizing implementation cost was a mission from SAP Enterprise Support right from the beginning, and it matured over the years. The SAP modification justification check offers insight to whether a company's uniquely developed custom code is still required or if it can be replaced by innovations that SAP provided in the meantime. The SAP Accelerated Innovation Enablement service helps users understand in detail how SAP's innovations work, and if they fit into the customer solution. Both services are delivered by SAP solution experts. The full value becomes obvious if you combine both services into a package and let an SAP custom code maintainability check run upfront to identify areas of interest.

Replace custom code

Maximizing time-to-value for the customers' lines of business is the other part where customers may expect help from SAP Enterprise Support. A complete toolset is provided, surrounded by required services and methodologies, to organize/structure the software change, reduce the test scope, automate testing, and minimize downtime. All this is subsumed in Application Lifecycle Management. Before, during, and after

Maximize time-to-value

go-live, it is essential that the new solution is working on its promises via the SAP integration/validation approach, and can be handed over to "normal" operations.

The circle is closed and the next innovation cycle can start. SAP's customers decide what to do next, and SAP Enterprise Support will help again on the innovation journey, no matter if it is SAP HANA, mobile, SAP Business Suite, or cloud-integration scenarios.

Innovate and implement innovation
Different examples have been given on how customers will additionally profit from the broad variety of tools, services, and methodologies that are delivered with SAP Enterprise Support. The unique delivery platform of this expertise, SAP Solution Manager, helps customers to effectively and efficiently perform operations and to innovate and implement faster. But only the combination with other elements of SAP Enterprise Support, the living collaboration with the support advisory center and support experts, as well as the empowerment part via the SAP Enterprise Support Academy (see Section 6.3.2), completes the picture of the most holistic support offering in the market.

Additional Support Options

Personalized support
SAP Enterprise Support covers the broadest customer base, and sometimes this creates the need for a more individualized and personalized support, as well as helps in situations when the customer must decide between a "make" or a "buy." This is why SAP offers SAP Premium Support Engagements, where additional customer requirements are being addressed that are not covered by the SAP Enterprise Support maintenance agreement described previously.

SAP Premium Support Engagements
- SAP ActiveEmbedded is an active partnership and supports our customers in the implementation, operations, and innovation lifecycles.

- SAP MaxAttention, a strategic support engagement for continued and effective business operations, is an additional option for our largest customers. SAP MaxAttention offers the highest level of collaboration and co-innovation with SAP Support.

Both types of SAP Premium Support Engagements are carried out through embedded SAP Support teams (experts embedded into SAP customers' IT operations organization), engineering services performed by professionals worldwide with unparalleled expertise, and "SAP support control centers" (a shared pool of experts at SAP) to help in operation questions (operations control center), in implementation questions (implementation control center) and in critical situations (mission control center). With regard to SAP Rapid Deployment solutions, the Innovation Control Center (ICC) is of highest relevance and is explained later in this chapter.

For the largest customers that do not find their fit in SAP Premium Support Engagement, SAP offers specialized support that targets this customer group via SAP Product Support for Large Enterprises. It supports customers in key areas such as continuous improvement and innovation and message handling.

Summary

SAP Enterprise Support is the universal maintenance offering that provides quick and easy access for all customers through all phases of the software lifecycle. SAP Enterprise Support aims to help SAP customers implement better, operate better, and innovate better. This happens through:

- Collaboration, such as customers' access to support experts and 24/7 support that offers help in critical situations.

- Automation capabilities provided by SAP Solution Manager, with tools, methodologies, and services to automate what can be automated and provide support experiences via roadmaps.

- Empowerment via the unique SAP Enterprise Support Academy that provides learning from experts and acts as a one-stop shop for accessing and consuming a wide range of services and educational content.

- With regard to SAP Rapid Deployment solutions, it means full support and the logical complement to further reduce the software-to-service ratio.

SAP Premium Support Engagement is the maintenance offering that offers personalized support and a deepened engagement through an onsite component, engineering services, and control centers, to bring fast value to customers, relieve them during critical situations, and closely connect them to the SAP support organization.

SAP Product Support for Large Enterprises is an offering that targets the special needs of SAP's biggest customers.

Further information on SAP Enterprise Support can be found on the SAP Service Marketplace at *http://service.sap.com/enterprisesupport*.

6.2.2 Reduce Implementation and Operational Costs with SAP Maintenance

Software to service ratio

As the market leader in enterprise application software, SAP helps companies of all sizes and industries run better. SAP empowers people and organizations to work together more efficiently and use business insights more effectively to stay ahead of the competition. To achieve this, SAP developed its comprehensive portfolio of solutions in the market categories of application software, analytics, mobile solutions, cloud solutions, and database solutions. Direct input and feedback from SAP customers and user groups is used to validate market trends and product spaces, specify and test new versions of the software, and improve the solutions in productive use.

SAP is committed to providing the very best in customer support. The proactive maintenance offering, comprised of the range of aforementioned services, tools, and methodologies from SAP, helps in optimizing business processes, minimizing risks, managing the lifecycles of customer's applications, and accelerating innovation. The following subsections will provide an overview of key SAP offerings that accelerate the time to innovation and reduce costs of implementation.

For customers investing into innovation and deploying them autonomously, SAP Enterprise Support with AIE is the right choice. Where onsite expertise from SAP is desired, the premium support engagement, SAP MaxAttention, with the ICC approach is the key value driver.

Drive Fast Adoption of SAP Enhancement Packages: Accelerated Innovation Enablement (AIE)

SAP's standard software offerings are evolving constantly according to the business requirements of their customers. That is why it is important to stay ahead of new functionality that SAP provides with new value releases through SAP Enhancement Packages (EhP) or SAP Rapid Deployment solutions, and to understand how these standard processes can replace expensive custom code in the existing system landscape.

SAP Enterprise Support addresses one of the key challenges when starting to build a customer-specific roadmap to value: How can I identify functionality relevant to my business, and what's the best way to implement it?

Customers may choose between different methods of mapping the individual innovation requirements with SAP's software enhancements that are shipped via SAP Enhancement Packages, SAP Rapid Deployment solutions, Support Packages, or SAP Notes. The options range from different self-services, such the SAP Solution Browser and the SAP Improvement Finder, to a service option for a direct expert touch point, called SAP Accelerated Innovation Enablement. These options will be explained here.

SAP's entry point to find improvements and innovations quickly is the SAP Service Marketplace. Access SAP improvements and innovations directly at *http://service.sap.com/findinnovation*. The site provides an overview of SAP's current products and solutions, as well as planned innovations (roadmaps). In addition, it provides access to tools and services that help identify customer-specific business value.

In order to give customers a maximum choice in how to approach and adopt innovation, SAP has been building a series of self-service tools to identify new functionality with dedicated focus on the different applications comprised in the SAP Business Suite.

The starting point is the solution browser (*http://service.sap.com/solutionbrowser*):

- The solution browser can help to discover new functionality across all core SAP application releases and respective SAP enhancement packages (i.e., SAP CRM, SAP ERP, SAP SCM, and SAP SRM).
- Functionality between a customer's existing release and any selected release up to SAP Business Suite 7 and the latest enhancement packages are outlined.

SAP Improvement Finder (*www.sapimprovementfinder.com*):

▶ SAP Improvement Finder helps users discover improvements delivered through SAP's Customer Connection program with user groups, addressing only a selection of focus topics. These improvements are delivered via support notes and support packages, and enhance SAP product versions that customers are using today.

▶ Furthermore, SAP provides customer-tailored services to support customers in identifying functional value based on their existing system usage.

Both the solution browser and the SAP Improvement Finder help identify appropriate business functions and features, whereas actual recommendations on SAP ERP business functions in relevance to the individual business are provided by the SAP Business Function Prediction Finder.

The new version of the business function prediction for SAP ERP and especially SAP ECC 6.0 (*http://service.sap.com/bfp*) is a self-service to more easily discover the SAP ERP business functions relevant for a customer's business. Business functions are part of the SAP Enhancement Package strategy, and can be activated selectively based on customers' demand. The service is free of charge and gives tailored recommendations dependent on how a customer is using the SAP ERP system today.

The brand-new offering, business scenario recommendations for SAP Business Suite powered by SAP HANA (*www.suiteonhana.com*), gives customers advice on which business scenarios in the SAP Business Suite applications benefit from SAP HANA. For a sample report see Figure 6.2.

With the modern SAP HANA platform, SAP helps companies to transform their entire business in real-time, with minimal disruption for smarter business innovations, faster business processes, and simpler business interactions. The offering is tailored to specific customer systems and free of charge.

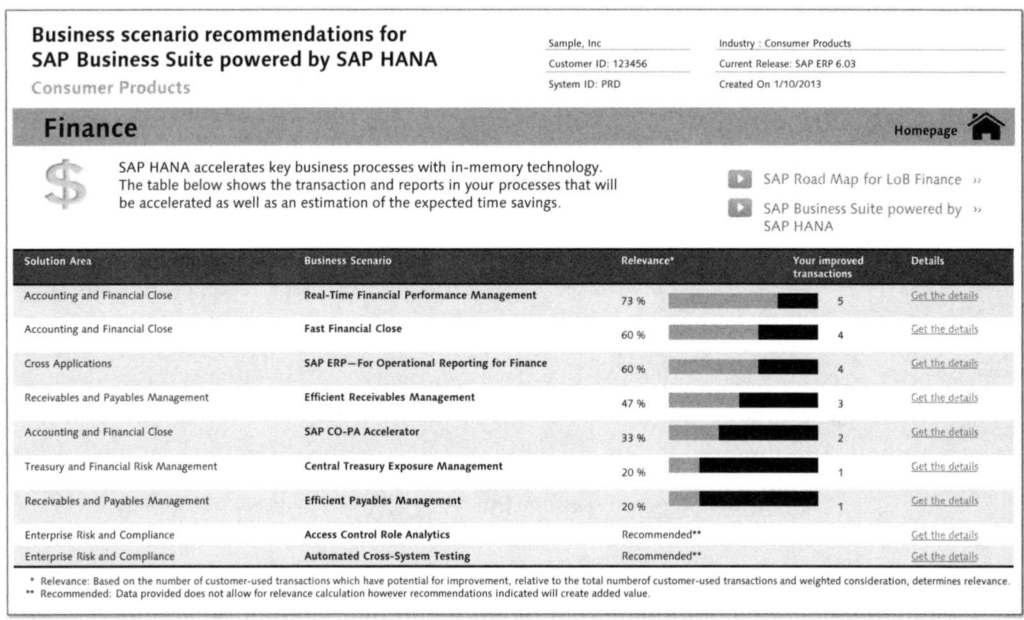

Solution Area	Business Scenario	Relevance*	Your improved transactions	Details
Accounting and Financial Close	Real-Time Financial Performance Management	73 %	5	Get the details
Accounting and Financial Close	Fast Financial Close	60 %	4	Get the details
Cross Applications	SAP ERP—For Operational Reporting for Finance	60 %	4	Get the details
Receivables and Payables Management	Efficient Receivables Management	47 %	3	Get the details
Accounting and Financial Close	SAP CO-PA Accelerator	33 %	2	Get the details
Treasury and Financial Risk Management	Central Treasury Exposure Management	20 %	1	Get the details
Receivables and Payables Management	Efficient Payables Management	20 %	1	Get the details
Enterprise Risk and Compliance	Access Control Role Analytics	Recommended**		Get the details
Enterprise Risk and Compliance	Automated Cross-System Testing	Recommended**		Get the details

Figure 6.2 Sample Report: Business Scenario Recommendation for SAP Business Suite Powered by SAP HANA

Direct engagement

Are you looking for a direct expert touch-point to validate your findings? With SAP Accelerated Innovation Enablement (AIE) as part of SAP Enterprise Support and accessible via the academy, the customer can benefit from direct engagement with SAP's experts who assist and enable customers to evaluate the innovation capabilities of the latest SAP Enhancement Package. SAP provides up to five days to remotely access an SAP solution engineer per calendar year.

With AIE live-expert sessions, SAP solution architects remotely inform customers about the latest innovation contained in SAP Enhancement Packages. This also includes live demos of the new functionality and how it may be deployed for the business-process requirements. The live expert sessions are offered in different areas (e.g., SAP ERP, SAP CRM, SAP SCM) and are either available as one-on-one sessions for one customer only, or as sessions for a few customers—where the benefit comes from joint discussions.

AIE expert-on-demand
In case additional questions remain open, these questions can be addressed to SAP experts via AIE expert-on-demand requests. AIE expert-on-demand sessions address one special area to be answered by one expert. It is recommended to start with AIE live-expert sessions to build up general knowledge on SAP Enhancement Packages before booking an AIE expert-on-demand session.

In focus are specific questions concerning the new functionalities on the latest enhancement package, and technical questions about architecture or installation of enhancement packages.

The overall session catalogue and the request templates for AIE services can be found under *http://service.sap.com/aie*.

Drive Accelerated Innovation with SAP Premium Engagement: Innovation Control Center (ICC)

Maintainability
After finding the right SAP solution that meets the requirements of the business, it is important to ensure maintainability of the solution long-term and stay innovative by constantly profiting from new SAP enhancements. To ensure this, customers should avoid unnecessary modifications. In the long-term, unnecessary custom code leads to a higher complexity of the landscape, an increased total cost of ownership (TCO), and it becomes a roadblock for business transitions, innovations, and upgrades. Therefore it is crucial to identify and use SAP Best Practices during a rapid-deployment solutions implementation, and to get feedback from SAP *before* required changes are made to the standard software.

This comes from personalized support and a deep engagement through an on-site component called the Innovation Control Center (ICC). An ICC is relevant for new implementations with new or existing customers and is exclusively available through SAP Premium Engagement (SAP ActiveEmbedded or SAP MaxAttention) in order to drive accelerated innovation.

Speed implementation
The ICC is designed to speed up the implementation timelines dramatically while unlocking innovation for the business. Through the center, which is located on-site and led by an expert from the SAP Active Global

Support (SAP AGS) organization, the customer gains access to SAP software experts who have a direct line to SAP development (SAP mission control center). This extremely close collaboration between the ICC and the SAP back office serves as the cornerstone for fulfilling the Innovation Control Center's charter: lowering the cost of implementation. Considering the evolution of offerings from SAP AGS, the ICC is the logical next step in providing customers with full support and comprehensive functional expertise starting from the very first days of the blueprinting phase of the implementation project.

The overall approach of the engagement runs the customer through the following activities:

Engagement approach

1. The starting point is a scoping and requirements workshop, the blueprinting phase, followed by an evaluation and mapping against the existing rapid-deployment solutions.

2. In continuation, SAP can build a cloud-based value prototype in order to support the overall blueprint evaluation. The prototype allows the customer to identify further perceived gaps and discuss to what extent custom code can be reduced or avoided ("zero modifications"). The aim is to reduce development, deployment and maintenance effort. In return the SAP response provides a full summary of all recommendations including necessary enhancement points to be used, if a standard solution should not be sufficient.

3. After the customer's decision, the prototype can be transitioned to the customer sandbox environment. The end result, depending on the blueprint complexity, is the transition to the customer production system.

Targets of an ICC include the following:

ICC targets

- Maximize the usage of standard functionality: position best practices.

- Avoid unnecessary custom code (explicitly modifications).

- Secure the implementation project: protect customer investment. Validate all integration aspects end-to-end.

- Get ready for the operations phase: prepare for smooth, non-disruptive operations.

ICC components

A classic ICC consists of the following components (depending on project phase), including the following (see Figure 6.3):

- Zero modification.
- Integration validation.
- Preparation of an operations control center (OCC).
- Optional: application lifecycle management (ALM), rapid prototyping.

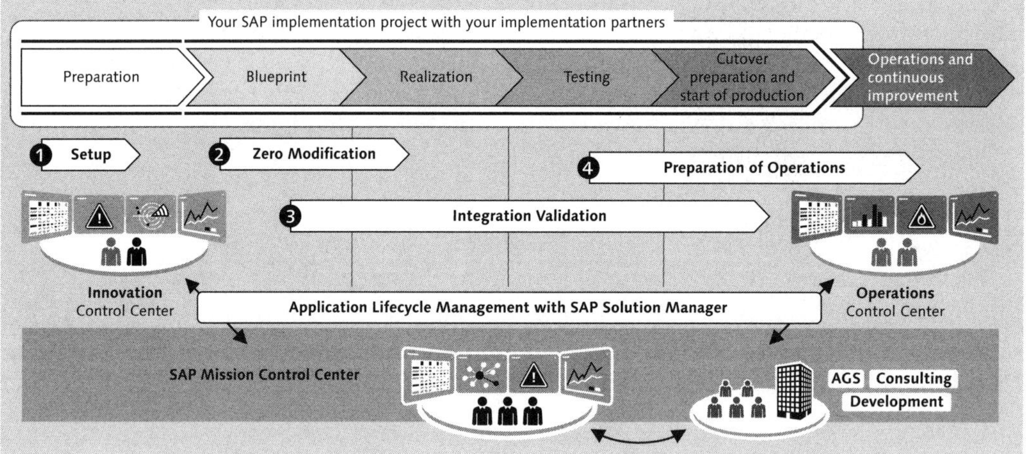

Figure 6.3 Different Components of an Innovation Control Center Structured by Project Phases

ICC setup

The set-up phase is necessary to integrate the ICC into the existing project organization at the customer and to establish the communication with the project. Roles and tasks of an ICC will be defined in detail, together with SAP. SAP Solution Manager will be set up as communication medium to dispatch perceived project gaps to the SAP mission control center at SAP. Additional dashboards are offered in SAP Solution Manager to monitor the technical progress of the implementation process (e.g., blueprint analyzer, see Figure 6.4). The detailed practical instructions will be aligned during the initial scoping and requirements workshop.

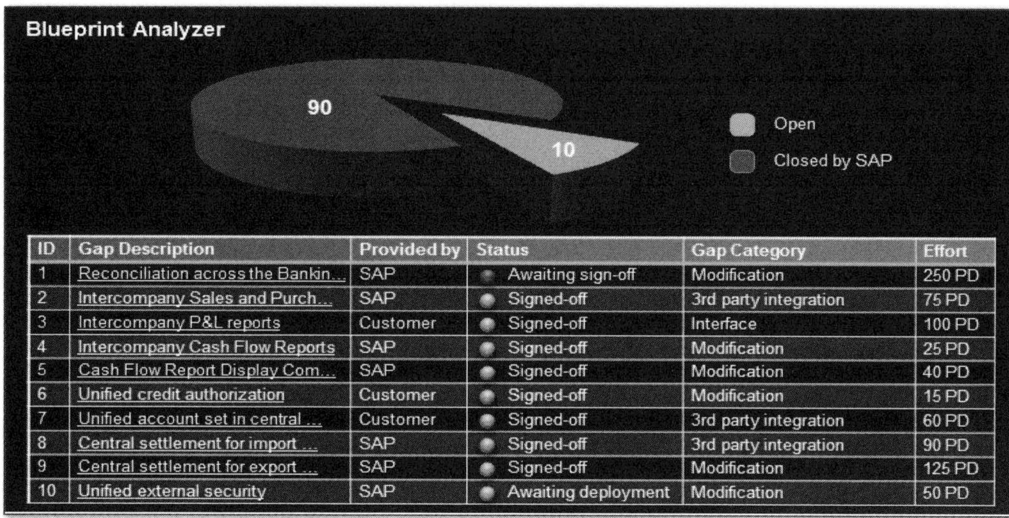

ID	Gap Description	Provided by	Status	Gap Category	Effort
1	Reconciliation across the Bankin...	SAP	Awaiting sign-off	Modification	250 PD
2	Intercompany Sales and Purch...	SAP	Signed-off	3rd party integration	75 PD
3	Intercompany P&L reports	Customer	Signed-off	Interface	100 PD
4	Intercompany Cash Flow Reports	SAP	Signed-off	Modification	25 PD
5	Cash Flow Report Display Com...	SAP	Signed-off	Modification	40 PD
6	Unified credit authorization	Customer	Signed-off	Modification	15 PD
7	Unified account set in central ...	Customer	Signed-off	3rd party integration	60 PD
8	Central settlement for import ...	SAP	Signed-off	3rd party integration	90 PD
9	Central settlement for export ...	SAP	Signed-off	Modification	125 PD
10	Unified external security	SAP	Awaiting deployment	Modification	50 PD

Figure 6.4 Blueprint Analyzer Creates Transparency of the Gap Validation in an Innovation Control Center

Zero modification is a new offering of SAP AGS to get as close to SAP standard as possible by avoiding unnecessary modifications. Thus SAP provides an optimization of a business blueprint and supports the alignment with SAP Best Practice solutions in an early project phase (see Figure 6.5). By applying as many best practices as possible, customers minimize implementation and operations efforts. To manage this, an experienced ICC lead of SAP AGS will be employed in the project to filter and document the gaps, and forward relevant gaps to the functional experts in the underlying SAP mission control center.

Implementing complex solution landscapes and mission-critical business-process scenarios can be a challenging task that is typically distributed across many teams and stakeholders. To cover a full and ongoing validation of the defined target processes including integration aspects to cover data consistency and interface monitoring of an SAP solution, SAP AGS offers integration validation (IV) as a key component of an ICC as shown in Figure 6.4. The setup of the IV is part of the ICC and therefore addressed in the initial scoping and requirements workshop.

Business Process	Data Consistency			Exception Management Instrumentation		Exception Management Procedures			System Integration & Queues	Performance & Scalability		End of Day & Volume Processing
	No user can create inconsistencies by any means	Transactional Consistency - All postings belonging together are posted or not at all	Data consistency across systems can be proactively checked	All exceptions are logged and exceptions raised to the end user with the appropriate context information	End-to-End Process completion trace available for all systems – SAP and non-SAP	All exceptions creates an alert	All exceptions are creating an incidents and incident resolution is tracked	There are guided procedures for managing exceptions	All queues are monitored with regard to processing completion and errors. (Business process monitoring)	End-to-End Business Process Performance trace enabled	Business process KPIs are defined and reported	Parallelization and restart ability are implemented and tested
Order to Cash												
Procure to Pay												
Production to Order												
Production to Stock												
Material Resource Planning												
Supply Network Planning												
Month End Closing												
Goods Receivable												

Figure 6.5 Integration Validator Dashboard: Transparency to what Degree KPIs for Target Processes are Already being Met

Integration validation

IV supports in:

▶ Introducing solutions into production smoothly while maintaining ongoing operations with minimal disruption.

▶ Combining best practices in one standardized, project-based delivery approach.

▶ Validating end-to-end processes with regard to technical integration aspects: data consistency, exception management, system integration, volume processing, and performance.

Operations control center

One aim of the ICC concept is to ensure that the new application can be supported safely and efficiently during productive usage. Therefore, IT operations should be optimized and already automated before go-live during implementation. Preparing an operations control center (OCC) is another component of an ICC.

An OCC is comprised of a small team of IT operators, who work on the alerts in a guided way (event management). It provides dashboards that report the status of the business processes and related IT landscapes. A continuous improvement process can be included, which optimizes the overall operational setup depending on newly identified business requirements.

6.3 Services for Enablement

Enablement for customers and partners is an essential service as everyone implementing, using, or operating solutions needs to have the right skills. Depending on topics like solution or processes, its target groups can range from simple information updates, knowledge transfer, to complete formal education curricula and certifications.

Almost every month, SAP releases new and enhanced business solutions to the market. SAP's portfolio is continuously broadened, and release cycles are shortened to respond to the rapidly changing business demands of SAP's clients. In order to simplify and speed up the time-to-market and time-to-value of SAP solutions, SAP has introduced new ways of packaging best practices and simplifying the implementation experience that was explained earlier in this book.

However, implementation and operations teams need to have fundamental know-how about the capabilities of SAP Rapid Deployment solutions and the underlying SAP solutions. All customer solution lifecycle phases have their task-specific knowledge demands (see Figure 6.6).

Knowledge demands

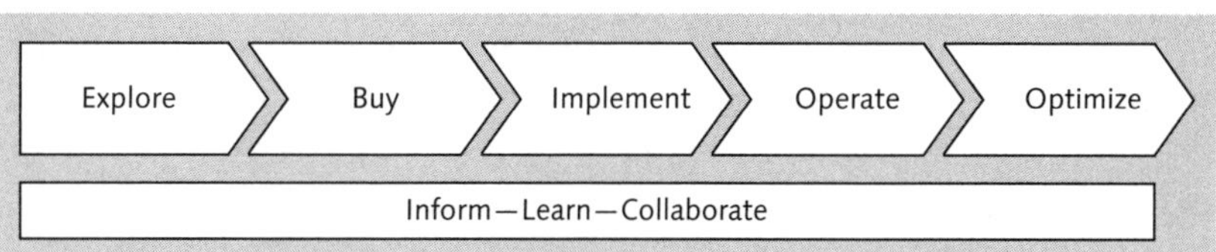

Figure 6.6 Customer Solution Lifecycle Supported by Continuous Learning

For all these needs, SAP provides a comprehensive knowledge transfer and education portfolio as well as information, collaboration, and support services. The offerings are continuously enhanced to reflect project experiences and to develop best practices. It is crucial to SAP to harvest

Comprehensive knowledge portfolio

the knowledge in order to simplify and scale the adoption while increasing the scope and relevance of SAP Rapid Deployment solutions packages.

6.3.1 SAP Ramp-Up Knowledge Transfer: Supporting SAP Solution Launches

As stated previously, the focus on SAP solutions makes SAP offerings much easier and less expensive to consume. This requires a best-practice approach to knowledge management. SAP solutions are created by assembling products and content across SAP's entire portfolio—a great deal of knowledge is required to effectively drive a solution business along the customer lifecycle.

When launching a new solution to the market, it is essential to orchestrate information-delivery and enablement of SAP's workforce and the SAP ecosystem. The enablement demand starts months before the formal release to customers, as the first customers participating in the SAP solution ramp-up need to be engaged. Therefore SAP has introduced the Ramp-Up Knowledge Transfer (RKT). RKT is embedded into SAP's standard development process (which is called "product innovation lifecycle") as a product standard.

The RKT scope, in the form of learning maps as well as the enablement content, needs to be provided at project quality gates before the ramp-up phase can start. The content—often created by product managers and developers—comes in hands-on formats like how-to guides, as rapid e-learning (e.g., demos, presentations with voiceovers) and also in the form of live/remote workshops and sandbox systems.

Depending on the solution, KPIs are defined by how many consultants in which role need to be enabled, and fulfillment is monitored during the ramp-up phase. Thus SAP can ensure that with the start of the first customer implementation projects in ramp-up, a sufficient number of SAP technical, solution, and business transformation consultants (SAP and SAP Partners) are enabled to support the implementation projects.

In most cases, a new solution is not fully "new" but a new release to an existing foundation. Generally it is sufficient to complement a project team with a certain number of consultants who are already enabled on the new solution as well. With the start of individual customer implementations in ramp-up, the knowledge available at the "release to customer" point can only be seen as an initial foundation to start maturing and completing the implementation content towards best practices.

During the first implementation projects, it is elementary that implementation teams collaborate closely with the development and support teams to solve product issues, improve the RKT enablement content (which is an important input in the SAP Education training material), and jointly enhance implementation procedures, eventually to define best practices in any format (e.g., as part of SAP Rapid Deployment solutions, SAP Solution Manager content, implementation and upgrade guides, enterprise cloud-based deployments).

Ramp-up customers get access to the RKT content free via their ramp-up coaches and project leads. Customers and partners can also access the content, either via the SAP Learning Hub including all digital assets from SAP Education as a subscription—or separately as online knowledge products. Customers can find further information and how to purchase SAP online knowledge products on the SAP Service Marketplace (SMP) (*https://service.sap.com/okp*).

6.3.2 SAP Education: Accelerating Time-to-Market and Time-to-Value

Every year, SAP Education trains about 300,000 partners and customers in SAP skills. As a growth company, SAP needs to increase the availability of IT skill sets, particularly of SAP-relevant skill sets, to create a market that is ready to embrace and adopt new SAP innovation as it rolls out.

SAP Education has put a lot of emphasis in offering the newest, most effective, and most engaging training methods to its customers. It has evolved over the years in step with advancements in the training and education market, starting years ago with traditional, classroom-style training, and evolving to offer e-learning, in-context, and just-in-time training and mobile learning. E-learning has proved to be an extremely cost-effective method of education for organizations.

Company ROI With both traditional classroom and new training initiatives, companies have seen excellent return on investment. According to analyst firm IDC, the application of 1.5% of project cost to training improves project success by 30%. In addition, every dollar spent on training yields an approximate 15% gain in productivity. Companies have also noticed the opportunity cost of untrained employees: A CompTIA 2012 report states that employers cite an IT skills gap as negatively impacting their productivity (41%), customer engagement (32%), and security (31%).

SAP Innovation Curriculum In recent years, SAP broadened its portfolio of offerings, including the introduction of flexible online learning. In addition, SAP introduced the SAP Innovation Curriculum for emerging innovation such as SAP HANA and SAP mobility solutions. IDC remarks that "unlike most ven-dors...SAP makes training available along with the beta-testing release of the software to both 'test' the training and provide the ecosystem and early-adopting clients with the best opportunity for successfully deploy-ing the new software."

SAP Learning Hub In 2012, SAP launched the SAP Learning Hub, a subscription-based offering that provides 24/7 access to the electronic learning curriculum of SAP Education. SAP hosts private and public versions of SAP Learning Hub. Enterprise Edition is a private environment for either partners or customers to increase flexibility to consume SAP's learning content while also lowering costs. Customer Edition and Partner Edition are public versions designed to support SAP centers of expertise in either enterprises or partner organizations.

Figure 6.7 illustrates all SAP Education service and software offerings supporting the plan/build/run phases of SAP solutions.

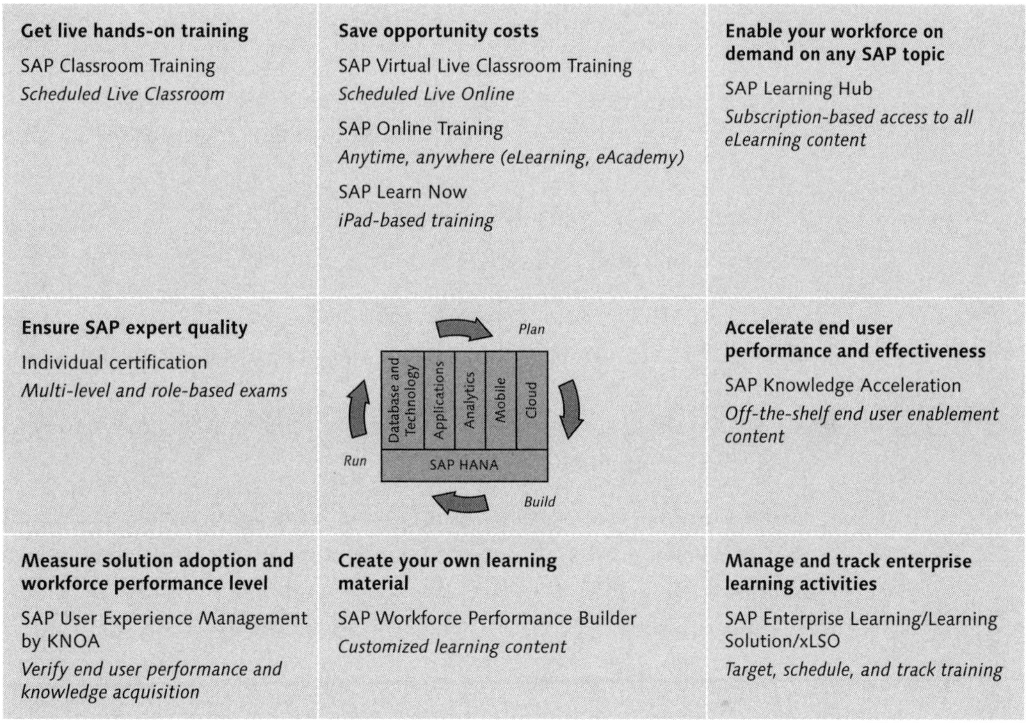

Figure 6.7 SAP Education Addressing Requirements in Each Phase of Business

6.3.3 SAP Certifications: Key for Achieving Technology Value

SAP Education offerings for industry-recognized certification can make the SAP workforce invaluable to customers that want to speed business adoption and enhance the value of their SAP investments.

In general, associate and professional certification exams are available: *Associate certifications* are for those who are new to SAP solutions. They cover the fundamental knowledge requirements for an SAP consultant, ensuring the successful acquisition of broad SAP solution knowledge and skills. They help people to:

Associate/professional

▶ Gain an externally recognized mark of excellence that clients seek.

▶ Establish differentiation in a crowded marketplace.

▶ Execute tasks with confidence and skill.

Professional certifications require proven project experience, business process knowledge, and a more detailed understanding of SAP solutions. They help:

- Demonstrate experience and expertise through a rigorous testing process.
- Promote a more globally applicable accreditation.
- Lead as well as execute tasks and engagements.

SAP Education is working closely with the SAP Certification & Enablement Influence Council to enhance the value of certification and improve the exams. An increasing number of customers and partners are now looking towards certification as a reliable benchmark to safeguard their investments.

Various options for accessing training and knowledge are available. SAP Education provides a choice of in-classroom or virtual live classroom training on a public schedule, or corresponding e-learning or mobile learning offerings.

Certification-specific trainings
In particular, new starters on a topic can prepare most efficiently for an SAP certification exam by leveraging certification-specific trainings in a streamlined sequence as:

- SAP Academy (classroom delivered academy curriculum).
- SAP eAcademy (self-paced online learning experience, including access to asynchronous 5/24 help-desk support and training systems over a certain time period to practice their knowledge and prepare for the certification).

6.3.4 SAP Education Software: Improve Learning Management, Knowledge Transfer, and Performance

Solutions
Customers can also benefit from education-related software products that help drive down customers total cost of ownership and increase motivation and productivity of employees. Currently SAP Education offers the following solutions:

- SAP Workforce Performance Builder is SAP's new solution for creating, editing, and distributing process documentation, context-sensitive user help, rapid e-learning, and test scripts. Once you build the content, you can distribute it as e-learning (standalone or in your learning management system), online help, mobile, integrated in SAP Solution Manager or on-screen guide—giving you flexible deployment options. Through automation like rerecording and multiple outputs (docu, training, simulations) it makes the learning and help content creation much more effective—and in the end, the end users become more skilled and confident in using SAP solutions.

- SAP Knowledge Acceleration software is pre-built, web-based learning and knowledge support that can be quickly deployed to users via a server, intranet, or CD. It can be used out of the box, or customized using SAP Workforce Performance Builder. Knowledge Acceleration is available for many SAP and SAP BusinessObjects solutions.

- The SAP User Experience Management application by Knoa is the only product to measure the end user experience and performance customers encounter with their SAP solution. It tracks response time, errors, workflows, and user behavior, and presents data in dashboards and built-in SAP BusinessObjects reports. The data can be used to improve training, but also the whole support processes.

- SAP Learning Solution and SAP Enterprise Learning enable you to plan, implement, and control learning strategy across the extended enterprise with a comprehensive learning environment. SAP's Learning Management System integrates business processes, content development, and delivery of learning linked to employee performance. SAP Enterprise Learning also provides virtual classroom functionality.

- With the add on for external learning (xLSO) customers can easily provide learning to external target groups like dealers, customers, or suppliers and improve quality, productivity, and time to market.

- Fully integrated with SAP Learning Solution and SAP Enterprise Learning, the SAP Learning Assistant mobile app is a native application for mobile learning that provides access to learning content from anywhere, online and offline, and via the Apple iPad. SAP Learning Solution or SAP Enterprise Learning are required with this app.

- SAP Learn Now is a mobile learning app for the Apple iPad that enables users to consume mobile optimized courses that have been purchased through the SAP Training and Certification Shop.

Further information about SAP Education can be accessed via:

- SAP Education global website on *http://www.sap.com* • TRAINING & EDUCATION
- SAP Education Community in the SAP Community Network: *http://scn.sap.com/community/training-and-education*
- Twitter: *http://www.twitter.com/saplearn* or *http://www.twitter.com/sapedu*

6.3.5 SAP Enterprise Support Academy: Expert-to-Expert Training

For customers, the SAP Support Portal plays a central role—next to SAP Solution Manager, which was mentioned in previous chapters. This portal delivers, for example, support-relevant applications like message handling as well as information like SAP Notes.

Additionally, support customers can access the SAP Enterprise Support Academy (*http://service.sapcom/esacademy*). Customers can access expert led e-learning or knowledge-transfer assets for self-study regarding the current IT and support offers from SAP.

A rich mix of service and learning offerings—based on 40 years of customer interactions—are available. The SAP Enterprise Support Academy is focusing on all customers that have chosen SAP Enterprise Support—independent of the experience with SAP system landscapes or specific applications or support tools.

One example is in expert-guided implementations, where experts demonstrate how customers can configure and deploy specific tasks in SAP Solution Manager. Thus employees of customer IT departments are enabled to foster their skills and knowledge. The SAP Enterprise Support Academy supports in implementing application lifecycle management ("Build SAP like a Factory") according to valid IT service management-standards as well as in the sustainable operations ("Run SAP like a Factory").

Service- and knowledge-transfer contents are accessible via different categories:

- Role: alignment of offerings according to focus of task.

- Phase of software lifecycle: implementation, operations, upgrade, or innovation.

- Method or delivery-format of single contents.

Knowledge-Transfer Methods

The offered contents can either be accessed on a self-paced timeframe, or expert-led. The following methods and channels are available.

SAP Best Practices Library for Operations

The best-practice library is a resource that contains guides for products, databases, and operating systems. Different documents describe the experiences and insights from implementations and operations of solutions from the SAP Business Suite or SAP BusinessObjects. Through this resource, customers have direct access to expert knowledge around the clock, as download is enabled for immediate or later use.

Meet the Expert Sessions

The interactive, expert-led format highlights the different areas of operations in overview and offers detailed insight into single topics. Questions are answered immediately by SAP experts. The delivery occurs virtually and in different languages. The replay library, with recordings of past sessions, offers an extensive catalog next to virtual, live sessions.

Accelerated Innovation Enablement

The SAP Enterprise Support Academy also offers access to service offerings for an efficient usage of SAP Enhancement Packages. The service offering contains an evaluation of the SAP Enhancement Package technology and the new features of the SAP Business Suite. This is offered as live-expert or expert-on-demand sessions with solution architects from SAP. A summary at the end completes each session.

Expert-Guided Implementation Sessions

These are virtual workshop sessions that guide customers through the technical steps of the implementation using SAP Best Practices. They are a unique combination of training and direct configuration in the specific

Virtual workshop sessions

customer landscape, together with access to experts on demand. Focus areas are foundational configuration, setup of business-process monitoring, and management of customer-specific developments. They also contain the configuration of SAP Solution Manager and the setup of a single work center as well as the preparation for using self-services.

Guided Self-Services

With guided self-services, the SAP Enterprise Support Academy offers proven and standardized methods to analyze and optimize customer systems. The step-by-step guides are offered through SAP Solution Manager and are always accessible. They contain the optimization of the most important areas, like system performance, management of data volume, change management, security, and business processes.

QuickIQs

Short recorded tutorials transfer expert knowledge on configuration or changes of system settings. The QuickIQ tutorials are created with SAP Workforce Performance Builder—SAP's authoring tool for context-sensitive documentation and e-learning.

Run SAP Partner Academy

The SAP Partner program makes collaboration between partners and SAP easier. It is a basis to cover the demand for solutions and services in the segments of large enterprise customers, as well as for the growing segment of small and mid-sized customers. SAP's goal is to deliver world-class solutions and services—through SAP itself, or via SAP Partners. Therefore different programs were established to monitor service quality. SAP customers can rely on a consistent level of professionalism, technical expertise, and understanding of their specific requirements by the SAP Partners that support them.

Up-skilling One of the basic elements of the SAP Partner program is up-skilling, or continuous training. This is guaranteed via the Run SAP Partner Academy, which, like the SAP Enterprise Support Academy, combines established solutions with advanced online content and enablement that is specifically tailored to the partner (see Figure 6.8 outlining the key elements).

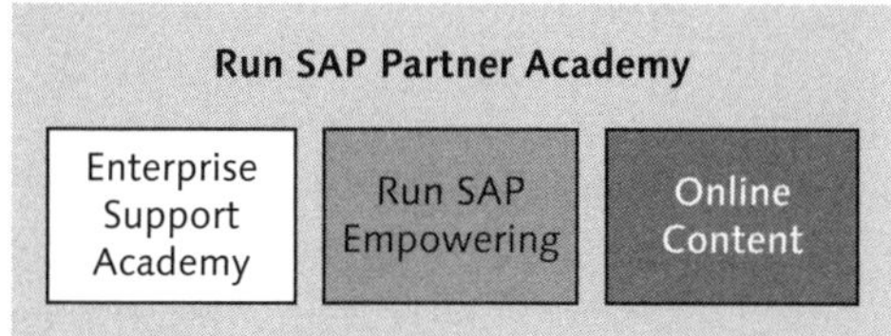

Figure 6.8 Key Elements of Run SAP Partner Academy

The Run SAP Partner Academy enables SAP Partners to access the contents and solutions from the SAP Enterprise Support Academy. This guarantees that partners have the same knowledge level on the same foundation as SAP Enterprise Support customers.

In most cases, SAP Partners need a more extensive knowledge to be a trusted advisor for their customers. This is ensured, as the Run SAP program partner can register for webinars that are tailored to partner needs—and get direct knowledge transfer from SAP experts. Additionally, partners can register for boot camps that can last from a few days to several weeks. The boot camps are not based on online knowledge transfer, but on intense training of partners at SAP locations.

The offering is enhanced through special online content for the partners, which enables them to access best practices or documentation on SAP Solution Manager as a managed service.

6.3.6 SAP Rapid Deployment Solutions Enablement Program

As part of an SAP Rapid Deployment solutions, enablement content is available as an accelerator to make project delivery faster and easier. It mainly targets implementation consultants—end-user training needs to be driven by the customer.

The enablement content of the SAP Rapid Deployment solutions for partners consists of two offering types: free and premium service assets. Premium assets can be purchased by partners to speed up the rapid-deployment-solution specific implementation project.

Free Assets: "Solution Discovery"

The "Solution Discovery" free assets consist of:

▶ Sales presentations

▶ Collaterals

▶ Web presence

▶ Demos

▶ Training materials

These free assets can be accessed directly through SAP Service Marketplace for each SAP Rapid Deployment solution package. Partners need to go to the Service Marketplace, find the solution they are interested in, and download the Solution Discovery free content.

Premium Services Assets: "Solution Deployment"

The premium services assets, also referred to as "Solution Deployment," speed up the implementation and reduce partner's workload for rapid-deployment solutions packages. The assets can be purchased by SAP Partners through their local SAP Education office.

Asset contents   The assets consist of SAP-supported best practices that are pre-configured into each solution's process scope and applied to project delivery containing the following:

▶ Step-by-step implementation guides.

▶ Guides to chart the course of a successful implementation.

▶ Tools and accelerators each step of the way.

▶ E-learning courses to speed up the knowledge transfer for the particular rapid-deployment solution package.

Learning map   Besides this SAP Rapid Deployment solutions-specific content, there is also a generic learning map where partners can get a basic introduction to SAP Rapid Deployment solutions, their pricing, and the rapid-deployment solutions partner framework. Furthermore, they provide detailed knowledge transfer on generic topics in SAP Rapid Deployment solutions implementation methodology:

▶ Technical concepts plus tools.

▶ Implementation steps in Solution Builder.

- Implementation steps in SAP Solution Manager.

- SAP Rapid Deployment solutions demo options and use of SAP NetWeaver Business Client.

- Cross topics.

Further information can be found at: *http://partner.sap.com/rds*

6.3.7 SAP University Alliance and SAP Student Academy: Next-Generation SAP Experts

SAP University Alliance (UA) provides connections between students, customers, partners, and SAP experts. The University Alliances Program opens up the world of SAP to more than 1,350 universities worldwide. Through the program universities gain access to a wide range of opportunities to engage with SAP. Associate members can take part in competitions and contests, send students to our Innojams, Codejams and Design Thinking events, get involved with Co-Innovation projects with customers and partners in the SAP universe, and get directly involved in research and the development of new SAP solutions. Full members have all this and can also gain access to full SAP solutions from business analytics to mobility, SAP HANA to BPM.

SAP University Alliance

As part of SAP's strategy to close the SAP skills gap in the information and communications technology (ICT) market and foster co-development with university students, a new online training offering has been developed specifically for university students: SAP Student Academy. Based on SAP eAcademy (comprehensive online training offering from SAP Education preparing for SAP certifications), SAP Student Academy will provide a strong value proposition to universities and students to become more employable through early in-study completion of SAP certifications. The offering will cover core SAP certification tracks in SAP's major market categories of business applications, database and technology, analytics, and mobility.

SAP Student Academy

Further information can be found at:

- *http://www.sap.com/corporate-en/our-company/university-alliances/index.epx*

- SAP Community network: *http://scn.sap.com/community/uac*

6.3.8 Educating the Crowd: openSAP "Enablement of Innovation Adoption at Scale"

While the academic world has rapidly adopted the massive open online course (MOOC) concept, enterprises have yet to grasp the enormous potential it offers when it comes to mass education and enablement. Based on the success of the openHPI lecture on in-memory data management, SAP is introducing enterprise MOOCs with a mass-education platform called openSAP (see Figure 6.9).

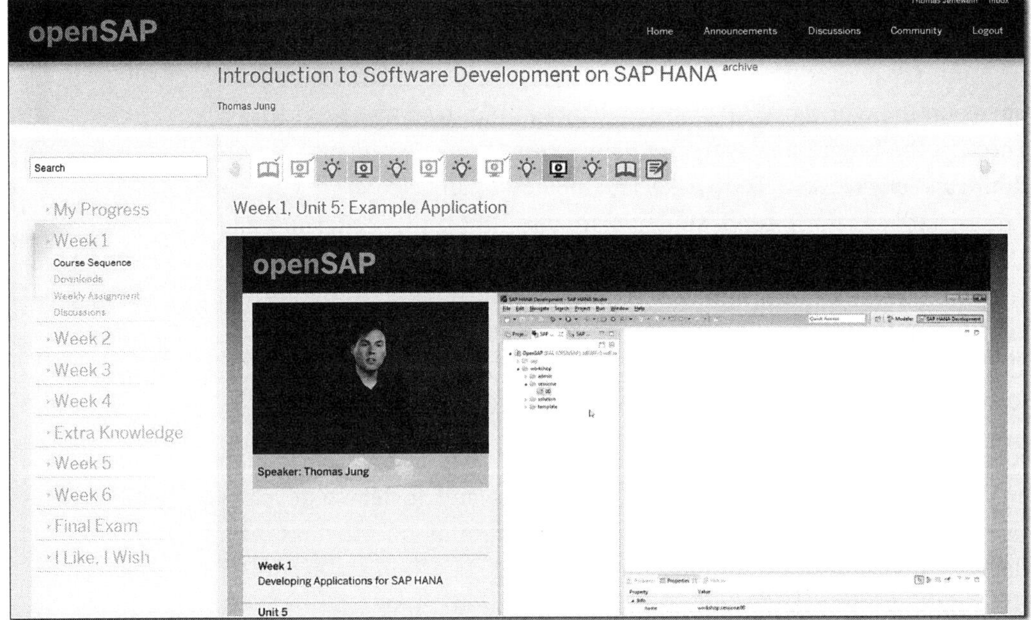

Figure 6.9 openSAP: Introduction to Software Development on SAP HANA

Features of openSAP Courses

The key difference between MOOCs and other types of e-learning lies in the way MOOCs demand commitment by leveraging tried and trusted classroom concepts in an online-delivery format. OpenSAP uses these concepts in the following ways:

▸ Courses have a defined duration (typically six weeks) to which students need to adhere.

- Courses are based on lectures (delivery through video), supporting material (slide decks, handouts), and self-tests.

- Students need to submit homework on a weekly basis and adhere to deadlines. The homework is graded and contributes to the points required to receive a statement of accomplishment.

- Students can discuss the course content in an online forum.

- Courses end with a final exam.

The average duration of the video lectures is 90 minutes per week. Combined with additional self-study and homework, the average effort required to complete an openSAP course successfully will be half a day per week. This makes it easy for students to combine courses with their other responsibilities.

Delivery of openSAP Course Content

Students will have to register with openSAP to access the course content. The content is then delivered online through the openSAP website (*http://open.sap.com*).

For the first course, 40,386 learners were enrolled after two months—9,383 course participants earned a graded record of achievement. The numbers show the opportunities in scaling and speeding up enablement. SAP plans to leverage this method even further for innovation adoption at scale—leveraging it for rolling out new innovations and strategies into the SAP ecosystem.

Next Generation "Informing—Learning—Collaborating" Experience

SAP is innovating achievements in continuous and flexible learning, and they constantly improve their enablement programs and services. SAP adopts, or even shapes, new market trends. More and more mobile learning tools and contents are becoming available. SAP Education works on using SAPs modern cloud based learning management system to offer enablement content free and via subscription in a consistent and engaging user experience. Massive open online courses, as well as the increased support of social and informal learning, will certainly also play a bigger role there. It is nothing new to suggest that most learning happens on the job or in social interaction. However, now new technology, like mobile devices and social networks (like SAP Jam) are available, which makes it possible to support those informal and social learning scenarios much better. Stay tuned for upcoming learning and education innovations—you can inform yourself by clicking on the links that we've mentioned throughout this section.

6.3.9 Information and Collaboration

The information section is a guide to information available from SAP. There is indeed a lot of information available, covering all aspects of a typical implementation process. However, it might be challenging to find the right information. With the variety of resources available, users rarely feel confident that they've really found everything. Sometimes it might be even unclear where to start.

Available resources include:

- SAP Help Portal
- SAP.com
- SAPPartnerEdge.com
- SAP EcoHub
- SAP Community Network (SCN)
- SAP experts

In the following subsections, we'll also detail the different resources that are available for you to pursue further, more specific information that is beyond the scope of this book.

Online Resources

In this section, we'll detail the resources that you can find online.

- *sap.com/rds*
- SAP Service Marketplace
  The SAP Service Marketplace provides a repository where customers and SAP Partners can obtain information and access programs and other materials. It is the central access point to all relevant information about SAP products and services, regardless of which website

(e.g., SAP Solution Explorer or SAP Help Portal) this information is hosted on.

http://service.sap.com/solutionpackages

▶ Rapid Deployment Center: *http://rapid.sap.com*

▶ Find your solution: *http://www.sap.com/resources/solutions-rapid-deployment/solutions-by-business.epx*

▶ SAP Solution Explorer: *https://rapid.sap.com/se/*

▶ SAP EcoHub

SAP EcoHub is your trusted source for discovering, evaluating, and buying targeted solutions from SAP and SAP Partners. The community-powered online marketplace supports you in finding enterprise software and services that can help your organization improve the efficiency of core processes, increase business agility, and capitalize on new opportunities. SAP EcoHub is frequently updated with new product information, expert advice, and special offers.

http://ecohub.sap.com/store/rds/

▶ SAP Solution Configurator: *http://www.sapconfigurator.com/*

▶ SAP Support Portal

Business applications and analytics solution and platform support, including software download, license key requests, customer messages, and SAP Notes database. The SAP Support Portal is your one stop for all support- and service-related needs. Access your software, request license keys, get technical support, and find the documentation you need to run your business better.
Service.sap.com/support

▶ SAP Help Portal

SAP online product documentation library and information design at SAP. *help.sap.com*

▶ SAP experts: SAP Solution Manager hub

The SAP Solution Manager hub is the most in-depth resource for independent, real-world guidance for your SAP Solution Manager activities. Get detailed instruction on topics that include: change request management, solution monitoring and reporting, services and support, implementation and rollout management, upgrade management, roadmaps, testing, and more.

All expertise at SAPexperts.com is independent and 100 percent validated by a board of technical advisors. All content is intended to explain even the most complex SAP tasks and projects in a way that's easy to understand.

For SAP Partners

SAP provides SAP PartnerEdge, which is the primary online destination for all SAP Partners who build, develop, sell, implement, service, and support SAP solutions. You can access this at *partneredge.sap.com*

Books

We recommend consulting the book *SAP Solution Manager* by Marc O. Schäfer and Matthias Melich (3rd edition SAP PRESS, 2012). SAP Solution Manager has quickly become one of the most important and all-encompassing tools needed by clients today. But what can it really do for you? How can it help you with project implementation or operation of the final solution? What is important for users to know, whether they are an administrator or a project team member? What functions has SAP expanded in the new 7.1 release, or developed from scratch?

The answers to these and many other questions can be found in this book. The authors discuss every functional area of SAP Solution Manager, explain its features, and use screenshots to illustrate the many aspects of the software. Whether you are interested in implementation and documentation; maintenance and testing; or monitoring, technical operation, and management problems, after reading this book, you will understand what SAP Solution Manager can do for you.

Collaboration and Social Media

There are many sites and resources that you might be familiar with, but not recognize as an essential source of technical information. We'll outline them in the following subsections.

SAP Community Network (SCN)

SCN provides the following benefits:

- Learn from the brightest in the SAP ecosystem. There are over 1 million articles, documents, and e-learning content on all SAP solutions and services.

- Solve problems by posting questions in the discussion forums, or search past questions. Since 2003, 8.7 million entries have been made.

- Connect and grow your network with real SAP experts, over 2.5 million members from over 200 countries.

- Start building your online reputation!

http://scn.sap.com/community/rapid-deployment

SAP Idea Place (SCN)

Co-innovate the future with SAP. Idea Place facilitates co-innovation with SAP, customers, partners, universities, and students through innovation campaigns based on new technologies, solutions, and markets.

ideas.sap.com

Customer Connection

Customer Connection is a simple process directed at incrementally enhancing and improving the products and solutions SAP customers are using today. It offers SAP customers the opportunity to suggest small enhancements to products and solutions in mainstream maintenance, providing a fast and non-disruptive delivery via SAP Notes and support packages. Customer Connection is structured along focus topics, which are suggested by SAP or the participating user groups.

cw.sdn.sap.com/cw/community/influence

SAP User Groups

SAP user groups are independent, not-for-profit organizations. Made up of SAP customers and partners, they are dedicated to educating members, facilitating customer involvement, and influencing SAP's strategy.

User groups provide a valuable channel through which SAP gathers feedback concerning the problems and requirements of its users in all technical and functional areas of interest. User groups allow SAP and

SAP users to exchange information of mutual interest and value. Additionally, SAP users have the opportunity to share their experiences, knowledge, and ideas.

Find a user group at *sap.com/communities/user-groups/*

Americas' SAP Users' Group (ASUG)

As the world's largest independent community of SAP customers and providers, ASUG is the most trusted source for experience-driven education and peer networking, and it serves as the collective influential voice of customers shaping the future of SAP solutions.

www.asug.com

Follow SAP Rapid Deployment Solutions:

- Twitter (*https://twitter.com/#!/saprds*)
- *LinkedIn (http://www.linkedin.com/groups/SAP-Rapid-Deployment-Solutions-4252390?trk=myg_ugrp_ovr)*
- YouTube (*http://www.youtube.com/playlist?list=PL1EF9CB66021210AE&feature=view_all*)

6.4   Summary

SAP has given in-depth consideration to the types of services that are unique to the teams deploying solutions. With SAP's network of services, enablement infrastructure, and solution experts who know how to support deployment teams, the new deployment paradigm at SAP is already fully established within the services portfolio. From enabling team communications and providing specific platforms to connect with SAP expertise, to self-directed learning resources or one-on-one, high-touch support, the deployment team members have the tools, materials, and programs designed to meet their needs and facilitate success.

Partners are key to the success of SAP's customers. In the context of SAP Rapid Deployment solutions, partners are essential to scale the available portfolio and to deliver rapid-deployment solutions across the globe.

7   The Rapid Deployment Partner Program

Today's markets for IT and business solutions are far too vast for SAP to try to cover alone—regardless of sales, service, or implementation of the software and solutions they offer. This is one of the reasons the SAP Partner ecosystem and channels are critical and integral to the new deployment paradigm at SAP. SAP Partners are those technical and professional firms that are under specific contract, and have a robust series of qualifications and requirements that ensure compliance with quality and process standards, as well as regulatory and compliance requirements from SAP and the markets they serve. When an organization does business with an SAP Partner, they do so with high expectations. Furthermore, many SAP customers actually enjoy and prefer to implement new IT solutions with partners, especially those that are often specialized in their industry and work in close proximity to their customers across the globe.

With SAP's focus to serve their customers best and to provide them with the right solutions, well-aligned and supported partners are a key pillar in the business model—and that key pillar allows for co-innovation and an extended reach of the SAP portfolio into any company, from the largest of world-class companies to the most specialized agencies in remote locations of the world. SAP Partners are important in all aspects of the adoption of SAP innovations and best practices.

Key pillar

SAP supports the thousands of SAP Partners with a sophisticated infrastructure of support, services, and opportunities. With business frameworks such as SAP PartnerEdge and numerous others, partners and customers alike benefit from the support provided around these new, simplified engagements and the extensive resources SAP provides to help their partners consistently deliver exceptional quality.

SAP PartnerEdge, for example, has an SAP Rapid Deployment solutions resource center that supports partners as they deploy SAP's solutions, or as they use SAP rapid-deployment methodology to create their own *qualified* package offering for an SAP solution. While the SAP Partner framework supports these partners with all aspects of the sales, service, and deployment of SAP solutions, the next pages will focus on the deployment aspect of the SAP Partner program, more specifically the SAP Rapid Deployment solutions for the SAP Partner.

A Few Partner Facts (Dated July 2013)

- 1.100+ SAP Business One partner add-on solutions
- 700+ SAP Business All-in-One partner industry-specific solutions
- 169+ SAP Business ByDesign partner solutions (approximately half of them add-ons)
- 280+ partners active in the Mobile Apps and SAP HANA Cloud Applications Partner programs, which resulted already in 130+ partner apps certified and made available in the SAP Store
- 500+ partners qualified on 950+ rapid-deployment solutions offerings with 300+ of these available in the SAP Store
- Over 400 startups in 19 countries participating in the SAP Startup Focus program for SAP HANA

In this chapter, we'll provide an overview of what it means for SAP Partners to use SAP Rapid Deployment solutions and in what way/which levels they can engage with SAP to incorporate these solutions into their business, so that more customers can benefit from them. In addition, selected sample solutions from partners are listed to give an indication of the depth and breadth of the available portfolio.

7.1   SAP Rapid Deployment Solutions for Partners

SAP Rapid Deployment solutions not only represent a competitive offering for customers in order to step away from lengthy implementations of monolithic solutions that require extensive, manual customization with little control over cost and timelines—they also serve as a comprehensive framework for various types of partners to address their customers with attractive, innovative solutions and to conveniently educate themselves to go to market in a rapid timeframe. When looking into the framework, partners have the opportunity to adopt SAP Rapid Deployment solutions on three different levels to mirror their own business expertise and to translate this into respective market offerings. We'll discuss these three levels in the following sections.

Adopt solutions on three levels

7.1.1   Adopting the Methodology to Conduct State-of-the-Art Implementations

Rapid-deployment solutions follow a dedicated methodology to add speed and predictability to an SAP implementation. This methodology becomes visible on two different levels:

1. In the form of a step-by-step guide that is available for each individual solution, outlining each and every activity necessary to implement the pre-defined scope of the package.

   Methodology levels

2. In the form of the overarching accelerated SAP methodology, outlining a best-practices-based way to run an implementation project in which rapid-deployment solutions are used—not only addressing the hard facts, but also the "soft" ones.

SAP Partners adopting SAP Rapid Deployment solutions on this level engage with SAP to learn about the methodology and how to use it in their own projects. The end result for you: A higher level of standardization without limiting flexibility, a higher level of quality and transparency in an implementation, and a solid foundation to leverage SAP Rapid Deployment solutions—be it a single package or a combination of multiple packages that form the base for a larger implementation with a broader scope, in which a significant set of delta requirements is put on top.

7.1.2 Adopting the Delivery of SAP Rapid Deployment Solutions

Delivering rapid-deployment solutions goes beyond the pure adoption of the underlying and overarching methodology. SAP Partners that qualify to deliver rapid-deployment solutions commit to the same principles that SAP is committing to: Running implementation projects in a fixed-price, fixed-scope manner. Customers engaging with such partners can consequently enjoy a much higher level of speed and predictability in their implementations—not just in projects where the live solution later mirrors the scope of the rapid-deployment solution implemented, but also when one or several rapid-deployment solutions represent a first milestone in a larger project.

List of qualified partners

Qualified partners that are entitled to deliver rapid-deployment solutions are listed in several web-based directories to give customers choices and insight—the most important one being the SAP EcoHub at *http://ecohub.sap.com/store/rds/,* which has a dedicated store with all relevant partners as well as related information (see Figure 7.1).

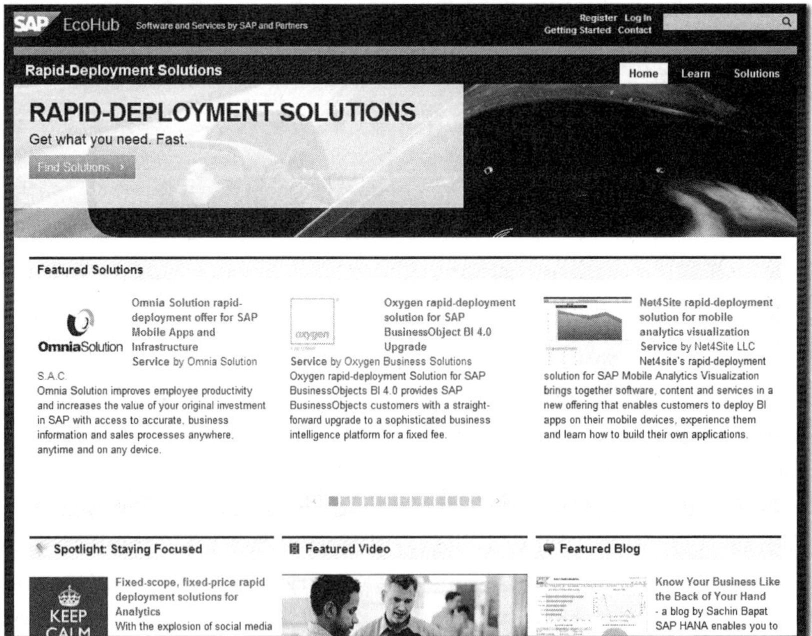

Figure 7.1 Qualified Partners on SAP EcoHub

Already, a vast amount of SAP Rapid Deployment solutions-based implementation projects are being conducted by partners.

7.1.3 Bringing It All Together: Partner-Led Rapid-Deployment Solutions

Sometimes, following a profound methodology or delivering rapid-deployment solutions is not enough to address individual customer requirements. And despite the continuous growth of the SAP Rapid Deployment solutions portfolio, there of course can be cases where there is no matching solution to start an implementation with.

This is where partners' ability to build their own rapid-deployment solutions comes into play. By leveraging best-practice content from SAP Rapid Deployment solutions and the corresponding packaging and deployment-tool framework, and bundling it with the unique business expertise that the partner brings to the table, the portfolio of SAP Rapid Deployment solutions grows to include unique, partner-specific, qualified rapid-deployment solutions that follow the same principles and deliver upon the same promises as the SAP offerings.

SAP Partners can complement the wide array of SAP-built solutions that help customers start, grow, and innovate against business needs across lines of businesses, industries, mobility, database and technology, cloud, and analytics with their own preconfigured solutions based on SAP software. For example, at the time of publication, there are partner-created solutions in:

- Industry
  - Consumer products (178)
  - Cross industry (176)
  - Automotive (171)
  - High tech (168)
  - Retail (167)
  - Chemicals (160)
  - Wholesale distribution (159)
  - Industrial machinery and components (158)

- Professional services (158)
- Engineering, construction and operations (148)
- Utilities (148)
- Telecommunications (145)
- Oil and gas (139)
- Healthcare (135)
- Life sciences (133)
- Mill products (132)
- Public sector (130)
- Aerospace and defense (129)
- Travel and logistics services (125)
- Banking (124)
- Mining (122)
- Insurance (118)
- Defense and security (116)
- Media (115)
- Higher education and research (106)
- Solution Area
  - SAP Business All-in-One (5)
  - SAP ERP (5)
- Line of Business
  - Sales (92)
  - Service (84)
  - Operations (72)
  - Marketing (70)
  - Finance (68)
  - Human resources (67)
  - Information-technology management (67)
  - Supply chain (67)
  - Purchasing (64)

- ▸ Manufacturing (55)
- ▸ Product development (45)
- ▸ Sustainability (32)
- ▸ Regional Availability
  - ▸ Europe (117)
  - ▸ Asia (78)
  - ▸ North America (68)
  - ▸ South America (36)
  - ▸ Worldwide availability (19)
  - ▸ Australia/Pacific Rim (17)
  - ▸ Central America (11)
  - ▸ Middle East (10)
  - ▸ Africa (2)

Samples of these types of solutions are listed in Table 7.1. These solutions cover technologies, industries, and even specific locations.

Partner Qualified Rapid-Deployment Solution Title	Service Offered by SAP Partner
Acorel implementation service for SAP Web Channel Experience Management rapid-deployment solution	Acorel B.V.
ATOS Belgium implementation service for SAP CRM rapid-deployment solution	ATOS
Bluefin Solutions (UK) implementation service for SAP G/L Financial Planning rapid-deployment solution	BLUEFIN SOLUTIONS
HCL AXON implementation service for SAP Visual Enterprise rapid-deployment solution	HCL AXON

Table 7.1 Sample of SAP Partner-Qualified Rapid Deployment Solution Offerings on the SAP EcoHub (July 2013)

Partner Qualified Rapid-Deployment Solution Title	Service Offered by SAP Partner
Hisoft rapid-deployment offer for SAP BusinessObjects for implementation of data services, BI platform, and rapid marts to SAP	BESURE TECHNOLOGY CO., LTD.
HP Singapore implementation service for rapid database migration to SAP Sybase ASE	HP SINGAPORE
KPIT Cummins implementation services for SAP CRM rapid-deployment solution	KPIT CUMMINS INFOSYSTEMS
Net4Site rapid-deployment solution for mobile analytics visualization	NET4SITE LLC
Omnia Solution rapid-deployment offer for SAP Mobile Apps and Infrastructure	OMNIA SOLUTION
Taiwan Application Service packaged offering for SAP HANA Profitability Analysis rapid-deployment solution	TAIWAN APPLICATION SERVICE
Velixis implementation service for SAP HANA Operational Reporting rapid-deployment solution	VELIXIS NV
Westernacher implementation service for SAP Service Parts Planning rapid-deployment solution	WESTERNACHER CONSULTING AG

Table 7.1 Sample of SAP Partner-Qualified Rapid Deployment Solution Offerings on the SAP EcoHub (July 2013) (Cont.)

Partner-led rapid-deployment solutions are owned and actively sold by the partner, with the exception of the software license if the partner doesn't have value-added reseller status. With partner-led rapid-deployment solutions, partners leverage SAP's concepts, tools, and templates, described in earlier chapters of this book, to deliver on the SAP Rapid Deployment solutions promise of a defined solution scope, fixed implementation duration, and a fixed-service price. Figure 7.2 shows an example of how the latest SAP innovations assist SAP Partners.

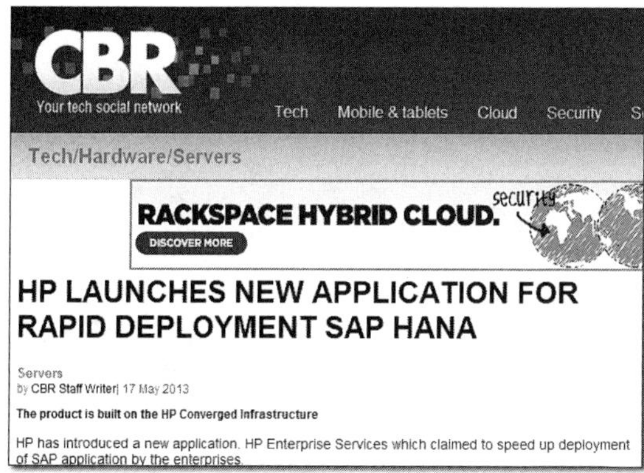

Figure 7.2 SAP Partners Leverage SAP Rapid Deployment Solutions Concepts, Tools, and Templates with the Latest SAP Innovations, such as SAP HANA

SAP Partners and SAP can join together with a unique synergy that provides customers with a magnitude of rapid-deployment solutions that cover a broad range of countries, industries, lines of business, technologies, analytics, and innovations, as shown in the figure above. Furthermore, partner-led rapid-deployment solutions are not limited to the packages that the specific partner qualifies and offers. Customers who choose a partner-qualified rapid-deployment solution have the option to connect to the rest of the individual partner-solutions portfolio on the EcoHub, such as third-party add-ons or non-SAP software solutions.

Customer choice and flexibility

Hundreds of partner-led rapid-deployment solutions already exist, giving customers a great level of choice and confidence. Like the partner-based service offerings for SAP Rapid Deployment solutions, all partner-led solutions are listed on SAP EcoHub.

Rolta on SAP Rapid Deployment Solutions

"With these new rapid-deployment solutions from Rolta, clients can expect to receive thoughtful guidance, rapid deployment for improved time-to-value, and industry-leading ROI...Customers will now have ready access to these solutions also through the vast SAP sales channels, thus enabling our clients to experience high success rates quickly."
—*Preetha Pulusani, president, Rolta Americas*

7.2 Getting There Fast: Enablement and Qualification

Partners adopting SAP Rapid Deployment solutions require qualification. This helps to ensure that customers receive high-quality results—repeatedly. However, the path toward qualification is smooth, since all qualification-related information is published on the prime web platform for partners: SAP PartnerEdge as shown in Figure 7.3—to be found at *http://sappartneredge.com*.

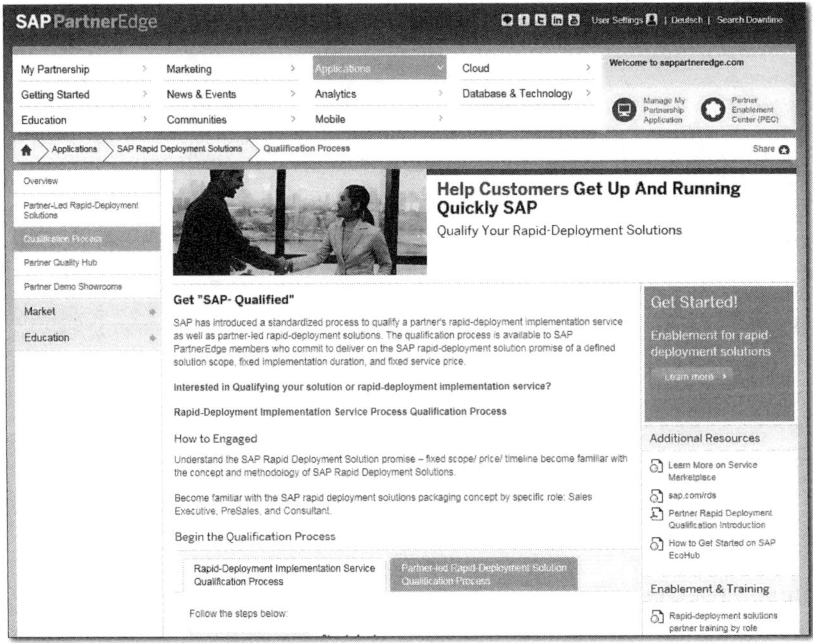

Figure 7.3 Qualification Information on SAP PartnerEdge

Self-service education   Dedicated self-service education material equips sales executives, pre-sales representatives, and consultants to get started with the fundamentals of packaging and delivering packaged solutions to market at their own pace. Unlike many other solutions, content within SAP Rapid Deployment solutions is in principle available to all partners—not just in the form of e-learning, but also in tangible delivery assets, based on which partners can easily learn and also define their business and portfolio focus in conjunction with SAP Rapid Deployment solutions.

7.2.1 Core Methodology Program

There is a core SAP rapid-deployment methodology program targeted to support SAP-qualified partner deployment-team members. These programs cover topics such as:

- SAP Rapid Deployment solutions implementation methodology.
- Technical concepts and tools.
- Implementation steps in Solution Builder.
- Implementation steps in SAP Solution Manager.
- SAP Rapid Deployment solutions demo options.

There are workshops for SAP Partners that have goals for creating qualified rapid-deployment solution offerings. These sessions are led by an SAP expert who provides enablement so teams can:

- Understand the specifics of the SAP Partner-qualification process.
- Work within the building-block architecture.
- Perform packaging in the Solution Builder.
- Customize packages.
- Understand SAP Partner deployment options.
- Use SAP Solution Manager.
- Personalize the Solution Builder.

These offerings are complemented with interactive workshops, classes, and live expert sessions, many of which are open to all partners; however, others are exclusively for SAP-qualified partners on an "invite only" basis.

7.2.2 Enablement

SAP recognizes that it is important for the partner ecosystem to keep updated on the latest market trends, technologies, and solutions. Enablement is key to staying current in order to offer the most up-to-date advice, recommendations, and services to customers. SAP offers enablement to SAP Partners on specific SAP Rapid Deployment solutions. These live and recorded sessions are available via the Partner Enablement Center as part of the SAP PartnerEdge (see Figure 7.4), and

Live/recorded sessions

partners have all such information at their fingertips—including the possibility to register for future sessions and to stay up to date with new enablement offerings.

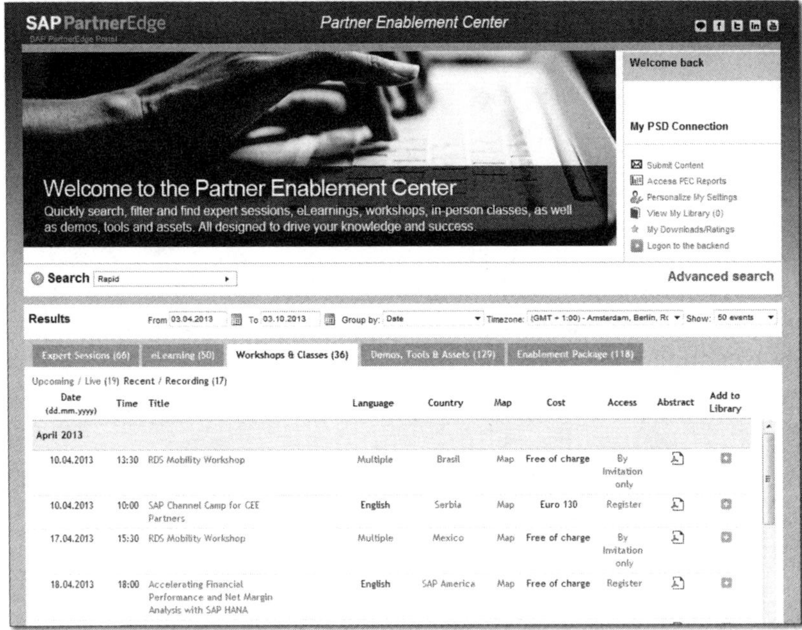

Figure 7.4 Partner Enablement Center

7.2.3 Qualification

Obtaining qualification to deliver projects based on SAP Rapid Deployment solutions or for rapid-deployment solutions they created on their own is not the only benefit for SAP Partners. Partners also collaborate with SAP during the development of SAP Rapid Deployment solutions, for example by providing essential market and scope information, or even by being part of the development teams that create SAP Rapid Deployment solutions, getting first-hand enablement information in return, and an even quicker market entry.

We'll now discuss a sample partner case that will illustrate the SAP Partner benefits related to SAP Rapid Deployment solutions. Partners of all sizes, including local, regional, and global are able to become qualified and deliver value to their customer base.

7.3   Sample Partner Case: F.I.T. Consulting

F.I.T. Consulting is an SAP-based solution and service provider, delivering customer and industry-focused business solutions. Founded in 1999 in Istanbul, Turkey-based F.I.T. has grown internationally with offices in the Netherlands, Turkey, and Cyprus, and services customers on a global scale from these key locations. To offer clients cost-effective solutions for challenging business issues, F.I.T. invests a substantial amount of time and money in developing innovative solutions and implementation approaches. F.I.T. effective business solutions help clients to support their business processes and cultivate long-term relationships with their most valuable customers.

F.I.T. has a strong focus on innovation and productization; applying the latest technologies and implementation approaches in product development, resulting in more or less standard solutions. These solutions are clearly defined, fixed-price offerings, increasing transparency and predictability in customer implementation projects. When SAP introduced SAP Rapid Deployment solutions, they were looking for partners to adopt the solutions to help them turn these into proven solution and gather best-practice implementations. F.I.T. was approached by SAP, and was immediately interested by the fact that the rapid-deployment solution methodology was very much in line with F.I.T.'s own strategy. F.I.T. strives to be the first partner in Turkey to adopt new technologies, solutions, or methodologies into customer projects and was eager to take this challenge to apply rapid-deployment solutions in real-life cases.

7.3.1   How the Engagement Started

As trusted partner of SAP Turkey, F.I.T. was motivated to adopt some of the rapid-deployment solutions into their solution portfolio. The responsible ecosystem and channels contact pulled F.I.T. into a partner-enablement session, which made the company realize the value behind SAP Rapid Deployment solutions offerings. F.I.T. is always interested in innovative new solution methodologies, especially if the principle behind the solution is to introduce easy-to-adopt SAP solutions. One of the most-heard critiques on SAP is the lack of flexibility and the complexity in enhancing functionality. These ready-to-use solutions, easy to deploy, with a fixed price and a clear scope, offer real value to customers in the short term, and this triggered F.I.T.'s enthusiasm to include them in their solution portfolio.

7.3.2 How the Qualification Went

F.I.T. first received the basic information on the new SAP Rapid Deployment solutions methodology and joined additional enablement sessions. Then, during a conference call, all required qualification-related deliverables were introduced and explained in detail. Templates were offered, especially for the business plan, which was rated as very helpful. F.I.T. worked on defining their own rapid-deployment solutions and created the required deliverables (e.g., solution presentation, solution whitepaper, and solution business plan). The Ecosystem & Channels Solution Center reviewed provided deliverables, including the online company profile, and the first qualification became a fact: F.I.T. was the first in Turkey with a qualified rapid-deployment solution for Sybase ASE system migration. After the first successful qualification, the second and third were less complex and established within a short time span.

7.3.3 Qualifications for F.I.T.

F.I.T. has three rapid-deployment solutions qualified so far:

1. **F.I.T. Sybase ASE rapid-deployment solution**
   The "System Migration Service" is a fixed-price service offering aimed at migrating an existing SAP solution to the ASE database for one productive three-system landscape. The F.I.T offering enables the customer to have the entire SAP landscape run on Sybase ASE, and realizes this via a transparent, fixed-price implementation offer.

2. **F.I.T. Afaria rapid-deployment solution**
   Installing the Afaria platform offers a single point of control over all mobile devices within your company regarding provisioning, production, and decommissioning of apps. The F.I.T. solution enables increased control over your mobile devices, improved device management, easy mobile-application onboarding, and increased analytics.

3. **F.I.T. Business Communications Management rapid-deployment solution**

   Boost customer satisfaction with our rapid-deployment solution for SAP Business Communications Management. An integrated package of contact-center software and implementation services, this solution is designed for rapid results. F.I.T. offers a fast track to a better customer experience, reducing response time by offering increased insight control on call-forwarding and flexible assignments of agents to queues, for example.

Together with the Ecosystem & Channel Solution Center, F.I.T. already managed to publish several success stories, such as a Betek implementation, which was the first Sybase Arafia rapid-deployment solution implementation in Turkey! And for their successful F.I.T. Business Communications Management rapid-deployment solution implementation at Aslanoba Webnak, another success story was created.

7.3.4   Experiences and Expectations

F.I.T. is convinced that the clearly defined, fixed-price nature of rapid-deployment solutions, together with their predictability and short-term deliverables, will become increasingly interesting to customers around the world. Their close cooperation with SAP Turkey over the entire project duration very much helped to accelerate qualification. At this moment, however, F.I.T. still sees potential in the market to develop a deeper understanding around SAP Rapid Deployment solutions. F.I.T. believes it will take a little bit more time for customers to see the showcases and proven value, and then the interest will increase. In parallel, F.I.T. is planning additional qualifications for rapid-deployment solutions.

7.4   Sample Partner Case: Fujitsu

As a partner with SAP for over 40 years, Fujitsu is constantly asked by their customers for more cost-effective ways to get the most out of their investment in SAP software without a huge impact to their IT budgets. Early on, Fujitsu saw how SAP Rapid Deployment solutions could drastically reduce implementation efforts compared to the classic whiteboard approach, since the solution scope is based on well-defined best practices, and is more efficient than defining custom-specific processes that could also affect any upgrade efforts. In addition, their clients aren't always looking for a large implementation, upgrade or optimization effort. Most often, it is a smaller project focused on a specific line of business that an SAP Rapid Deployment solution can cover. This allows for faster, easier, and less costly projects with quicker return on investment and minimal risk.

7.4.1   How the Engagement Started and Developed

Fujitsu had weekly conversations with many departments within SAP, so it was the product teams that Fujitsu first reached out to. From there, other departments got involved as well. The process greatly improved over the years and is a thorough and detailed one. The process guides partners to focus on what is really necessary and not just required from a customer's standpoint. It also provides information from which to build collateral and marketing strategies once the rapid-deployment solution is approved. In the end, Fujitsu became qualified for SAP Rapid Deployment solutions in the areas of mobility, enterprise operations management, analytics, and SAP HANA.

Some qualifications coincided with the ramp-up to customers, which is why Fujitsu can be seen as a very early adopter. Some were so close that some colleagues in SAP weren't even aware that the solution was qualified. Fujitsu is a manufacturer, a user of SAP, and 84 percent of their SAP customers are in the manufacturing industry. Their focus for the last 12 months was to work side by side with SAP to build on their enterprise operations management capabilities (Manufacturing Integration and Intelligence, Manufacturing Engineering, 3D Visual Enterprise, Sustainability, Environmental Health & Safety Management, Project Management, Quality Management, etc.). When asked to work directly with SAP to help test the solution, Fujitsu jumped right at it. Fujitsu wants to be in forefront of SAP Partners in bringing these innovative solutions to their customers.

In addition to the Condition-based Maintenance (CBM) solution, Fujitsu also qualified their rapid-deployment solution for asset analytics. These are just the first two of many that will make up the Fujitsu solution offering for SAP Idea to Performance Global Trade Management strategy, specifically in responsive manufacturing and operational excellence. An example of this can be seen in the winning solution of SAP-MSFT Innovation Award at SAPPHIRE in 2013, which allows machine-to-machine automated processing providing real-time operations and consumer data on mobile and gesture-controlled screens. This solution utilizes the cash budget management rapid-deployment solution along with additional SAP and Microsoft technologies such as: SAP 3D Visual Enterprise, SAP Manufacturing Integration and Intelligence (MII), SAP mobility, SAP Rapid Deployment solutions, Microsoft Windows 8, and Microsoft Kinect for Windows.

7.4.2 Experiences and Expectations

By now, Fujitsu has been able to enhance their pipeline with new opportunities due to the strong talking points these qualifications have allowed their sales teams to have with new and existing customers. Fujitsu is also looking to get qualified for four additional solutions by the end of the year; most likely in the area of SAP ECC (ERP Central Component), Manufacturing Engineering (ME), Customer Relationship Management (CRM), and industry solution-CPG (Consumer Packaged Goods).

7.5 Sample Enablement Session

SAP has a wide variety of enablement offerings to support partners on their way to qualification. Such offerings span across the entire engagement lifecycle with a partner, starting from providing high-level information to create the right level of awareness, down to tailored support implementation projects (see Figure 7.5).

In the following sections, we'll go over a list of selected enablement offerings that help partners choose where to go from a business perspective and how to get qualified. These offerings primarily are offered in a face-to-face mode and they are complementary to the regular solution/product training that SAP offers.

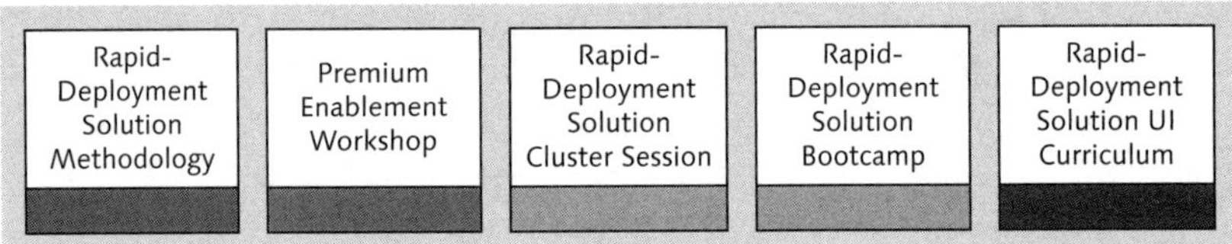

Figure 7.5 Premium Enablement Areas that Compliment Regular Training

7.5.1 SAP Rapid Deployment Solutions Methodology Premium Enablement Sessions

These sessions focus on equipping partners with all the knowledge required to build and to deploy rapid-deployment solutions—either from SAP or partner solutions.

Workshop In a two-day workshop, partners are enabled to understand SAP Rapid Deployment solutions concepts, find and download SAP Rapid Deployment solutions packages, identify implementation steps, run implementation project using these solutions, activate a package using the Solution Builder and SAP Solution Manager, to build partner rapid-deployment solutions offerings, to understand solutions demo offerings, and to get insights from data migration packages.

In a deep-dive workshop, partners that decided to build their own package are enabled to build a partner rapid-deployment solution. The starting point of the session is the introduction in the registration and qualification process end-to-end, where you can find information in the channel partner portal. Partners learn about the options for how to build their solution so that they can select the right option for their business case (BC). In the technical part of the workshop, partners get an introduction into the building block concept and how to reuse it in their build project. Partners get hands-on experience with the Solution Builder and how to use the BC API to build their solution. Furthermore, they learn about personalization (e.g., enterprise structure) and how to create documentation and attach documents to new building blocks. To round off the workshop, participants are guided through the steps on how to set up a scenario map, how deploy the solution, and how to integrate to SAP Solution Manager.

7.5.2 SAP Rapid Deployment Solutions Premium Enablement Workshops

Enablement offerings provide partners with essential information on key areas within the SAP Rapid Deployment solutions portfolio, so that partner can choose what to focus on, business-wise. Sessions are provided upon partner requests and partner priorities, which is why the examples below do not necessarily represent the full breadth and depth of available enablement workshops.

The first example is on mobility. "Mobility" is a buzzword people can rarely escape nowadays, whether in the consumer space or the business environment. But, the actual adoption and deployment of enterprise mobility solutions by customers are not as common as we think, as many customers do not know where, when, or how to begin the journey. Using SAP Rapid Deployment solutions mobile packages as the key enablers, the workshop aims to help partners approach their customers and help them get started with enterprise mobility in bite-sized chunks.

Mobility

In this case, SAP Rapid Deployment solutions packages are the safest way to a customer's mobility adoption, as they come with a promise for a fixed scope, cost, and time implementation.

Another key focus area for enablement is business intelligence. In this session, partners are introduced to SAP Best Practices, the components of a rapid-deployment solution, and the solution-adoption model. Next, the workshop introduces the SAP Rapid Deployment solutions analytics portfolio, including SAP HANA and mobile analytics. A focus is set on the SAP Rapid Deployment solution for BI adoption, including a demo of visualization options, presenting deliverables, installation steps, demo options, and outlook for future versions. In a hands-on section for this package, participants are trained how to deploy and visualize an SAP NetWeaver Business Warehouse (BW) report.

BI

The workshop also provides an overview and demo of related, out-of-the-box analytic solutions from SAP, including embedded analytics, business content released with Edge analytics edition, and standard analytic content for the SAP Business Suite delivered on SAP HANA.

SAP HANA

With SAP HANA a strategic priority, another enablement offering is focused on this area. The SAP HANA consulting boot camp introduces the basics of the SAP HANA technology and architecture to consultants who will be participating in SAP HANA-based rapid-deployment solutions implementation projects. The workshop covers the scope of the available SAP HANA-based rapid-deployment solutions packages, and gives an overview of the SAP Rapid Deployment solutions methodology.

In conjunction with analytics, the premium enablement workshop on SAP BusinessObjects Edge Rapid Marts illustrates the SAP BusinessObjects rapid-deployment solution for implementation of SAP Data Services, the BI platform, and rapid marts, also in combination with SAP HANA as an additional option. It includes the solution overview and hands-on installation. A deep-dive into rapid marts provides insights into prebuilt analytical reporting and analysis, along with extraction routines, transformations, loading, universes, and initial reports.

SAP Rapid Deployment solutions cluster sessions

For partners seeking detailed knowledge around the scope of the various SAP Rapid Deployment solutions and their interdependencies, SAP Rapid Deployment solutions cluster sessions are provided. In alignment with current requests from partners, the following cluster sessions are provided, with others upon request:

- Banking
- Extended Warehouse Management
- Migration to SAP NetWeaver BW powered by SAP HANA
- Optimizing Enterprise Performance Management with SAP Rapid Deployment solutions
- Financial Performance/Net Margin Analysis with SAP HANA

User experience and user interface optimization is a priority across the entire SAP Rapid Deployment solutions portfolio—and not only there. For this reason, dedicated enablement offerings exist to introduce the various options partners have around user experience, enabling them to choose the best option for their business, how to avoid modifications to the software, and to add their own user interfaces that blend the experience from the partner with the one from the SAP solution. Topics covered are as follows:

- Page builder
- Floorplan manager
- Side panel
- Personal object worklists
- SAP UI5
- SAP screen personas
- Technical setup for UI topics
- SAP NetWeaver business client entry pages

7.6 Summary

Complementing ordinary enablement and training offerings, premium enablement for SAP Rapid Deployment solutions provides SAP Partners with a perfect opportunity to quickly assess the relevance for their business and to get hands-on experience to come up with their own offerings or to deliver high-quality deployments for their customers.

A   SAP Rapid-Deployment Solutions: Packages

SAP Rapid Deployment solutions address a wide range of solution clusters across SAP's entire portfolio, spanning industries and lines of businesses across all five categories. In each cluster, typically several solutions are available to support a company's adoption path in a modular way, be it with a solution to get started new in the solution cluster, or to expand an existing footprint.

An easy way to explore which solutions are available to address a specific area of interest is via the industry value maps.

Say, for example, a consumer products company is interested in a solution to manage demand in their supply chain. Via SAP Solution Explorer (*http://www.sap.com/solutionexplorer*) upon selecting CONSUMER PRODUCTS and SUPPLY CHAIN MANAGEMENT, you'll immediately find SAP's solution offering for this business priority in the industry value map.

Upon choosing these options, you'll be presented with a description of SAP's offering to manage demand in a consumer products environment, but that there are two SAP Rapid Deployment solutions supporting this adoption—one for demand planning and one for demand-signal management.

Overall, SAP Rapid Deployment solutions are available for the following solution areas:

- SAP ERP entry packages.
- SAP Business Suite powered by SAP HANA.
- Line-of-business-specific packages:
  - Sales and marketing, customer relationship management on SAP HANA.
  - Supply chain management.
  - Procurement including Ariba.
  - Products.

> ► Human resources including SuccessFactors.
>
> ► Financials.
>
> ► Enterprise asset management.

- Industry-specific packages:

  > ► Discrete manufacturing.
  >
  > ► Energy and resources industries.
  >
  > ► Consumer products.
  >
  > ► Service industries.
  >
  > ► Financial services.
  >
  > ► Retail.
  >
  > ► Public services.

- Mobile packages.

- Technology packages:

  > ► Technology enabler DB, SAP NetWeaver, Integration.
  >
  > ► Cloud integration.
  >
  > ► Analytics packages (outside the lines of business and industry analytics covered under the section above).
  >
  > ► BI & BW on SAP HANA.
  >
  > ► EPM, GRC.
  >
  > ► Enterprise information management.

- SAP Business All-in-One packages.

In the following sections, we'll provide tables of the specific solutions that are available for each major area, list the languages the solution is available in, and provide a short product description.

A.1   SAP ERP Rapid-Deployment Solutions

NameSAP	Languages	Short Description
SAP ERP Finance and Controlling rapid-deployment solution	EN; RU; AR; DE; ES; PT	Supports the accounting requirements of an organization by providing a complete record of all business transactions and financial reporting for multiple accounting standards.
SAP ERP for Trading rapid-deployment solution	EN; RU; AR; DE; ES; PT	Gain insight into financial performance, supply chains, inventory cycles, and trading processes. By running an integrated software-and-service solution, you can quickly and affordably identify business opportunities, anticipate risks, and outline a predictable path for realizing your enterprise-software objectives.
SAP Business All-in-One rapid-deployment solution	EN; DE; EL; HE; HR; IT; NO; PL; SV; AR; ES; FR; JA; KO; NL; PT; RU; TH; TR; UK; ZH	Refer to SAP Business All-in-One section in this appendix.
SAP ERP for Manufacturing rapid-deployment solution	EN; RU; AR; DE; ES; PT	Optimize your most important manufacturing operations. With this integrated solution, you can streamline your core end-to-end business processes: order-to-cash, forecast-to-stock, time-to-market, and procure-to-pay. You can also improve your financial management performance.

Table A.1 ERP Entry Packages, Including SAP ERP on SAP HANA

NameSAP	Languages	Short Description
SAP ERP for Manufacturing in China rapid-deployment solution	EN; ZH	Improve how you manage your most important business processes—from procure-to-pay, make to stock, order-to-cash—fully integrated with efficient financial processes. By implementing an integrated software-and-service package, you can identify the many drivers and processes shaping manufacturing performance. You can also automate procurement transactions, optimize financial margins, and manage suppliers, capital, and risks.
SAP ERP Subsidiary Rollout rapid-deployment solution	EN	This rapid-deployment solution streamlines core business processes across subsidiaries and integrates them with corporate headquarters by standardizing processes, improving data management and operational efficiency, increasing transparency and efficiency, and reducing IT costs across your organization.

Table A.1 ERP Entry Packages, Including SAP ERP on SAP HANA (Cont.)

A.2   SAP Business Suite Powered by SAP HANA

Name	Languages	Short Description
SAP CRM rapid deployment-solution powered by SAP HANA	EN	The SAP CRM rapid-deployment solution powered by SAP HANA brings together software and services to give you essential marketing, sales, and service functionality, powered by superior loading and reporting performance and real-time data access through the in-memory technology of SAP HANA.

Table A.2 SAP Business Suite Powered by SAP HANA

Name	Languages	Short Description
SAP ERP for Finance and Controlling rapid-deployment solution powered by SAP HANA	EN	Take a comprehensive approach to financial and management accounting—with an integrated solution for finance and controlling that is powered by SAP HANA. Get the enterprise-resource planning functionality you need to reduce risk and create a predictable path for the future, with support for everything from general ledger to overhead-cost accounting. With the SAP ERP for Finance and Controlling rapid-deployment solution powered by SAP HANA, we are simply combining the best suite of applications and the next-generation, best-performing platform for doing real-time business.
SAP ERP for Manufacturing rapid-deployment solution powered by SAP HANA	EN	Optimize your most important manufacturing operations—with our integrated solution for finance and controlling powered by SAP HANA. With this integrated solution, you can streamline your core end-to-end business processes: order-to-cash, forecast-to-stock, time-to-market, and procure-to-pay. You can also improve your financial management performance. With the SAP ERP for Manufacturing rapid-deployment solution powered by SAP HANA, SAP is simply combining the best suite of applications and the next-generation, best-performing platform for doing real-time business.

Table A.2 SAP Business Suite Powered by SAP HANA (Cont.)

Name	Languages	Short Description
SAP ERP for Trading rapid-deployment solution powered by SAP HANA	EN	Gain insight into financial performance, supply chains, inventory cycles, and trading processes with our integrated solution for trading powered by SAP HANA. By running an integrated software-and-service solution, you can quickly and affordably identify business opportunities, anticipate risks, and outline a predictable path for realizing your enterprise-software objectives. The SAP ERP for Trading rapid-deployment solution powered by SAP HANA can be used with the new lightning-quick, in-memory platform SAP HANA, or without. With this package, we are simply combining the best suite of applications and the next-generation, best-performing platform for doing real-time business.
SAP HANA Live rapid deployment solution	EN	The SAP HANA Live rapid-deployment solution enables real-time reporting on operational data from SAP Business Suite applications. This rapid-deployment solution provides pre-built reporting content for easier and faster analysis of operational data on the SAP HANA platform with best-practices enablement content and fixed-scope and fixed-timeline service offering.

Table A.2 SAP Business Suite Powered by SAP HANA (Cont.)

Name	Languages	Short Description
Rapid database migration of SAP Business Suite to SAP HANA	EN	This rapid-deployment solution supports the migration of an existing SAP Business Suite installation to the SAP HANA database system without disruption of the existing Business Suite scenarios. This new deployment approach—provided with SAP's rapid-deployment solutions, which leverage out-of-the-box accelerators and predefined scope—will help accelerate your adoption of SAP HANA to supercharge your SAP Business Suite. The simplified process eliminates any migration guesswork and uncertainties regarding realization timeline, due to automation of steps as well as planning security due to standardization of the approach.
SAP HANA Analytics for Heterogeneous Data rapid-deployment solution	EN	Get detailed insight into sales and purchasing results in a heterogeneous business-system landscape. Reports and information spaces allow easy access to data from SAP, Oracle, and JDE business systems via a single point of entry on SAP HANA.
Rapid data migration to SAP ERP and SAP CRM	EN	Accelerate data migration with pre-built best-practices content for over 100 critical master and transactional-data objects. Migrate your data from any system to SAP ERP and CRM powered by SAP HANA and have high-quality legacy data to use at full potential in SAP Business Suite powered by SAP HANA.

Table A.2 SAP Business Suite Powered by SAP HANA (Cont.)

A.3   Line-of-Business Rapid Deployment Solutions

Name	Languages	Short Description
SAP Business Communications Management rapid-deployment solution	EN	Boost customer satisfaction—quickly—with our rapid-deployment solution for SAP business communications management. An integrated package of contact-center software and implementation services, this solution is designed for rapid results.
SAP CRM Interaction Center rapid-deployment solution	EN	This process enables service agents and managers to streamline the service process to resolve customer issues. It provides agents tools to process service requests during customer interaction, avoiding unnecessary callbacks or follow-ups.
SAP CRM rapid-deployment solution	EN; DE; ES; PT; ZH; IT; JA; FR; RU; AR	Attract, win, and retain customers with the rapid deployment of SAP CRM software—and begin to see benefits in a matter of weeks.
SAP Mobile Sales rapid-deployment solution	EN; DE; ES; FR; JA; PT; ZH; RU	The SAP Mobile Sales rapid-deployment solution mobilizes your sales force, so they can address customer needs faster and more cost-effectively. By making it easier to manage communication and all customer-related activities on the road, you can increase sales productivity and efficiency.
SAP Business Collaboration rapid-deployment solution	EN; ZH	The rapid-deployment solution provides an extensive integration of SAP JAM into the SAP Customer Relationship Management (SAP CRM) for Sales, supporting collaborative and people-centric CRM processes.

Table A.3 Sales and Marketing Solutions

Name	Languages	Short Description
SAP CRM rapid-deployment solution powered by SAP HANA	EN	The SAP CRM rapid-deployment solution powered by SAP HANA brings together software and services to give you essential marketing, sales, and service functionality, powered by superior loading and reporting performance and real-time data access through the in-memory technology of SAP HANA.
SAP Business-to-Business Sales rapid-deployment solution	EN	This solution package includes capabilities to enable the complete sales process to run on the Internet. Organizations can provide customers with interactive and easy-to-use web shops, and streamline sales and fulfillment operations to enable an end-to-end order-to-cash process.
SAP CRM Service Management rapid-deployment solution	EN; DE; ES; PT; ZH; FR; JA; RU	This rapid-deployment solution provides support for field service planning, execution, and confirmation as well as for complaints and returns management. Preconfigured functionality and templates accelerate implementation time.
SAP HANA CRM Analytics rapid-deployment solution	EN; ES; PT	Based on SAP CRM, SAP NetWeaver BW, and SAP HANA, this rapid-deployment solution provides insights into sales, marketing, and service. It includes role-based reports and dashboards to provide you these insights flexibly, right at your fingertips.

Table A.3 Sales and Marketing Solutions (Cont.)

Name	Languages	Short Description
SAP Rapid Deployment Solutions for Demand-Driven Supply Chain		
SAP Supply Network Planning rapid-deployment solution	EN; DE; ES; PT; RU; ZH	This rapid-deployment solution allows you to create a feasible midterm supply plan that integrates procurement, distribution, and production planning dimensions across the entire supply chain.
SAP Advanced Production Scheduling rapid-deployment solution	EN; DE; ES; PT; RU; ZH	Advanced-production scheduling fully combines your existing material requirement planning in the SAP ERP application with sophisticated, detailed scheduling in the SAP APO component with limited replication of master data to SAP APO. You can graphically optimize the production plan while safeguarding the investments made in SAP ERP.
SAP Demand Signal Management rapid-deployment solution	EN	Increase the demand visibility into your supply chain and get a holistic view on your markets—now—with our software-and service-package for SAP demand signal management, which is powered by the SAP HANA platform. Manage massive volumes of external demand data and internal data, and transform them into a single source of truth.
SAP Demand Planning rapid-deployment solution	EN; DE; ES; PT; RU; ZH	Boost your supply-chain management effectiveness—quickly—with our demand-planning software-and service-package. Manage dynamic customer demand and meet delivery commitments by relying on leading-edge forecasting technology, analytics, best practices, and a robust alert system.

Table A.4 Supply Chain Management Solutions

Name	Languages	Short Description
SAP Global ATP Check rapid-deployment solution	EN; DE; ES; PT; RU; ZH	Provide the right amount of products that have been requested at the right time and deliver more value to your customers by relying on the SAP SCM rapid-deployment solution for global available-to-promise (ATP) check. The solution can help you confirm and process orders smoothly, and resolve back-order issues more quickly.
SAP Supply Network Collaboration rapid-deployment solution for supplier collaboration	EN; DE	The SAP supply-network collaboration (SNC) application lets you synchronize the flow of information between your company and its suppliers. This rapid-deployment solution provides you with a fast and predictable implementation of the main processes of SAP SNC: purchase-order processing, release processing, and supplier-managed inventory.
SAP Supply Network Collaboration rapid-deployment solution for customer collaboration	EN	Improve your vendor-managed inventory (VMI) relationship with your distributors and retailers and move toward more responsive replenishment planning to take better control of inventory at customer locations.
SAP Collaborative Replenishment between Manufacturers rapid-deployment solution	EN	The solution covers the material-replenishment process between manufacturing companies. It supports the VMI process with consigned/non-consigned material, material tracking by batch and integration with SAP ERP. The solution includes an enhanced version of SAP/SNC and a fixed-cost, three-month deployment effort.

Table A.4 Supply Chain Management Solutions (Cont.)

Name	Languages	Short Description
SAP Rapid Deployment Solutions for Logistics and Execution		
SAP Extended Warehouse Management rapid-deployment solution	EN; RU	The SAP Extended Warehouse Management (EWM) rapid-deployment solution helps you achieve supply-chain operational excellence and responsiveness. You can increase warehouse productivity and efficiency, improve the accuracy of inventory visibility, and achieve better space utilization. This EWM solution provides you with integrated warehousing and logistics, and provides a way for you to contribute to better customer service.
SAP Extended Warehouse Management for Retail rapid-deployment solution	EN	The SAP EWM solution helps you achieve supply-chain operational excellence and responsiveness in terms of high warehouse productivity and efficiency, accurate inventory visibility, better space utilization, integrated warehousing and logistics, and better customer service.
SAP Ocean Carrier Booking rapid-deployment solution	EN; RU	Plan, execute, and monitor ocean shipments, including container tracking. Support for booking ocean-vessel capacity, exchange of shipping instructions, and container visibility. Standard connectivity to ocean carriers or freight-forwarding companies with the SAP Information Interchange OnDemand.
SAP Transportation Charge Management for Shippers rapid-deployment solution	EN	The solution extends transportation execution by helping companies that ship goods to carry out freight-charge calculation, cost distribution, and carrier-invoice processing.

Table A.4 Supply Chain Management Solutions (Cont.)

Name	Languages	Short Description
SAP Freight Tendering for Shippers rapid-deployment solution	EN	Designed for companies that ship goods and manage constraints such as delivery dates, costs, and carrier availability. It helps get the best carrier option to execute a transport within an agreed timeframe against the lowest costs. It extends transportation execution through SAP ERP by enabling communication and information exchange with multiple carriers, including electronic connectivity to carriers.
SAP Transportation Planning for Shippers rapid-deployment solution	EN	Designed for companies that ship goods while managing constraints such as delivery costs, carrier availability, or time windows. The solution supports order consolidation, routing, scheduling, and carrier selection. It includes a set of rules and parameters to find the optimal transportation option.
SAP Rapid Deployment Solutions for Sales and Operations Business Planning		
SAP Sales and Operations Planning rapid-deployment solution	EN	Create synchronized supply and demand plans that are aligned with your financial and strategic goals.
SAP Rapid Deployment Solutions for Service Supply Chain		
SAP Service Parts Planning rapid-deployment solution	EN; DE; ZH	Better manage your customer relationships while reducing logistics costs—with SAP Service Parts Planning rapid-deployment solution. Align your sales, service, and marketing processes with your business needs. You can also use it to improve collaboration with suppliers and customers while you increase visibility and efficiency in service-parts planning.

Table A.4 Supply Chain Management Solutions (Cont.)

Name	Languages	Short Description
SAP Rapid Deployment Solutions for Supply Chain Monitoring		
SAP Order Tracking and Exception Management rapid-deployment solution	EN	SAP event-management rapid-deployment solution for order tracking and exception management offers visibility on the order-to-cash process. Extensive tracking and tracing functionalities allow process monitoring, automated exception resolution, and proactive alerting in tight integration with SAP ERP—in one single solution.
SAP Global Batch Traceability rapid-deployment solution	EN	SAP event-management rapid-deployment solution for order tracking and exception management offers visibility on the order-to-cash process. Extensive tracking and tracing functionalities allow process monitoring, automated exception resolution, and proactive alerting in tight integration with SAP ERP—in one single solution.

Table A.4 Supply Chain Management Solutions (Cont.)

Name	Languages	Short Description
SAP Supplier Life-cycle Management rapid-deployment solution	EN	Self-service functionality enables suppliers to register themselves and maintain their own company and contact data, add users as needed, upload attachments, and maintain all qualification requests and certificates. Automated workflow helps manage the approval process for new suppliers.

Table A.5 Procurement Solutions

Name	Languages	Short Description
SAP Commodity Procurement rapid-deployment solution	EN	With the SAP Commodity Procurement rapid-deployment solution, you can manage commodity-pricing rules, handle multiple invoice cycles, and integrate risk-relevant data of logistical documents to the SAP treasury risk-management application.
SAP SRM Operational Sourcing rapid-deployment solution	EN; DE; ES; FR; PT; RU; ZH	Operational sourcing solution enables: ▶ Automation of request for quotation process. ▶ Emails to multiple suppliers, requesting bids for specific goods and services. ▶ Online bid response by suppliers. ▶ Easy side-by-side comparison of competitive bids. ▶ Winning-bid selection and contract creation.
SAP Spend Performance Management rapid-deployment solution	EN; DE; ES; FR; PT; KO	Gain transparency across your enterprise and integrate your supply-chain and procurement activities quickly and affordably by managing spend performance.
SAP Integrated Procurement Contract Management rapid-deployment solution	EN; DE; PT; ES; FR	Integrated contract management solution enables: ▶ Contract lifecycle from contract creation to utilization. ▶ Increased contract usage during the procure-to-pay process. ▶ Reduced off-contract maverick spending and savings leakage. ▶ Improved visibility of contracts to employees and purchasing team.

Table A.5 Procurement Solutions (Cont.)

Name	Languages	Short Description
SAP SRM rapid-deployment solution for self-service procurement	EN; DE; ES; FR; PT; RU; ZH	Improve productivity and reduce risks by empowering your employees with the essential self-service procurement functionality they need to shop online for goods and services and approve requisitions.
SAP SRM User Interface Add-on rapid-deployment solution	EN	A user experience to create shopping carts from catalogs with little or no training. The user interface has a familiar look and feel, and features that users enjoy from online shopping experiences. Users can search across internal and external catalog content to quickly find products and services.
SAP Business Suite integration with the Ariba Network rapid-deployment solution	EN	Connect your back-end SAP software securely and reliably to the Ariba Network. Go live with the first wave of suppliers with preconfigured integration for the procure-to-pay process and Ariba Procurement Content.

Table A.5 Procurement Solutions (Cont.)

Name	Languages	Short Description
SAP Environmental Incident Management rapid-deployment solution	EN	SAP Environmental Incident Management will stand up the most critical incident management functions of component extension 3.0 for SAP EHS Management, including recording of injuries, near misses, and safety observations, incident investigation, regulator reporting, and analytics. It also includes optional enhanced content for 17 configurable tables.

Table A.6 Products Solutions

Name	Languages	Short Description
SAP ERP for Manufacturing rapid-deployment solution	EN; AR; DE; ES; PT; RU; ZH	The SAP ERP rapid-deployment solution for Manufacturing optimizes your most important manufacturing operations. With this integrated solution, you can streamline your core end-to-end business processes: order-to-cash, forecast-to-stock, time-to-market, and procure-to-pay. You can also improve your financial management performance.
SAP Manufacturing Execution for Discrete Manufacturing rapid-deployment solution	EN	The SAP Manufacturing Execution for Discrete Manufacturing rapid-deployment solution is a predefined configuration bringing together software and services that enable delivery of core shop floor execution processes.
SAP MII Batch Manufacturing rapid-deployment solution	EN	SAP MII for Batch Manufacturing rapid-deployment solution enables batch manufacturing industries to achieve excellence in manufacturing execution, manufacturing performance & plant-to-ERP integration quickly and affordably, reduces risk, and puts our manufacturing industries on a predictable path to attain their manufacturing excellence vision.
SAP Quality Issue Management rapid-deployment solution	EN	The SAP Quality Issue Management rapid-deployment solution replaces nonintegrated manual methods for handling quality problems. With an integrated and centralized approach to handling quality issues, you can enhance visibility, reduce the cost of poor quality, and strengthen the continuous improvement process.

Table A.6 Products Solutions (Cont.)

Name	Languages	Short Description
SAP Internal Project Staffing and Cost Management rapid-deployment solution	EN	The SAP ERP rapid-deployment solution for internal project staffing and cost management supports end-to-end business processes to plan and settle employees' time and costs to internal orders or projects. It lets you track and document staffing decisions, forecast resource needs, and control time and expense recording.
SAP KANBAN Process rapid-deployment solution	EN	The scenario Manufacturing with KANBAN Supply into Production focuses on a lean production control method within a repetitive manufacturing environment using Kanban processing for lean replenishment with the the flavour supplier Kanban, flow manufacturing and move Kanban.
SAP PLM for Discrete Manufacturing rapid-deployment solution	EN; DE; FR; JA; ZH	SAP PLM for Discrete Manufacturing rapid-deployment solution provides the technical foundation for using the SAP Product Lifecycle Management (SAP PLM) application. You can optimize product development processes to speed up release of products to market using an intuitive web user interface where you can easily access all your PLM objects in a personalized way.
SAP PLM for Process Manufacturing rapid-deployment solution	EN; DE; FR; JA; ZH	SAP PLM for Process Manufacturing rapid-deployment solution provides comprehensive formulation functionality combined with specification management, compliance check and labeling capabilities.

Table A.6 Products Solutions (Cont.)

Name	Languages	Short Description
SAP Product Structure Synchronization for Bills of Materials rapid-deployment solution	EN; DE; FR; JA	SAP Product Structure Synchronization rapid-deployment solution works as a generic engine to support the transformation (complex restructuring) of bills of materials, with full tracking to provide guidance for continuous updates.
SAP Visual Enterprise rapid-deployment solution	EN; DE	SAP Visual Enterprise rapid-deployment solution visualizes product knowledge for better and faster product navigation, combining 3-D visual information with relevant data from SAP Business Suite applications. The solution enables 3-D visual navigation, including 3-D animation of procedures for assembly or disassembly sequences.
SAP Project Portfolio Management rapid-deployment solution	EN; ZH; DE; ES; FR; PT	SAP Project Portfolio Management rapid-deployment solution helps deliver projects on time and on budget and ensures continuous alignment of projects with your strategic business goals.
SAP Portfolio Management for Innovation and Product Development rapid-deployment solution	EN	SAP Portfolio Management for Innovation and Product Development rapid-deployment solution supports you in managing projects and resources for development projects, covering project proposal, initiation, planning, execution, and resource staffing for development projects.
SAP IT Portfolio and Project Management rapid-deployment solution	EN	The SAP Portfolio and Project Management rapid-deployment solution for IT management provides support for managing projects and resources for IT, covering project proposal, initiation, planning, execution, and capacity planning and resource staffing for recurring and single IT projects.

Table A.6 Products Solutions (Cont.)

Name	Languages	Short Description
SAP Commercial Project Management rapid-deployment solution	EN; DE; FR; RU	The SAP® Commercial Project Management rapid-deployment solution contains best practices and cross-industry preconfigured content for commercial project management. It covers project workspace, project cost and revenue planning, as well as issue and change management. In addition, it offers how-to guides as implementation accelerators.
SAP Maintenance Operations rapid-deployment solution	EN	SAP Maintenance Operations rapid-deployment solution is the easy entry point for customers running SAP ERP, but not yet leveraging core functionalities of SAP Enterprise Asset Management, allowing customers to benefit from the rich functionality SAP ERP provides with regards to managing the assets from a maintenance perceptive.
SAP 3D Visual Enterprise Asset Management rapid-deployment solution	EN; DE	Supports the business scenarios maintenance and repair procedures, technical publication authoring and publishing, and visual learning and training. It enables 3D-animated, step-by-step procedural instructions, as well as 3D model-driven document authoring and standards compliance. It also allows using visual information for search and query.
SAP Multiresource Scheduling rapid-deployment solution	EN; DE; ES; PT	SAP Multiresource Scheduling rapid-deployment solution is a fast way to implement a powerful resource planning solution for the service, plant maintenance, and project business. It provides scheduling of different resource types from one planning tool that leverages the existing SAP software infrastructure.

Table A.6 Products Solutions (Cont.)

Name	Languages	Short Description
SAP Asset Analytics rapid-deployment solution	EN; DE	SAP Asset Analytics rapid-deployment solution empowers you to gain visibility into the operation of physical assets, take proactive steps to avoid interruptions and downtime, effectively forecast and plan to maximize asset utilization, and optimize asset performance to compete in the marketplace.
SAP Asset Data Quality rapid-deployment solution	EN	SAP Asset Data Quality rapid-deployment solution allows you to assess, validate and continuously monitor the quality of your asset master data. Simplify management of your asset data quality with SAP's industry-leading EIM tools and predefined content.
SAP Condition-Based Maintenance rapid-deployment solution	EN	SAP Condition-Based Maintenance enables your organization to implement a condition-based maintenance (CBM) strategy based on the real-time assets and equipment conditions obtained from embedded sensors and/or external tests and measurements. This improves upon the more traditional time-based or counter-based maintenance strategy by automating maintenance work orders and minimizing risks of catastrophic asset failure.
SAP Work Manager rapid-deployment solution	EN	SAP Work Manager rapid-deployment solution accelerates the implementation with preconfigured content to integrate SAP Work Manager with SAP EAM (Plant Maintenance) backend-system to improve time-to-value proposition of SAP Work Manager mobile app. The package enables required configurations to mobilize 1) Work Orders 2) Notifications and 3) Timesheets using customer-based data.

Table A.6 Products Solutions (Cont.)

Name	Languages	Short Description
SAP Real Estate Management rapid-deployment solution	EN; DE; ZH	With this solution, you can quickly and affordably implement and automate real estate-related business processes. You can effectively align cross-functional stakeholders to manage real estate in a collaborative way and deliver on strategic goals.
SAP Capital Project Accounting rapid-deployment solution	EN	SAP Capital Project Accounting rapid-deployment solution supports planning, executing, and controlling capital investment projects in SAP ERP. The solution supports capital project accounting requirements that use work breakdown structures integrated in core ERP processes and enterprise accounting.

Table A.6 Products Solutions (Cont.)

Name	Languages	Short Description
SAP Employee and Manager Self-Service rapid-deployment solution	EN; DE; IT; PT; FR; KO; NL; ES; JA; RU; ZH	The SAP ERP rapid-deployment solution for employee and manager self-service enables you to quickly and efficiently streamline your HR processes. Leveraging your Microsoft SharePoint portal, it provides your employees and managers with web-based access to HR information, processes and services. The SAP ERP rapid-deployment solution for employee and manager self-service enables you to quickly and efficiently streamline your HR processes. Leveraging your existing SAP NetWeaver portal, it provides your employees and managers with web-based access to HR information, processes and services.

Table A.7 Human Capital Management (HCM) and SuccessFactors Solutions

Name	Languages	Short Description
SAP E-Recruiting rapid-deployment solution	EN; PT; DE; ES; JA; ZH	The SAP E-Recruiting rapid-deployment solution streamlines and standardizes the process of hiring talented individuals from within and outside the organization, speeding up the time-to-hire and tracking processes of a global talent pool to help maximize retention rates and reduce recruiting costs.
SAP HR Core Functions for China rapid-deployment solution	EN; ZH	This solution provides a template for HR processes and structures based on best practices and localized for enterprises in China. It provides the foundation for your human capital management (HCM) functions across the organization. The solution also includes support for organizational management, personnel administration, time management, and payroll processes. This rapid-deployment solution also incorporate the latest SAP HR renewal functionality, to enhance the user experience and flexibility, and to reflect the modern user interface technology.
SAP Personnel Administration and Organizational Management rapid-deployment solution	EN	A global template for your HR processes and structures, based on SAP Best Practices, facilitates employee life-cycle management. The solution provides the foundation for your human capital management solution across the organization, including self-services, forms, and processes.
SAP HCM Shared Service Framework rapid-deployment solution	EN; DE; ES; FR; IT; PT	The SAP shared service framework rapid-deployment solution for human capital management is an entry point for efficient and convenient shared-services functions across a global organization. Employees can create a service request, freeing up time for their managers and HR staff.

Table A.7 Human Capital Management (HCM) and SuccessFactors Solutions (Cont.)

Name	Languages	Short Description
SAP Executive HR Reporting rapid-deployment solution	EN; DE; ES; FR; JA; PT; RU; ZH	An executive HR reporting cockpit at your fingertips. It contains predefined dashboards that visualize more than 40 key human capital management (HCM) metrics. Reliable data provides clear insights into the workforce, allows detailed monitoring, and enables you to react proactively to unfavorable situations.
SAP Advanced HR Analysis rapid-deployment solution	EN;DE; ES; FR; IT; JA; PT; RU	With over 20 predefined types of analysis that cover all HR processes, the SAP Advanced HR Analysis rapid-deployment solution enables you to drill down into details and explore your workforce data to answer questions, uncover problems, and validate hunches more quickly.
SAP ERP HCM Integration to SuccessFactors rapid-deployment solution	EN; JA; KO; ZH	Integrate your SAP ERP human capital management (SAP ERP HCM) solution and SuccessFactors Business Execution (BizX) Suite with flexible and automated data exchange. These cover basic employee, compensation planning, recruiting, and workforce analytics. Integrated data is the basis for running hybrid end-to-end "pay-for-performance" and "attract-to-hire" processes.
SAP HR Core Functions for United Arab Emirates rapid-deployment solution	EN; AR	A package of localized HR functionality and services for the United Arab Emirates, based on best business practices, provides the foundation for your HR vision. It includes templates and end-to-end processes across organizational management, personnel administration, time management, and payroll.

Table A.7 Human Capital Management (HCM) and SuccessFactors Solutions (Cont.)

Name	Languages	Short Description
SAP HR Core Functions for Kingdom of Saudi Arabia rapid-deployment solution	EN; AR	A package of localized HR functionality and services for the Kingdom of Saudi Arabia, based on best business practices, provides the foundation for your HR vision. It includes templates and end-to-end processes across organizational management, personnel administration, time management, and payroll.

Table A.7 Human Capital Management (HCM) and SuccessFactors Solutions (Cont.)

Name	Languages	Short Description
SAP HANA Net Margin Analysis rapid-deployment solution	EN	The SAP HANA Net Margin Analysis rapid-deployment solution helps reduce direct and indirect costs to maximize overall net margin across all combinations of product, customer, sales organization, and channel.
SAP Collections and Dispute Management rapid-deployment solution	EN; DE; ES; PT; RU; ZH	With the SAP Collections and Dispute Management rapid-deployment solution, you can: ▸ Implement and automate receivables, management business processes quickly and affordably. ▸ Efficiently manage disputes that arise because of customer invoices. ▸ Proactively manage and collect overdue receivables. ▸ Reduce and positively impact your bad debt risk and exposure.
SAP Commodity Risk Management rapid-deployment solution	EN; DE; ES; PT; ZH	With the SAP Commodity Risk Management rapid-deployment solution, you can manage and assess the price risk of commodity positions and handle the financial transactions used to hedge this risk.

Table A.8 Financial Solutions

Name	Languages	Short Description
SAP Financial Close and Disclosure Management rapid-deployment solution	EN; ZH	This rapid-deployment solution supports an integrated, end-to-end enterprise performance-management financial consolidation process that complies with IFRS or U.S. GAAP.
SAP Real Estate Management rapid-deployment solution	EN; DE; ZH	With the SAP Real Estate Management rapid-deployment solution, you can quickly and affordably implement and automate real estate-related business processes. You can effectively align cross-functional stakeholders to manage real estate in a collaborative way and deliver on strategic goals.
SAP Treasury and Risk Management rapid-deployment solution	EN; DE; ES; PT; ZH	The SAP Treasury and Risk Management rapid-deployment solution brings together software and services in a new offering that enables you to achieve excellence in treasury quickly and affordably. You will get the core treasury functionality up and running with a low-cost, fixed-scope implementation based on SAP Best Practices. By fixing the scope, the requirements definition process is streamlined and the focus is on scope validation and solution deployment. By using the solution, you can quickly reduce manual work, automate your processes, streamline your accounting and operational compliance, and improve your risk management.

Table A.8 Financial Solutions (Cont.)

Name	Languages	Short Description
SAP Financials Shared Service Framework rapid-deployment solution	EN; ZH; DE; ES; FR; PT	The SAP Financials Shared Service Framework rapid-deployment solution significantly lowers the entry barrier for a shared service delivery infrastructure by reducing both implementation time and risk to a minimum with a fixed-scope engineered service from SAP at a predictable price.
Financial Solution on SAP HANA		
SAP HANA Operational Reporting rapid-deployment solution	EN; DE; ES; FR; JA; RU; ZH	SAP HANA Operational Reporting rapid-deployment solution can help you generate insightful reports from the business areas of sales, financials, shipping, purchasing, and master data—in real time. The quick-time-to-value implementation of models and reports enables customers to go live in about six to eight weeks. In addition to using SAP BI tools, mobile devices can now be leveraged as well.
SAP HANA Operational Reporting rapid-deployment solution (Cont.)	EN; DE; ES; FR; JA; RU; ZH (Cont.)	This rapid-deployment solution uses the SAP HANA platform to process high volumes of ERP data at unparalleled speed—for faster, smarter decisions and increased productivity.
SAP HANA Net Margin Analysis	EN; ES; FR; PT	The SAP HANA Net Margin Analysis rapid-deployment solution provides preconfigured data modeling and over 100 predefined metrics in more than a dozen dashboards and reports. The solution, powered by SAP HANA, provides your organization with high-level visibility of net margin and costs across the entire customer, product, sales channel, and organizational landscape.

Table A.8 Financial Solutions (Cont.)

Name	Languages	Short Description
SAP HANA Accelerated Finance and Controlling rapid-deployment solution	EN	This rapid deployment solution, based on SAP HANA, ensures optimal performance—even with high data volumes. It also helps establish an extendable, solid foundation for financial, CO-PA, overhead management, material ledger, and production cost analysis reporting without disrupting current SAP ERP landscape.
SAP HANA Financials for Public Sector rapid-deployment solution	EN; DE; ES	A rapid deployment solution that offers easy and real-time access to financial and budget figures covering public sector financials (FI, CO, FM, GM, and US Fed) and public sector collection disbursement (PSCD).
SAP Financial and Regulatory Reporting for Banking rapid-deployment solution	EN	The European Banking Authority mandates specific financial reporting (FINREP). Most banks doing business in Europe are also required to comply with International Financial Reporting Standards (IFRS). This solution provides an integrated financial and regulatory reporting platform for both FINREP and IFRS.

Table A.8 Financial Solutions (Cont.)

Name	Languages	Short Description
SAP Maintenance Operations rapid-deployment solution	EN	SAP Maintenance Operations rapid-deployment solution provides the standard maintenance processes based on the SAP Enterprise Asset Management (SAP EAM) solution.

Table A.9 Enterprise Asset Management Solutions

A.4   Industry-Specific Packages

Name	Languages	Short Description
SAP AMI Integration for Utilities rapid-deployment solution	EN; DE	The SAP AMI Integration for Utilities rapid-deployment solution offers essential standard business processes for integration with SAP AMI for utilities. With the rapid-deployment solution, you can set up a baseline for your specific implementation more quickly than a traditional approach allows.
SAP Energy Demand-Side Management for Utilities rapid-deployment solution	EN	The solution provides specialized functionality to manage the lifecycle of demand-side management (DSM) programs, including design, enrollment, monitoring, and reporting. It also provides a central place for all DSM programs and associated information.
SAP EAM for Power Plants rapid-deployment solution	EN; ZH	This scenario describes the whole process of typical overhaul maintenance in the power industry, including project setting up, approval, project planning and budgeting, scheduling, creating maintenance orders, project monitoring, and settlement.

Table A.10 Energy and Resources Industries Solutions

Name	Languages	Short Description
SAP Trade Promotion Planning and Optimization rapid-deployment solution	EN	The SAP Trade Promotion Planning and Optimization rapid-deployment solution enables you to deploy promotion pre-assessments, agreements, and detailed promotion planning, quickly and affordably.

Table A.11 Consumer Products Solutions

Name	Languages	Short Description
SAP Billing and Revenue Innovation Management rapid-deployment solution	EN	The SAP Billing and Revenue Innovation Management solution enables you to define innovative tariffs and launch new business models quickly. With the rapid-deployment solution, you can set up a baseline solution for your specific implementation more quickly than a traditional approach allows.
SAP Multiresource Scheduling rapid-deployment solution	EN; DE; ES; PT	The SAP Multiresource Scheduling rapid-deployment solution is a fast way to implement a powerful resource-planning solution for service, plant maintenance, and project business. It provides scheduling of different resource types from one planning tool that leverages the existing SAP software infrastructure.
SAP Internal Project Staffing and Cost Management rapid-deployment solution	EN	The SAP ERP rapid-deployment solution for internal project staffing and cost management supports end-to-end business processes to plan and settle employees' time and costs to internal orders or projects. It lets you track and document staffing decisions, forecast resource needs, and control time and expense recording.

Table A.12 Service Industries Solutions

Name	Languages	Short Description
SAP Loans Management for Banking rapid-deployment solution	EN; ES; PT	Gain the functionality you need to better manage different loan products. By implementing an integrated banking software-and-service package to support the entire lifecycle of a loan, you can reduce loan risks and improve your processes for distributing loans, processing payments, managing changes, and closing accounts.
SAP Deposits Management rapid-deployment solution	EN; ES; PT	SAP brings together software and services in a new offering that gives you essential deposits-management functionality quickly and affordably.
SAP Branch Agreement Origination for Banking rapid-deployment solution	EN; DE; ES; FR; IT; PT	SAP Marketing, Sales, and Service for Banking rapid-deployment solution for branch-agreement origination covers the sales cycle specific to financial services, including origination of loan agreements. Embedded in the cross-industry SAP CRM application, it provides an integrated and customer-oriented approach from the front office to the back office.
SAP Sales Management for Insurance rapid-deployment solution	EN; DE; ES; FR; PT	The rapid-deployment solution supports a predefined role for insurance sales agents with features and functions they really need. Customers want a vertical customer-relationship management solution with fast, simple, and smooth automation of customer-related processes and insurance-specific content.

Table A.13 Financial Services Solutions

Name	Languages	Short Description
SAP Planning for Retail rapid-deployment solution	EN	SAP Planning for Retail rapid-deployment solution helps retailers perform consistent end-to-end planning, from channel financial, location-to-merchandise/open-to-buy planning, using real-time, demand-driven forecasts, common data, and key performance indicators across the entire process.

Table A.14 Retail Solutions

Name	Languages	Short Description
SAP Citizen Contact Center for Public Sector rapid-deployment solution	EN; DE; ES; FR2	The SAP CRM rapid-deployment solution for citizen contact center is a multichannel contact center. It will allow governments to be more responsive and efficient by giving their citizens quick and easy access to all services and information in a consistent manner while providing the highest levels of customer service.
SAP Budgeting and Planning for Public Sector rapid-deployment solution	EN	The purpose of this rapid-deployment solution is to address a key planning need of public-sector customers of SAP. Customers want to leverage transaction and master data in SAP ERP, make planning flexible and integration easy.

Table A.15 Public Services Solutions

A.5   Mobile Packages

Name	Languages	Short Description
SAP Mobile Analytics rapid-deployment solution	EN; ES; FR; JA; PT; ZH	The solution extends your investments in SAP BusinessObjects BI and the SAP mobile platform: It installs the mobile BI server and creates custom reports. It implements developer kits for charts embedded in mobile workflow. It enables you to build mobile analytics apps that use big data in SAP HANA.
SAP Mobile Platform rapid-deployment solution	EN; ES; PT; RU	A rapid-deployment solution package that focuses on the implementation of SAP's mobile platform in a development and production environment. It includes the platform runtime and design-time component setup, configuration and validation as well as integration with SAP business and operational systems.
SAP Afaria rapid-deployment solution	EN; RU	Get SAP's award-winning mobile device- and application-management system, Afaria, deployed and configured for your enterprise in just a few days. Secure your mobile devices throughout their lifecycle in your company. Empower your employees to become more productive with mobile enterpise apps.
SAP Mobile Apps and Infrastructure rapid-deployment solution	EN	This integrated offering of software, best practices, and services deploys instant-value productivity mobile apps and SAP Fiori apps into your landscape quickly, so you can begin to realize reduced costs and improve employee efficiency immediately.

Table A.16 Mobile Solutions

A.6   Technology Packages

Name	Languages	Short Description
Rapid database migration of SAP NetWeaver BW to SAP HANA	EN	The rapid database migration of SAP NetWeaver BW to SAP HANA enables customers to replace the actual underlying relational database of their SAP NetWeaver BW system with SAP HANA as a database.
Rapid data load for SAP HANA applications	EN	This solution provides pre-defined content to load specific data sources for the SAP Customer Engagement Intelligence solution into SAP HANA platform. It includes all requirements, components, and load jobs for SAP Data Services software, as well as reports and mappings of specific objects to load into SAP HANA.
SAP NetWeaver Identity Management rapid-deployment solution	EN; DE	This solution reduces total cost of ownership by simplifying assignment of roles and privileges to users and reduces risk through compliance checks and remediation. With its predefined content, customers are able to implement the SAP NetWeaver Identity Management component in a short timeframe.
SAP Master Data Governance rapid-deployment solution	EN; DE	This solution delivers the fast track to adopt SAP master data governance for supplier, material, and customer in the organization, to gain end-to-end insight in master data CRUD (create, read, update, delete) processes across the landscape, and integrates with SAP Information Steward rapid-deployment solution for data-quality analysis.

Table A.17 Technology Enabler DB, NetWeaver, Integration

Name	Languages	Short Description
SAP Electronic Data Interchange rapid-deployment solution	EN	Collaborate with your business partners using business-to-business electronic data interchange (EDI) to automate your order-to-cash and procure-to-pay processes within the value chain.
SAP Side Panel Content for SAP NetWeaver Business Client rapid-deployment solution	EN	The SAP rapid-deployment solution of side-panel content in SAP NetWeaver Business Client software offers packaged content to enhance the user's experience with SAP applications. It provides context-related business content, including master data, analytics, and related services, along with supplementary information (including external) and takes SAP ERP transaction data to the next level.
Rapid database migration to SAP Sybase Adaptive Service Enterprise (ASE)	EN	This rapid-deployment solution provides an end-to-end solution for migrating an existing SAP Business Suite application running on any SAP-supported database to SAP Sybase Adaptive Server Enterprise (ASE) database without disruption to any existing scenarios.
Rapid database migration of SAP Business Suite to SAP HANA	EN	The rapid database migration of SAP Business Suite to SAP HANA enables customers to replace the actual underlying relational database of their SAP Business Suite system with SAP HANA as a database.

Table A.17 Technology Enabler DB, NetWeaver, Integration (Cont.)

Name	Languages	Short Description
SAP Invoice Management by OpenText rapid-deployment solution	EN	SAP Invoice Management by OpenText rapid-deployment solution provides a scalable, low-cost solution for your invoice-to-pay operations. As a comprehensive front-end invoice-to-pay solution, it provides key benefits for your accounts-payable operations, such as improved invoice processing time, reduced cycle times, manual data keying, preconfigured exception handling, and approval work-flow functionality.

Table A.17 Technology Enabler DB, NetWeaver, Integration (Cont.)

Name	Languages	Short Description
SAP Business Suite Integration with the Ariba Network rapid-deployment solution	EN	Connect your back-end SAP software securely and reliably to the Ariba Network. Go live with the first wave of suppliers with preconfigured integration for the procure-to-pay process and Ariba Procurement Content.
SAP ERP HCM Integration to SuccessFactors rapid-deployment solution	EN; JA; KO; ZH	Integrate your SAP ERP human capital management (SAP ERP HCM) solution and SuccessFactors Business Execution (BizX) Suite with flexible and automated data exchange. These cover basic employee, compensation planning, recruiting, and workforce analytics. Integrated data is the basis for running hybrid end-to-end "pay-for-performance" and "attract-to-hire" processes.

Table A.18 Cloud Integration Solutions

Name	Languages	Short Description
SAP Information Interchange OnDemand rapid-deployment solution	EN	Connect your back-end SAP software securely and reliably to the SAP Information Interchange OnDemand solution and benefit from preconfigured integration for business-to-business processes, such as order-to-cash and procure-to-pay.

Table A.18 Cloud Integration Solutions (Cont.)

Name	Languages	Short Description
SAP Customer Usage Analytics rapid-deployment solution	EN	SAP Customer Usage Analytics rapid-deployment solution provides accelerated insight on services consumed by customers. With this solution, marketing and financials teams can obtain real-time visibility on customer activities and easily explore service usage patterns and financial results.
SAP HANA Commodity Risk Analytics rapid-deployment solution	EN	The solution provides your organization with instant visibility into commodity risk-related information across multiple lines of business. This enables your business to address commodity position risks appropriately at all levels.
SAP Shopper Insight rapid-deployment solution	EN	SAP rapid-deployment solution for shopper insight leverages SAP HANA to provide daily sales analytics that enable retailers to make business decisions in real time. Fast-track implementation of a daily flash scorecard on top of the SAP POS Data Management application helps deliver a fast return on investment.

Table A.19 Analytics Packages (Outside LoB and Industry Analytics)

Name	Languages	Short Description
SAP HANA Net Margin Analysis rapid-deployment solution	EN; ES; FR; PT	The SAP HANA Net Margin Analysis rapid-deployment solution helps reduce direct and indirect costs to maximize overall net margin across all combinations of product, customer, sales organization, and channel.
SAP HANA Sentiment Intelligence rapid-deployment solution	EN	Gain insights into market trends and customer perception of your brands and products. Get in direct touch with your most vocal customers by combining visibility into campaigns, promotions, and service entries residing in SAP applications with unstructured text data.
SAP Asset Analytics rapid-deployment solution	EN	SAP Asset Analytics software empowers you to gain visibility into the operation of physical assets, take proactive steps to avoid interruptions and downtime, effectively forecast and plan to maximize asset utilization, and optimize asset performance to compete in the marketplace.
SAP Predictive Analytics Adoption rapid-deployment solution	EN	The solution delivers sample content that your organization can quickly leverage for selected sales and marketing, retail, or manufacturing predictive analysis scenarios.

Table A.19 Analytics Packages (Outside LoB and Industry Analytics) (Cont.)

Name	Languages	Short Description
SAP Condition-Based Maintenance rapid-deployment solution	EN	SAP Condition-Based Maintenance rapid-deployment solution enables your organization to perform maintenance only when necessary by arming maintenance teams with sophisticated intelligence and comprehensive asset health dashboards. The solution also enables manual and automatic triggering of maintenance workflow leveraging through native integration with the SAP Enterprise Asset Management (SAP EAM) solution.
SAP HANA Customer Engagement Intelligence rapid-deployment solution	EN	The SAP Customer Engagement Intelligence suite of applications enables B2B customers to maximize revenue and margin. It provides decision assistance for sales and marketing across customers, products, and channels. In addition, it offers high-volume, real-time, predictive segmentation for B2C.

Table A.19 Analytics Packages (Outside LoB and Industry Analytics) (Cont.)

Name	Languages	Short Description
Rapid database migration of SAP NetWeaver BW to SAP HANA	EN	The rapid database migration of SAP NetWeaver BW to SAP HANA enables customers to replace the actual underlying relational database of their SAP NetWeaver BW system with SAP HANA as a database.

Table A.20 Business Intelligence and SAP NetWeaver Business Warehouse on SAP HANA Solutions

Name	Languages	Short Description
SAP NetWeaver BW Near-Line Storage rapid-deployment solution	EN	The SAP NetWeaver BW Near Line Storage rapid-deployment solution provides a complete data-archiving solution that enables extract, transform, and load (ETL) reporting, and lookup capabilities. The near-line storage technology will secure write-protected data, partitioned by age and/or time, resulting in a leaner, low-cost, more easily maintainable online SAP NetWeaver BW application.
SAP HANA CRM Analytics rapid-deployment solution	EN; ES; PT	Based on SAP CRM, SAP NetWeaver BW, and SAP HANA, this rapid-deployment solution provides insights into sales, marketing, and service. It includes role-based reports and dashboards to provide you these insights flexibly, right at your fingertips.
SAP Demand Signal Management rapid-deployment solution	EN	Increase the demand visibility into your supply chain and get a holistic view on your markets—now—with SAP's software-and-service package for SAP Demand Signal Management, which is powered by the SAP HANA platform. Manage massive volumes of external demand data and internal data and transform them into a single source of truth.
SAP Enterprise Risk Reporting for Banking rapid-deployment solution	EN	The SAP Enterprise Risk Reporting for Banking rapid-deployment solution enables best practices for the implementation of risk-management reporting for banks within SAP BusinessObjects business intelligence software.

Table A.20 Business Intelligence and SAP NetWeaver Business Warehouse on SAP HANA Solutions (Cont.)

Name	Languages	Short Description
SAP Business Intelligence Adoption rapid-deployment solution	EN	The SAP Business Intelligence Adoption rapid-deployment solution is a comprehensive package that helps customers choose the right reporting tool for the right reports. Software content helps to serve as a starting point for building better reports. Also, data reconciliation and availability helps users gain trust in the data warehouse environment, serving as a catalyst to adopt business intelligence tools. Simple visualization of data in desktop and mobile devices provides easy access to enterprise data.

Table A.20 Business Intelligence and SAP NetWeaver Business Warehouse on SAP HANA Solutions (Cont.)

Name	Languages	Short Description
SAP GTS for Trading in China rapid-deployment solution	EN; ZH	This rapid-deployment solution provides a complete trading solution based on SAP Best Practices, and localization for enterprises with import or export businesses in China. The solution streamlines trading processes and integrates with the SAP Global Trade Services application to ensure legal compliance.
SAP Access Control rapid-deployment solution	PT; ZH	Enforce best practices in role management with SAP BusinessObjects Access Control. Define business roles consistently, free of segregation of duties (SoD) and critical-access violations.

Table A.21 EPM and GRC Solutions

Name	Languages	Short Description
SAP Embargo Check and Sanctioned-Party List Screening rapid-deployment solution	EN	Services-driven offering that includes implementation accelerators providing baseline export functionality and a roadmap for expansion. Customers receive sanctioned party list (SPL) and embargo, the most widely used functionality, and can measure time-to-value in days or weeks instead of months or years!
SAP Value Realization Management rapid-deployment solution	EN; DE	The SAP rapid-deployment solution for value-realization management helps organizations establish, communicate, and monitor progress toward strategic goals, ensuring strategic alignment across the organization.
SAP Solvency II Regulatory Reporting rapid-deployment solution	EN; DE; FR; IT; NL	The solution gives an insurance undertaking a clear process for the creation of Solvency II quantitative reports (report to supervisor (RTS) and solvency and financial condition (SFCR)). It provides amodel for the collection of the data needed for quantitative reporting templates (QRT) and it supports the generation of QRTs in XBRL format.
SAP Strategic Financial Planning rapid-deployment solution	EN	Leveraging SAP Business Planning and Consolidation application, the SAP Strategic Financial Planning rapid-deployment solution allows the customer to model and measure the long-term financial health of their organization. It helps keep track of an ongoing financial model to track profit and loss, balance sheet, and cash flow for your company. Additionally, it performs ad-hoc modeling and measures the financial impact of one-time events or proposals.

Table A.21 EPM and GRC Solutions (Cont.)

Name	Languages	Short Description
SAP Financial Close and Disclosure Management rapid-deployment solution	EN	This SAP rapid-deployment solution supports an integrated, end-to-end enterprise performance management financial-close process that complies with either IFRS or U.S. GAAP. Standardization, automation, and better process management are the key words to a faster, less expensive, and more transparent financial closing cycle—from data collection and data processing to the last mile of finance, including XBRL reporting.
SAP G/L Financial Planning rapid-deployment solution	EN; ES; FR; PT	The SAP G/L Financial Planning rapid-deployment solution provides your organization with accelerated time-to-use of SAP flexible business-planning application. Built by SAP for SAP customers, this rapid-deployment solution will quickly leverage the data model in the G/L in SAP software to feed financial plans and statements in SAP Business Planning and Consolidation, version for SAP NetWeaver.

Table A.21 EPM and GRC Solutions (Cont.)

Name	Languages	Short Description
Rapid data migration to cloud solutions from SAP	EN	With rapid data migration to cloud solutions from SAP, you can safely and successfully migrate legacy data to SAP Customer OnDemand and SuccessFactors Employee Central.
Rapid data migration to SAP to Customer Relationship Management and Billing for Utilities	EN	With rapid data migration to SAP billing for utilities, you can safely and successfully migrate legacy data to SAP billing for utilities.

Table A.22 Enterprise Information Management Solutions

Name	Languages	Short Description
Rapid data migration to SAP ERP and SAP CRM	EN	Rapid data migration to SAP Customer Relationship Management enables a safe and trusted migration based on the highly acclaimed SAP CRM rapid-deployment solution, in a package that includes a fixed scope, specific for CRM data, with predefined services at a predictable price.
Rapid data migration to SAP Loans Management	EN; DE	Preconfigured, ready-to-use data migration solution for SAP Loans Management is based on SAP BusinessObjects Data Services and SAP Landscape Transformation to migrate legacy systems to SAP.
SAP Landed Cost Analysis rapid-deployment solution	EN; ES; PT; ZH	The SAP rapid-deployment solution for landed-cost analysis helps you extract and analyze cost data across multiple source systems to get a holistic view of landed costs for products. Identify cost trends, discover hidden costs, and optimize sourcing decisions to drive down product costs and improve overall margin.
SAP Asset Data Quality rapid-deployment solution	EN	SAP Asset Data Quality rapid-deployment solution allows you to assess, validate, and continuously monitor the quality of your asset master data. Simplify management of your asset data quality with SAP's industry-leading enterprise information management (EIM) tools and predefined content.

Table A.22 Enterprise Information Management Solutions (Cont.)

Name	Languages	Short Description
SAP Customer Data Integration rapid-deployment solution	EN; DE; ES; PT	Get a unified view of your customer data with SAP NetWeaver Master Data Management. (SAP NetWeaver MDM) software and SAP's service package. Consolidate and harmonize data from heterogeneous sources and provide everyone in your organization with reliable information for more effective sales, marketing, and service.
SAP Information Steward rapid-deployment solution	EN	Get detailed data quality insight in customer, supplier, and material master data records. Understand your data via advanced profiling, validate via business rule-driven analysis, and continuously monitor and measure your master data quality.
SAP HANA Data Services, Rapid Marts, and BI Platform rapid-deployment solution	EN	This solution provides quick installation of the SAP BusinessObjects Business Intelligence Platform and Data Services applications pre-configured to connect to the SAP HANA appliance software. Additonally, it includes one SAP BusinessObjects Rapid Mart for pre-built analytical reporting and analysis, extraction routines, transformations, loading, universes, and initial reports.

Table A.22 Enterprise Information Management Solutions (Cont.)

A.7 SAP Business All-in-One

The following tables provide the most recent release versions of the SAP Business All-in-One packages. There are baseline, industry-specific, and cross-industry packages.

The grouping by baseline/industry/cross-industry can also be seen here:

- *http://service.sap.com/bestpractices* is where you can locate the subpages in the left-hand navigation.
- The SAP Help portal provides the specific package information on all SAP Business All-in-One packages:
  - *http://help.sap.com/bp-baseline*
  - *http://help.sap.com/bp-industrypackages*
  - *http://help.sap.com/bp-crossindustrypackages*

Name	Country Versions	Languages
SAP Best Practices Baseline package (including versions for SAP HANA)	▸ Arabic Countries	▸ AR/EN
	▸ Argentina	▸ ES/EN
	▸ Australia	▸ EN
	▸ Belgium	▸ EN/FR/NL
	▸ Brazil	▸ PT/EN
	▸ Bulgaria	▸ BG/EN
	▸ Canada	▸ EN
	▸ Chile	▸ ES/EN
	▸ China	▸ ZH/EN
	▸ Colombia	▸ ES/EN
	▸ Croatia	▸ HR/EN
	▸ Czech Republic	▸ CS/EN
	▸ Denmark	▸ DA/EN
	▸ Ecuador	▸ ES/EN
	▸ Estonia	▸ EN
	▸ Finland	▸ FI/EN
	▸ France	▸ FR/EN
	▸ Germany	▸ DE/EN
	▸ Greece	▸ EL/EN
	▸ Hungary	▸ HU/EN
	▸ India	▸ EN
	▸ Indonesia	▸ EN

Table A.23 Baseline SAP Business All-in-One Packages (Q3 2013)

Name	Country Versions	Languages
SAP Best Practices Baseline package (including versions for SAP HANA)	▶ Israel	▶ HE/EN
	▶ Italy	▶ IT/EN
	▶ Japan	▶ JA/EN
	▶ Kazakhstan	▶ RU/EN
	▶ Korea	▶ KO/EN
	▶ Malaysia	▶ EN
	▶ Mexico	▶ ES/EN
	▶ Netherlands	▶ NL/EN
	▶ Norway	▶ NO/EN
	▶ Pakistan	▶ EN
	▶ Panama	▶ ES/EN
	▶ Peru	▶ ES/EN
	▶ Philippines	▶ EN
	▶ Poland	▶ PL/EN
	▶ Portugal	▶ PT/EN
	▶ Romania	▶ RO/EN
	▶ Russia	▶ RU/EN
	▶ Serbia	▶ SR/EN
	▶ Singapore	▶ EN
	▶ Slovak Republic	▶ SK/EN
	▶ South Africa	▶ EN
	▶ Spain	▶ ES/EN
	▶ Sweden	▶ SV/EN
	▶ Switzerland	▶ DE/EN/FR
	▶ Thailand	▶ EN
	▶ Turkey	▶ TR/EN
	▶ Ukraine	▶ UK/EN
	▶ United Kingdom	▶ EN
	▶ USA	▶ EN
	▶ Venezuela	▶ ES/EN
	▶ Vietnam	▶ EN

Table A.23 Baseline SAP Business All-in-One Packages (Q3 2013) (Cont.)

SAP also has multiple SAP Business All-in-One packages for various industries, such as banking, global trade, public sector, utilities, service industries, health care, life sciences, retail, consumer products, and wholesale. There are specialized packages as well, for engineering, mining, fabricated metals, automotive, construction, chemicals, high-tech, and industrial components. Cross-industry packages cover multiple industries with best practices for customer relationship management or enterprise information management. The specific packages for industries and cross-industries are listed in the following tables.

Name	Country Version	Languages
SAP Best Practices for automotive	Japan	JA/EN
SAP Best Practices for banking	China	ZH/EN
SAP Best Practices for building materials	USA	EN
SAP Best Practices for chemicals	Arabic countries	AR/EN
	Brazil	PT/EN
	China	ZH/EN
	France	FR/EN
	Germany	DE/EN
	India	EN
	Russia	RU/EN
	USA	EN
SAP Best Practices for apparel and footwear	China	ZH/EN
	India	EN
SAP Best Practices for food and beverage	Japan	JA/EN
	Russia	RU/EN
SAP Best Practices for consumer products	China	ZH/EN
	France	FR/EN
	India	EN

Table A.24 SAP Business All-in-One Packages for Industries

Name	Country Version	Languages
	United Kingdom	EN
	USA	EN
SAP Best Practices for consumer products and wholesale industries	Arabic countries	AR/EN
	Argentina	ES/EN
	Brazil	PT/EN
	China	ZH/EN
	Colombia	ES/EN
	France	FR/EN
	Germany	DE/EN
	India	EN
	Italy	IT/EN
	Japan	JA/EN
	Mexico	ES/EN
	Netherlands	NL/EN
	Spain	ES/EN
	USA	EN
SAP Best Practices for discrete manufacturing	Belgium	FR/NL/EN
	Brazil	PT/EN
	China	ZH/EN
	France	FR/EN
	Germany	DE/EN
	India	EN
	Italy	IT/EN
	Japan	JA/EN
	Korea	KR/EN

Table A.24 SAP Business All-in-One Packages for Industries (Cont.)

Name	Country Version	Languages
	Mexico	ES/EN
	Netherlands	NL/EN
	Spain	ES/EN
	USA	EN
SAP Best Practices for Engineering, Construction & Operations	India	EN
	USA	EN
SAP Best Practices for fabricated metals	France	FR/EN
	USA	EN
SAP Best Practices for global trade management	Germany	DE/EN
SAP Best Practices for healthcare	China	ZH/EN
	USA	EN
SAP Best Practices for semiconductor and photovoltaic companies	China	ZH/EN
	USA	EN
SAP Best Practices for electronics and component manufacturing	USA	EN
SAP Best Practices for industrial machinery and components	China	ZH/EN
	USA	EN
SAP Best Practices for pharmaceuticals	Global	EN
SAP Best Practices for medical devices	Global	EN
SAP Best Practices for mining	Australia	EN
SAP Best Practices for power plant construction	China	ZH/EN
SAP Best Practices for public sector	Canada	EN
	Germany	DE/EN
	USA	EN

Table A.24 SAP Business All-in-One Packages for Industries (Cont.)

Name	Country Version	Languages
SAP Best Practices for retail	Brazil	PT/EN
	France	FR/EN
	Germany	DE/EN
	India	EN
	Russia	RU/EN
	USA	EN
SAP Best Practices for service industries	Belgium	FR/NL/EN
	Brazil	PT/EN
	France	FR/EN
	Germany	DE/EN
	India	EN
	Mexico	ES/EN
	Netherlands	NL/EN
	Spain	ES/EN
	United Kingdom	EN
	USA	EN
SAP Best Practices for utilities	China	ZH/EN

Table A.24 SAP Business All-in-One Packages for Industries (Cont.)

There are cross-industry packages for SAP Business All-in-One. Those are listed in Table A.25.

Name	Country Version	Languages
SAP Best Practices for business planning and consolidation	Global	JA/EN
SAP Best Practices for business network integration	Global	DE/EN

Table A.25 SAP Business All-in-One Packages for Cross-Industry

Name	Country Version	Languages
SAP Best Practices for customer relationship management	Global	AR/DE/EN/ES/FI/FR/JA/PT/RU/ZH
SAP Best Practices for CRM service management	Global	DE/EN/ES/FR/JA/PT/RU/ZH
SAP Best Practices for CRM interaction center	Global	DE/EN/ES/FR/JA/PT/RU/ZH
SAP Best Practices for CRM territory management	Global	DE/EN/ES/FR/JA/PT/RU/ZH
SAP Best Practices for CRM data warehouse analytics	Global	DE/EN/ES/FR/JA/PT/RU/ZH
SAP Best Practices for data migration	Global	EN
Enablement kit for SAP NetWeaver Business Client	Global	EN
SAP Best Practices for environment, health, and safety management	China	ZH/EN
	India	EN
	USA	EN
SAP Best Practices for e-commerce with SAP ERP	Global	DE/EN/ES/FR/PT/RU/ZH
SAP Best Practices for human capital management	China	ZH/EN
	USA	EN
SAP Best Practices for mobile apps and infrastructure	Global	EN
SAP Best Practices for planning and consolidation, version for SAP NetWeaver	Global	EN

Table A.25 SAP Business All-in-One Packages for Cross-Industry (Cont.)

Name	Country Version	Languages
SAP Best Practices for planning and consolidation, version for the Microsoft platform	Australia	EN
	China	ZH/EN
SAP Best Practices for subsidiary in one client	Global	DE/EN/FR/ZH
SAP Best Practices for self-service procurement	Global	EN/DE/ES/FR/ PT/RU/ZH
SAP Best Practices for operational sourcing	Global	EN/DE/ES/FR/PT/RU/ZH
SAP Best Practices for SAPUI5 enablement	Global	EN

Table A.25 SAP Business All-in-One Packages for Cross-Industry (Cont.)

Bernd Welz is an executive vice president at SAP and global head of the Solution & Knowledge Packaging organization responsible for enabling the customer adoption of SAP innovations at scale—in the cloud and everywhere. The team develops solution content for implementation, migration to the cloud and integration of hybrid solution landscapes and produces enablement content for SAP, customers, and partners.

Welz joined SAP in 1997 in Customer Support. Since then he held several global positions such as Head of Product Support, and Head of the SAP Cloud Program.

Before joining SAP, Welz was manager at Roland Berger Strategy Consultants, located in the Düsseldorf and London offices. As a strategy expert in IT, he managed IT strategy and process reengineering projects for various multi-national companies. Previous to this, Welz worked in research sponsored by the European Union applying Artificial Intelligence to production automation.

He graduated with a master of science in computer science from University of Massachusetts Amherst in the United States and completed his studies in Germany, receiving a PhD in computer science from the University of Karlsruhe.

As a senior vice president and chief product owner, **Stefan Hänisch** is responsible for all of SAP's solution package offerings for lines of business and industries (SAP Rapid Deployment Solutions, SAP Business All-in-One).

Stefan looks back at a track record of leadership roles spanning product and solution management, go-to-market, and consulting. Before joining the packaging business he headed up go-to-market, new product introduction, and field enablement for all industry solutions. Prior to this, he owned the SAP CRM Marketing and Trade Promotion Management product lines. He also worked several years in consulting inside and outside SAP. He holds a master's degree in management and engineering from the University of Karlsruhe, Germany.

Stefan Kätker is a senior vice president at SAP and head of the Taxonomy & Content Architecture unit within Solution and Knowledge Packaging. Stefan is responsible for the SAP corporate taxonomy, the content architecture of SAP's knowledge assets, and the solution implementation methodology based on rapid-deployment solutions.

He joined SAP in 2001 as a solution manager in the area of supplier relationship management. He's held various leadership positions spanning product innovation in the cloud, software engineering, business process engineering, and product architecture.

Before joining SAP, Stefan was with IBM from 1992 – 2001 in various roles in research, product development, and consulting. Stefan holds a master's degree in computer science from the University of Erlangen-Nürnberg, Germany and a PhD in computer science from the University of Frankfurt, Germany.

As a senior vice president and head of the Packaging Framework unit, **Thomas Reiss** is responsible for developing products and tools that enable efficient packaging of content and for enabling efficient consumption of the content via the simplified implementation experience.

Thomas joined SAP AG in 1993, starting with R/3 EDI and ALE development, and has since held several management positions in innovative product development: first for ALE development, then New Dimension and CRM integration, SAP Business ByDesign Business Configuration and Extensibility and finally, before taking on his current role in 2011, Thomas established and led the SAP-wide Product Security Initiative for two years.

Prior to joining SAP, Thomas spent two years as developer at BASF AG for computer security. Thomas holds a PhD and a master's degree in electrical and information sciences from the University of Cambridge, England.

Elvira Wallis is an SAP senior vice president of Packaged Solutions. She leads the Database & Technology (DB&T), Analytics, Cloud Integration, Mobile, UX SAP Rapid Deployment solutions packaging team. This team drives the innovations in SAP Best Practices content, services, and enablement packages with SAP's software. Each quarter, her team delivers new, upgraded, updated and translated packages that have saved some of the world's best performing businesses several millions of dollars in IT and productivity savings, performance improvements, and elevated competitive advantage.

B.1   Chapter Authors

The following is a listing of author by order of appearance in each chapter. These are SAP topic experts who worked many months to develop the materials in this book.

Bernd Welz, Executive Editor
Executive Vice President and Global Head of Solution & Knowledge Packaging

Chapter 1

Bernd Welz
Executive Vice President and Global Head of Solution & Knowledge Packaging

Chapter 2

Stefan Hänisch
Senior Vice President and Chief Product Owner, LoB & Industry Solution Packages, SAP AG

Stefan Kätker
Senior Vice President, Head of Taxonomy & Content Architecture, SAP AG

Elvira Wallis
Senior Vice President, Packaged Solutions

Markus Weber
Vice President, Solution and Knowledge Packaging

Eva Zauke
Vice President, SAP Solution and Knowledge Packaging BSQM

Chapter 3

Bharath Ajendla
SAP Rapid Deployment Solutions Product Owner

Jens Baumann
Vice President, Head of Solution Packaging for Finance and HR

Mark P. Burke
SAP Rapid Deployment Solutions Solution Owner

Frank Densborn
SAP Rapid Deployment Solutions Product Manager

Dirk Eyermann
Senior Package Owner for the package Mobile Apps and Infrastructure rapid-deployment solution

Darius Golshani
SAP Packaged Solutions Owner – Business Services

Jan Gruenen
Head of LoB SCM Rapid Deployment Solutions

Ulrich Hauke
Vice President, Head of Solution Packaging for SAP Business All-in-One and SAP ERP

Sumita Jayaraman

Henrik Kiessler

Mark Kleber
Director, CRM Packaged Solutions, Solution & Knowledge Packaging, SAP AG

Kim Mathaess
SAP Rapid Deployment Solutions Product Manager

Jan Musil
Global Project Management Practice Head, SAP Services

Sreedhar Muthuramalingam
Director, Business Analytics, Rapid Deployment Solutions

Joachim Plumbaum
Head of 360 Products and Manufacturing, Energy & Resources Industries Packages at SAP

Sunder Ramesh
Head of Solutions Package, HANA & Analytics Rapid-Deployment Solutions

Joern Rischmueller
Chief Product Expert, SAP AG

Oliver Schuck

Seema Thomas
Director, Customer LoB Packages

Sebastien Thugnet
Package Owner (EPM), Solution Assembly & Packaging, SAP Labs, LLC

Jan Zielinski
SAP Rapid Deployment Solutions Package Owner for ERP Foundation Packages

Chapter 4

Beate Eichhorn
Development Architect, SaKP Taxonomy & Content Architecture, SAP

Jens Freund
Chief Development Architect, SaKP Taxonomy & Content Architecture, SAP

Stefan Kätker
Senior Vice President, Head of Taxonomy & Content Architecture, SAP AG

Chapter 5

Thomas Reiss
Senior Vice President and Head of Packaging Framework, SAP AG

Jan Musil
Global Project Management Practice Head, SAP Services

Marc Oliver Schäfer
Director, Product Management

Chapter 6

Kurt R. Bauer
SVP/Executive Knowledge Productization Services

Dirk Dobiey

Oleg Figlin
Director, Services Delivery Operations

Dr. Heike Laube
Senior Director, Global Head Support Academy

Jörg Rudat
Chief Support Architect, Upgrades and Innovation at SAP AGS

Maximilian Veith
Chief Support Architect and Global Enterprise Support Program Lead

Chapter 7

Miho Birimisa

Book Production

Florian Biehlig
Senior Developer, Packaging Framework, SAP AG

Christina Galbreath
SAP EAM Rapid Deployment Solutions Cluster Rollout Lead

Julian Rayner
Media Production Specialist

Index

A

AcceleratedSAP (ASAP), 22, 48
Accelerators, 47, 144
Activation monitor, 263
Adapter framework, 98
Agile ASAP, 248
  lifecycle, 249
Agile delivery, 248
AIE
  expert-on-demand requests, 286
  live-expert sessions, 285
Analytics portfolio, 329
Application Incident Management, 267
Application Lifecycle Management
  (ALM), 251
Application management phases, 259
ASAP
  benefits to deployment teams, 245
  for assemble-to-order projects, 248
  six phases, 249
  taxonomy, 246
ASAP methodology, 244, 274, 313
  agile delivery, 248
  hierarchy structure, 247
  in SAP Solution Manager, 259
  key characteristics, 246
Assemble screen, 241
Assemble-to-order, 26, 36, 50
  content architecture principles, 217
  deployment strategy, 102
  finance, 142
  high-level WBS, 244
  implementation project, 233
  innovation, 103
  rapid deployment best practice, 251
  relation, 222
  SAP ERP, 120
  software implementation projects, 217
Asset harmonization, 195
Asset type, 194
  defragmentation, 195

Asset type, 194 (Cont.)
  inventory (ATI), 190, 194
Automate, 278

B

Baseline build, 103, 249
Best practice
  depart from/extend, 19
  library, 299
  midmarket, 23
  processes, 20
BI software, 152
Bidding teams, 238
  scope definition screen, 239
Bill of materials, 190
Blueprint, 22
Blueprint Analyzer, 289
Blueprinting, 19, 67, 125
  phase, 55
Building block
  activity, 198, 199, 262
  layers, 208
Business gaps, 119
Business priorities, 212
  strategic, 212
  supporting/enabling, 212
Business process, 265, 269
  document, 169
  operations, 267
Business Process Description (BPD), 40
Business scope, 201

C

Case study
  chemical industry, 87
  discrete manufacturing, 130
  food processor and marketer, 102
  food-production enterprises, 142
  German football governing agency, 108
  large enterprise, 94

Case study (Cont.)
   manufacturer, paper, 137
   mobile mining sector, 165
   producer and exporter of paper, 137
   small and medium-sized monitors, 121
   telecommunications, 125
Channel Partner Portal, 328
Cloud
   services, 27
   technologies, 51
   test-drive solution, 72
Cloud-based quick start, 122
Cloud-based value prototype, 287
Cluster, 200
   core enablement, 207
   implementation content, 201
   services, 204
   software, 201
Collaborative project execution, 257
Commodity Management end-to-end
   solution, 214
Common deployment strategy, 117
Content architecture, 186
   objectives, 188
Content management, 187
Content modeling, 189
Content re-structuring, 220
Corporate taxonomy, 214
Custom code
   maintainability check, 279
   management, 268
   replace, 278
Customer blueprint, 22
Customer solution lifecycle, 291
Customer-specific mobile apps, 167

D

Dashboards, 100
Data migration, 93
Database migration, 36, 57, 63, 85
Deliverable-based view, 245
Deliverables, 246
Demo, 54

Deploy phase, 252, 259
Design phase, 252
Design-based project approach, 55
Disjointed configuration space, 60

E

e-learning, 297
Enablement, 291, 321
   Business Intelligence, 329
   mobility, 329
   offerings, 327
   rapid marts, 330
End-to-end services approach, 102
End-to-end solution, 214
   catalog, 227
   definition, 230
End-user perspective
   process description, 41
Engineered services, 272
   combine with multiple solutions, 50
   deliver remotely, 276
   three-tiered resource deployment
     structure, 276
Enhancements, 102
Enterprise Performance Management,
   157
EPM Add-in for Excel, 161
Executive view, 227
Expert view, 230
Expert-guided implementations, 298

F

F.I.T. Afaria rapid-deployment solution,
   324
F.I.T. BCM rapid-deployment solution,
   325
F.I.T. Consulting, 323
F.I.T. Sybase ASE rapid-deployment
   solution, 324
Fit/gap analysis, 19, 51
Fixed-scope style, 115
Fujitsu, 325

G

German Football governing agency, 108
Go-to-market content, 47
Greenfield, 58, 59, 126
Guided self-services, 300

H

Harvesting content, 239
HR forms–based communication, 183
Human capital management, 180

I

ICC, 238
  gap validation, 289
  integration validation, 289
  targets, 287
Implementation
  best-practice based, 20
  collaborative, 251
  Content cluster, 39
  delta requirements in ASAP, 250
  expert-guided, 299
  iterative, 248
  methodology, 244
  minimize cost, 279
  parallel, 146
  *pre-assembled rapid-deployment
    solution*, 54
  pre-defined services, 47
  reduce cost/risk, 234
  scrum approach, 248
  speed timeline, 286
  standard accelerators, 274
  support, 279
  support with SAP Solution Manager,
    259
Implementation building block, 198,
  199, 262
  layered architecture, 208
Implementation project, high-level
  assemble-to-order WBS, 244
Incremental approach, 116
Incremental content design, 208

Industry packages, 45
Industry value map, 66, 68
  consumer products, 213
Infrastructure enhancements, 57, 62
Infrastructure requirements, 190
Innovation Control Center→ICC
Installation, accelerate, 52
Integrated system landscape, 52
Integrating unstructured data, 124
Integration Validator Dashboard, 290
IT Infrastructure Library (ITIL), 252
IT innovations, 30
IT/business user, communication, 29

K

Kennametal, 29
Knowledge assets, 187, 193
Knowledge documents, 185
Knowledge-transfer methods, 299

L

Landscape
  add component to existing, 59
  add new business scenario, 60
  add new solution to existing, 60
Lean project structure, 136
Lifecycle management automation, 90
Lifecycle workbench, 45
Local requirements, 123
Localized, disconnected systems, 114

M

Maintenance management, 267
Make-to-order, 272
Marketing, 108
Meta model, 189, 197
  entities, 211
Mobile Analytics, 329
Mobile Apps and Infrastructure, 164
Mobility applications, 176
Modeling environment
  integrate with enterprise data, 88
Multisystem landscape, 52

N

New delivery mechanism, 51
New implementation paradigm, key essentials, 34

O

Ontology, 189
openSAP, 304
Operate phase, 252
Operations control center, 290
Optimize phase, 252
Organizational change management, 106
Out-of-the box deployment, 37
Overlap, 61

P

Paradigm, evolution, 21
Partner-created solutions, list of, 315
Partner-led Rapid-Deployment Solutions, 80, 315, 318
Phase, 246
  bid, 218
  deploy, 73
  explore, 68
  implementation, 218
  run, 77
  scope, 70
Planning platform, 134
Positioning instrument, 214
Pre-assembled rapid-deployment solution, 51
  basis for implementation, 54
  demo environment, 54
  image scope, 52
  installation image, 52
  KPIs/monitoring objects, 76
  test drive, 54
  usage scenarios, 54
Preassembled software, 122
Pre-configuration data, deployment options, 57
Pre-configuration settings, 40, 261

Pre-configured best practice functionality, 19
Pre-configured task lists, 90
Pre-defined implementation services, 47
Pre-defined models, 244
Pre-defined scope, 274
Pre-delivery checklist, 145
Premium services assets, 302
Production landscape, reduce downtime, 90
Project
  lifecycle, 259
  overview, 253
  portal, 135
  scope item, 199
  team members, 257
Purchasing-volume dashboard, 153

Q

Qualification, 320, 322
  questionnaire, 89
  support for partners, 327
Quick Guide for Package Implementation, 44
Quotation management functionality, 117

R

Rainbow Chicken Limited, 102
Ramp-Up Knowledge Transfer (RKT), 292
Rapid Deployment Cockpit, 74, 251, 253
Rapid Deployment, key benefits, 28
Rapid-deployment solution
  activate customizing settings, 261
  ASAP for implementation, 244
  bill of material, clusters, 200
  BOM, 200
  business processes, 40
  combine multiple, 26, 52
  content architecture, 192, 196
  database migration packages, 64
  knowledge documents, 185
  master BOM, 201
  meta model, 197

Rapid-deployment solution (Cont.)
meta model and entities, 211
Methodology Premium Enablement Sessions, 328
overlap, 61
partner-based, 315
partner-led, 318
personalize, 126
pre-assembled, 50
pre-configuration content, 261
Premium Enablement Workshops, 329
scope items, 193
step-by-step guide, 313
Requirements phase, 252
Reuse and integration principles, 190
Run SAP Partner Academy, 301

S

SAP Accelerated Innovation Enablement (AIE), 279, 283, 285
SAP ActiveEmbedded, 280
SAP Advanced Delivery Management, 272
SAP Afaria, 177
SAP Best Practices, 38
as accelerator, 61
baseline package, 44
bundle with SAP software, 24
content for mid-market, 46
content platform, 38
industry packages, 45
lifecycle workbench, 45
link to go-to market structure, 66
package content, 39
package, key assets, 39
types, 44
SAP Business All-in-One, 23, 37, 45
partners/packages, 23
solution structure, 46
SAP Business Intelligence Adoption rapid-deployment solution, 151
SAP Business Planning and Consolidation, 158
SAP business process documents, 179

SAP BusinessObjects Web Intelligence reports, 94
SAP certifications, 295
SAP Commodity Risk Management rapid-deployment solution, 61
SAP configuration data, extract, 99
SAP content architecture
meta model, 190
SAP CRM
deploy, 113
deploy with SAP HANA, 108
rapid-deployment solution, 114
SAP Data Services, 96, 100
SAP Demand Planning, 130
SAP demo cloud landscape, 126
SAP EcoHub, 80
partner-led solutions, 319
SAP Partners, 314
SAP Education, 293
SAP Education Software, 296
SAP Enhancement Packages, 285
SAP Enterprise Learning, 297
SAP Enterprise Support, 277
Academy, 298
individual/personalized support, 280
SAP ERP
assemble-to-order, 120
integrate Multiresource Scheduling, 137
rapid deployment of, 101
SAP ERP backend system, evaluate new platform, 62
SAP Extended Warehouse Management rapid-deployment solution package, 42
SAP Fiori, 175
SAP HANA, 329
assemble-to-order finance, 142
Consulting Bootcamp, 330
data migration to SAP Business Suite, 93
database migration, 64
database migration to, 85
rapid deployment, 319
SAP HANA Enterprise Cloud, 20, 56, 77, 170, 234
leverage pre-assumbled solution, 261
SAP HCM solutions, 181

SAP implementation, speed/predictabi-
lity, 313
SAP Improvement Finder, 284
SAP Innovation Curriculum, 294
SAP Knowledge Acceleration, 297
SAP Landscape Transformation (SLT),
144
SAP Learn Now, 297
SAP Learning Assistant mobile app, 297
SAP Learning Hub, 294
SAP Learning Solution, 297
SAP MaxAttention, 280
SAP Mobile Platform, 62
SAP modification justification check, 279
SAP Multiresource Scheduling rapid-
deployment solution, 138
SAP NetWeaver BW, 151
  migrate landscape to system on SAP
    HANA, 85
  Post Copy Automation tool, 90
  system copy, 90
  time for reporting, 88
SAP NetWeaver Portal, 178
SAP Partner, 23, 79, 300, 311
  enablement and qualification, 320
  F.I.T. Consulting, 323
  Fujitsu, 325
  rapid-deployment methodology
    program, 321
SAP PartnerEdge, 308, 320
  Partner Enablement Center, 321
SAP Premium Support Engagements, 280
SAP Product Support for Large Enterprises, 281
SAP Rapid Deployment solutions, 15, 37
  address requirements, 24
  adopting the delivery, 314
  content, 25
  CRM, 115
  difference from engineered services, 273
  framework, 313
  methodology for speed/predictability,
    313
  partner program, 25
  partners, 313

SAP Rapid Deployment Solutions Enablement Program, 301
SAP Solution Configurator, 70, 232
  contact SAP, 236
  customers, 233
  document gaps, 238
  for bidding teams, 238
  review selection, 237
  scope phase, 72
SAP Solution Configurator for Business
  All-in-One, 232
SAP Solution Explorer, 27, 226
  industry value maps, 70
  SAP Solution Configurator, 233
  solution catalog/capabilities, 229
SAP Solution Manager, 28, 50, 76, 251,
  259, 280
  implement SAP Rapid Deployment
    solutions, 259
  operate solution, 265
  processes supported, 266
  project, 259, 265
  solution, 265
  upload implementation documents, 258
SAP Student Academy, 303
SAP Supply Chain Management rapid-
  deployment solution, 130, 135
SAP Support Portal, 298
SAP Sybase Unwired Platform, 167
SAP University Alliance, 303
SAP User Experience Management, 297
SAP Workforce Performance Builder,
  296
Scope, 232
  define, 249
  document, 47
  options, 241, 274
Scope items, 186, 198, 217, 234
  add to business scope, 235
  attributes, 193
  create network of, 221
  customer-specific, 239
  flow relation, 222
  link content to, 221
  network, 222
  select, 233

Scope items (Cont.)
  solution capability, 210
  structure content, 219
  structure content around, 218
Scope-validation workshops, 105
Scoping questionnaire, 110
Scrum approach, 248
Self-service data reconciliation, 156
Self-service tools, 283
Services assets, 47, 74
Simplified Rapid-Deployment Solution
  Experience, 66, 210
Software License Material, 216
Software Product Version, 216
Solution, 265
  browser, 283
  build best practice content, 239
  catalog of, 229
  complete catalog, 226
  components, 266
  deployment, 302
  documentation, 266
  expand existing, 35
  implementation, 73, 266
  launches, 292
  lifecycle, 252
  operate with SAP Solution Manager, 265
  scope, 232
  scope document, 110
  scope item, 199
  stable/integrated foundation, 35
  with disjointed configuration space, 60
  with overlapping configuration space, 61
Solution Builder, 261
  activate solution pre-configuration content, 261
  personalize structures, 263
Solution capability, 210, 229
  add to business scope, 235
  definition, 215
  grouping, 231
  represent concrete solutions, 214
  select, 233
Solution Configurator, 27, 28
Solution Discovery free assets, 302
Solution Implementation
  services, 276

Source system
  preparation, 64
  prepare, 86
Sprints, 250
Step-by-step guide, 48, 259
System landscape
  manage, 260

T

Task repository, 238
Tasks, 247
Taxonomy, 189
Technical operations, 267
Telecommunications billing system, 125
Template management, 266
Test and evaluation environment, 234
Test case, 267
Test management, 266
Three-tier landscape, 91, 147
Timeline, 55
Time-to-value, 279
Total cost of ownership, 34
Training guides, 179

U

Upgrade management, 268

V

Value maps, 228
Virtualization, 51

W

WBS, 47, 74, 238
  ASAP 8 methodology, 244
  assemble, 255
  item definitions, 247
  merge to single project, 50

Z

Zero modification, 289

■ For the executive: what SAP HANA is and how it can help you

■ For the practitioner: details on data modeling, data provisioning, and the SAP HANA client tools

■ For everyone: the latest and greatest developments—Suite on SAP HANA, advanced applications for SAP HANA, and more

Bjarne Berg, Penny Silvia

SAP HANA

An Introduction

HANA is shifting SAP into high gear—don't get left in the dust. In this updated edition of our best-selling book, explore the what, why, when, and how of SAP HANA. From building a business strategy to administering a system—and all the pit stops in between—you'll get the big picture you need to get started. Buckle up!

527 pp., 2. edition 2013, 69,95 Euro / US$ 69.95
ISBN 978-1-59229-865-5
www.sap-press.com

SAP PRESS
The SAP Blue Book
Are you ready?
The SAP® Blue Book
A Concise Business Guide to the World of SAP
SAP: what it is, how it works, and what it costs
Apply best practices to implementation planning and avoid common pitfalls
Gain maximum benefits, manage change, and learn how to thrive after go-live
Michael Doane
Galileo Press

■ Overcome implementation mistakes

■ Assess your SAP maturity and your users' skills

■ Build and sustain a Center of Excellence

Michael Doane

The SAP Green Book

A Business Guide for Effectively Managing the SAP Lifecycle

System up and running, project complete? Think twice! Read "The SAP Green Book" to learn how to continuously align your business with IT, and understand how best benefit from your SAP implementation. Written with the background of 15+ years of SAP implementation and post-implementation experience, this book is your guide to a truly successful and sustainable SAP project. Whether it's learning how to create a Center of Excellence, how to keep your end users up to date, or how to accelerate your ROI: This book is a must-read for all managers new to SAP!

265 pp., 2012, 29,95 Euro / US$ 29.95
ISBN 978-1-59229-407-7
www.sap-press.com